尾田栄一郎

Did you know? Apparently the reading comprehension rate of Japanese youth is among the highest in the world. Isn't that terrific? I mean, isn't that great? And do you know why that is? Even among the Japanese, the ones with the best reading comprehension are those who read manga. Isn't that terrific news? Seriously. Isn't it très magnifique? (←French style)

-Eiichiro Oda, 2002

**E**iichiro Oda began his manga career at the age of 17, when his one-shot cowboy manga **Wanted!** won second place in the coveted Tezuka manga awards. Oda went on to work as an assistant to some of the biggest manga artists in the industry, including Nobuhiro Watsuki, before winning the Hop Step Award for new artists. His pirate adventure **One Piece**, which debuted in **Weekly Shonen Jump** in 1997, quickly became one of the most popular manga in Japan.

**ONE PIECE VOL. 22**
**BAROQUE WORKS PART 11**

**SHONEN JUMP Manga Edition**

This graphic novel contains material that was originally published in English in **SHONEN JUMP** #76–78. Artwork in the magazine may have been slightly altered from that presented here.

STORY AND ART BY EIICHIRO ODA

English Adaptation/Lance Caselman
Translation/JN Productions
Touch-up Art & Lettering/Vanessa Satone
Additional Touch-up/Rachel Lightfoot
Design/Sean Lee
Editor/Yuki Murashige

ONE PIECE © 1997 by Eiichiro Oda. All rights reserved.
First published in Japan in 1997 by SHUEISHA Inc., Tokyo.
English translation rights arranged by SHUEISHA Inc.

Printed in the U.S.A.

Published by VIZ Media, LLC
P.O. Box 77010
San Francisco, CA 94107

10 9 8 7 6 5
First printing, September 2009
Fifth printing, January 2013

www.viz.com

THE WORLD'S MOST POPULAR MANGA
www.shonenjump.com

SHONEN JUMP MANGA

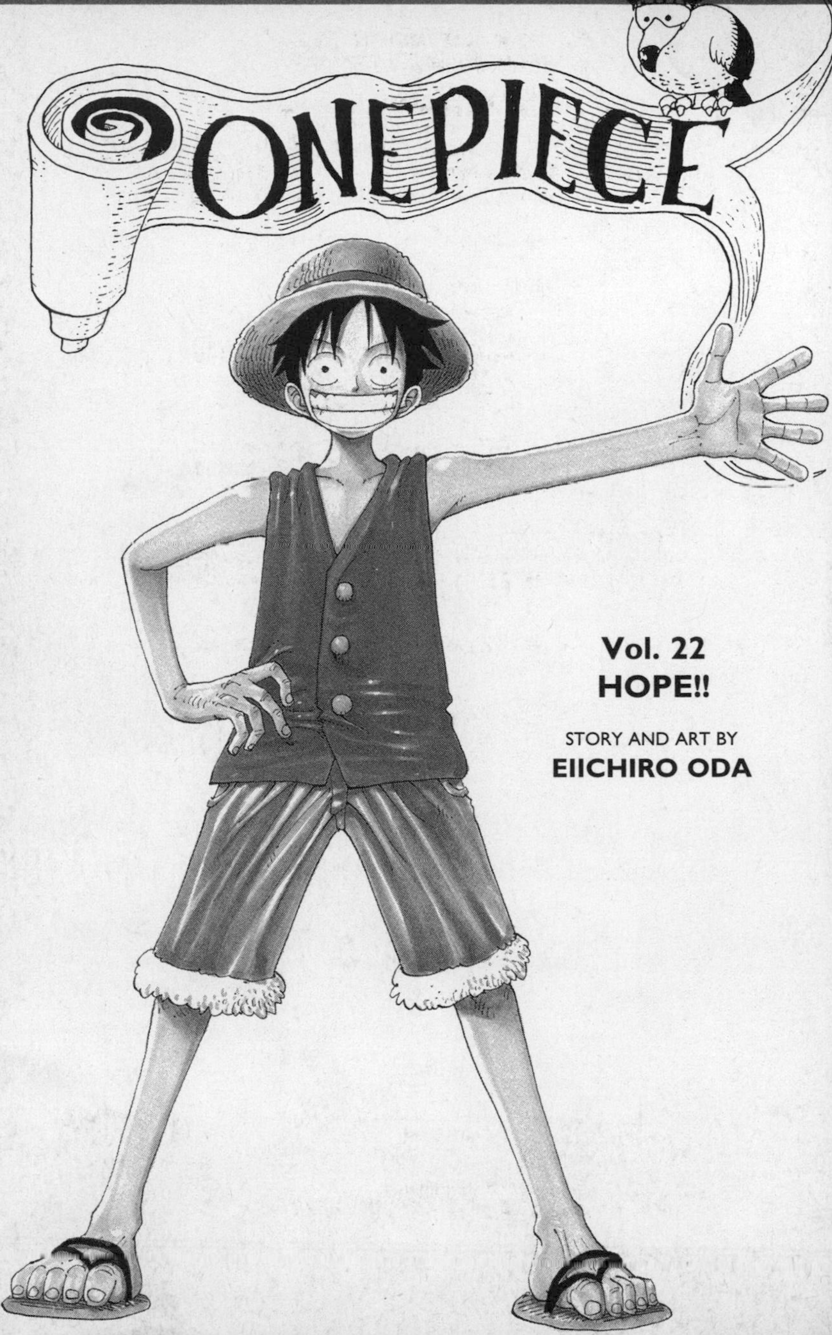
ONE PIECE

**Vol. 22**
**HOPE!!**

STORY AND ART BY
**EIICHIRO ODA**

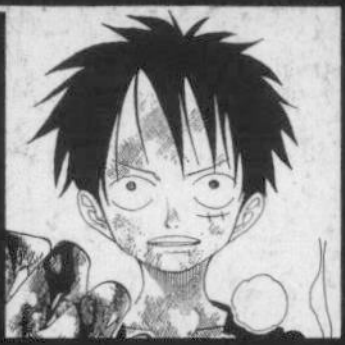

**Monkey D. Luffy**
Boundlessly optimistic and able to stretch like rubber, he is determined to become King of the Pirates.

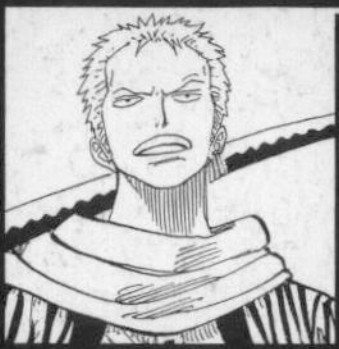

**Roronoa Zolo**
A former bounty hunter and master of the "three-sword" style. He aspires to be the world's greatest swordsman.

**Nami**
A thief who specializes in robbing pirates. Nami hates pirates, but Luffy convinced her to be his navigator.

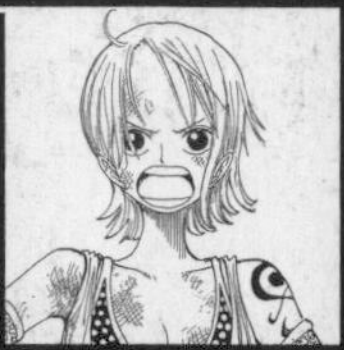

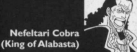

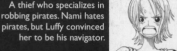

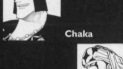

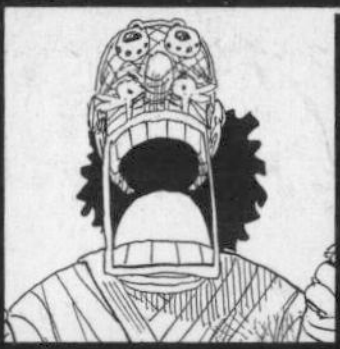

**Usopp**
A village boy with a talent for telling tall tales. His father, Yasopp, is a member of Shanks's crew.

**Sanji**
The big-hearted cook (and ladies' man) whose dream is to find the legendary sea, the "All Blue."

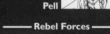

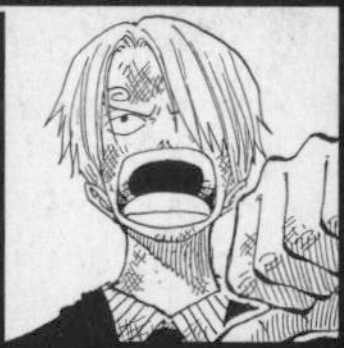

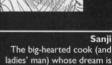

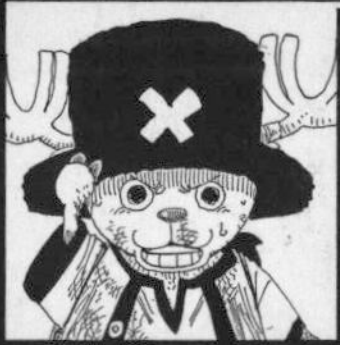

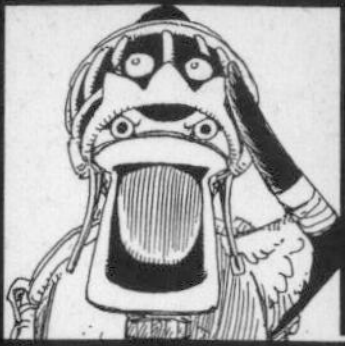

**Tony Tony Chopper**
A blue-nosed man-reindeer and the ship's doctor.

**Vivi**

**Karoo**

**——— Royal Forces ———**

**Nefeltari Cobra (King of Alabasta)**

**Chaka**

**Pell**

**——— Rebel Forces ———**

**Koza**

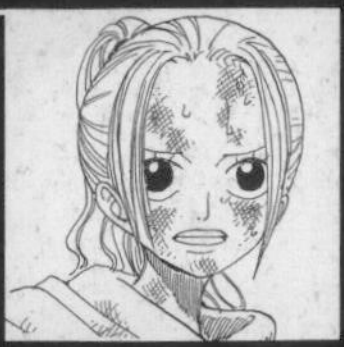

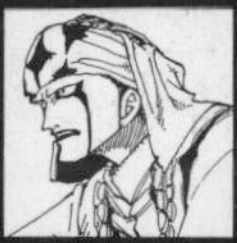

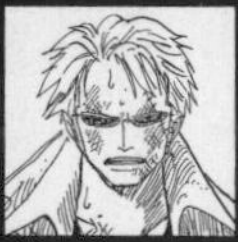

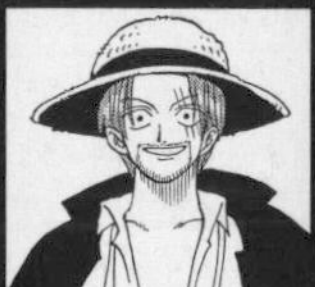

**"Red-Haired" Shanks**
A pirate that Luffy idolizes. Shanks gave Luffy his trademark straw hat.

**Volume 22** THE STORY OF

# ONE PIECE

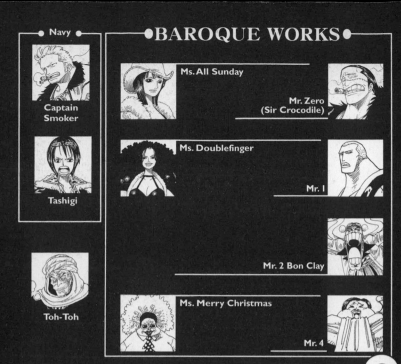

## Navy

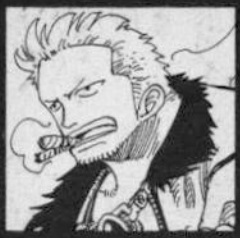

Captain Smoker

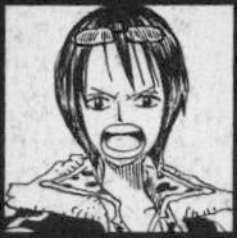

Tashigi

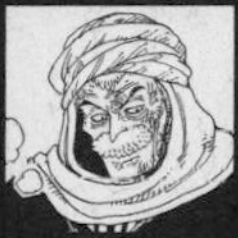

Toh-Toh

# BAROQUE WORKS

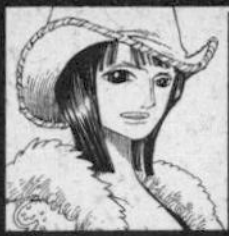

Ms. All Sunday

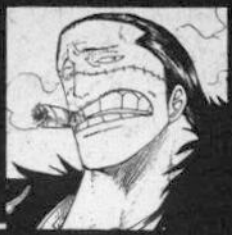

Mr. Zero (Sir Crocodile)

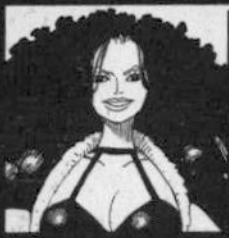

Ms. Doublefinger

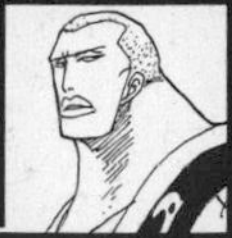

Mr. 1

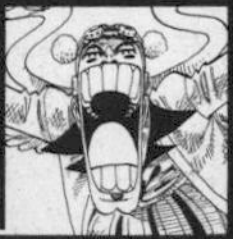

Mr. 2 Bon Clay

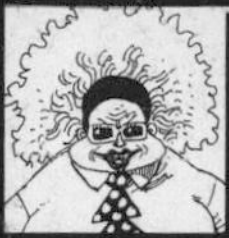

Ms. Merry Christmas

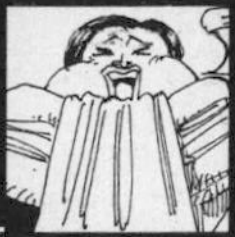

Mr. 4

Monkey D. Luffy started out as just a kid with a dream—to become the greatest pirate in history! Stirred by the tales of pirate "Red-Haired" Shanks, Luffy vowed to become a pirate himself. That was before the enchanted Devil Fruit gave Luffy the power to stretch like rubber, at the cost of being unable to swim—a serious handicap for an aspiring sea dog. Undeterred, Luffy set out to sea and recruited some crewmates: master swordsman Zolo, treasure-hunting thief Nami, lying sharpshooter Usopp, the high-kicking chef Sanji, and the latest addition, Chopper—the walkin' talkin' reindeer doctor.

Luffy and crew fight to help Princess Vivi save her war-torn and drought-ravaged kingdom from the evil Sir Crocodile and his secret criminal organization, the Baroque Works. Having finally reached the royal palace in Alubarna, Vivi devises a plan to end the civil war, only to be thwarted by the sudden arrival of Sir Crocodile, who reveals his true objective—to get his hands on the most destructive weapon of the ancient world, the Pluton! But first he intends to put an end to the rebellion himself by blowing up everyone near the palace, regardless of whose side they're on! With Luffy half-dead in the Alabastan desert and the rest of the crew taking on the Officer Agents in the streets of Alubarna, can anyone stop this fiend from realizing his evil plan?

BAROQUE WORKS

# ONE PIECE

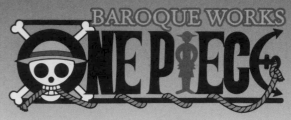

## Vol. 22
## Hope!!

## CONTENTS

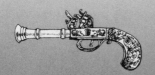

# Chapter 196:
# 1

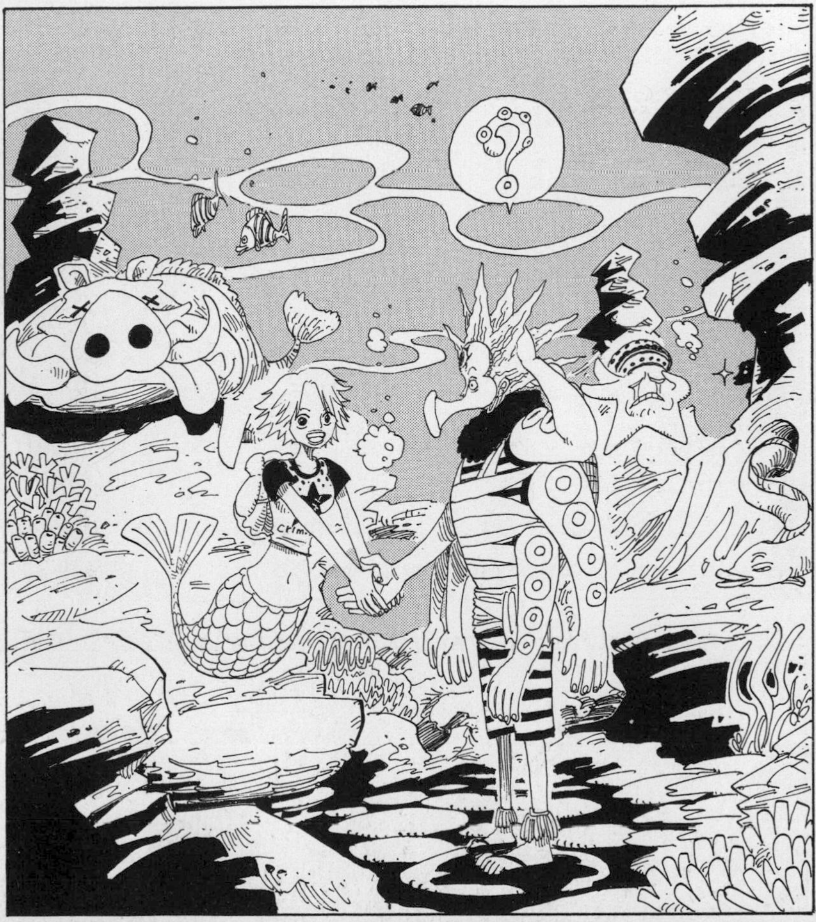

HACHI'S WALK ON THE SEAFLOOR, VOL. 13: "A SHADOW DRAWS NEAR HACHI, WHO SAVES SOMEONE WHO HAD BEEN EATEN BY A FISH, WHO HAD ALSO ALMOST BEEN EATEN BY A FISH"

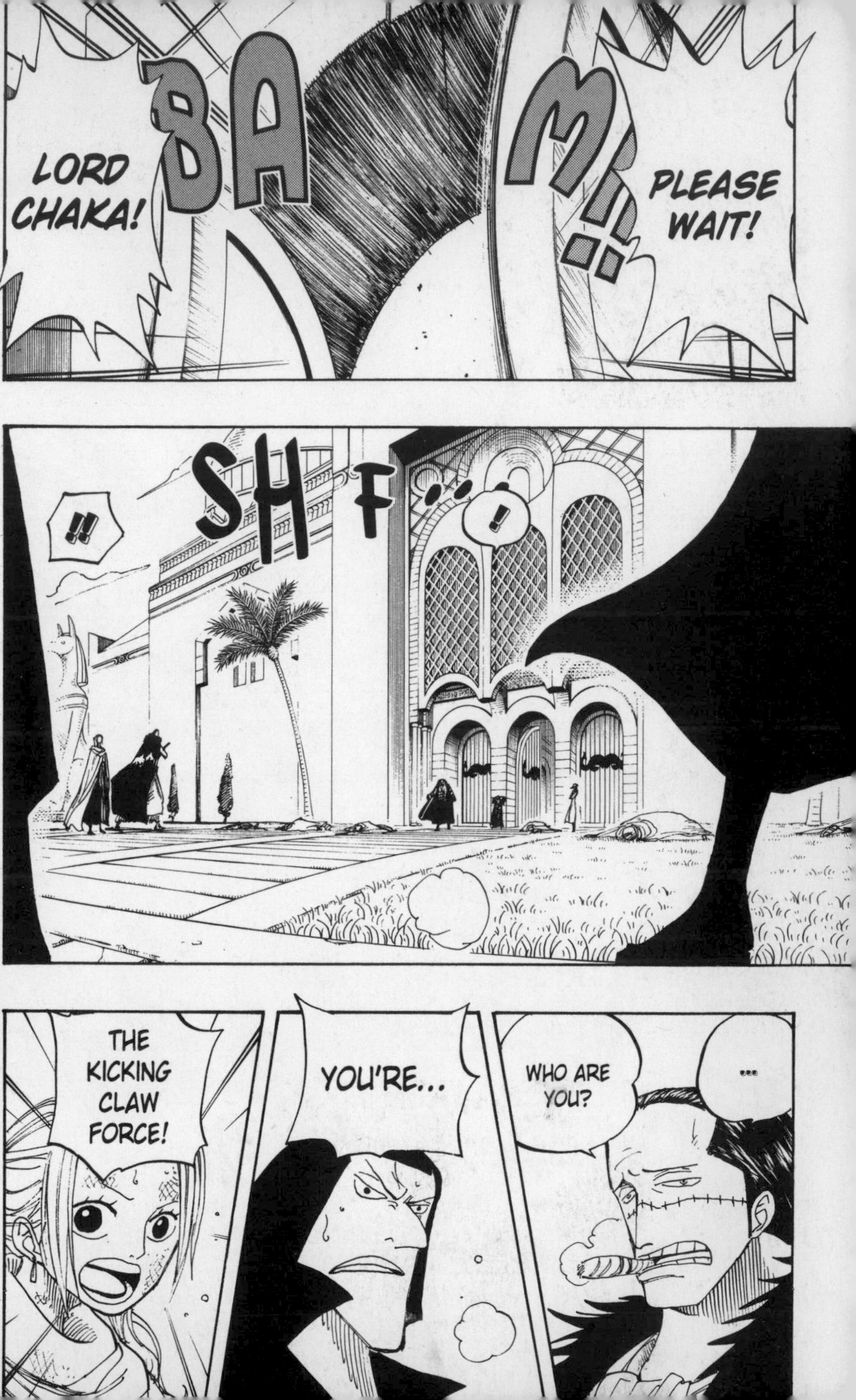
PLEASE WAIT!
BAM!!
LORD CHAKA!
...!
SHF
!!
...
WHO ARE YOU?
YOU'RE...
THE KICKING CLAW FORCE!

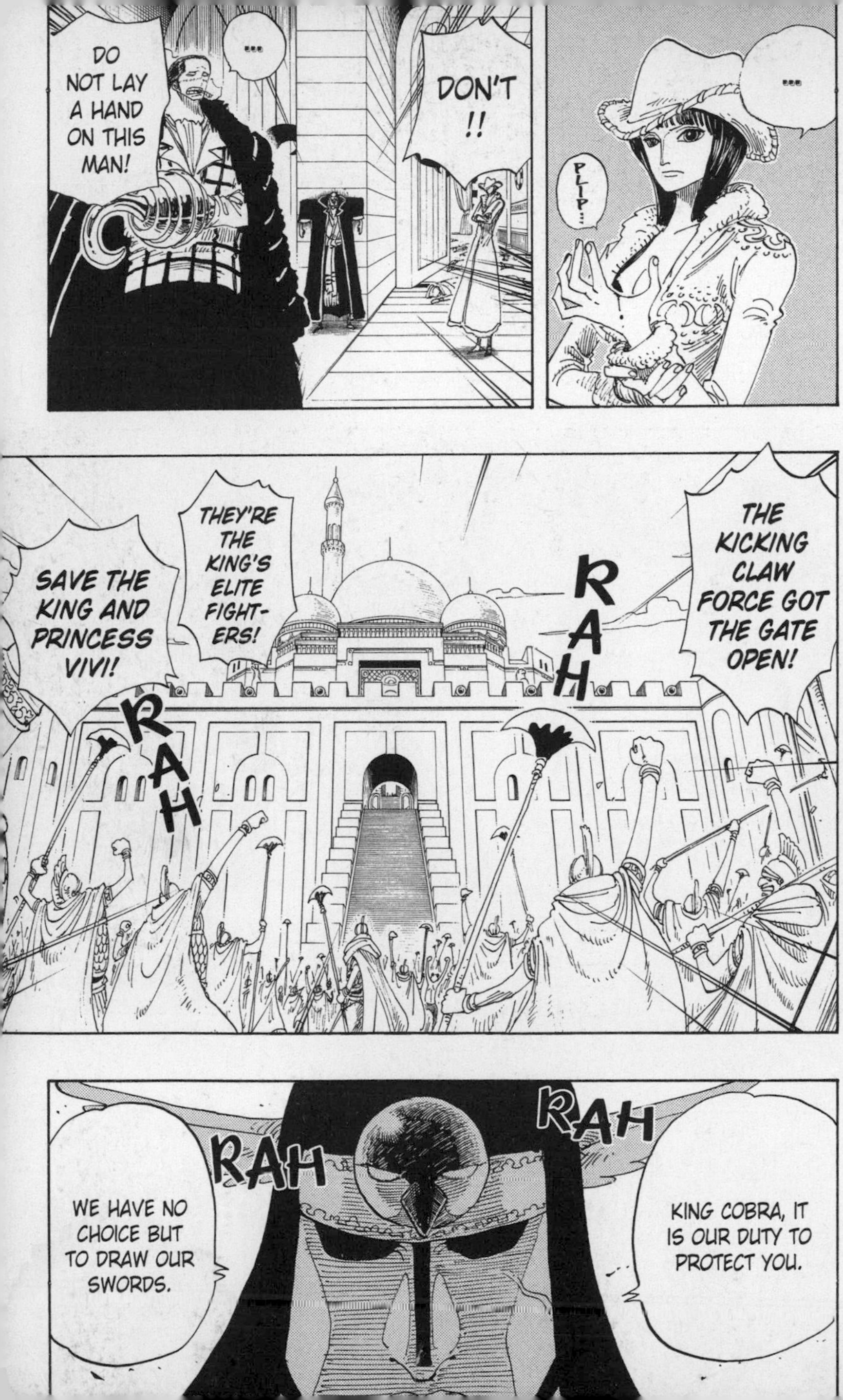
...
PLIP...
DON'T !!
...
DO NOT LAY A HAND ON THIS MAN!
THE KICKING CLAW FORCE GOT THE GATE OPEN!
RAH
THEY'RE THE KING'S ELITE FIGHTERS!
SAVE THE KING AND PRINCESS VIVI!
RAH
KING COBRA, IT IS OUR DUTY TO PROTECT YOU.
RAH
RAH
WE HAVE NO CHOICE BUT TO DRAW OUR SWORDS.

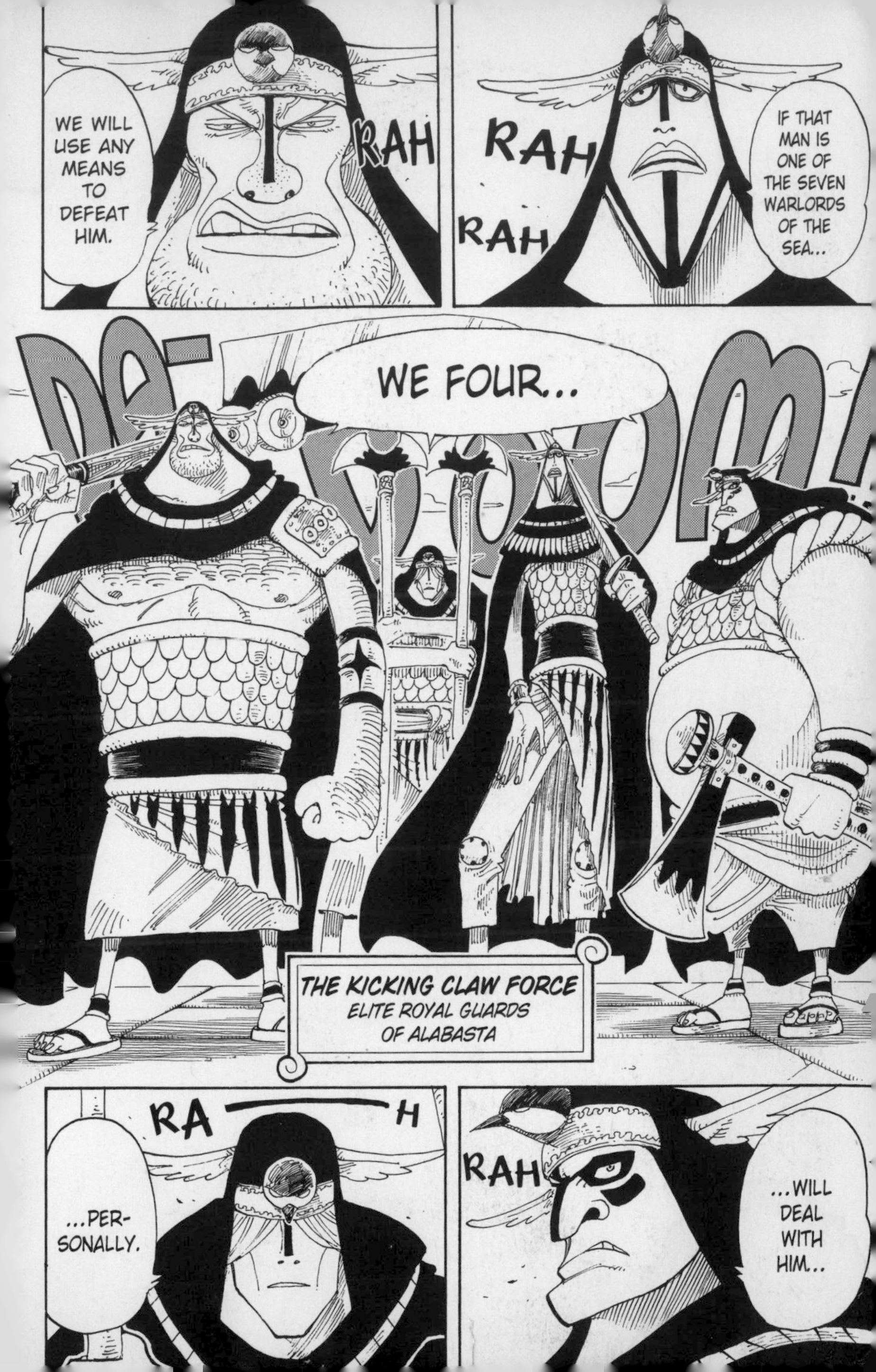

IF THAT MAN IS ONE OF THE SEVEN WARLORDS OF THE SEA...
RAH
RAH
RAH
WE WILL USE ANY MEANS TO DEFEAT HIM.
WE FOUR...
DE-
THE KICKING CLAW FORCE
ELITE ROYAL GUARDS OF ALABASTA
RAH
...WILL DEAL WITH HIM...
RA——H
...PER-SONALLY.

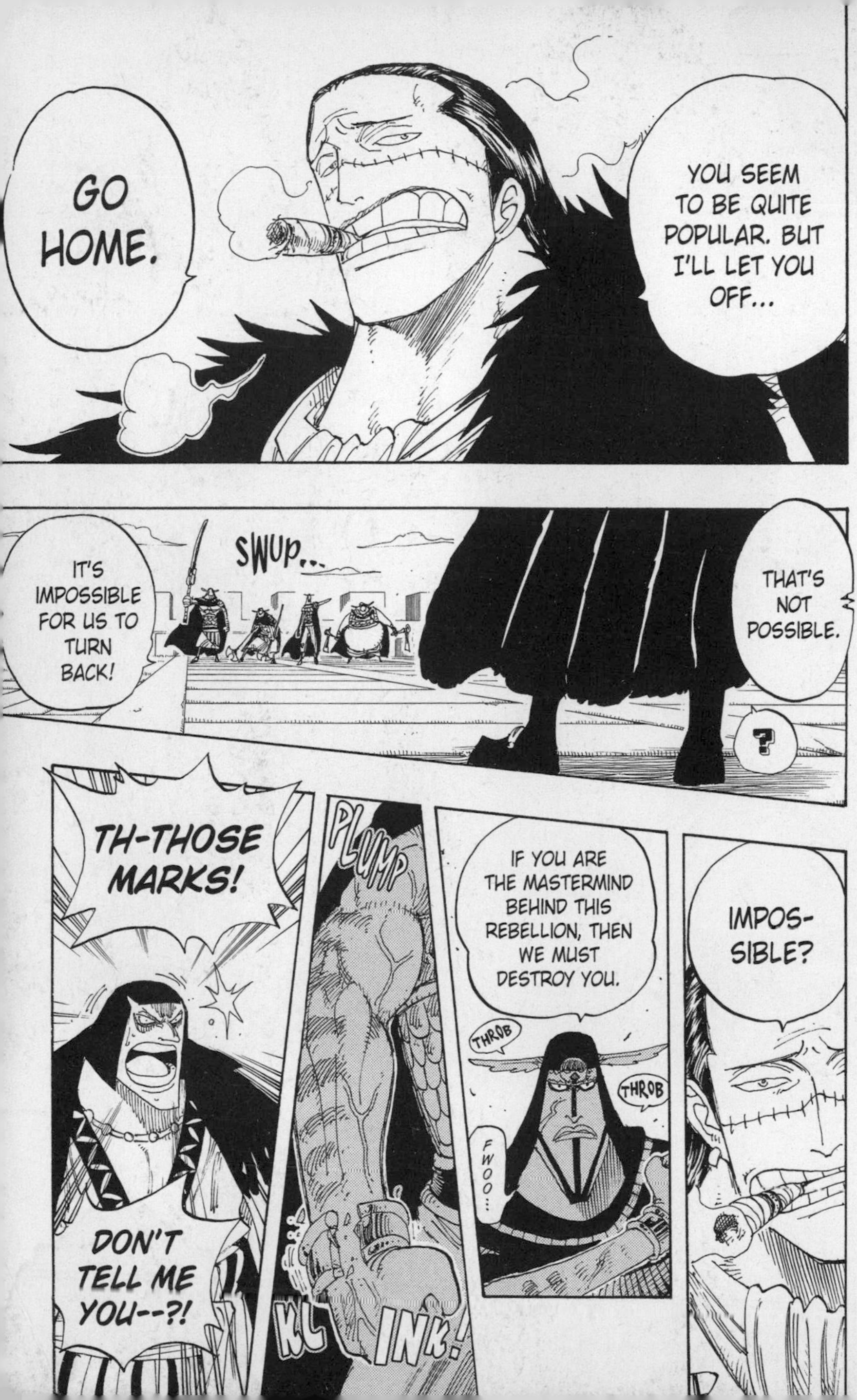
YOU SEEM TO BE QUITE POPULAR. BUT I'LL LET YOU OFF...
GO HOME.
THAT'S NOT POSSIBLE.
?
SWUP...
IT'S IMPOSSIBLE FOR US TO TURN BACK!
IMPOS-SIBLE?
IF YOU ARE THE MASTERMIND BEHIND THIS REBELLION, THEN WE MUST DESTROY YOU.
THROB
THROB
FWOO...
PLUMP
KLINK!
TH-THOSE MARKS!
DON'T TELL ME YOU--?!

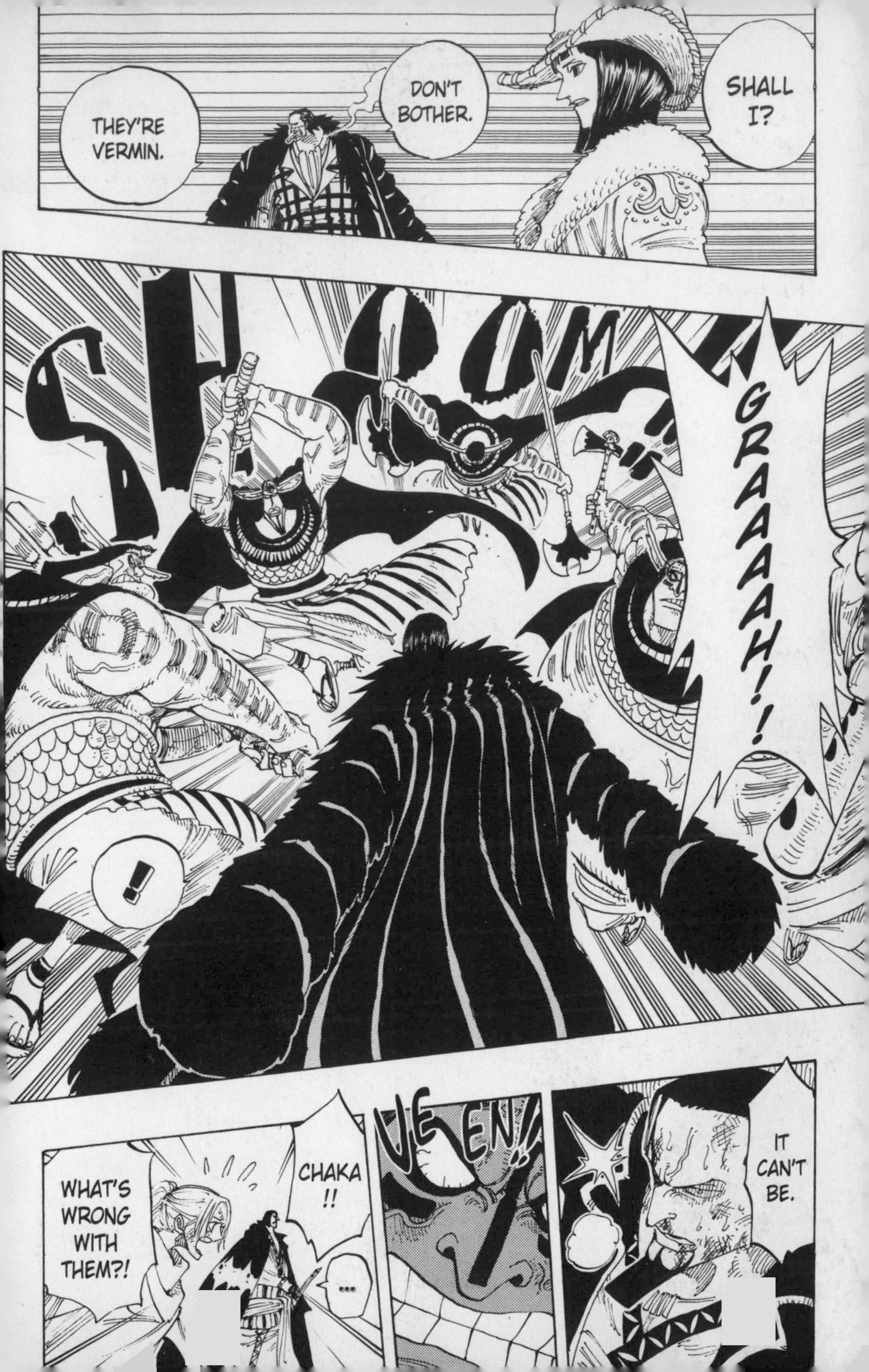
SHALL I?
DON'T BOTHER.
THEY'RE VERMIN.
GRAAAAH!!
!
IT CAN'T BE.
CHAKA!!
WHAT'S WRONG WITH THEM?!
...

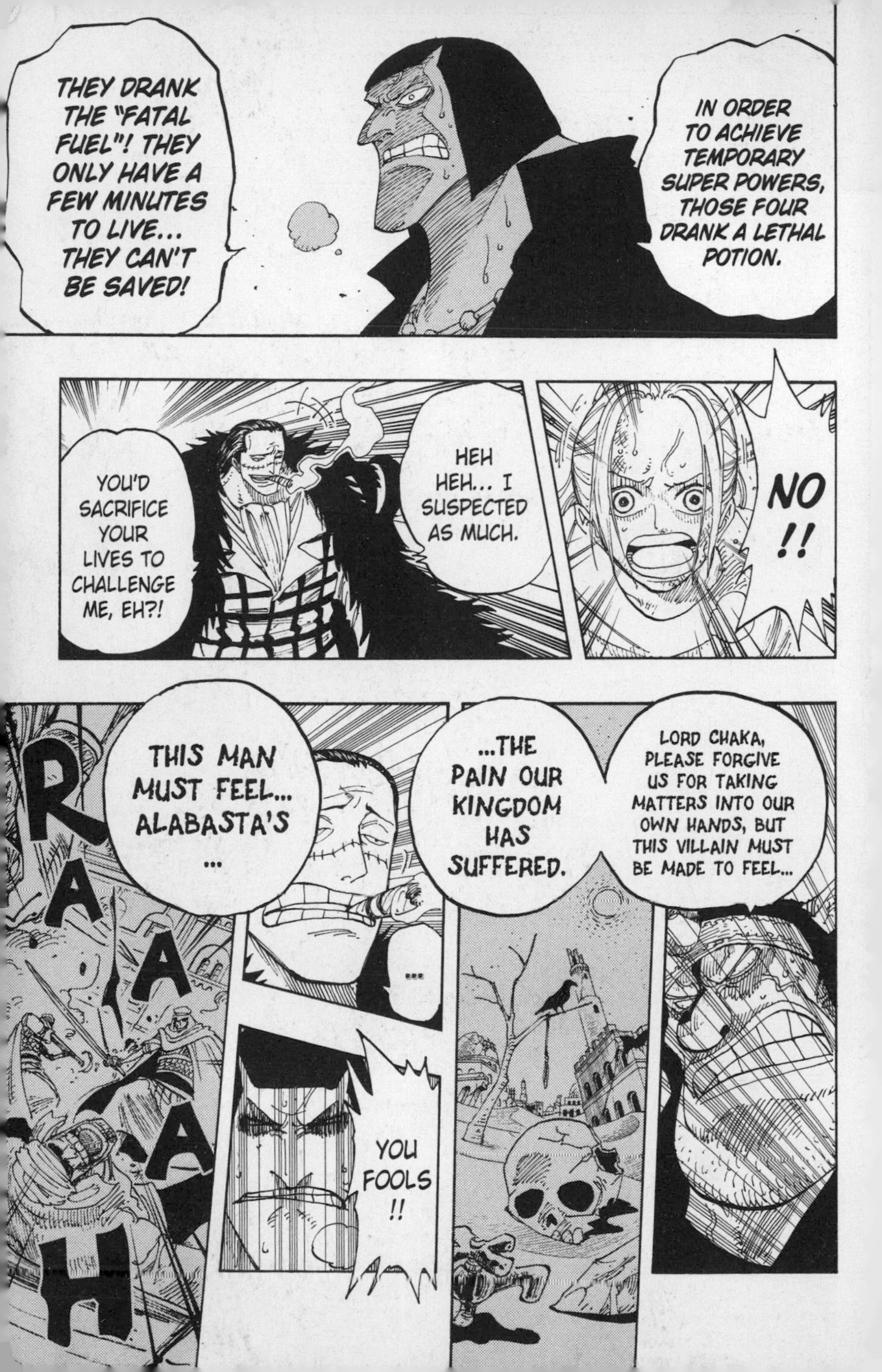
IN ORDER TO ACHIEVE TEMPORARY SUPER POWERS, THOSE FOUR DRANK A LETHAL POTION.
THEY DRANK THE "FATAL FUEL"! THEY ONLY HAVE A FEW MINUTES TO LIVE... THEY CAN'T BE SAVED!
NO !!
HEH HEH... I SUSPECTED AS MUCH.
YOU'D SACRIFICE YOUR LIVES TO CHALLENGE ME, EH?!
LORD CHAKA, PLEASE FORGIVE US FOR TAKING MATTERS INTO OUR OWN HANDS, BUT THIS VILLAIN MUST BE MADE TO FEEL...
...THE PAIN OUR KINGDOM HAS SUFFERED.
THIS MAN MUST FEEL... ALABASTA'S ...
...
YOU FOOLS !!
RAAAH

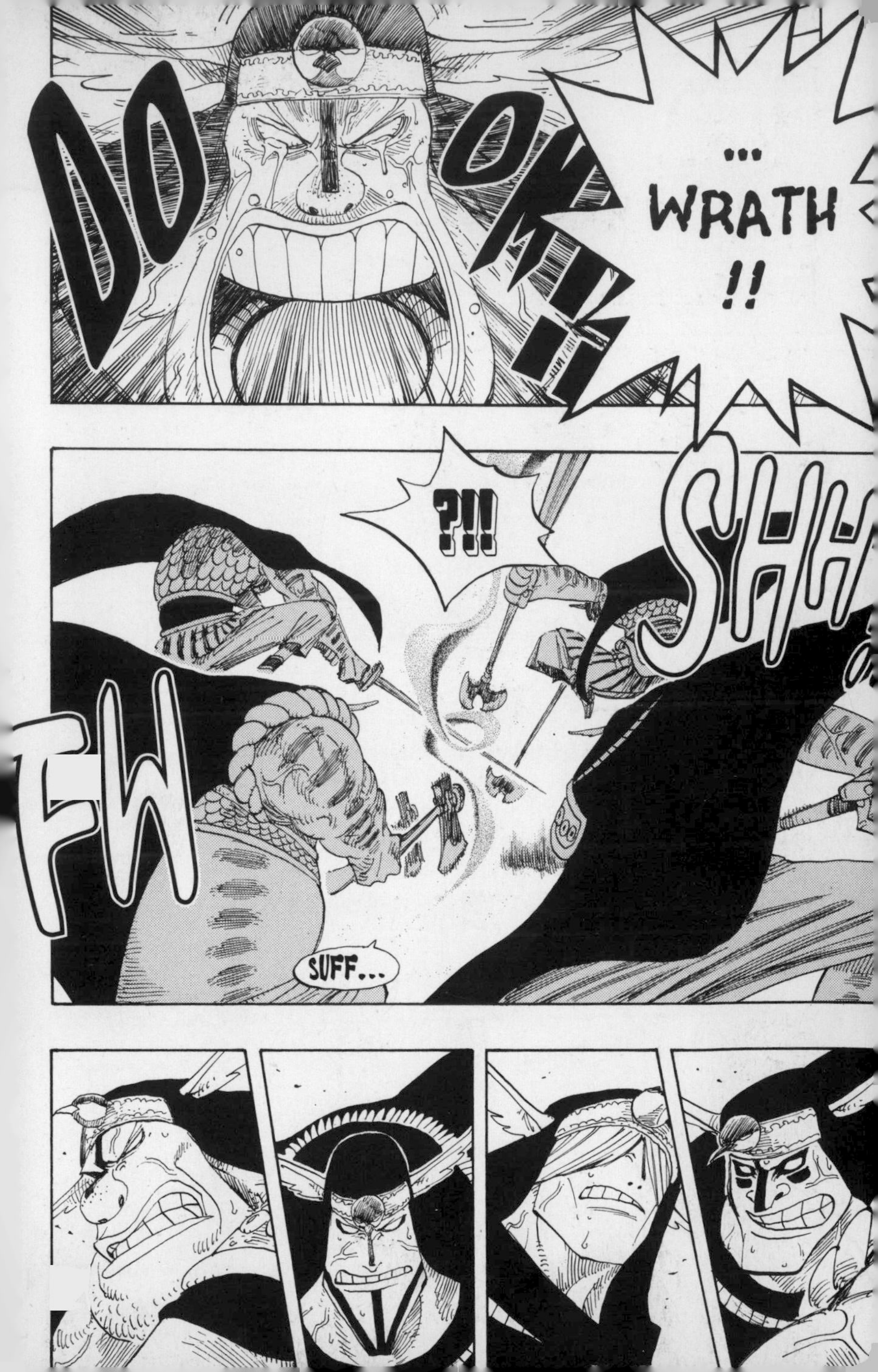
...WRATH !!
DO
SHH
?!!
FW
SUFF...

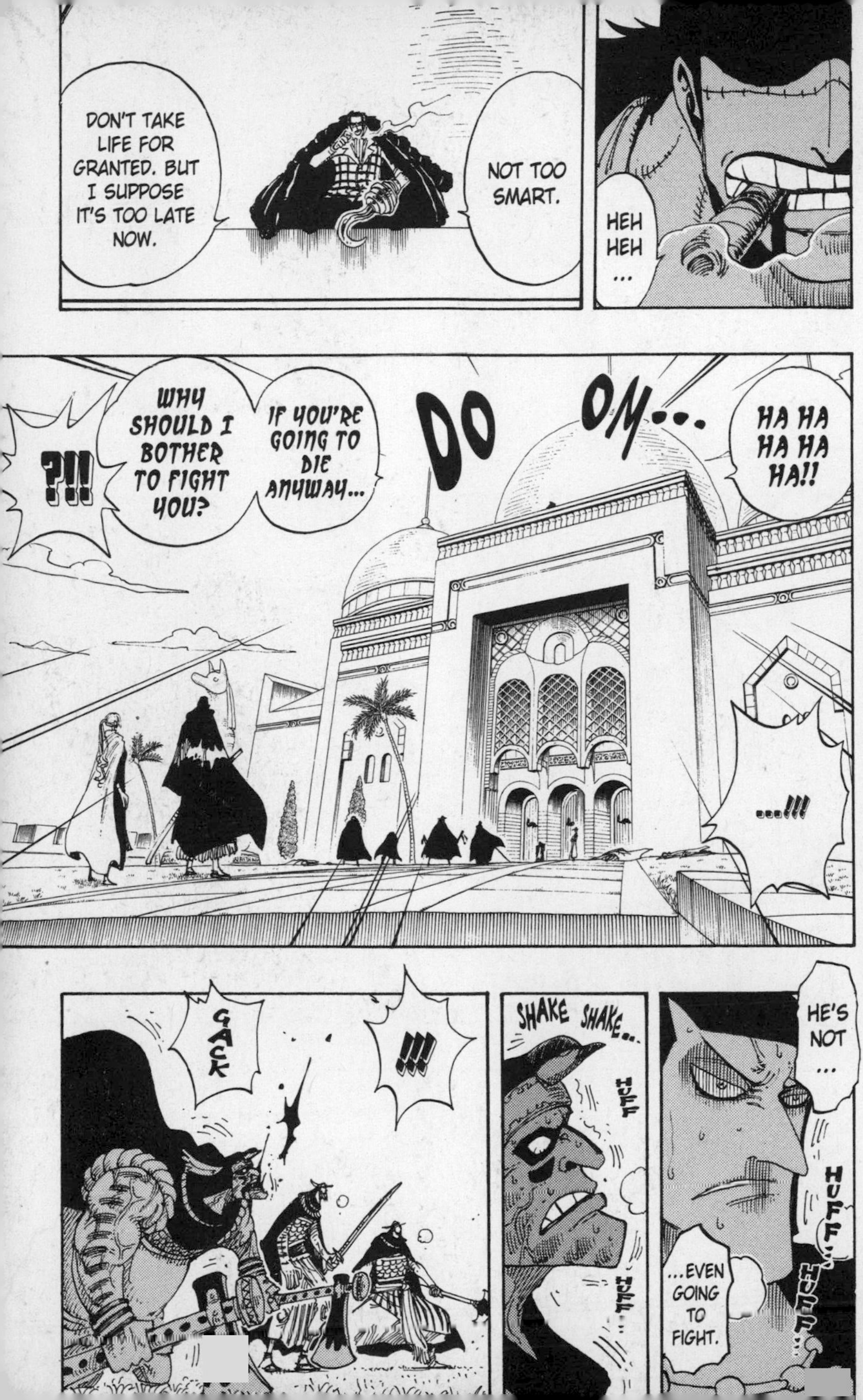
HEH HEH ...
NOT TOO SMART.
DON'T TAKE LIFE FOR GRANTED. BUT I SUPPOSE IT'S TOO LATE NOW.
HA HA HA HA HA!!
DO OM...
IF YOU'RE GOING TO DIE ANYWAY...
WHY SHOULD I BOTHER TO FIGHT YOU?
?!!
...!!!
HE'S NOT ...
HUFF HUFF HUFF...
...EVEN GOING TO FIGHT.
SHAKE SHAKE...
HUFF
HUFF...
!!!
GACK

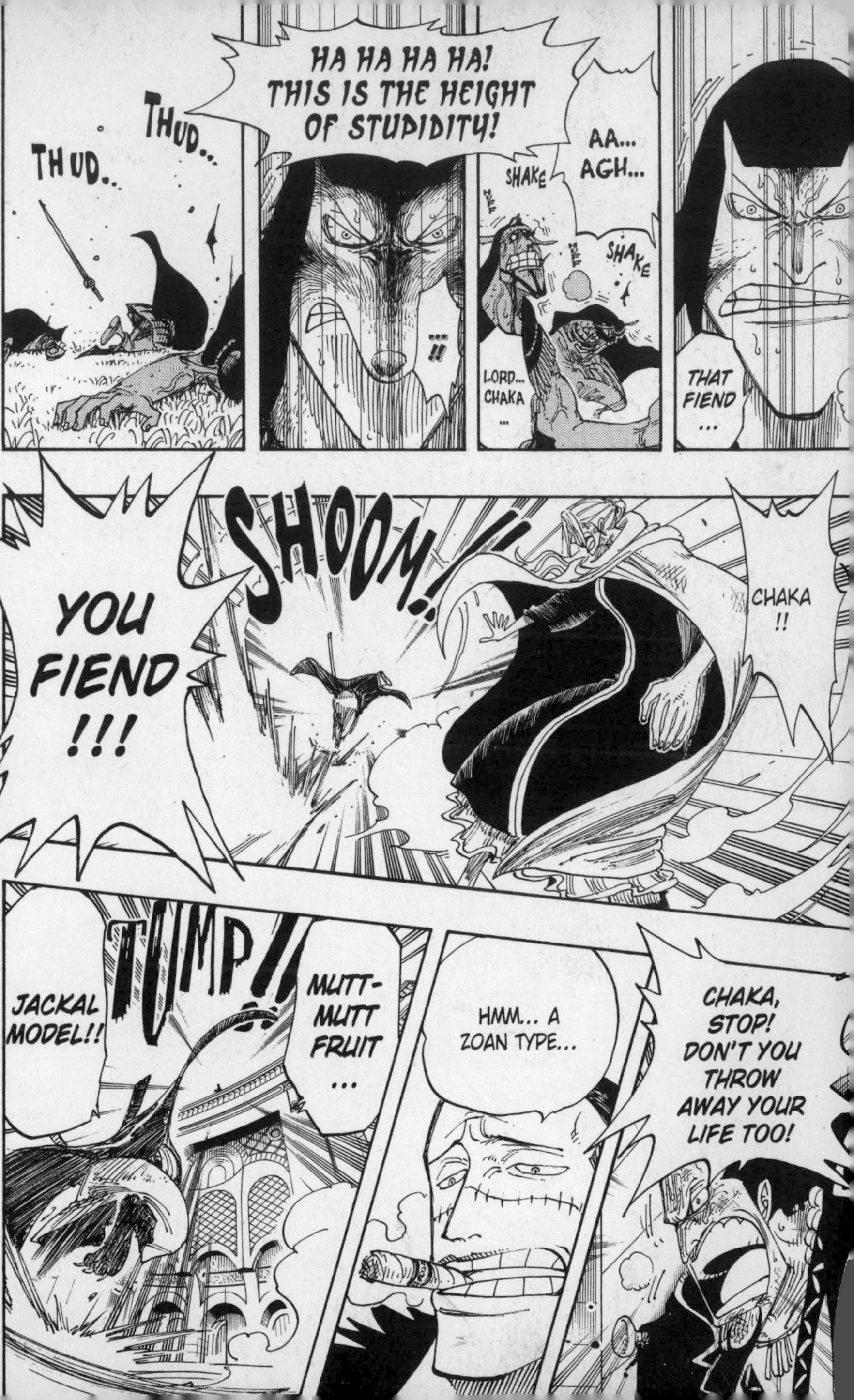
THAT FIEND ...
AA... AGH...
SHAKE
SHAKE
LORD... CHAKA ...
HA HA HA HA! THIS IS THE HEIGHT OF STUPIDITY!
...!!
THUD...
THUD...
CHAKA !!
SHOOM!!
YOU FIEND !!!
CHAKA, STOP! DON'T YOU THROW AWAY YOUR LIFE TOO!
HMM... A ZOAN TYPE...
MUTT-MUTT FRUIT ...
TUMP!!
JACKAL MODEL!!

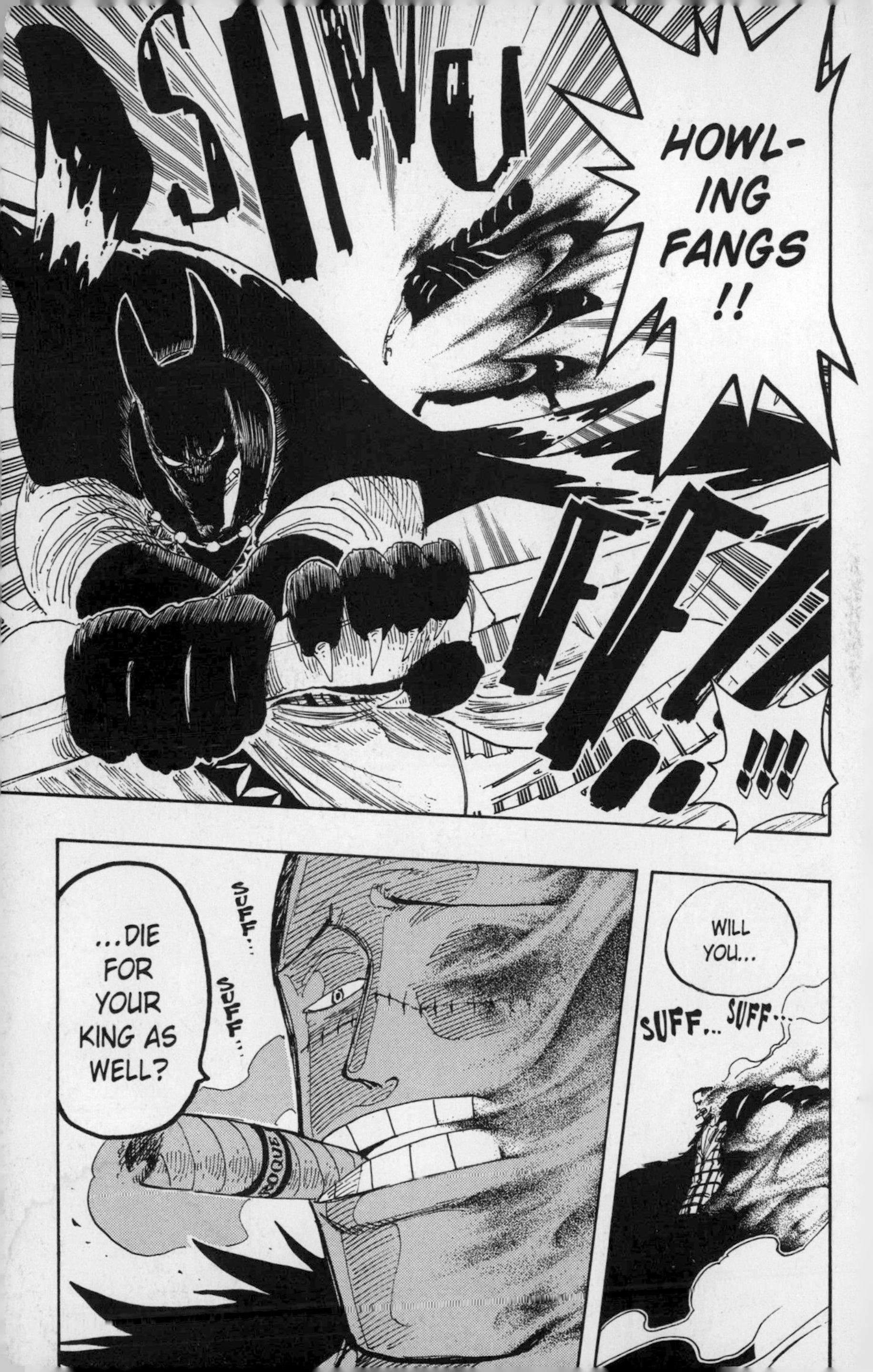
HOWL-ING FANGS!!
WILL YOU...
SUFF... SUFF...
...DIE FOR YOUR KING AS WELL?
SUFF... SUFF...

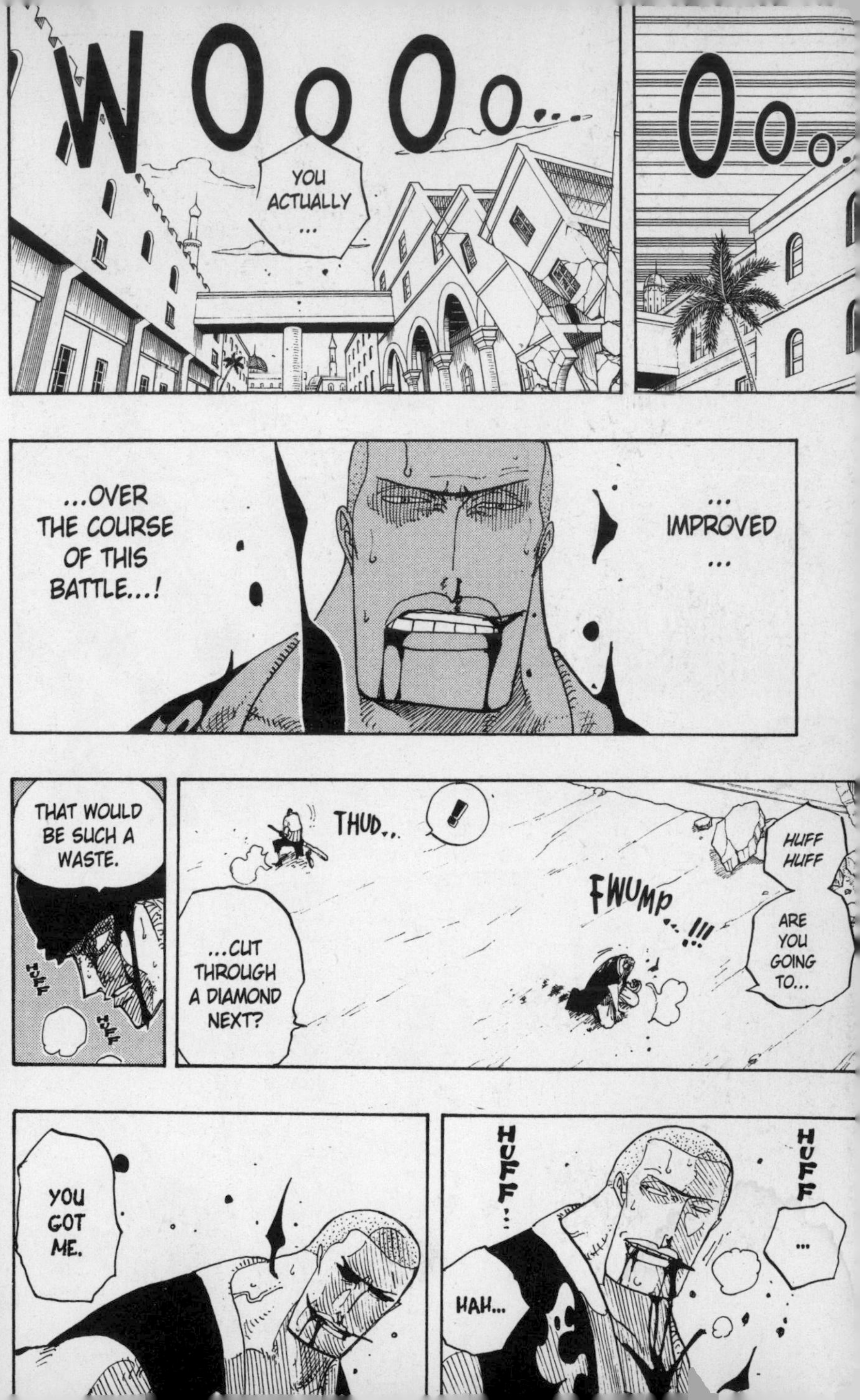
WOOOo... OOo.
YOU ACTUALLY ...
... IMPROVED ...
...OVER THE COURSE OF THIS BATTLE...!
HUFF HUFF
ARE YOU GOING TO...
FWUMP...!!!
!
THUD..
...CUT THROUGH A DIAMOND NEXT?
THAT WOULD BE SUCH A WASTE.
HUFF
HUFF
HUFF
...
HUFF...
HAH...
YOU GOT ME.

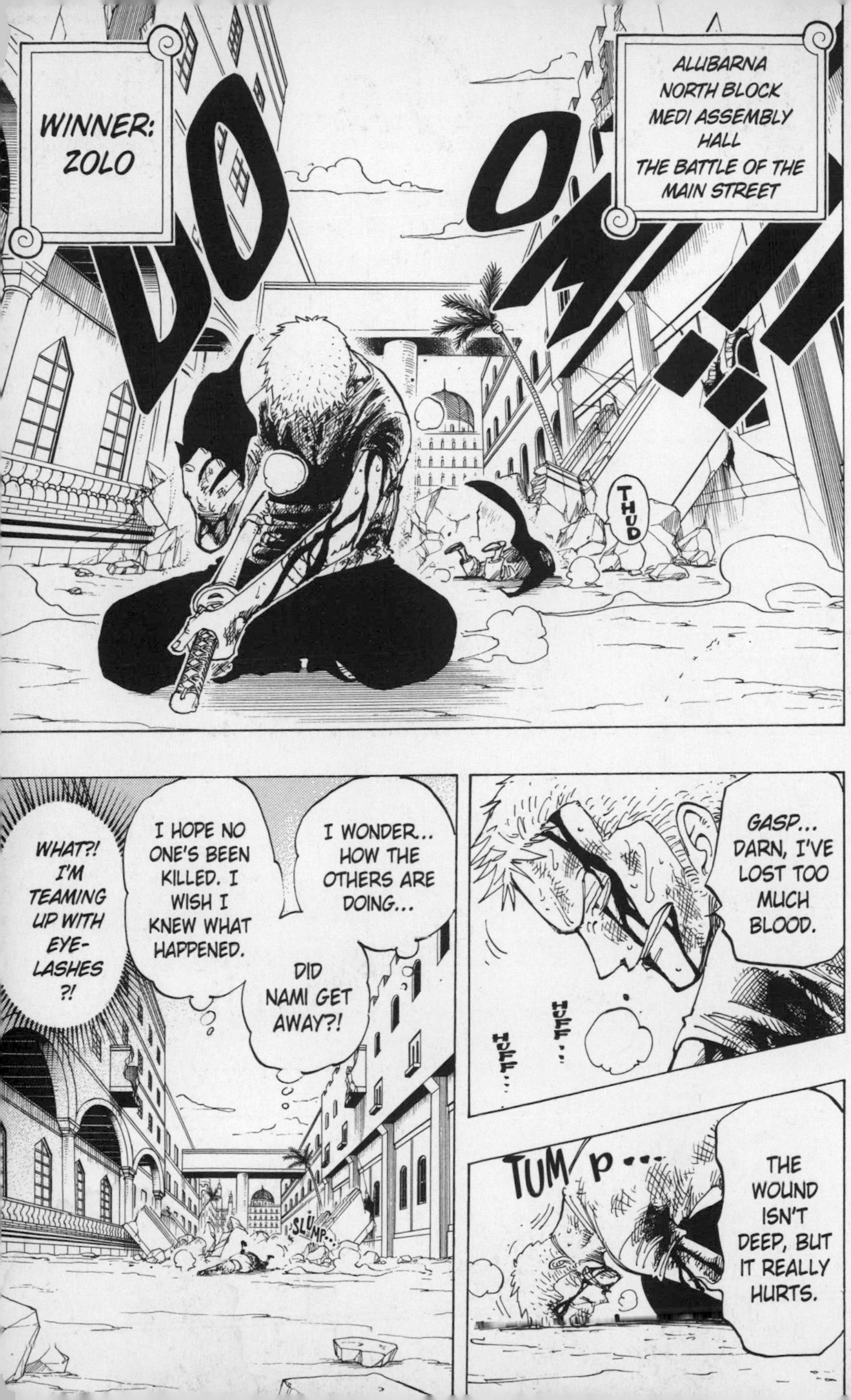
ALUBARNA NORTH BLOCK MEDI ASSEMBLY HALL THE BATTLE OF THE MAIN STREET
WINNER: ZOLO
DOOM...!!!
THUD
GASP... DARN, I'VE LOST TOO MUCH BLOOD.
HUFF...
HUFF...
TUMP...
THE WOUND ISN'T DEEP, BUT IT REALLY HURTS.
I WONDER... HOW THE OTHERS ARE DOING...
DID NAMI GET AWAY?!
I HOPE NO ONE'S BEEN KILLED. I WISH I KNEW WHAT HAPPENED.
WHAT?! I'M TEAMING UP WITH EYE-LASHES ?!
SLUMP...

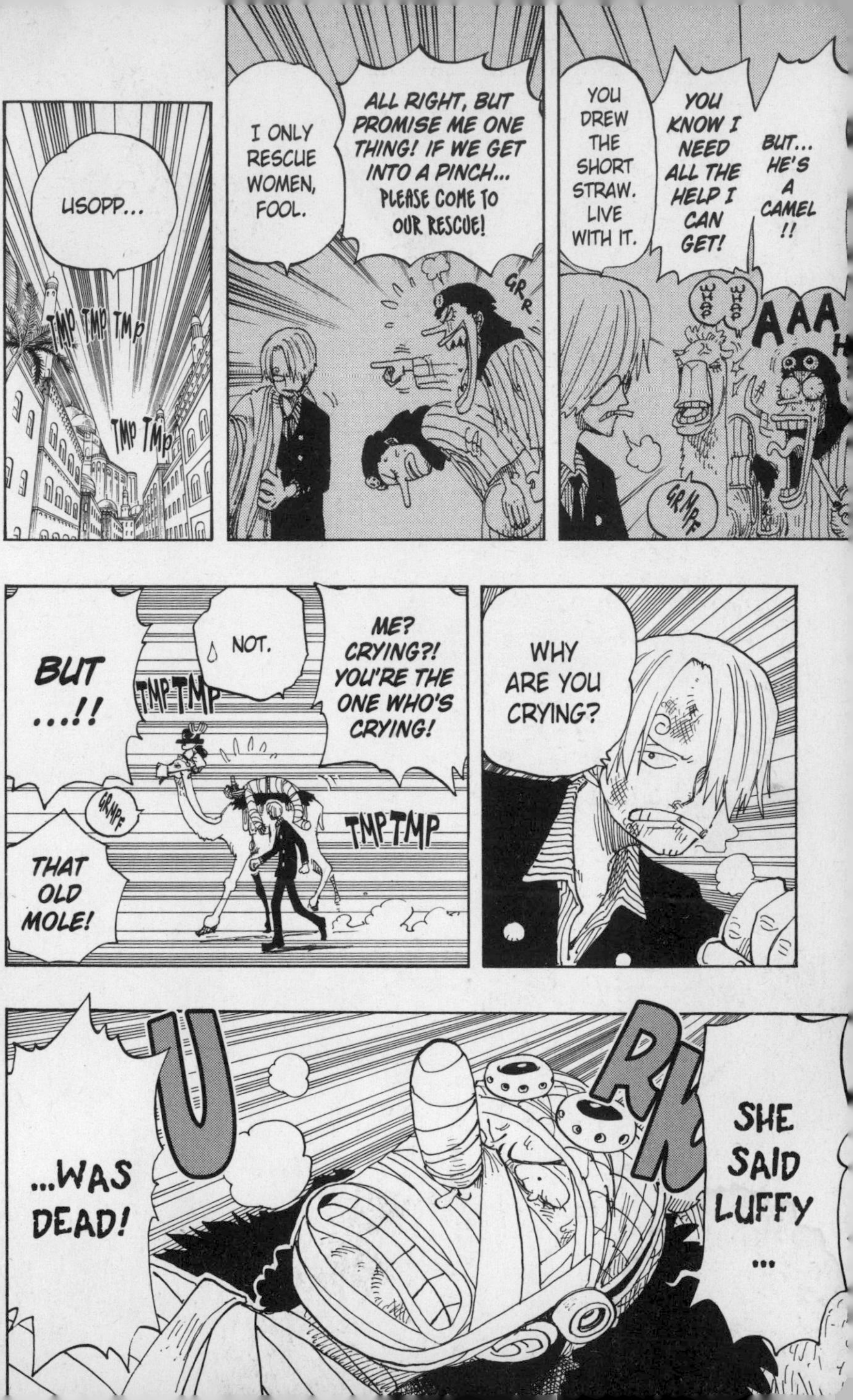
BUT... HE'S A CAMEL !!
YOU KNOW I NEED ALL THE HELP I CAN GET!
YOU DREW THE SHORT STRAW. LIVE WITH IT.
WHAP
WHAP
GRMPF
ALL RIGHT, BUT PROMISE ME ONE THING! IF WE GET INTO A PINCH... PLEASE COME TO OUR RESCUE!
I ONLY RESCUE WOMEN, FOOL.
GRR
USOPP...
TMP TMP TMp
TMP TMp
WHY ARE YOU CRYING?
ME? CRYING?! YOU'RE THE ONE WHO'S CRYING!
NOT.
BUT ...!!
TMP TMP
GRMPF
TMP TMP
THAT OLD MOLE!
SHE SAID LUFFY ...
...WAS DEAD!

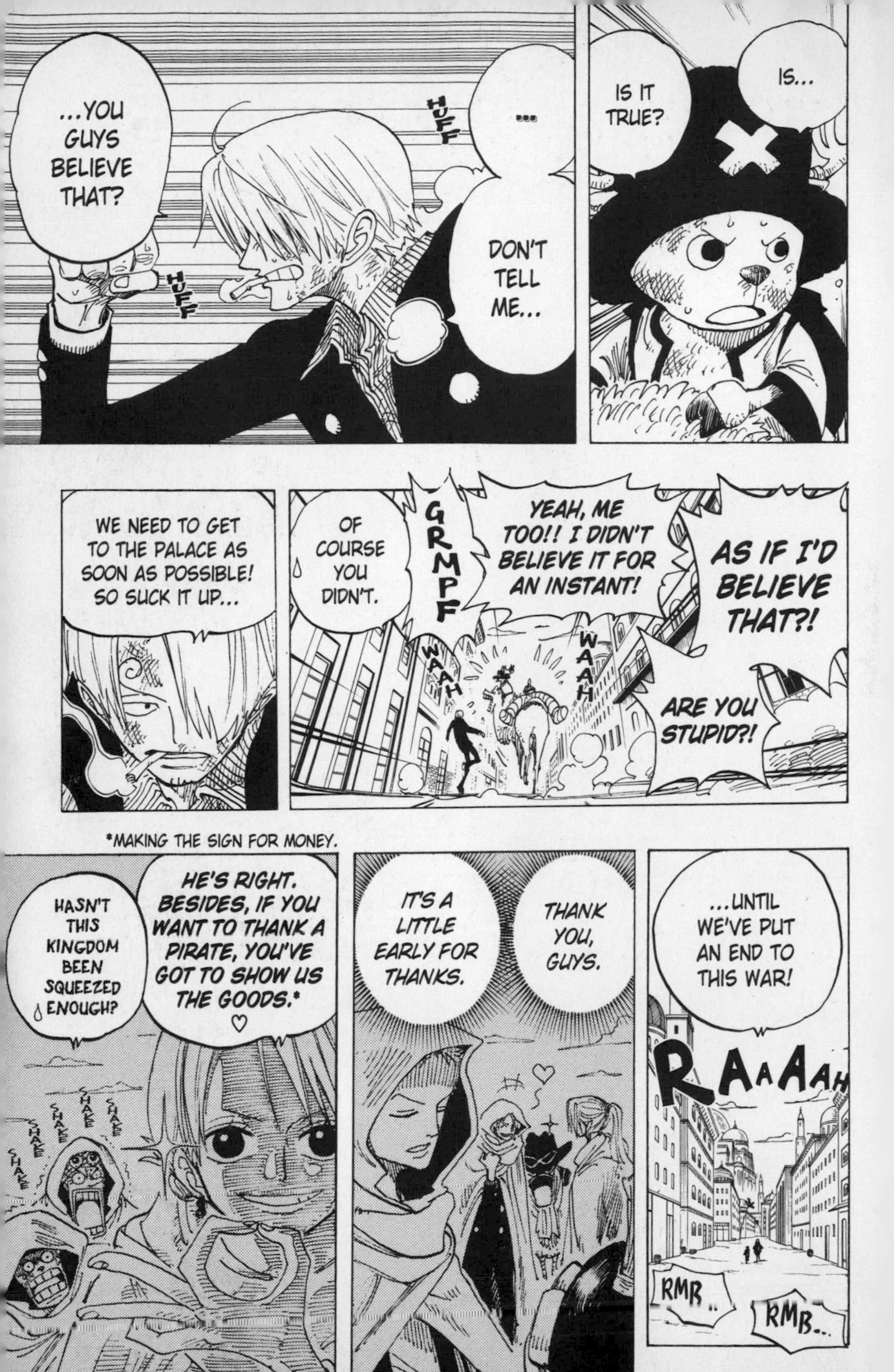
IS...
IS IT TRUE?
...
HUFF
DON'T TELL ME...
...YOU GUYS BELIEVE THAT?
HUFF
AS IF I'D BELIEVE THAT?!
YEAH, ME TOO!! I DIDN'T BELIEVE IT FOR AN INSTANT!
GRMPF
OF COURSE YOU DIDN'T.
WAAAH
WAAH
ARE YOU STUPID?!
WE NEED TO GET TO THE PALACE AS SOON AS POSSIBLE! SO SUCK IT UP...
...UNTIL WE'VE PUT AN END TO THIS WAR!
RAAAAH
RMB...
RMR...
THANK YOU, GUYS.
IT'S A LITTLE EARLY FOR THANKS.
HE'S RIGHT. BESIDES, IF YOU WANT TO THANK A PIRATE, YOU'VE GOT TO SHOW US THE GOODS.* ♡
HASN'T THIS KINGDOM BEEN SQUEEZED ENOUGH?
SHAKE
SHAKE
SHAKE
SHAKE

*MAKING THE SIGN FOR MONEY.

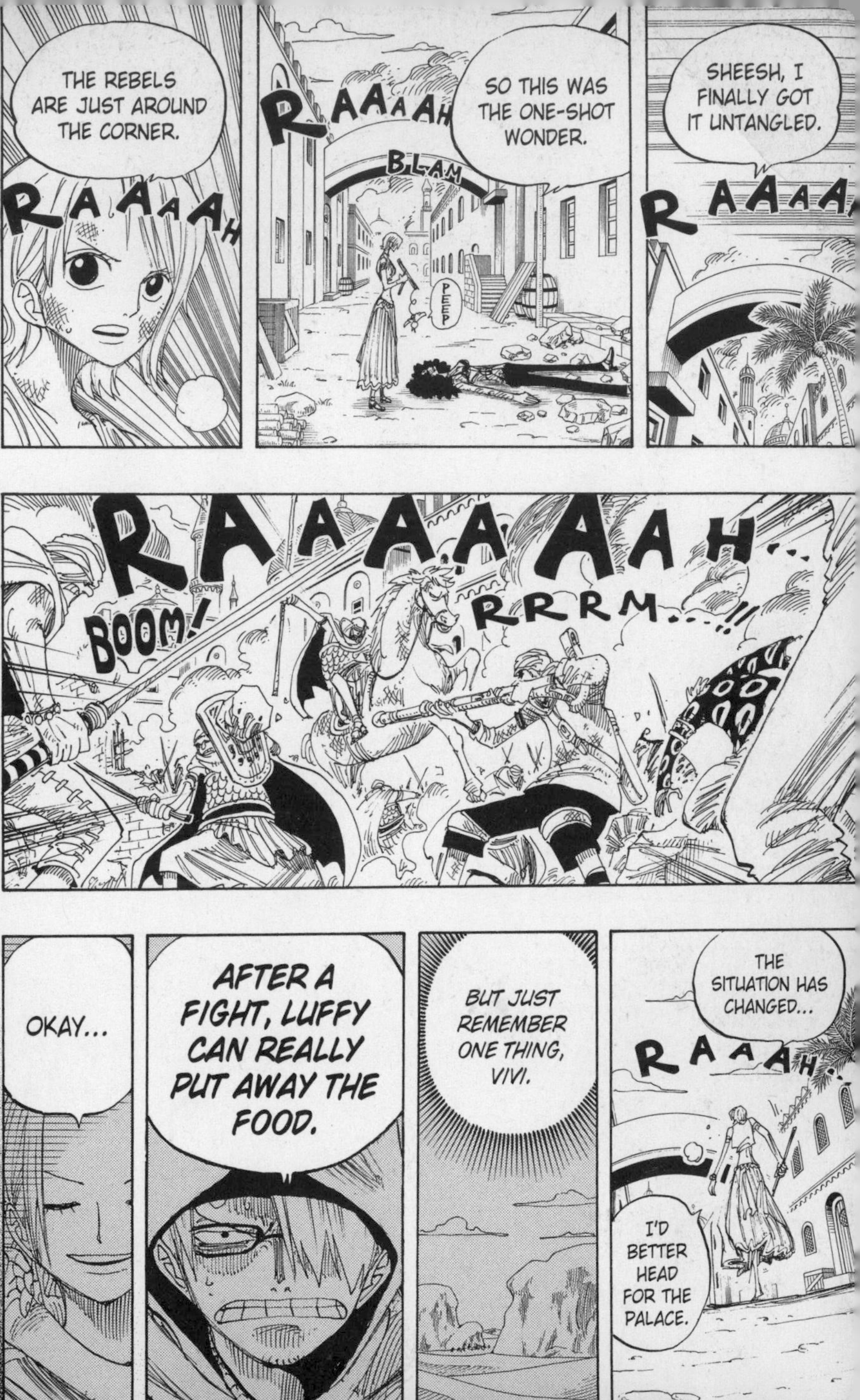
SHEESH, I FINALLY GOT IT UNTANGLED.
RAAAA
SO THIS WAS THE ONE-SHOT WONDER.
RAAAAH
BLAM
PEEP
THE REBELS ARE JUST AROUND THE CORNER.
RAAAAH
RAAAAAAH...
RRRM...!!
BOOM!
THE SITUATION HAS CHANGED...
RAAAH...
I'D BETTER HEAD FOR THE PALACE.
BUT JUST REMEMBER ONE THING, VIVI.
AFTER A FIGHT, LUFFY CAN REALLY PUT AWAY THE FOOD.
OKAY...

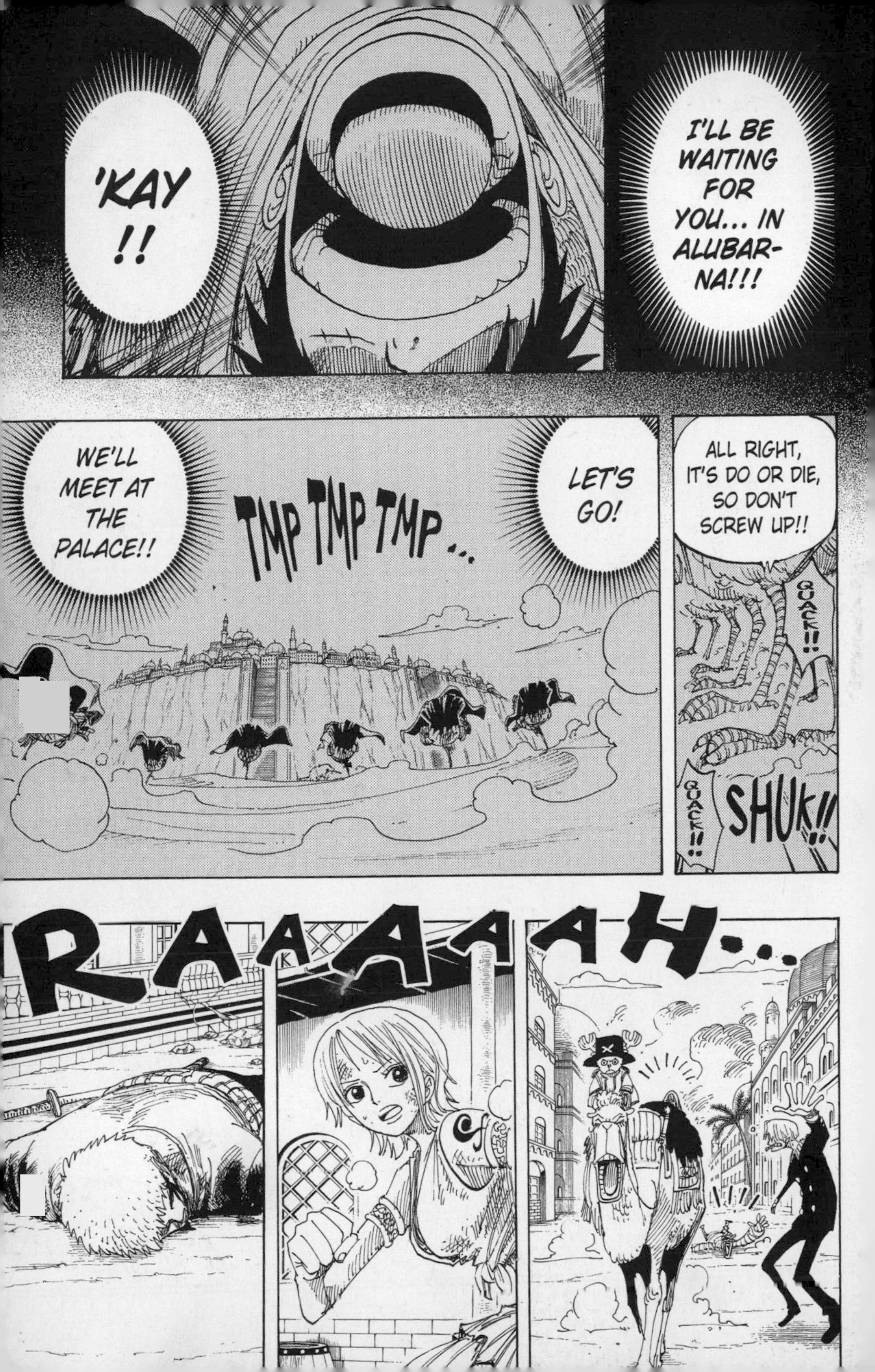
I'LL BE WAITING FOR YOU... IN ALUBARNA!!!
'KAY !!
ALL RIGHT, IT'S DO OR DIE, SO DON'T SCREW UP!!
GUACK!!
GUACK!!
SHUK!!
LET'S GO!
TMP TMP TMP...
WE'LL MEET AT THE PALACE!!
RAAAAAH...

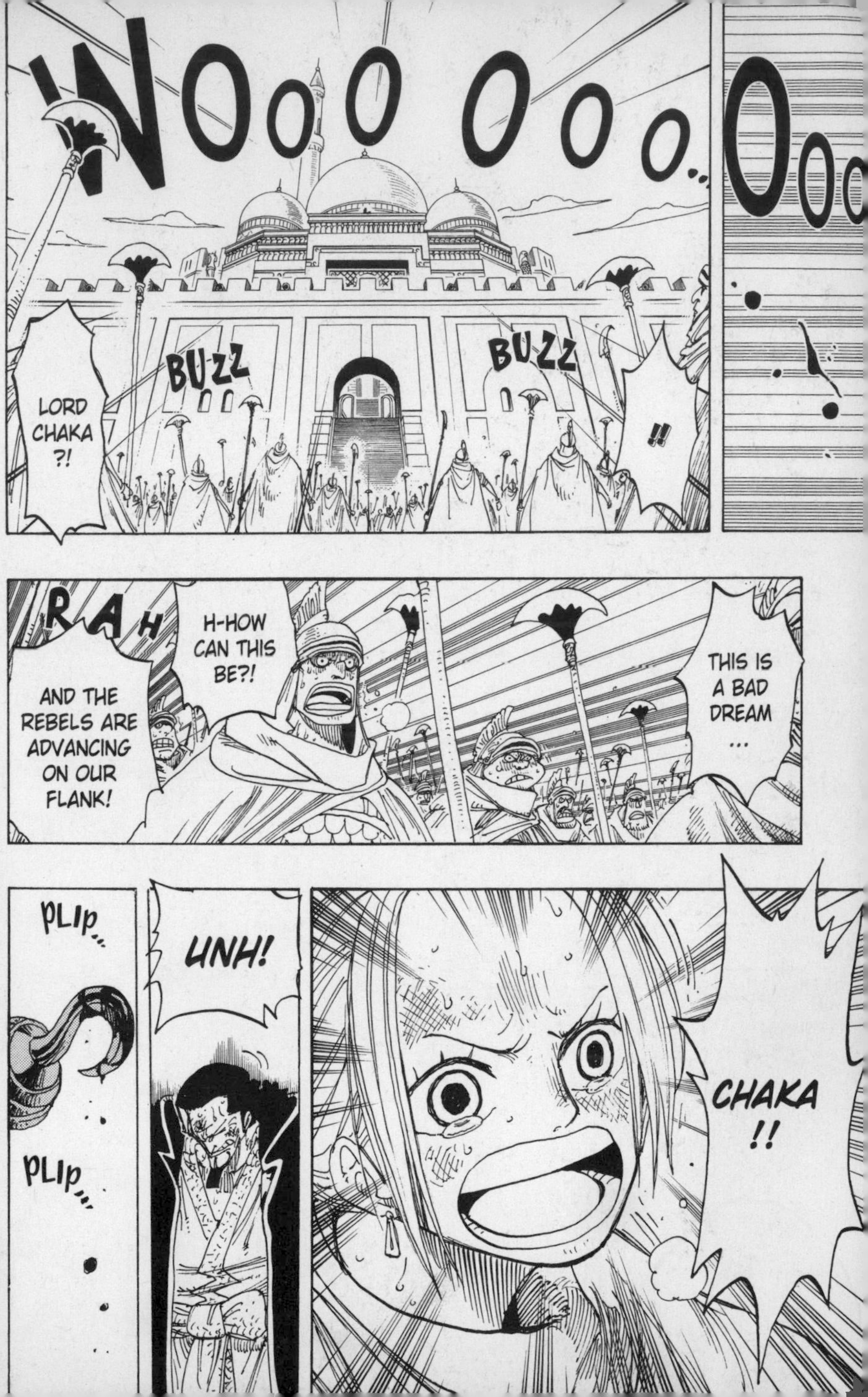
WOOOO OOOO...OOO
!!
BUZZ
BUZZ
LORD CHAKA ?!
THIS IS A BAD DREAM ...
H-HOW CAN THIS BE?!
RAH
AND THE REBELS ARE ADVANCING ON OUR FLANK!
CHAKA !!
UNH!
PLIP...
PLIP...

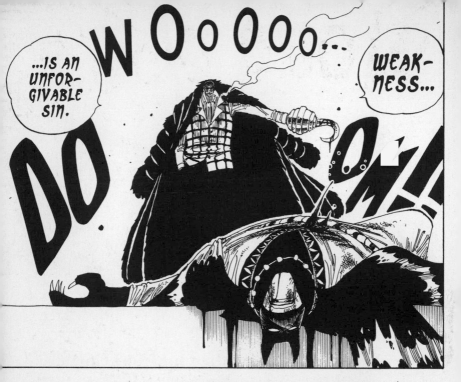

...IS AN UNFORGIVABLE SIN.

WOOoOOo...

DO

WEAKNESS...

HUH?

SH.F.

VIVI!!

TICK.. TICK..

PALACE SQUARE TIME UNTIL THE EXPLOSION...

25 MINUTES

TICK.. TICK..

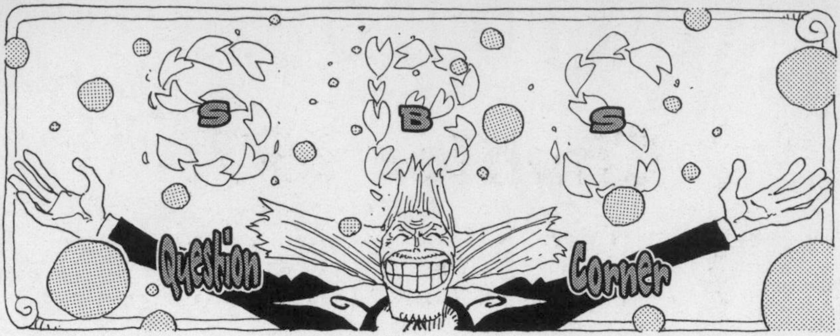
SBS
Question
Corner

Reader: Just now, I came upon a person in strange glasses lying in the street. So I bought him a beef bowl for lunch. Out of gratitude, he gave me an unusual ring with a sheet of instructions that read "How to Hypnotize People." So, since you've been having trouble lately getting the Question Corner started, I'm going to hypnotize you to help it go more smoothly.
Are you ready? Look closely at the ring. When I say "One, two, djanko!" you will begin the Question Corner immediately, no matter what.
Here I go. ♡ One, two, djanko!

**Whoa! Let's start the Question Corner!**

Oda: Whaat?! Did you hypnotize yourself?!

Reader: Oda Sensei! I love, love, love, love, love *One Piece!*
I go to the store every day to see if the latest volume has arrived. The waiting is agony! So would you list the dates when *One Piece* hits the stores?! Please!
--White Cat Pirates

Oda: Huh? That's a lot of trouble, but I understand. So for the sake of you fans that buy the graphic novel, I'm going to reveal the release schedule. Please note it in your calendars. *One Piece* comics are released in the following cycle: two months, two months, three months. So after three months, you'll know when the next two volumes will be released. Got that?*
[*This release schedule is for Japan. –Ed.]

Oda: Oh yes, I forgot. There was an error in Volume 21. I found it myself and I wanted to tell you about it right away. In the title drawing for the Question Corner I drew Crocus and Laboon again, like I did in Volume 18. Oh well. I must've had Crocus fever in Volume 21. Am I repentant? Yes, yes. (←I say this as I pick my nose.) Anyway, we'll continue in the next Question Corner.

# Chapter 197:

# THE LEADERS

KANJI ON CLOTHING SAYS "DEEP" -- ED.

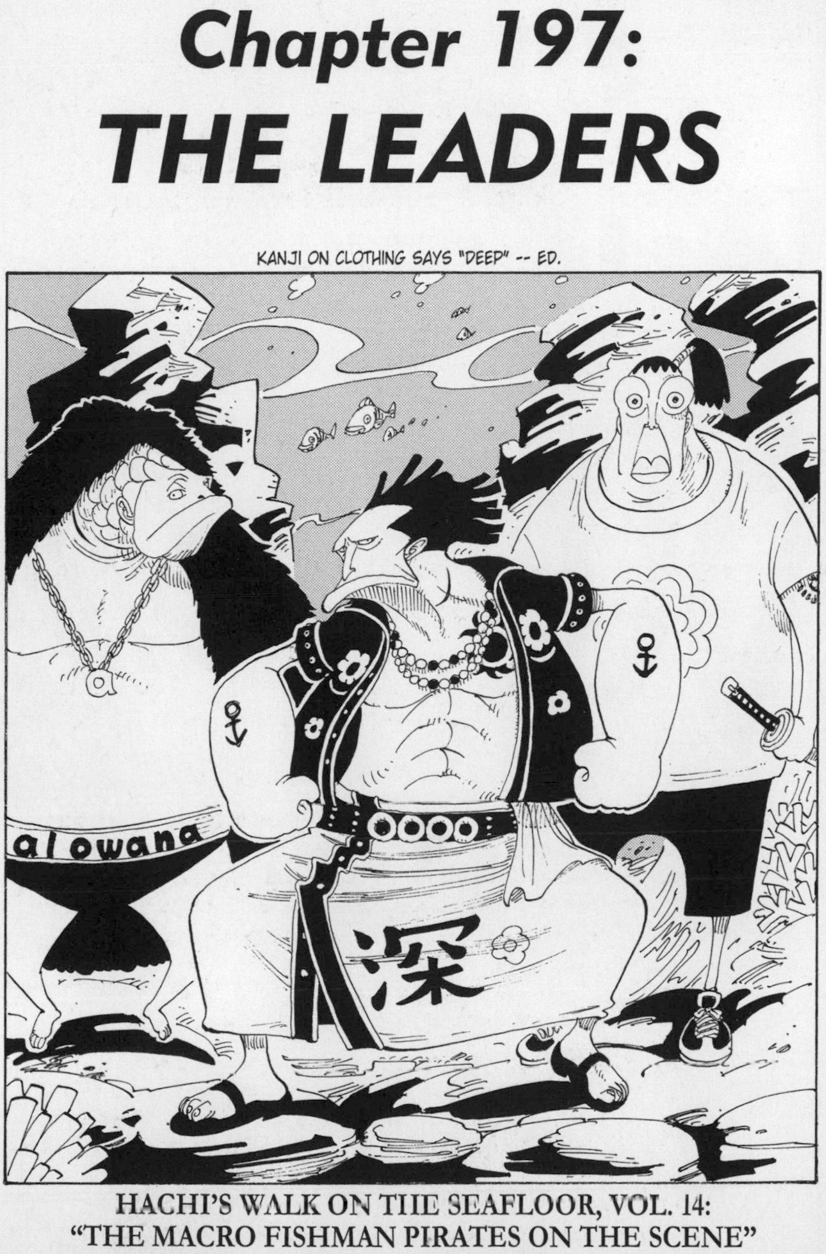
alowana
深

HACHI'S WALK ON THE SEAFLOOR, VOL. 14:
"THE MACRO FISHMAN PIRATES ON THE SCENE"

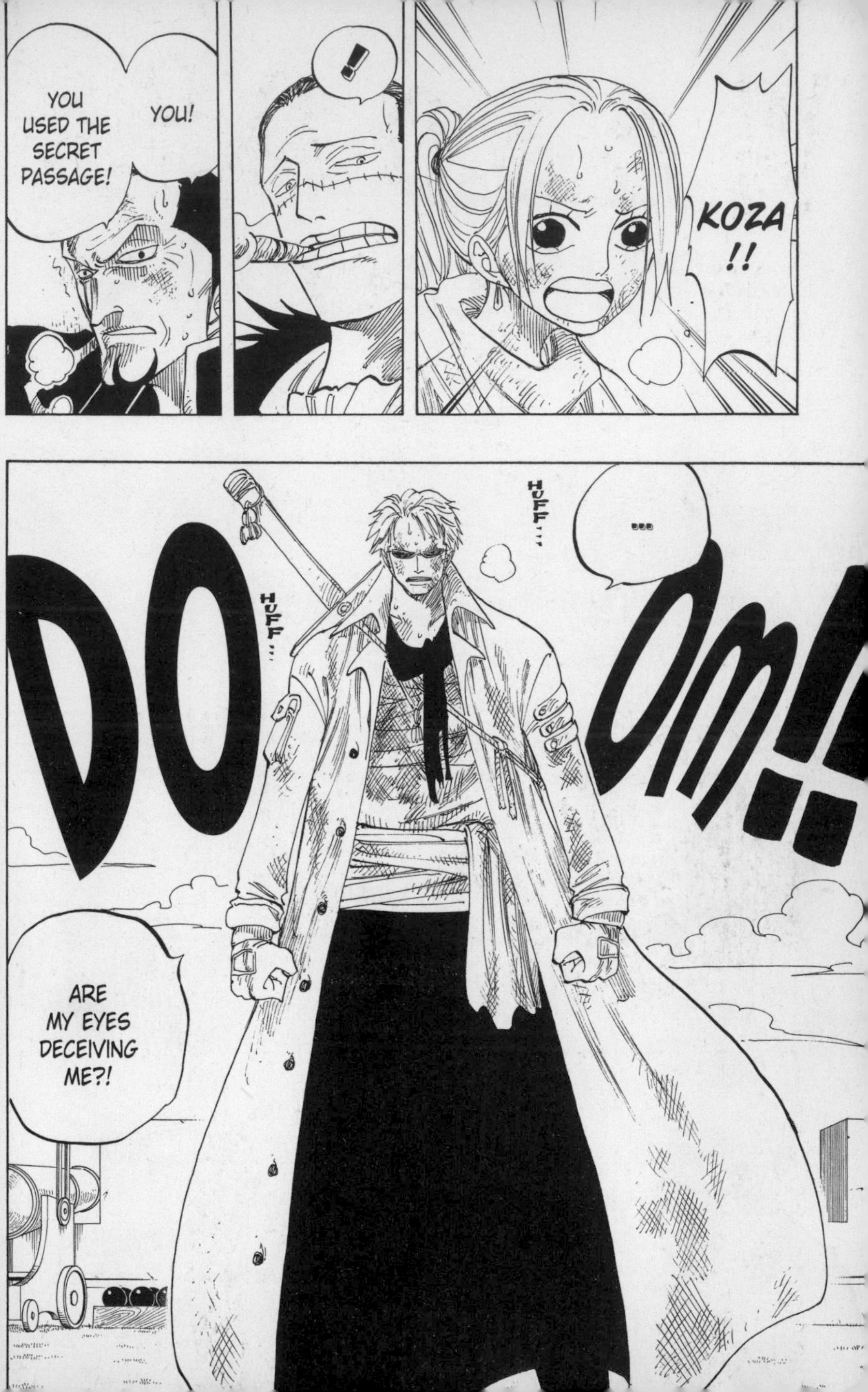
KOZA !!
!
YOU!
YOU USED THE SECRET PASSAGE!
...
HUFF...
HUFF...
DO
OM!!
ARE MY EYES DECEIVING ME?!

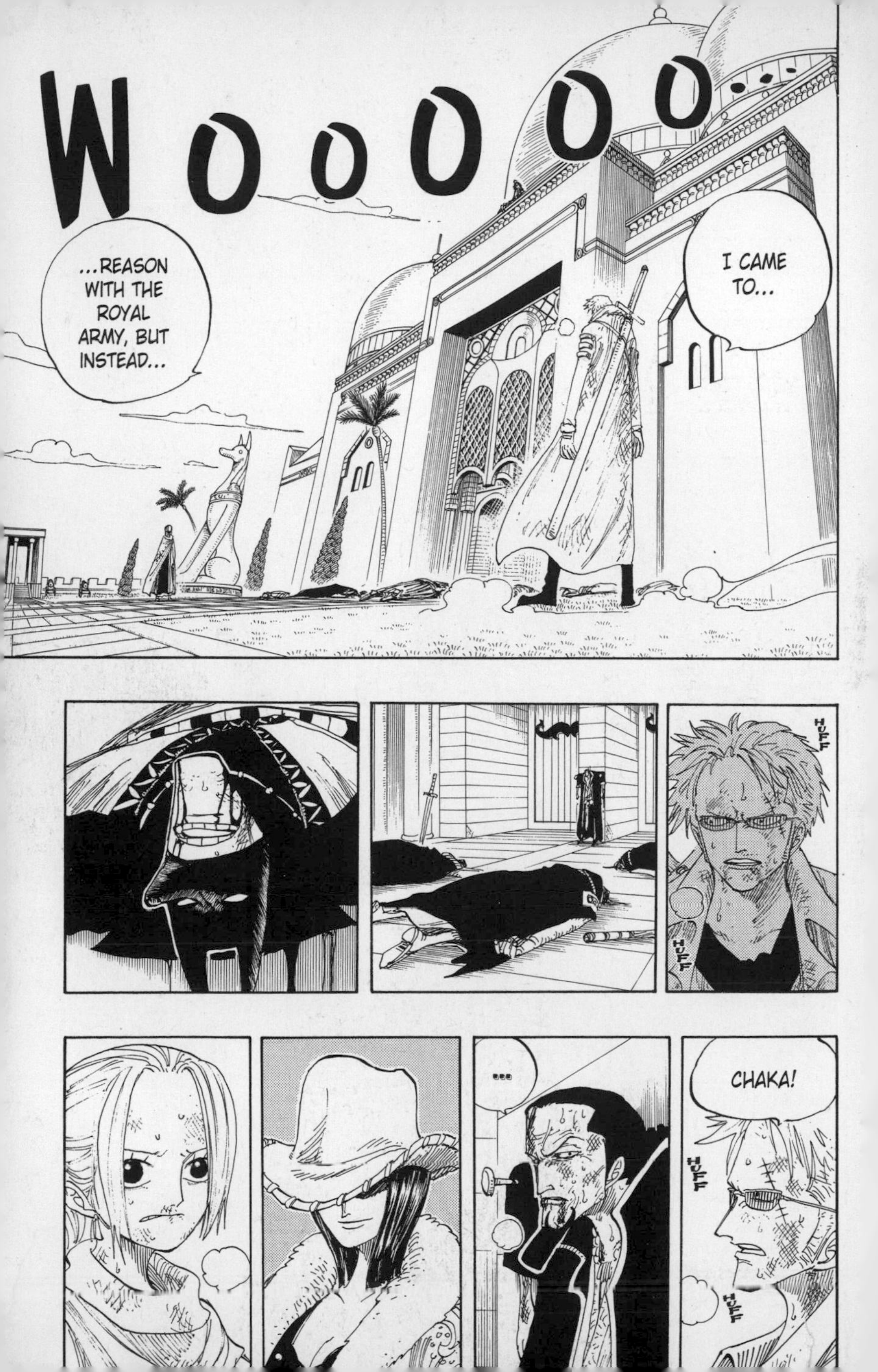
WOOOOOO...
I CAME TO...
...REASON WITH THE ROYAL ARMY, BUT INSTEAD...
HUFF
HUFF
CHAKA!
HUFF
HUFF
...

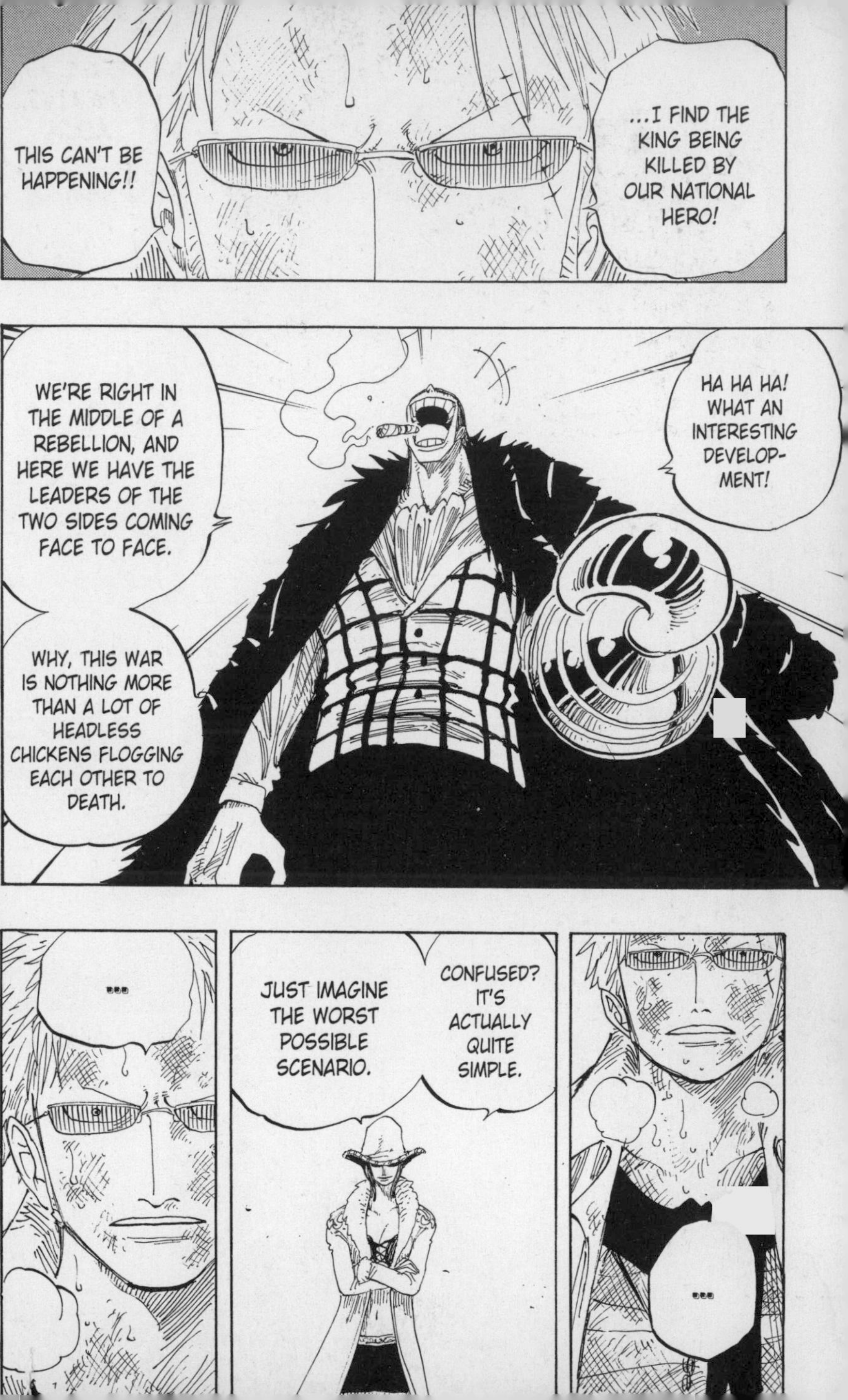
...I FIND THE KING BEING KILLED BY OUR NATIONAL HERO!
THIS CAN'T BE HAPPENING!!
HA HA HA! WHAT AN INTERESTING DEVELOP-MENT!
WE'RE RIGHT IN THE MIDDLE OF A REBELLION, AND HERE WE HAVE THE LEADERS OF THE TWO SIDES COMING FACE TO FACE.
WHY, THIS WAR IS NOTHING MORE THAN A LOT OF HEADLESS CHICKENS FLOGGING EACH OTHER TO DEATH.
...
CONFUSED? IT'S ACTUALLY QUITE SIMPLE.
JUST IMAGINE THE WORST POSSIBLE SCENARIO.
...

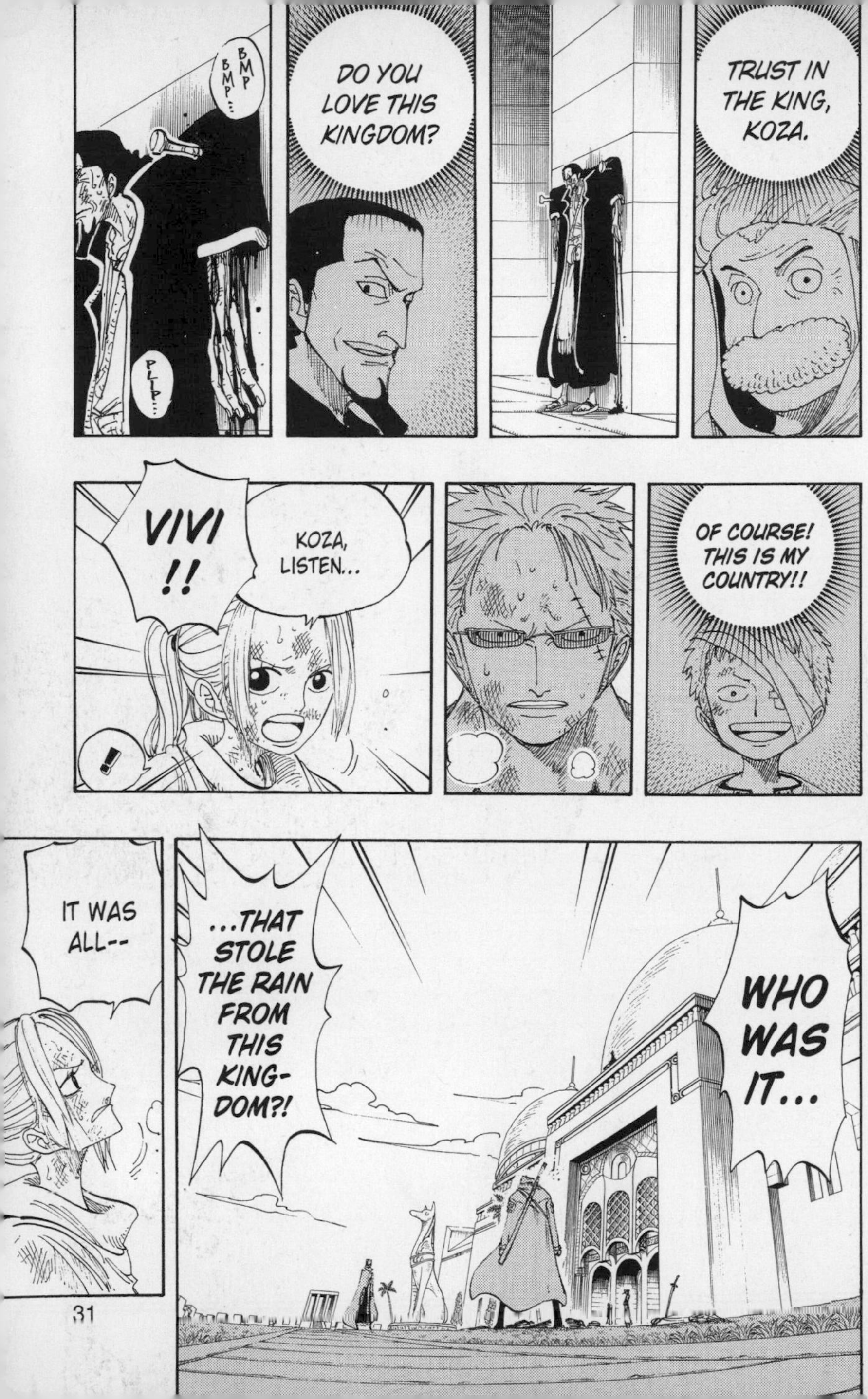
TRUST IN THE KING, KOZA.
DO YOU LOVE THIS KINGDOM?
BMP BMP...
PLIP...
OF COURSE! THIS IS MY COUNTRY!!
KOZA, LISTEN...
VIVI !!
!
WHO WAS IT...
...THAT STOLE THE RAIN FROM THIS KING-DOM?!
IT WAS ALL--

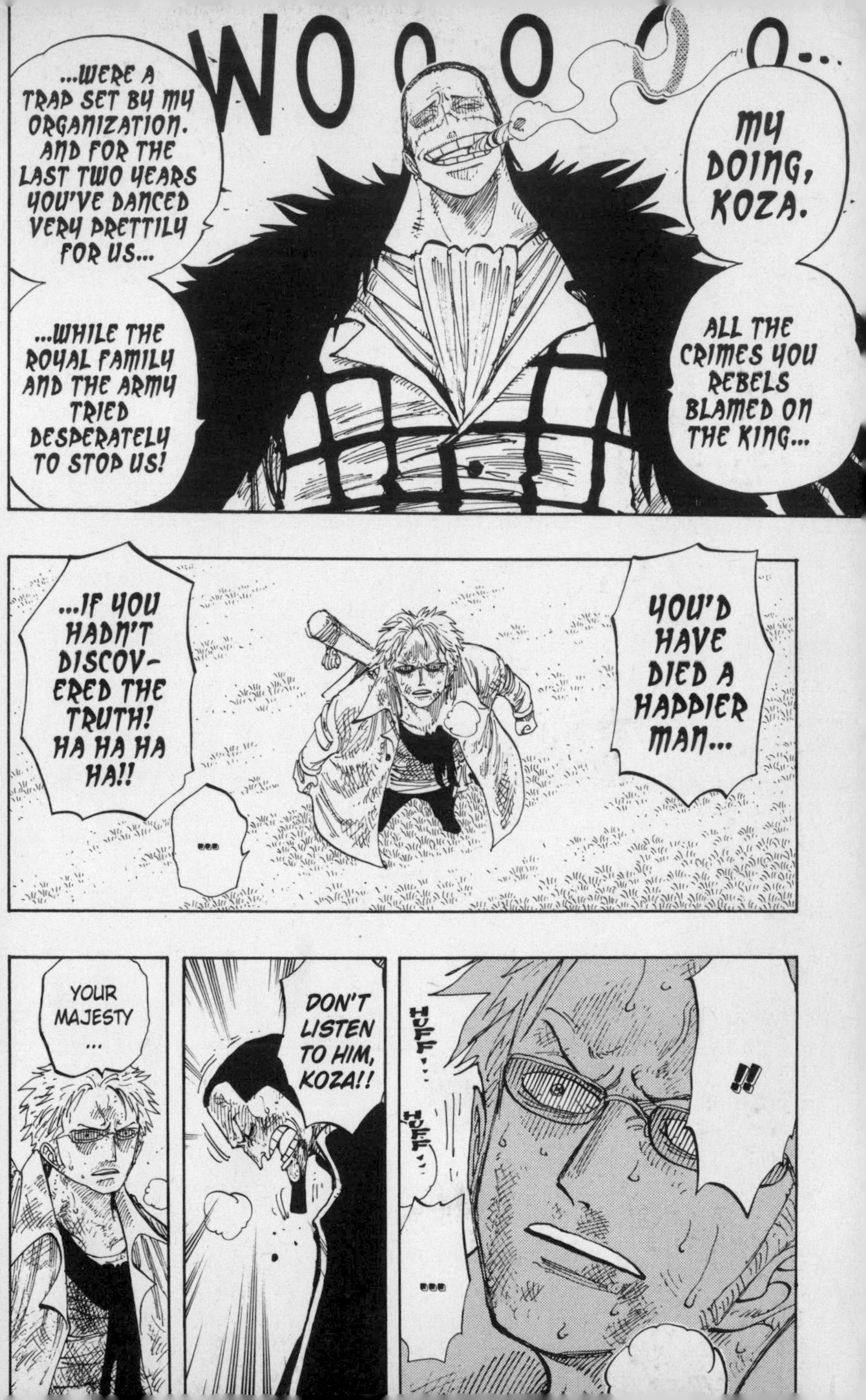
WOOOOO...
MY DOING, KOZA.
ALL THE CRIMES YOU REBELS BLAMED ON THE KING...
...WERE A TRAP SET BY MY ORGANIZATION. AND FOR THE LAST TWO YEARS YOU'VE DANCED VERY PRETTILY FOR US...
...WHILE THE ROYAL FAMILY AND THE ARMY TRIED DESPERATELY TO STOP US!
YOU'D HAVE DIED A HAPPIER MAN...
...IF YOU HADN'T DISCOVERED THE TRUTH! HA HA HA HA!!
...
!!
HUFF...
HUFF...
...
DON'T LISTEN TO HIM, KOZA!!
YOUR MAJESTY ...

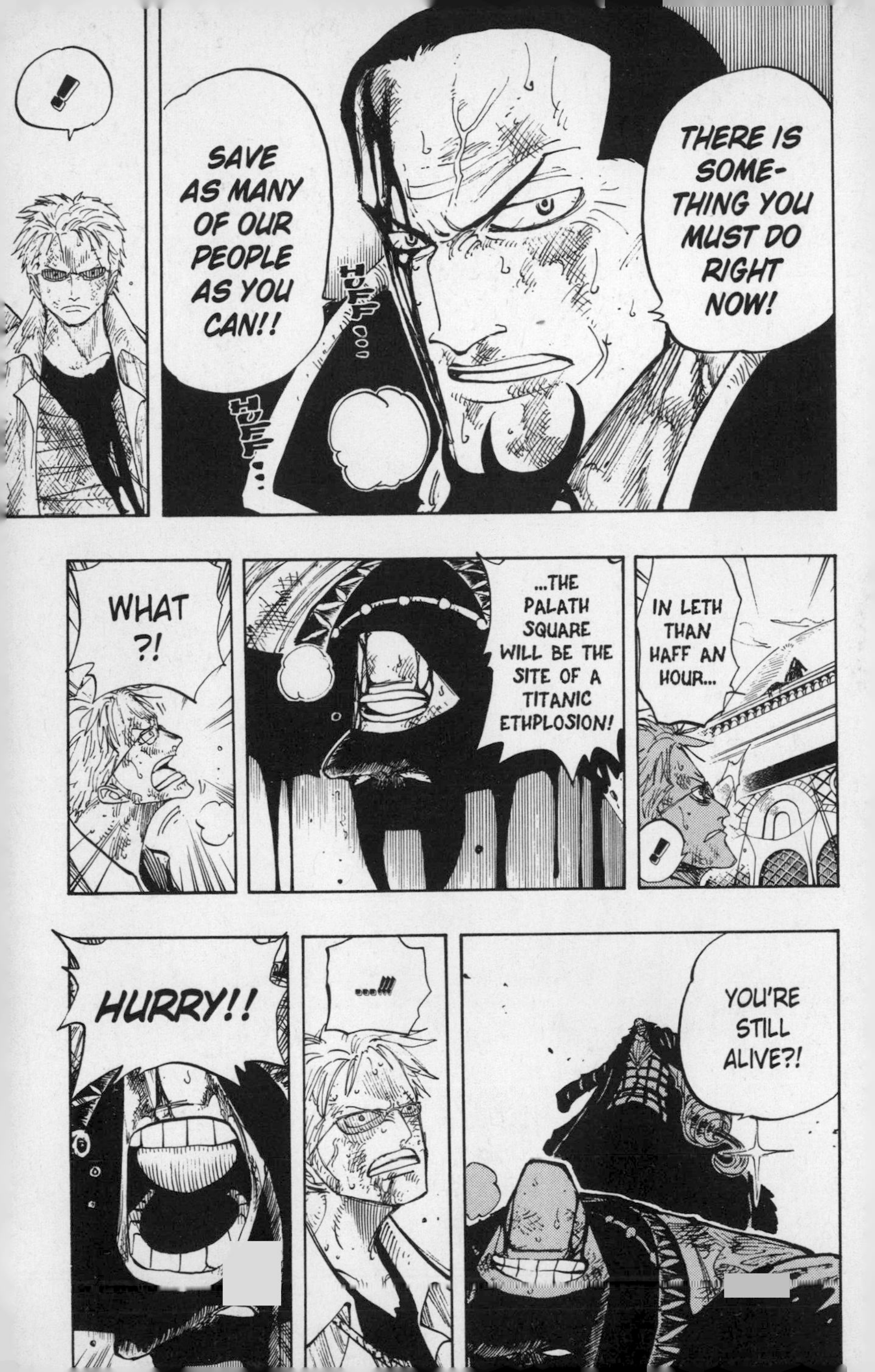
THERE IS SOME-THING YOU MUST DO RIGHT NOW!
SAVE AS MANY OF OUR PEOPLE AS YOU CAN!!
HUFF...
HUFF...
!
IN LETH THAN HAFF AN HOUR...
!
...THE PALATH SQUARE WILL BE THE SITE OF A TITANIC ETHPLOSION!
WHAT?!
YOU'RE STILL ALIVE?!
...!!!
HURRY!!

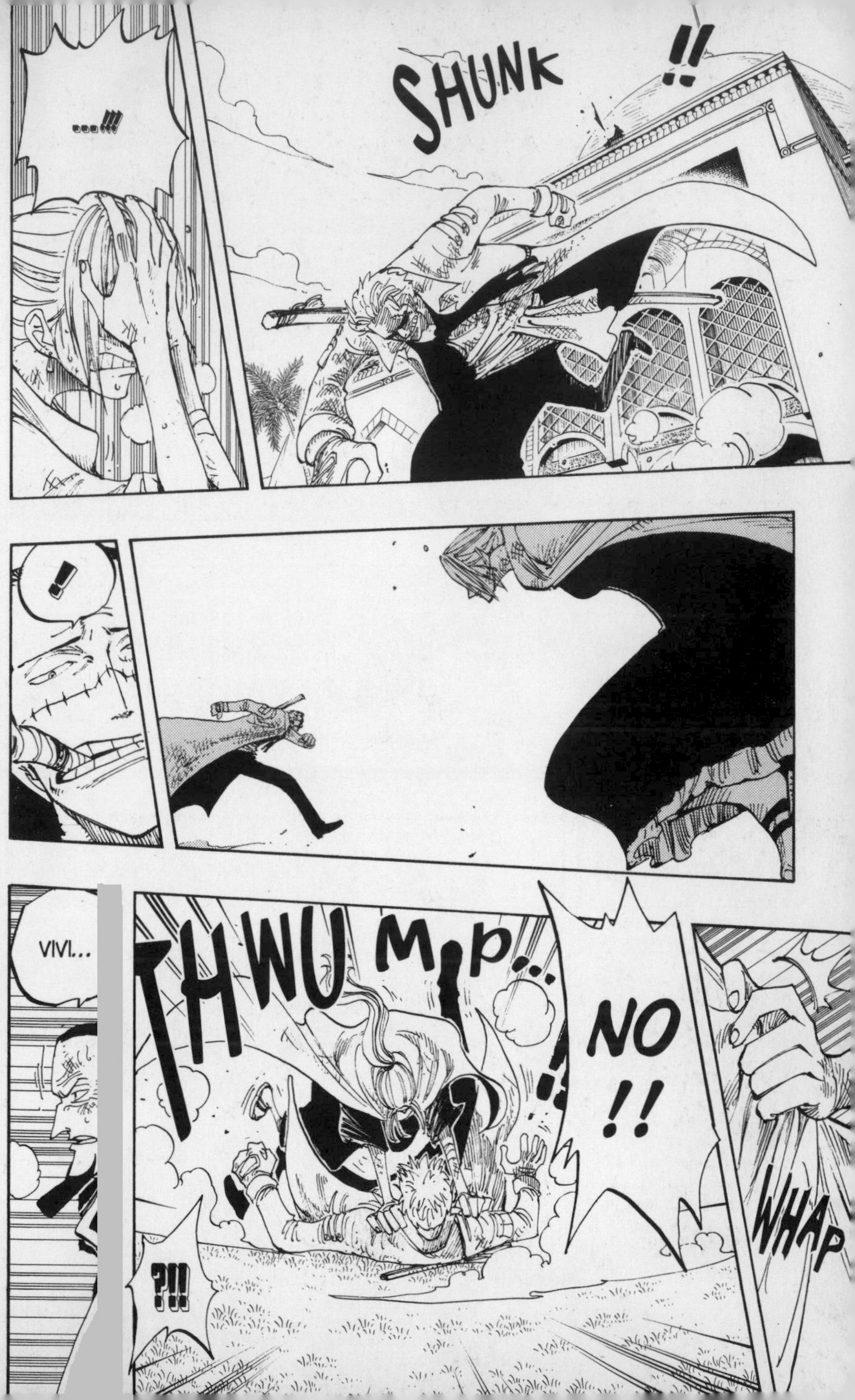
SHUNK!!
...!!!
!
WHAP
NO!!
THWUMP!!
?!!
VIVI...

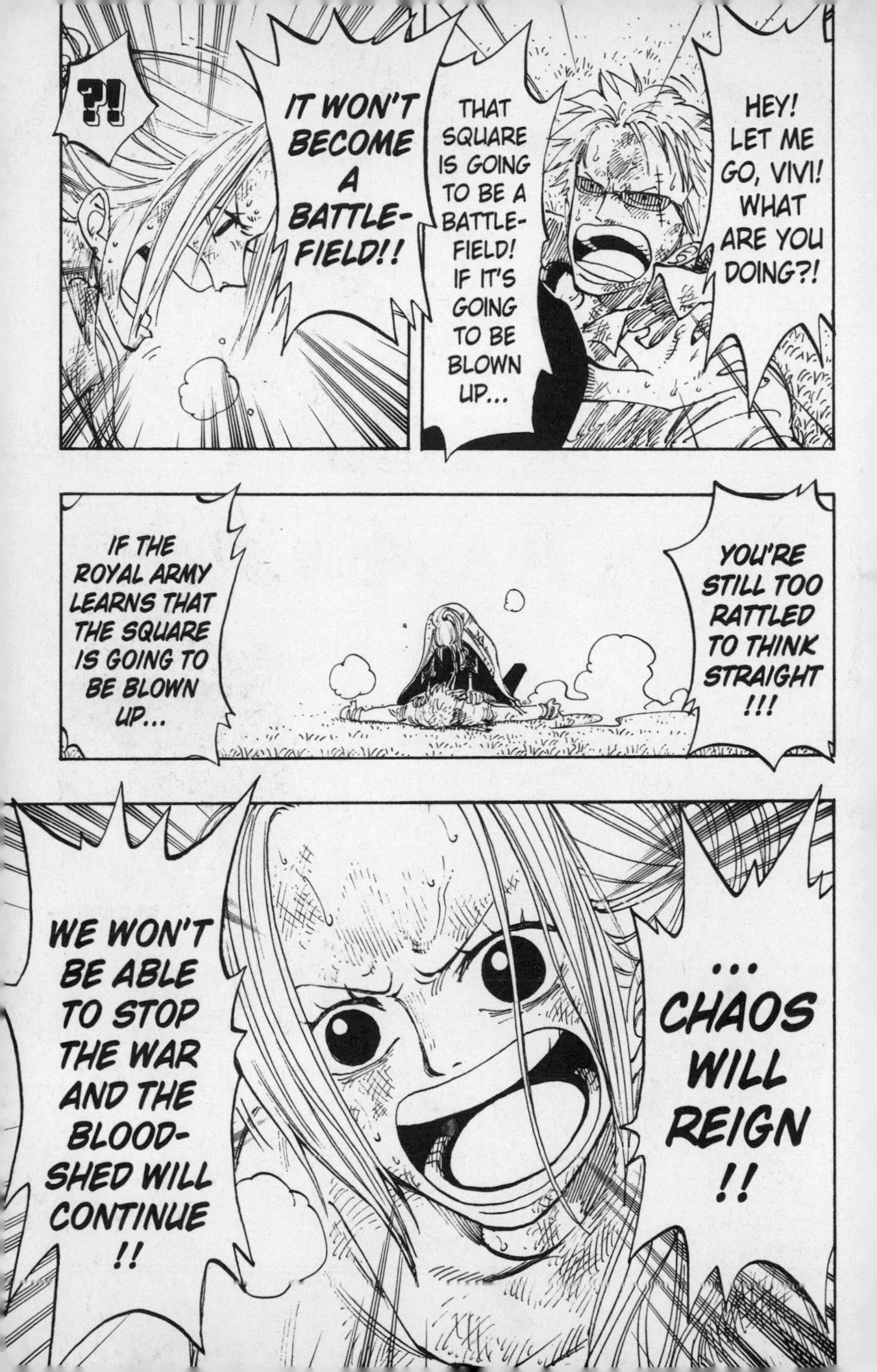
HEY! LET ME GO, VIVI! WHAT ARE YOU DOING?!
THAT SQUARE IS GOING TO BE A BATTLE-FIELD! IF IT'S GOING TO BE BLOWN UP...
IT WON'T BECOME A BATTLE-FIELD!!
?!
YOU'RE STILL TOO RATTLED TO THINK STRAIGHT!!!
IF THE ROYAL ARMY LEARNS THAT THE SQUARE IS GOING TO BE BLOWN UP...
...CHAOS WILL REIGN!!
WE WON'T BE ABLE TO STOP THE WAR AND THE BLOOD-SHED WILL CONTINUE!!

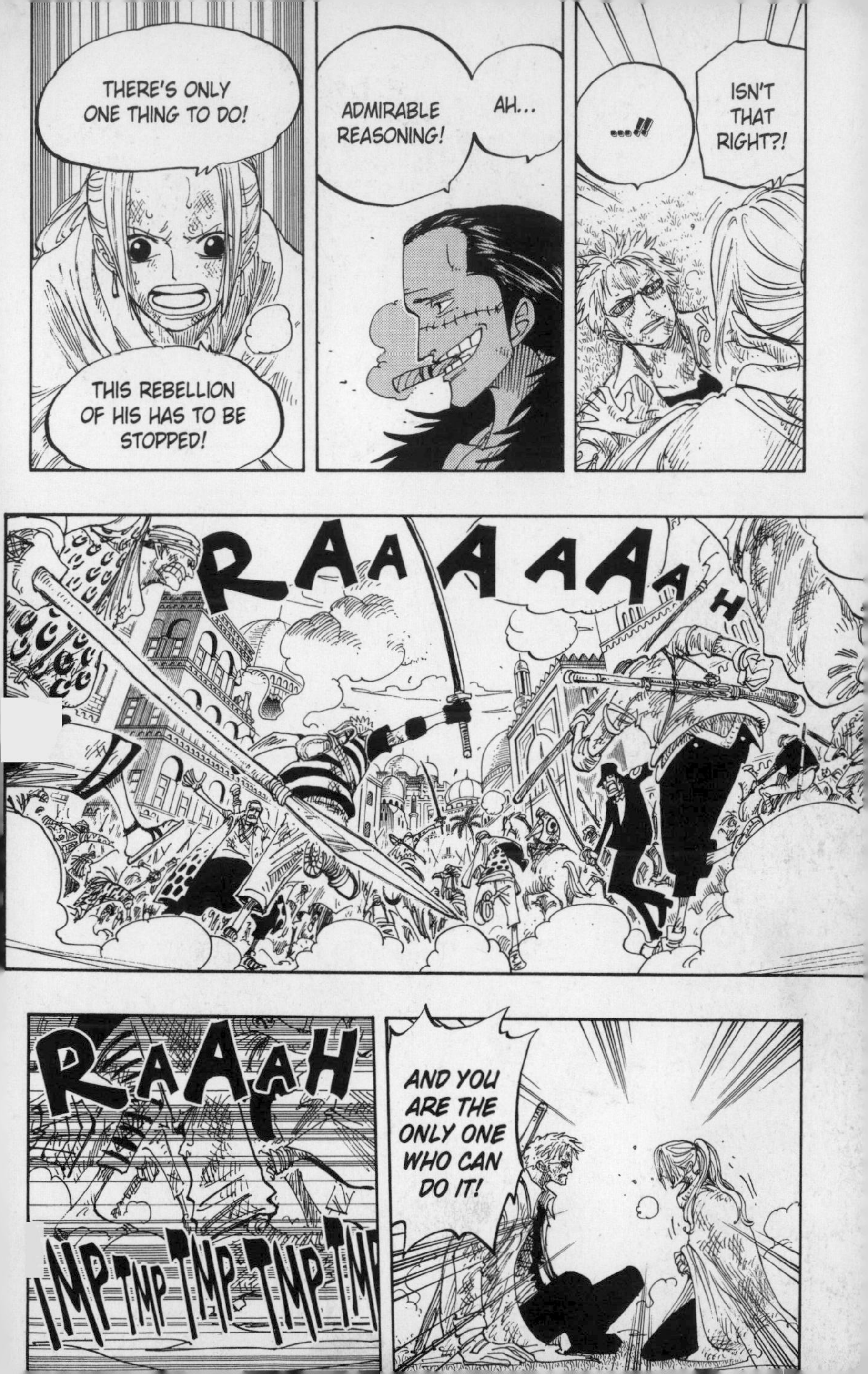
ISN'T THAT RIGHT?!
...!!
AH...
ADMIRABLE REASONING!
THERE'S ONLY ONE THING TO DO!
THIS REBELLION OF HIS HAS TO BE STOPPED!
RAAAAAAH
AND YOU ARE THE ONLY ONE WHO CAN DO IT!
RAAAH
TMP TMP TMP TMP

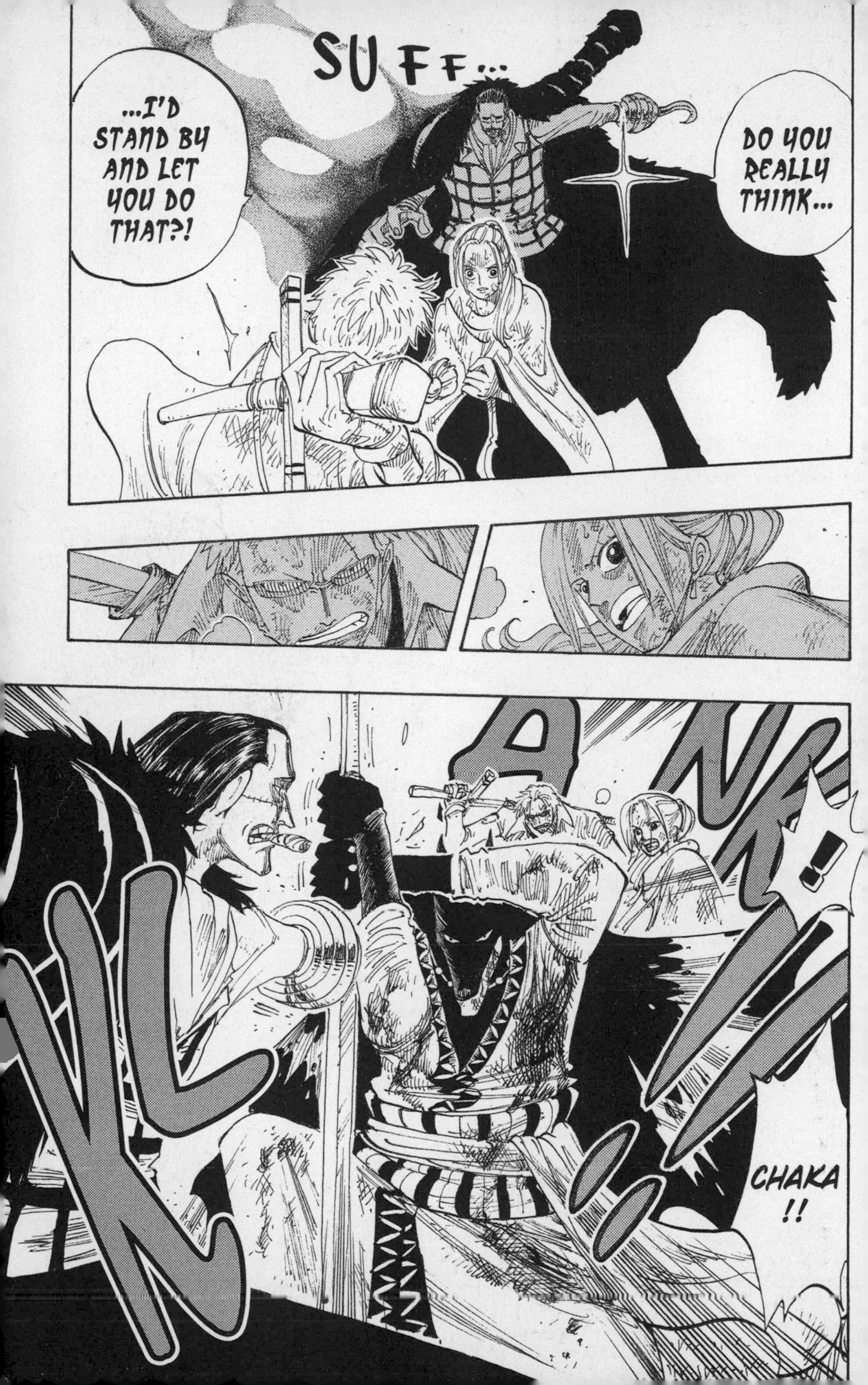
SU F F...
DO YOU REALLY THINK...
...I'D STAND BY AND LET YOU DO THAT?!
CHAKA!!
KLANK!

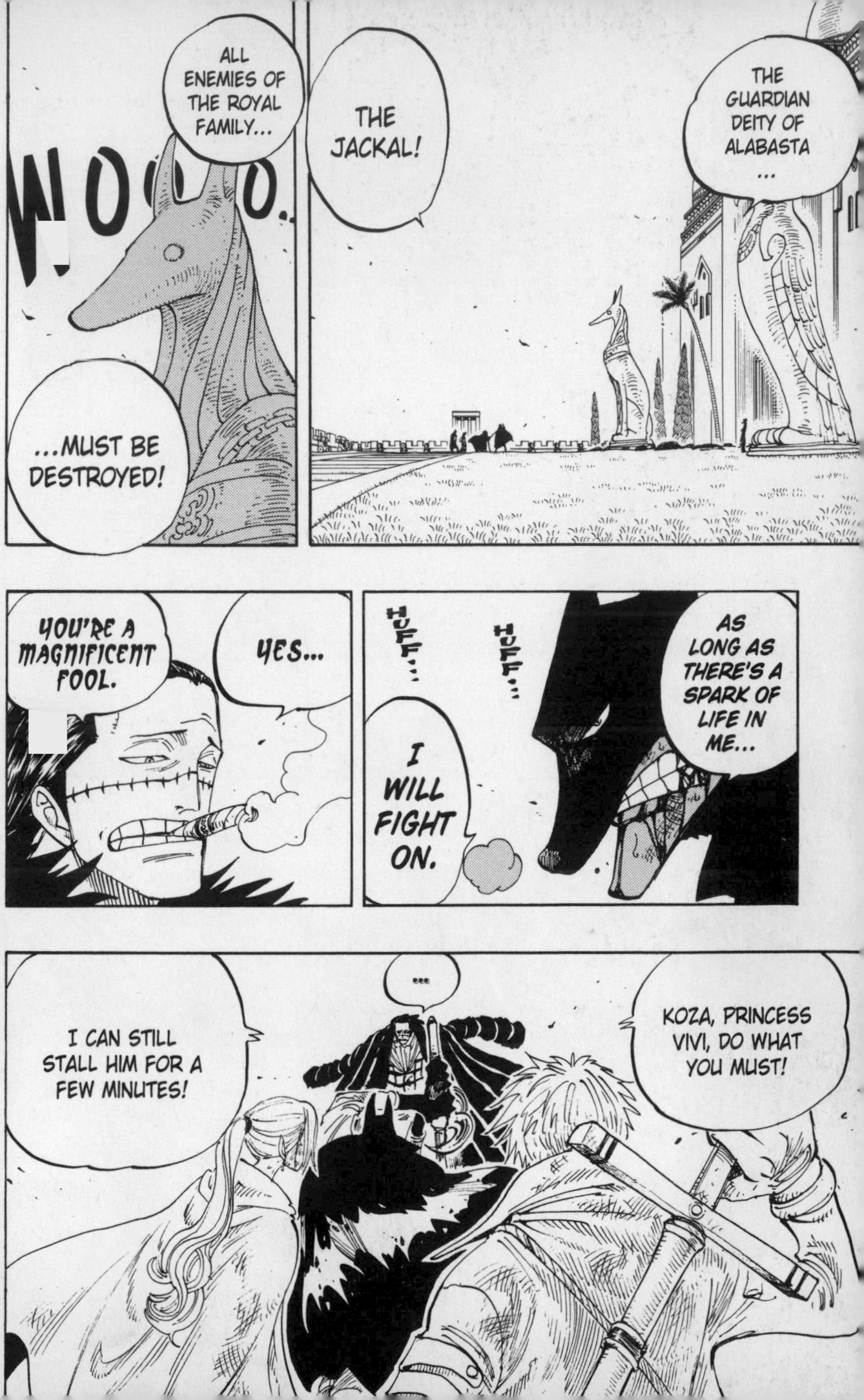
THE GUARDIAN DEITY OF ALABASTA ...
THE JACKAL!
ALL ENEMIES OF THE ROYAL FAMILY...
WOOOO..
...MUST BE DESTROYED!
HUFF... HUFF...
AS LONG AS THERE'S A SPARK OF LIFE IN ME...
I WILL FIGHT ON.
YES...
YOU'RE A MAGNIFICENT FOOL.
KOZA, PRINCESS VIVI, DO WHAT YOU MUST!
...
I CAN STILL STALL HIM FOR A FEW MINUTES!

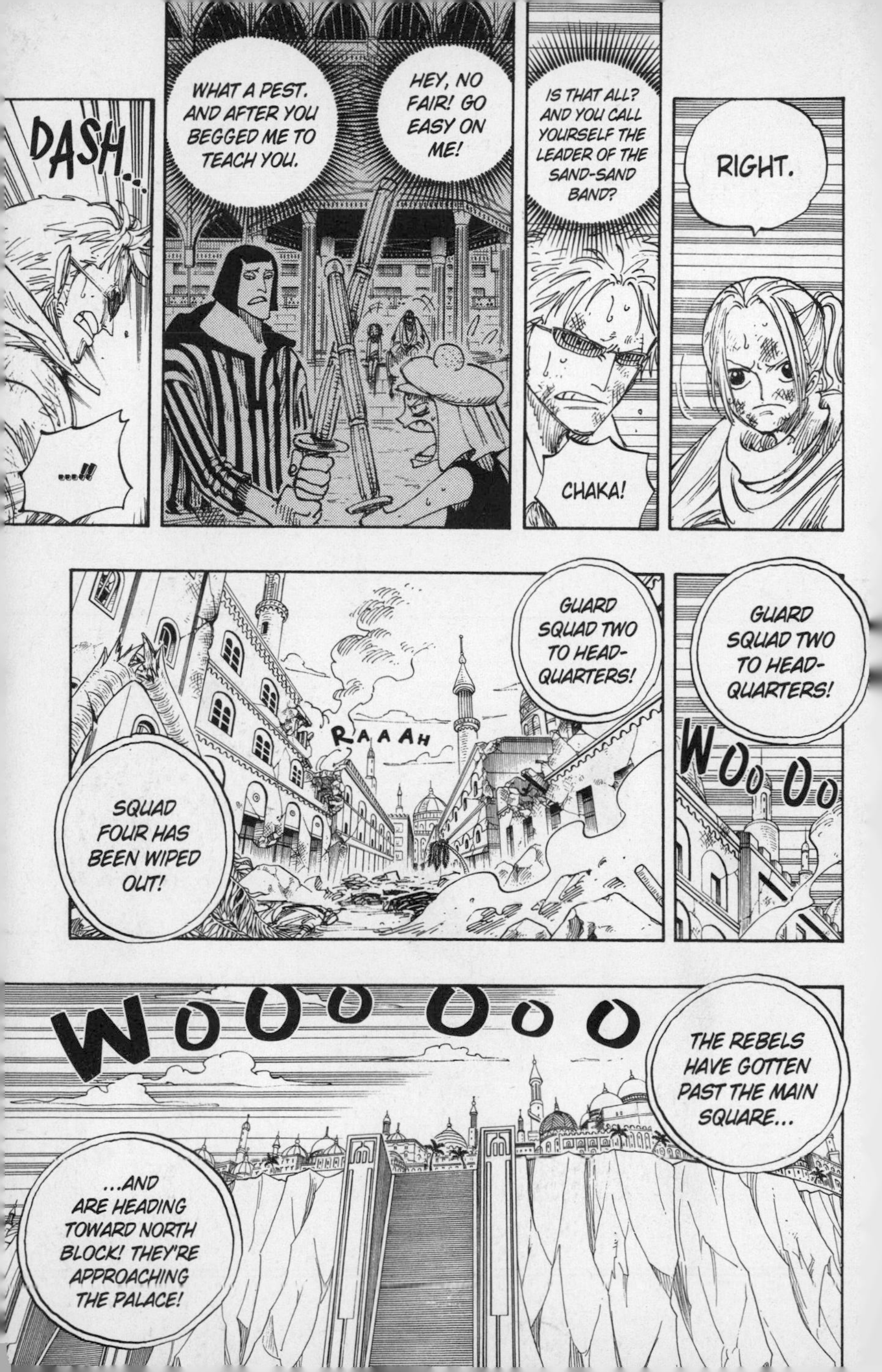
RIGHT.
IS THAT ALL? AND YOU CALL YOURSELF THE LEADER OF THE SAND-SAND BAND?
CHAKA!
HEY, NO FAIR! GO EASY ON ME!
WHAT A PEST. AND AFTER YOU BEGGED ME TO TEACH YOU.
DASH...
...!!
GUARD SQUAD TWO TO HEAD-QUARTERS!
WOOOO
GUARD SQUAD TWO TO HEAD-QUARTERS!
RAAAH
SQUAD FOUR HAS BEEN WIPED OUT!
THE REBELS HAVE GOTTEN PAST THE MAIN SQUARE...
WOOOO OOO
...AND ARE HEADING TOWARD NORTH BLOCK! THEY'RE APPROACHING THE PALACE!

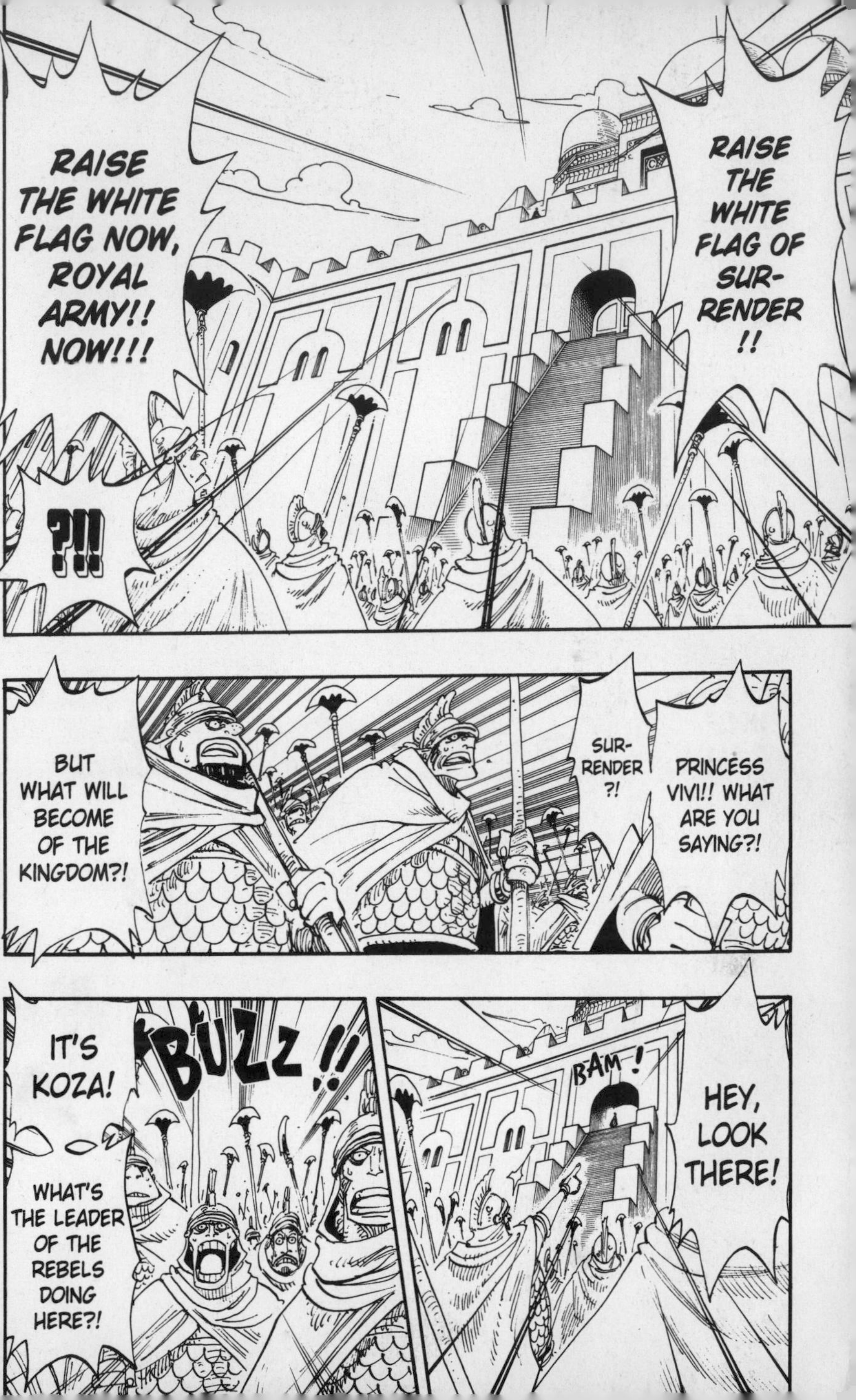
RAISE THE WHITE FLAG OF SUR-RENDER!!
RAISE THE WHITE FLAG NOW, ROYAL ARMY!! NOW!!!
?!!
PRINCESS VIVI!! WHAT ARE YOU SAYING?!
SUR-RENDER?!
BUT WHAT WILL BECOME OF THE KINGDOM?!
HEY, LOOK THERE!
BAM!
BUZZ!!
IT'S KOZA!
WHAT'S THE LEADER OF THE REBELS DOING HERE?!

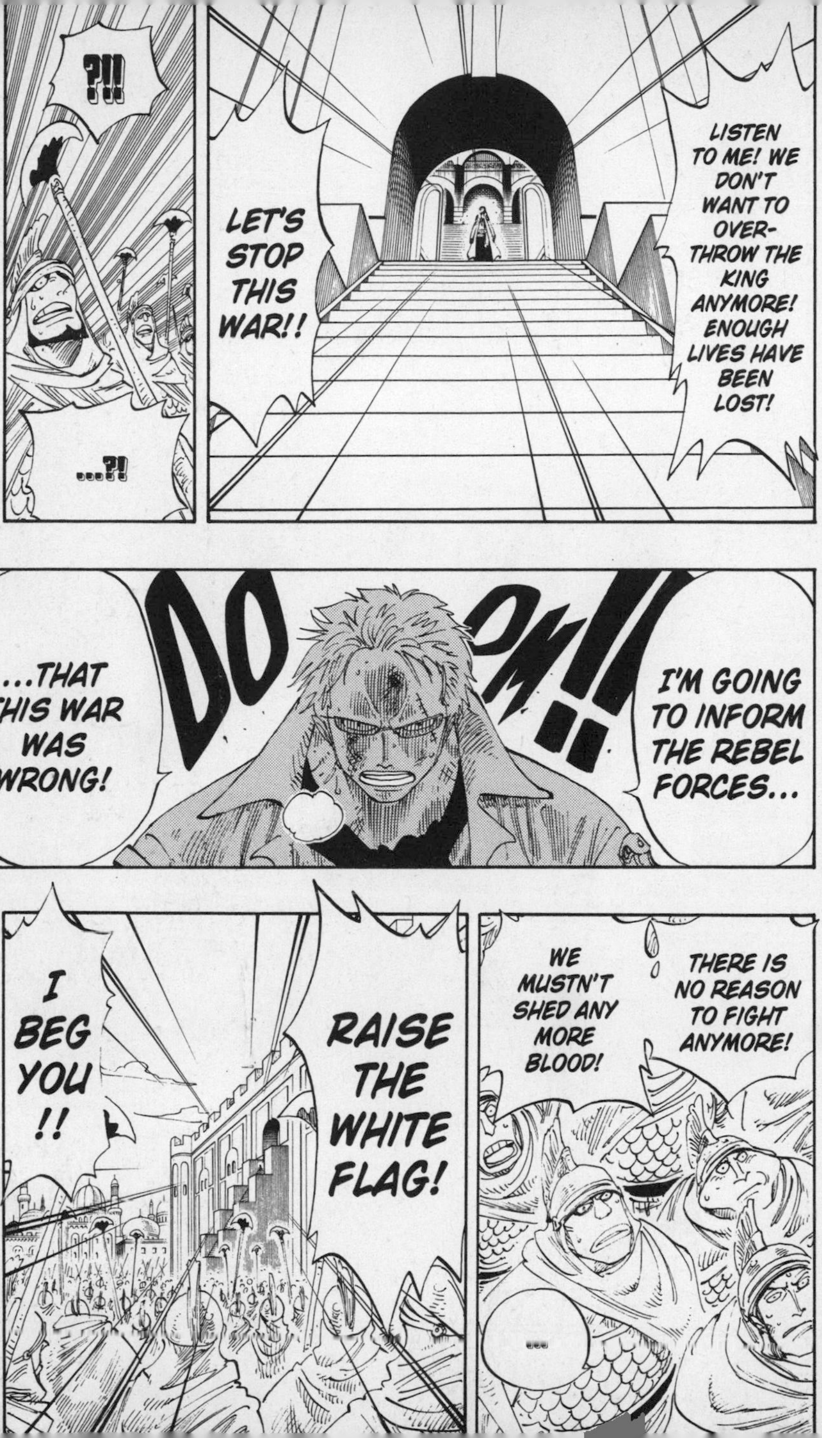
LISTEN TO ME! WE DON'T WANT TO OVER-THROW THE KING ANYMORE! ENOUGH LIVES HAVE BEEN LOST!
LET'S STOP THIS WAR!!
?!!
...?!
I'M GOING TO INFORM THE REBEL FORCES...
DOOM!!
...THAT THIS WAR WAS WRONG!
THERE IS NO REASON TO FIGHT ANYMORE!
WE MUSTN'T SHED ANY MORE BLOOD!
...
RAISE THE WHITE FLAG!
I BEG YOU!!

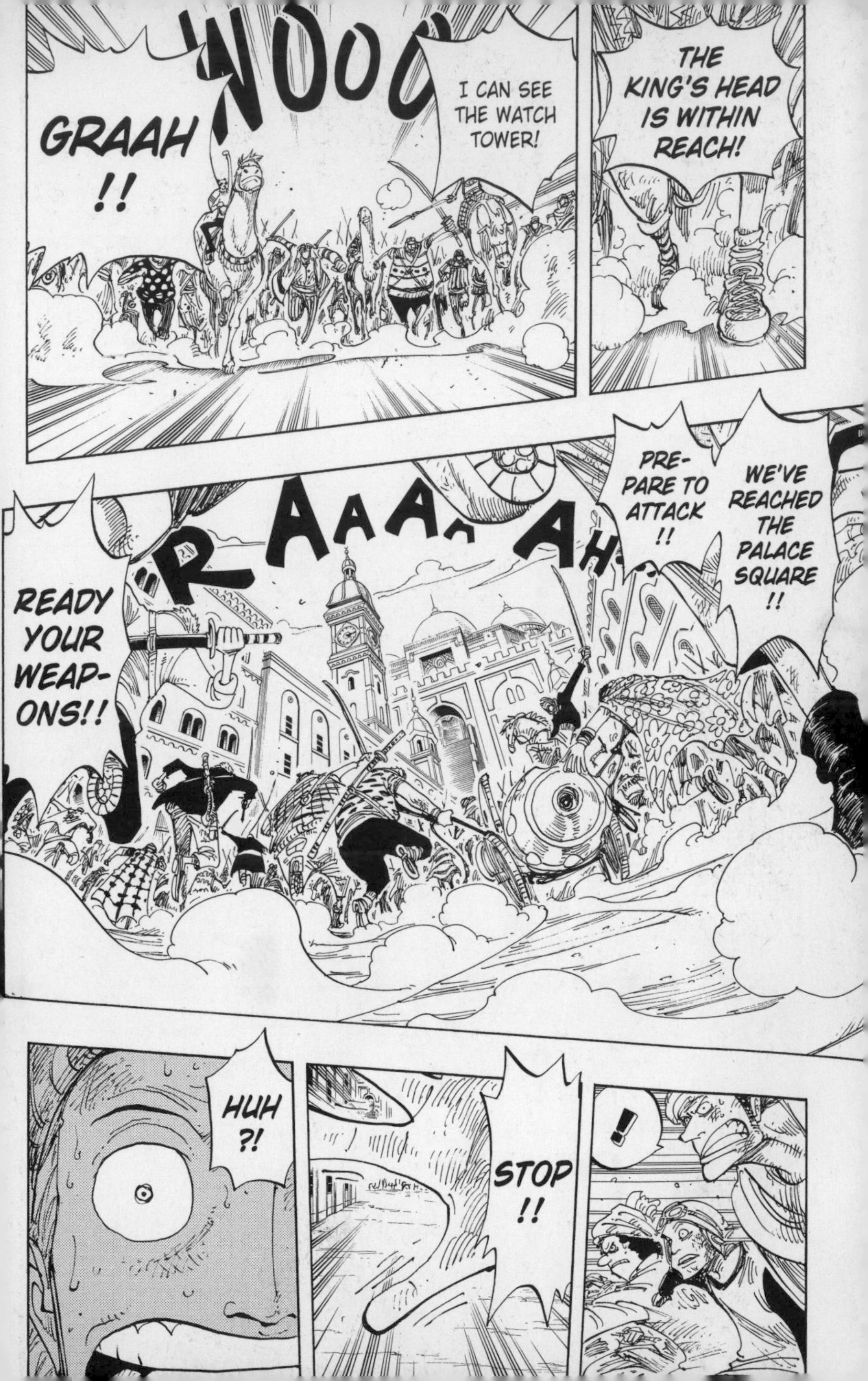
THE KING'S HEAD IS WITHIN REACH!
I CAN SEE THE WATCH TOWER!
WOOO
GRAAH !!
WE'VE REACHED THE PALACE SQUARE !!
PRE-PARE TO ATTACK !!
RAAAAH
READY YOUR WEAP-ONS!!
!
STOP !!
HUH ?!

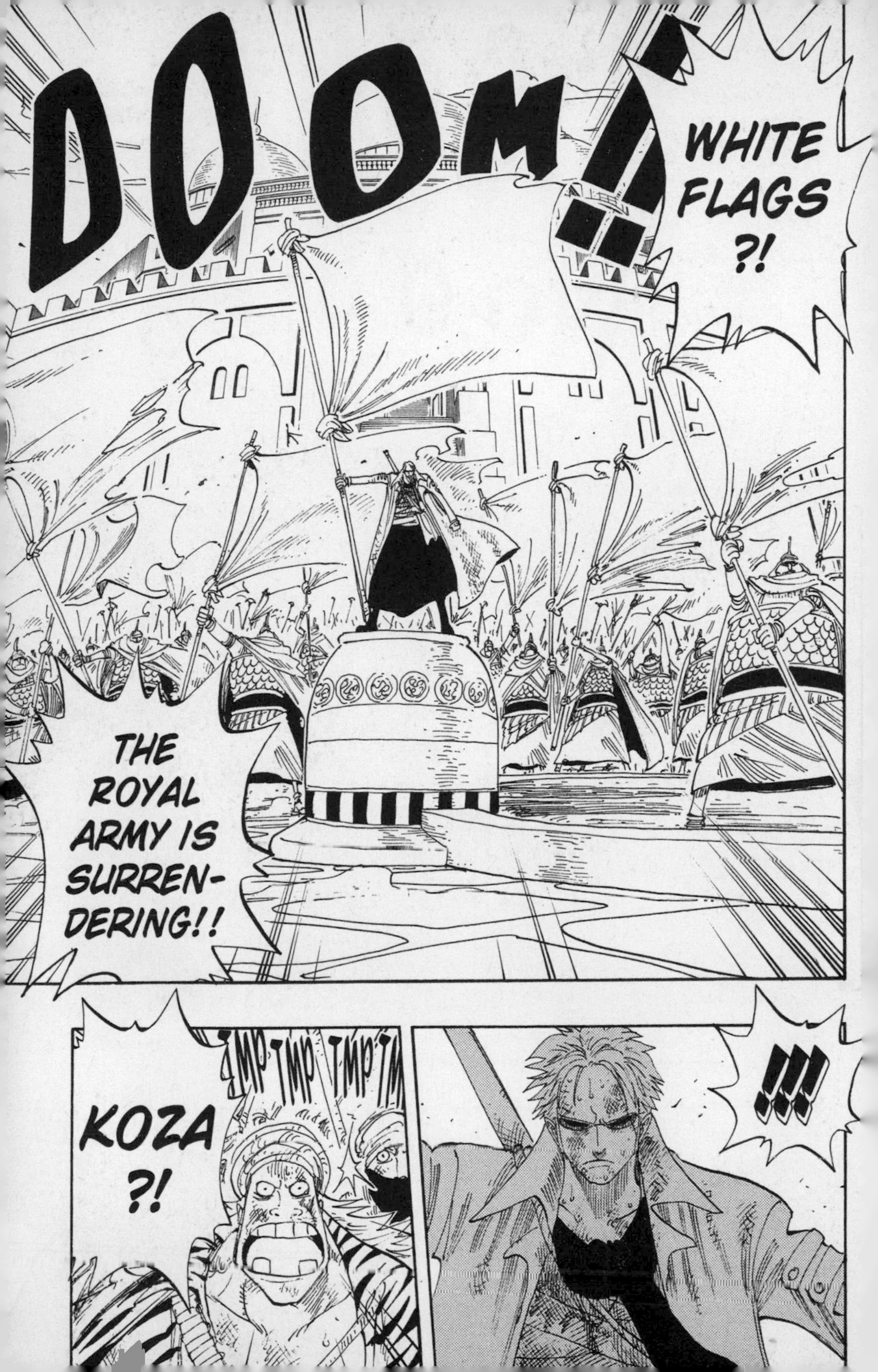
DOOM!!
WHITE FLAGS?!
THE ROYAL ARMY IS SURREN-DERING!!
!!!
TMP TMP
KOZA?!

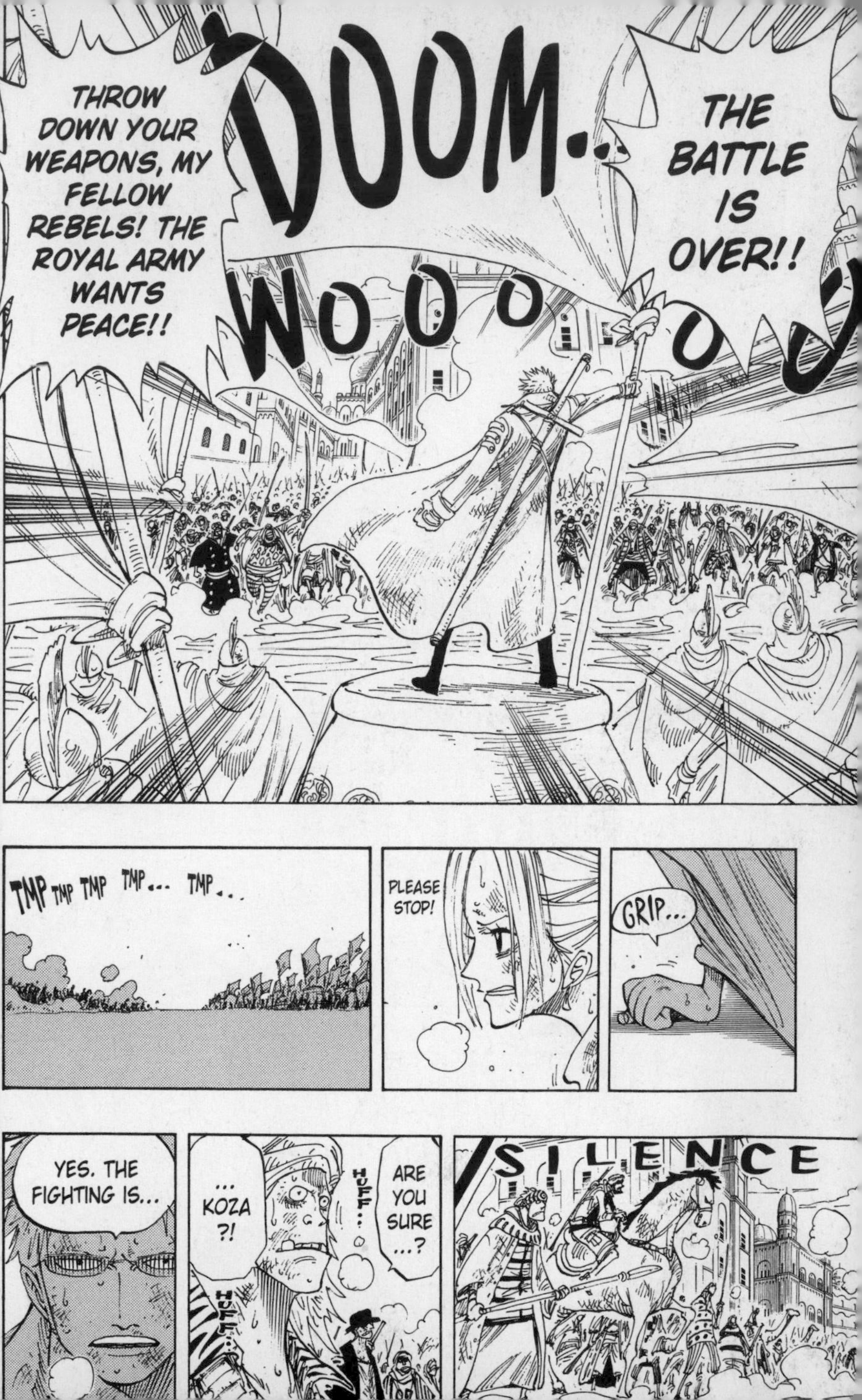
THE BATTLE IS OVER!!
DOOM..
THROW DOWN YOUR WEAPONS, MY FELLOW REBELS! THE ROYAL ARMY WANTS PEACE!!
WOOOOO
GRIP...
PLEASE STOP!
TMP TMP TMP TMP... TMP...
SILENCE
ARE YOU SURE ...?
HUFF...
... KOZA ?!
HUFF...
YES. THE FIGHTING IS...

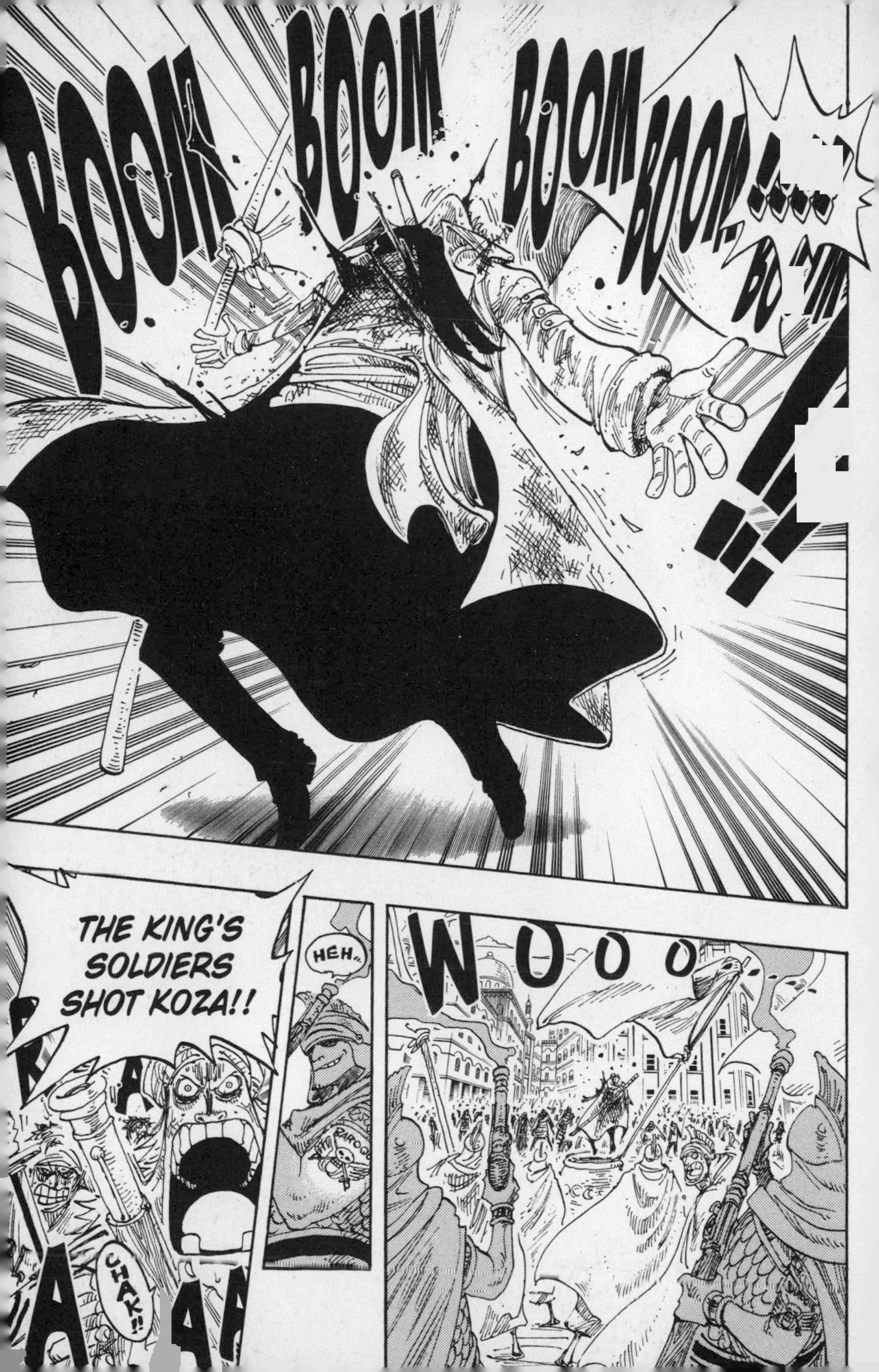
BOOM
BOOM
BOOM
BOOM!!!!
WOOO
HEH..
THE KING'S SOLDIERS SHOT KOZA!!
CHAK!!

# Chapter 198: 4:15 P.M.

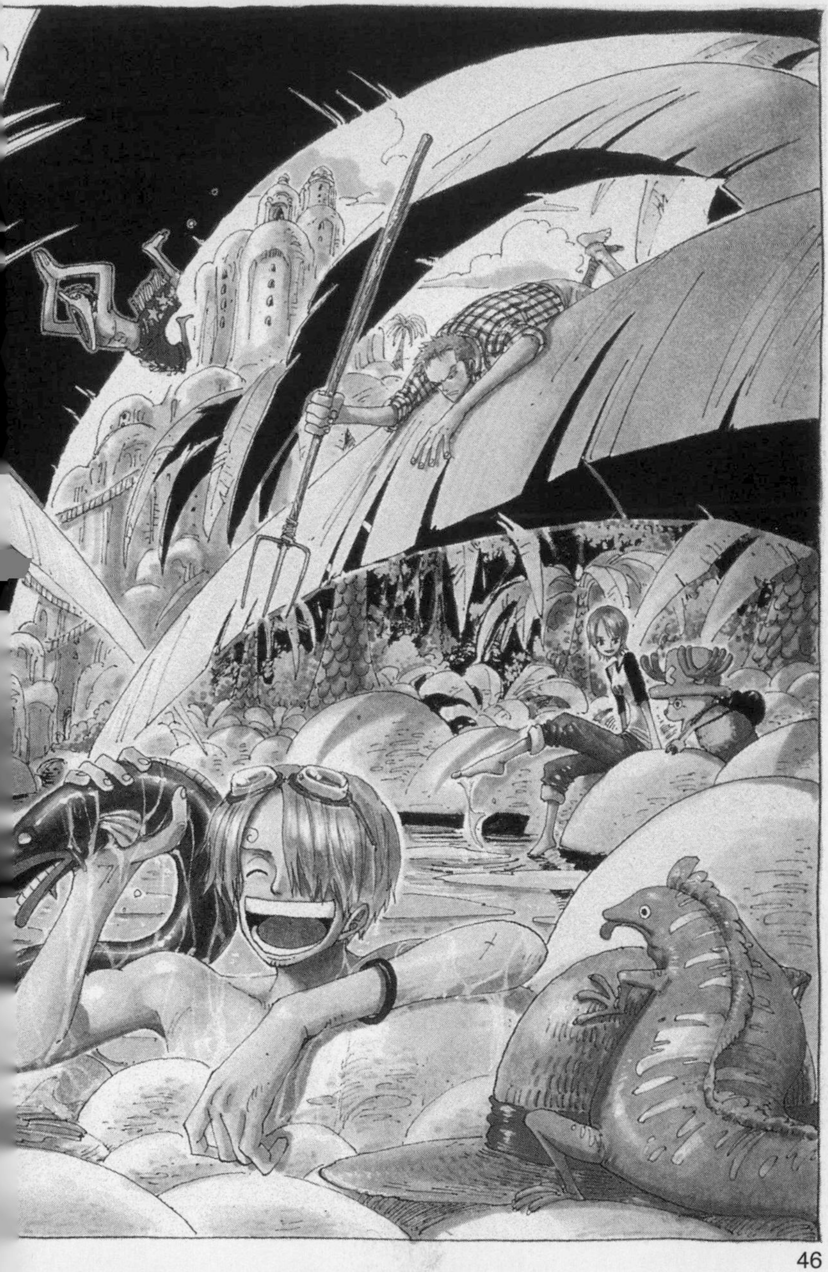

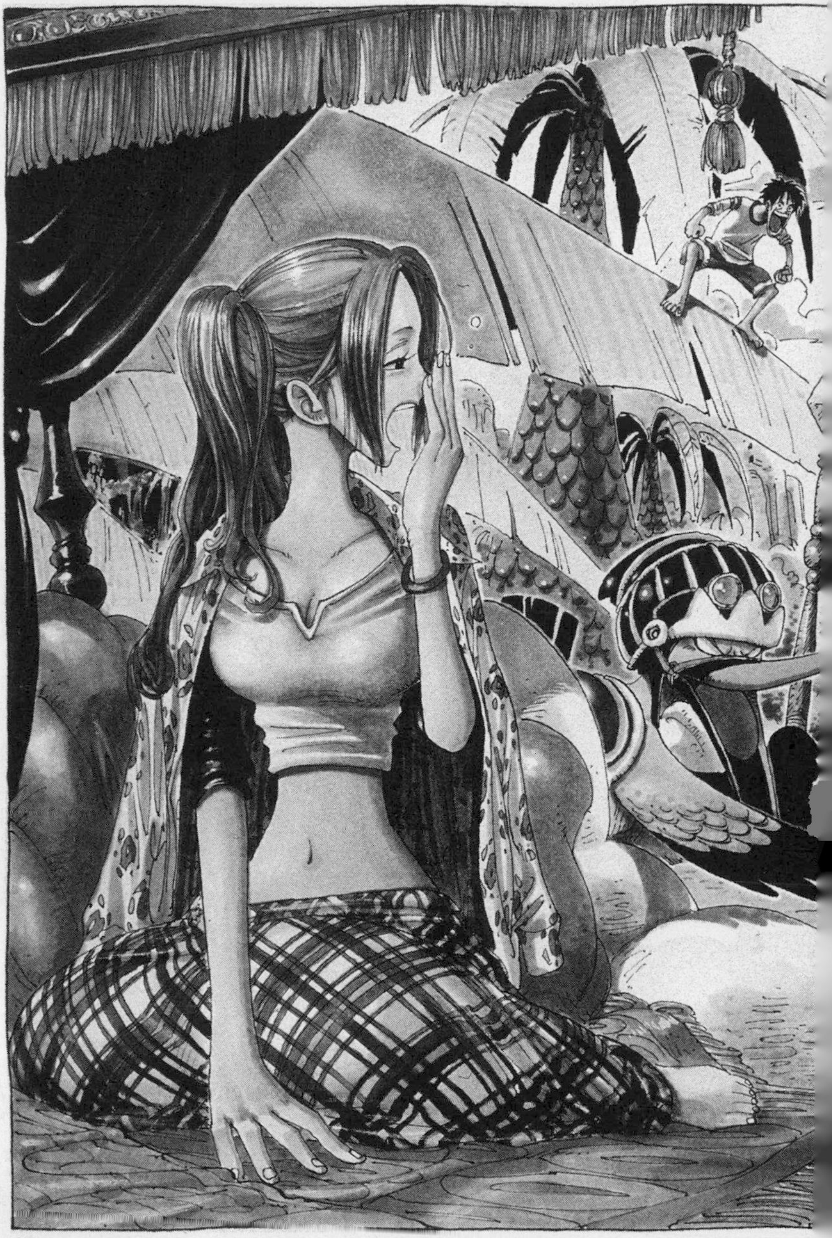

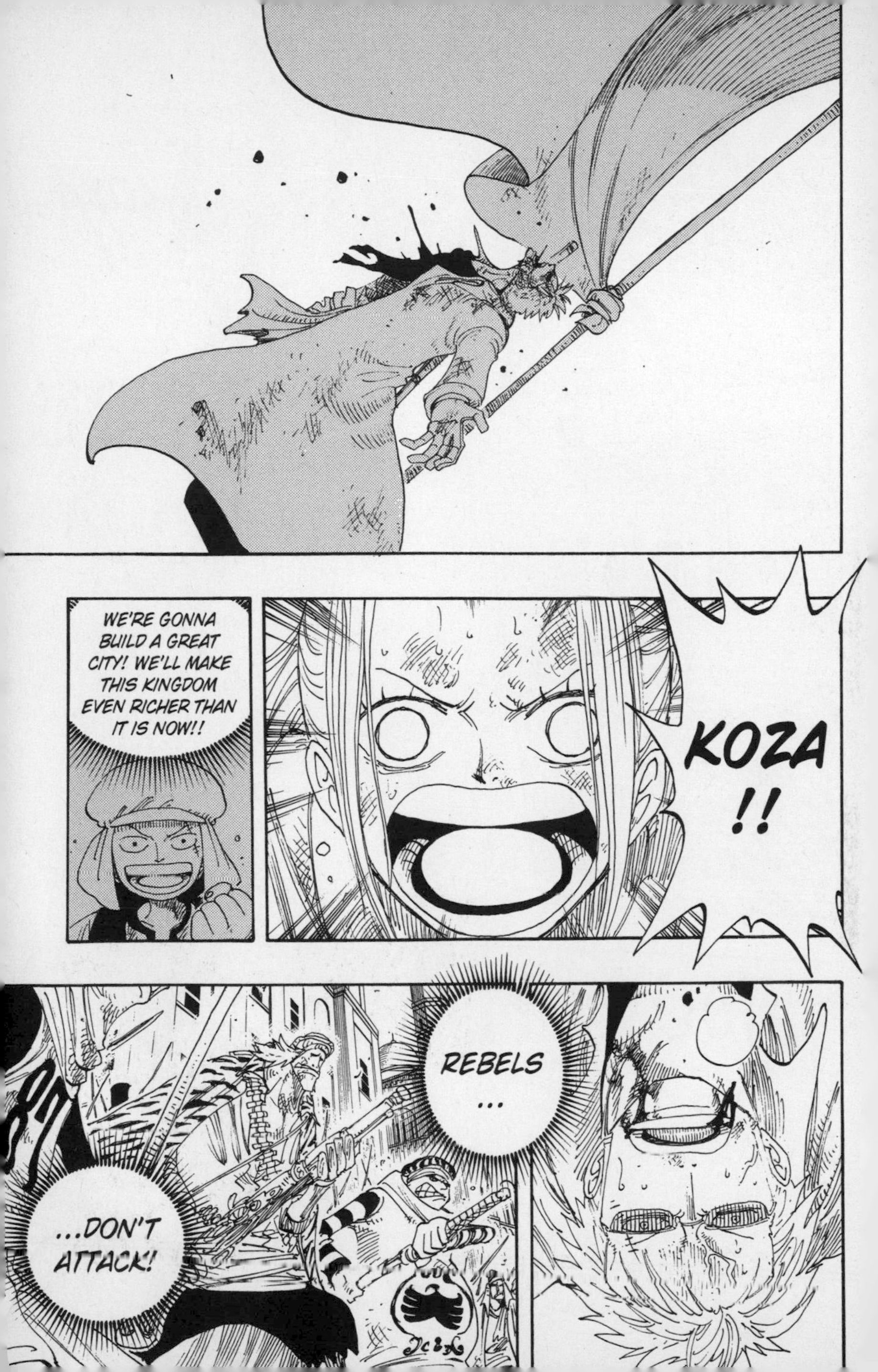

KOZA !!
WE'RE GONNA BUILD A GREAT CITY! WE'LL MAKE THIS KINGDOM EVEN RICHER THAN IT IS NOW!!
REBELS ...
...DON'T ATTACK!

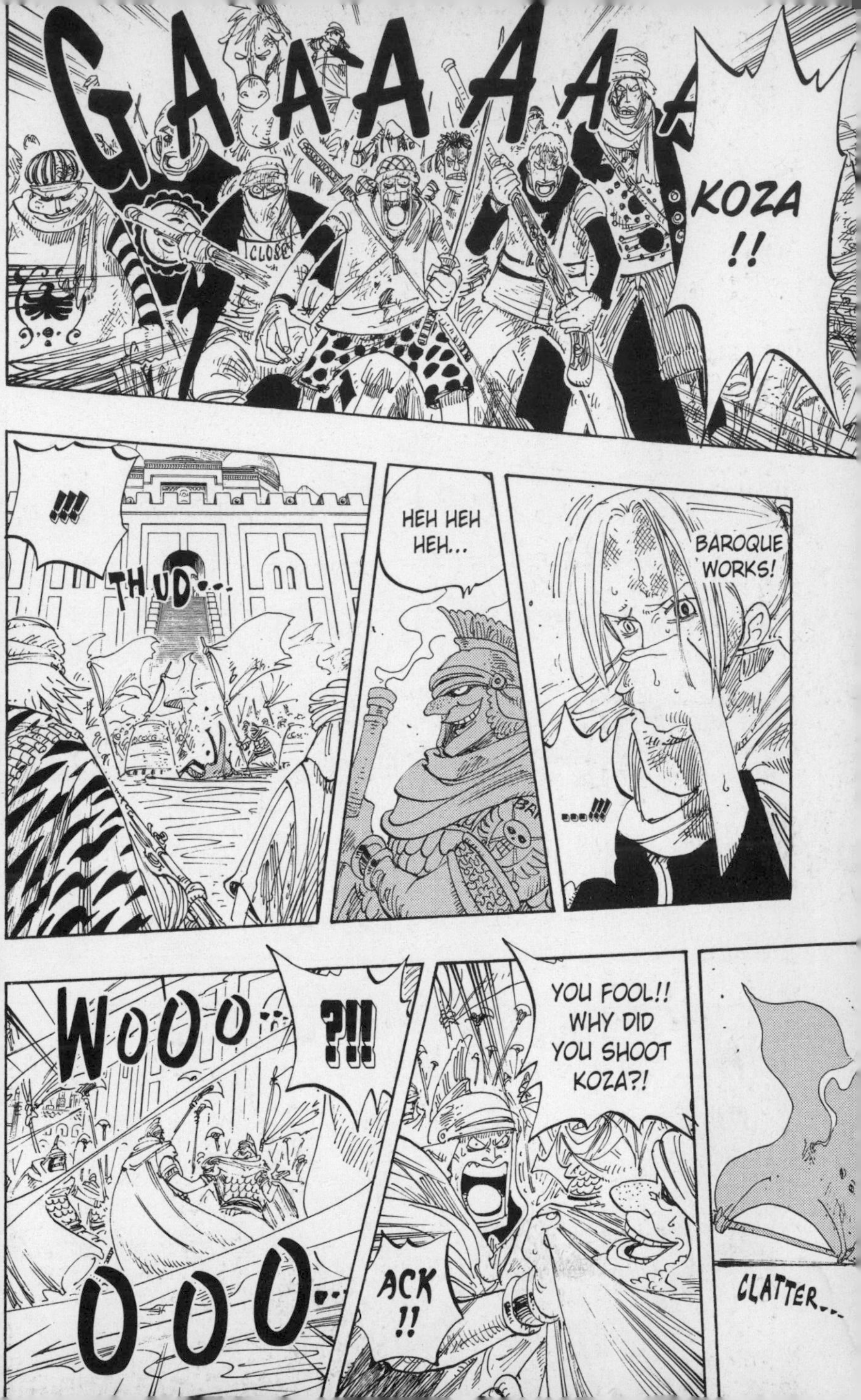
KOZA!!
GAAAAAA
BAROQUE WORKS!
...!!!
HEH HEH HEH...
!!!
THUD...
CLATTER...
YOU FOOL!! WHY DID YOU SHOOT KOZA?!
ACK!!
?!!
WOOOOOO...

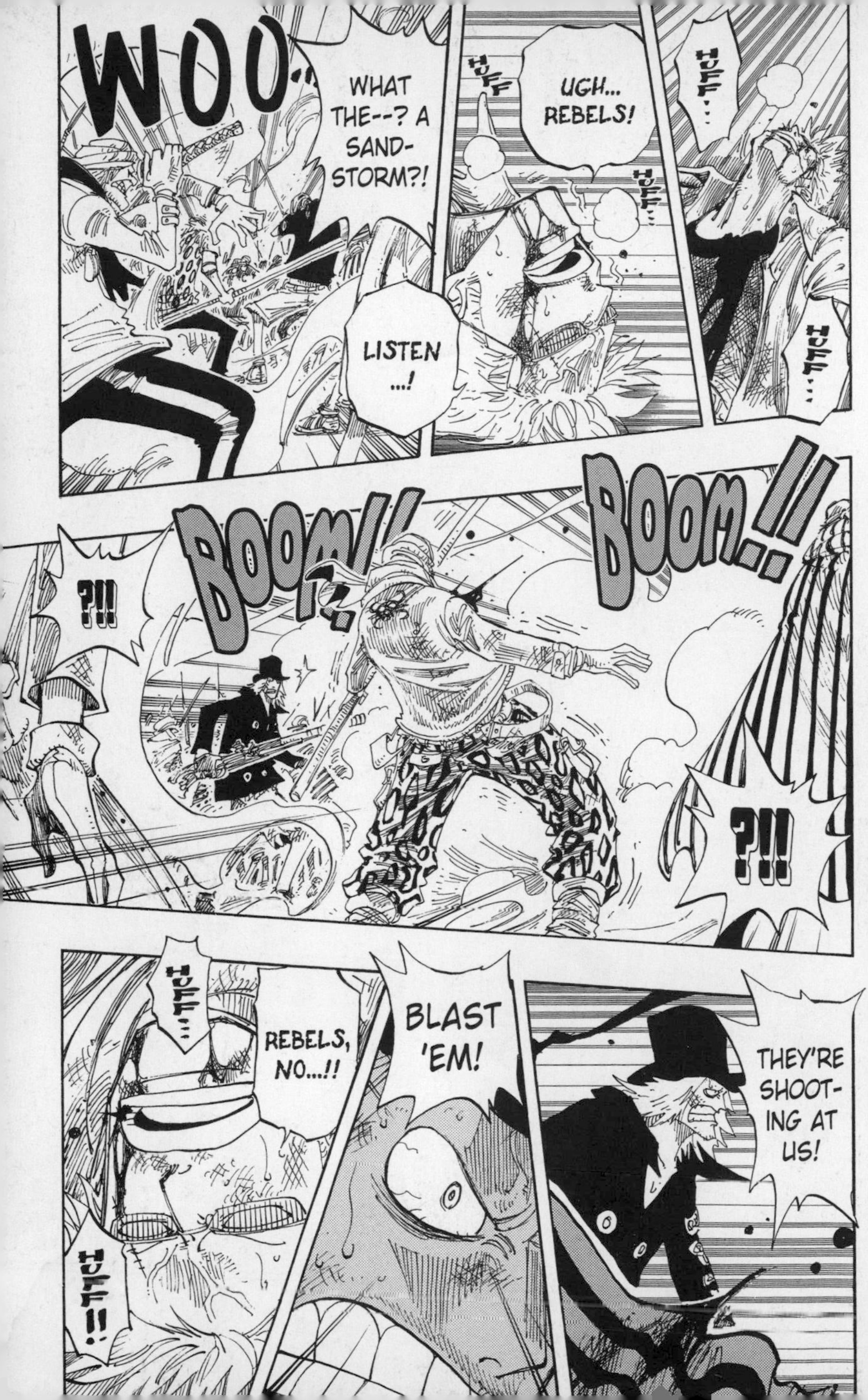
HUFF...
HUFF...
HUFF
UGH... REBELS!
HUFF...
WOO...
WHAT THE--? A SAND-STORM?!
LISTEN ...!
BOOM..!!
?!!
BOOM!!
?!!
THEY'RE SHOOT-ING AT US!
BLAST 'EM!
HUFF...
REBELS, NO...!!
HUFF!!

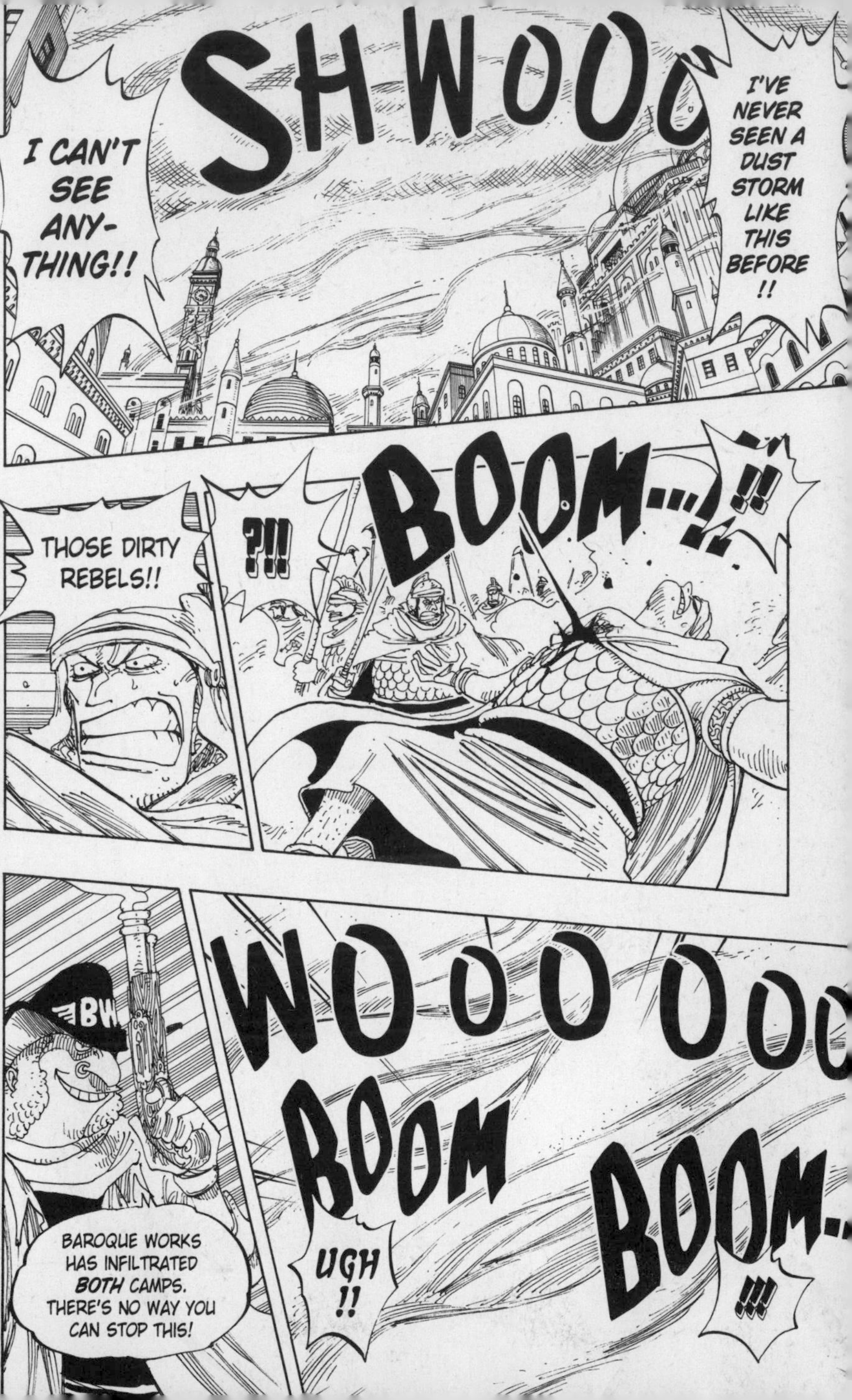
SHWOOO
I'VE NEVER SEEN A DUST STORM LIKE THIS BEFORE!!
I CAN'T SEE ANY-THING!!
BOOM...!!
?!!
THOSE DIRTY REBELS!!
WOOOOOO
BOOM
BOOM...!!!
UGH!!
BAROQUE WORKS HAS INFILTRATED *BOTH* CAMPS. THERE'S NO WAY YOU CAN STOP THIS!

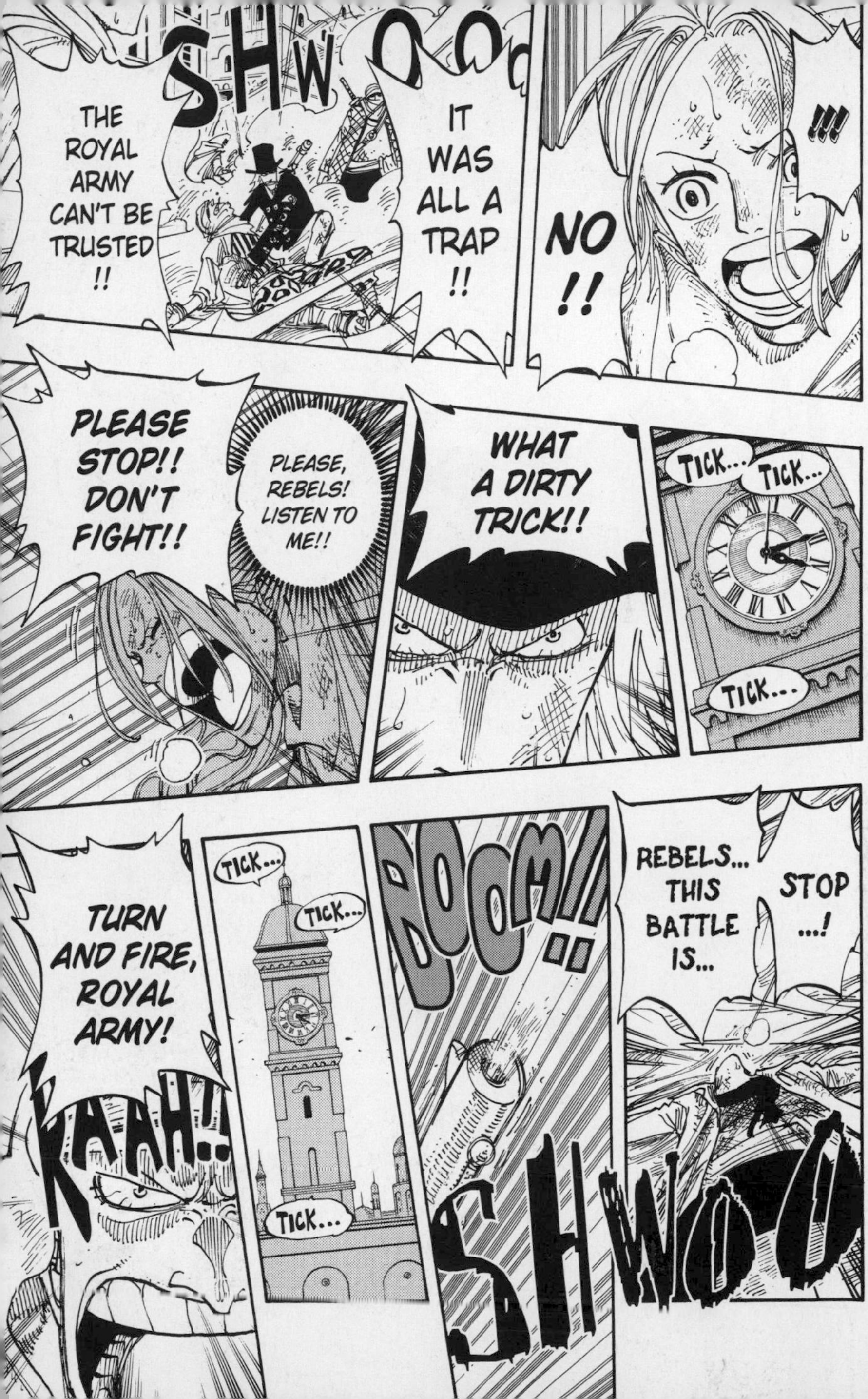
!!!
NO !!
SHWOOO
IT WAS ALL A TRAP !!
THE ROYAL ARMY CAN'T BE TRUSTED !!
TICK...
TICK...
TICK...
WHAT A DIRTY TRICK!!
PLEASE, REBELS! LISTEN TO ME!!
PLEASE STOP!! DON'T FIGHT!!
STOP ...!
REBELS... THIS BATTLE IS...
SHWOOO
BOOM!!
TICK...
TICK...
TICK...
TURN AND FIRE, ROYAL ARMY!
KAAH!!

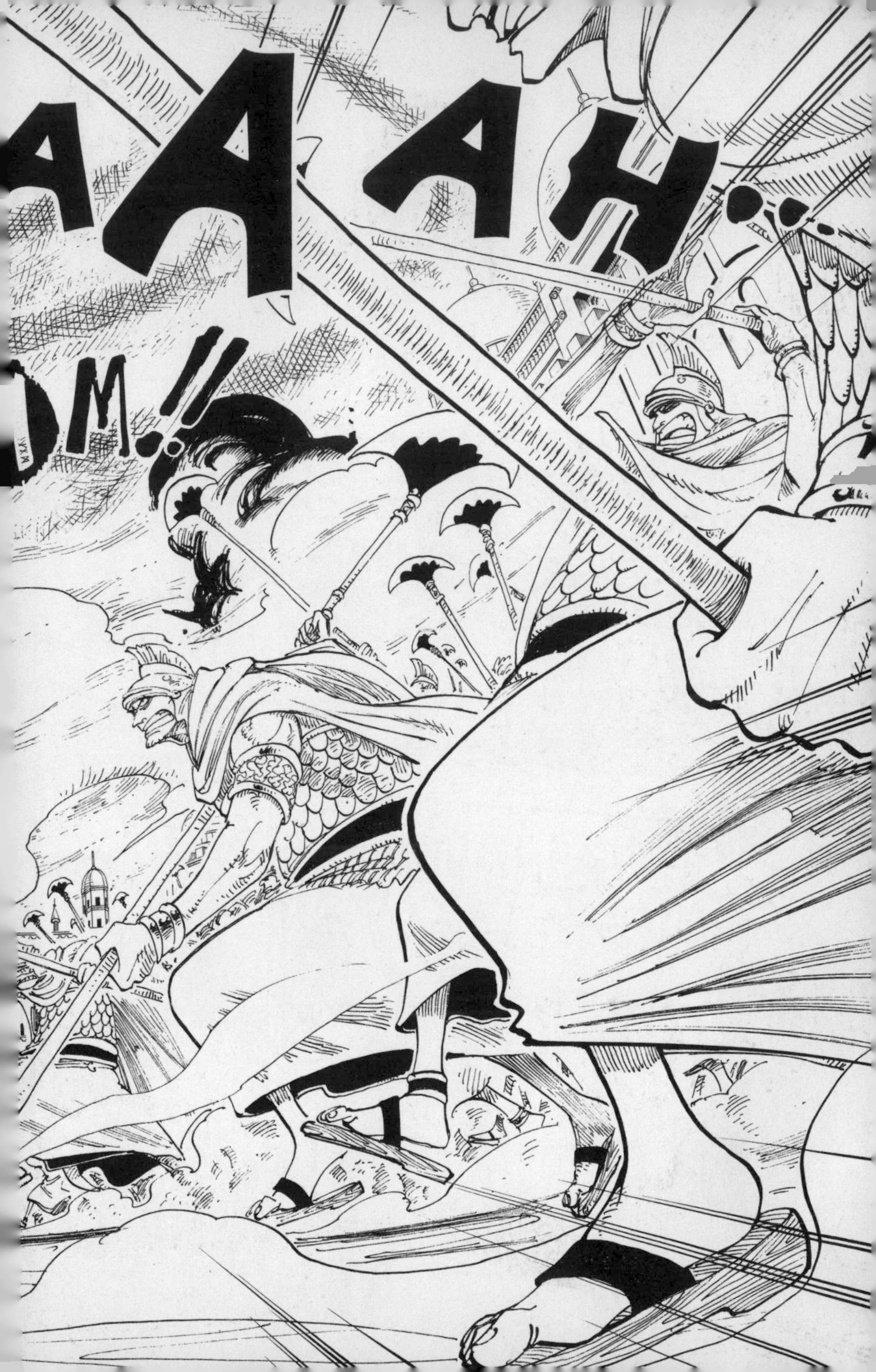
AAAH...
OM!!

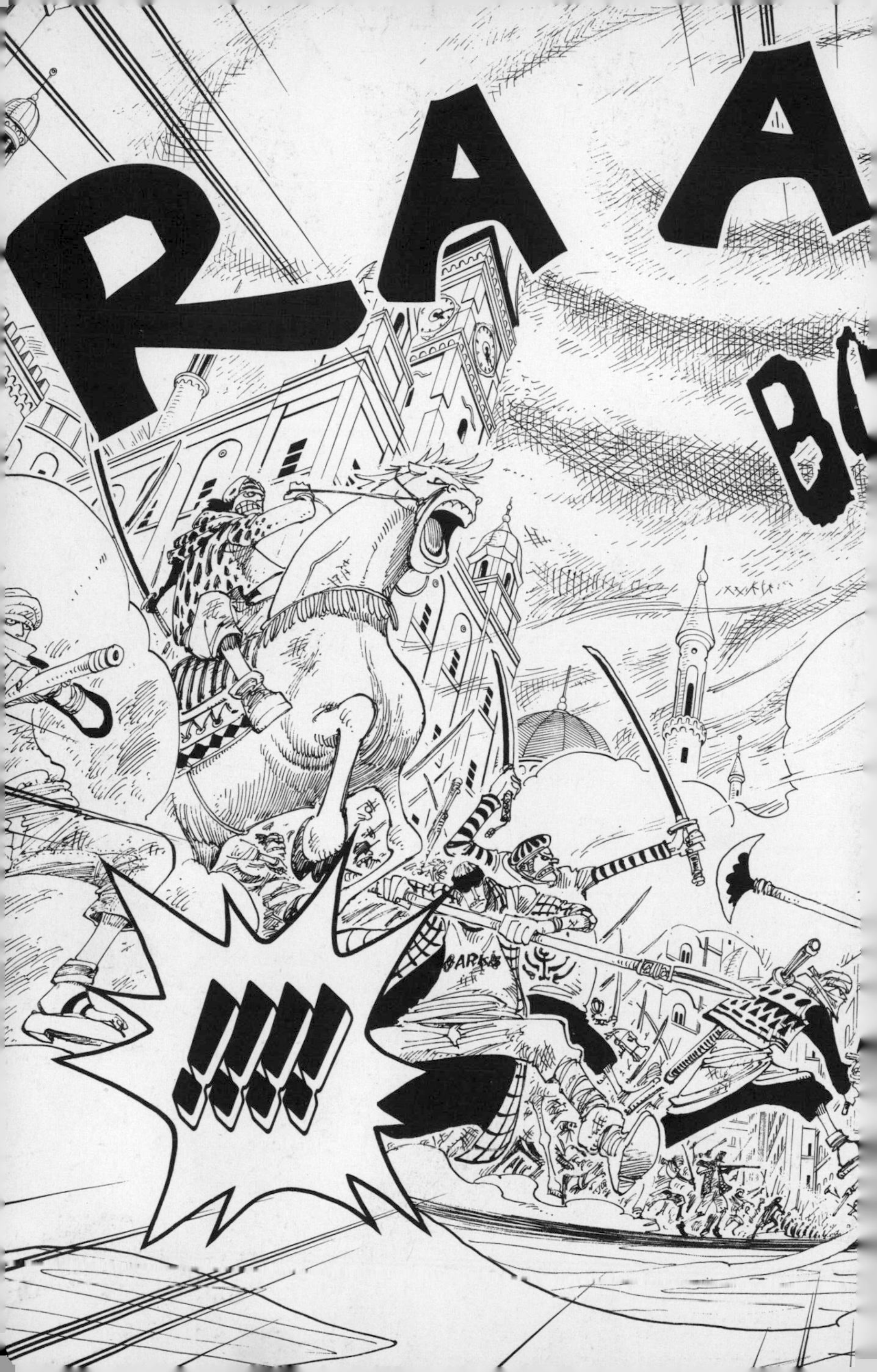
RAAA
!!!!

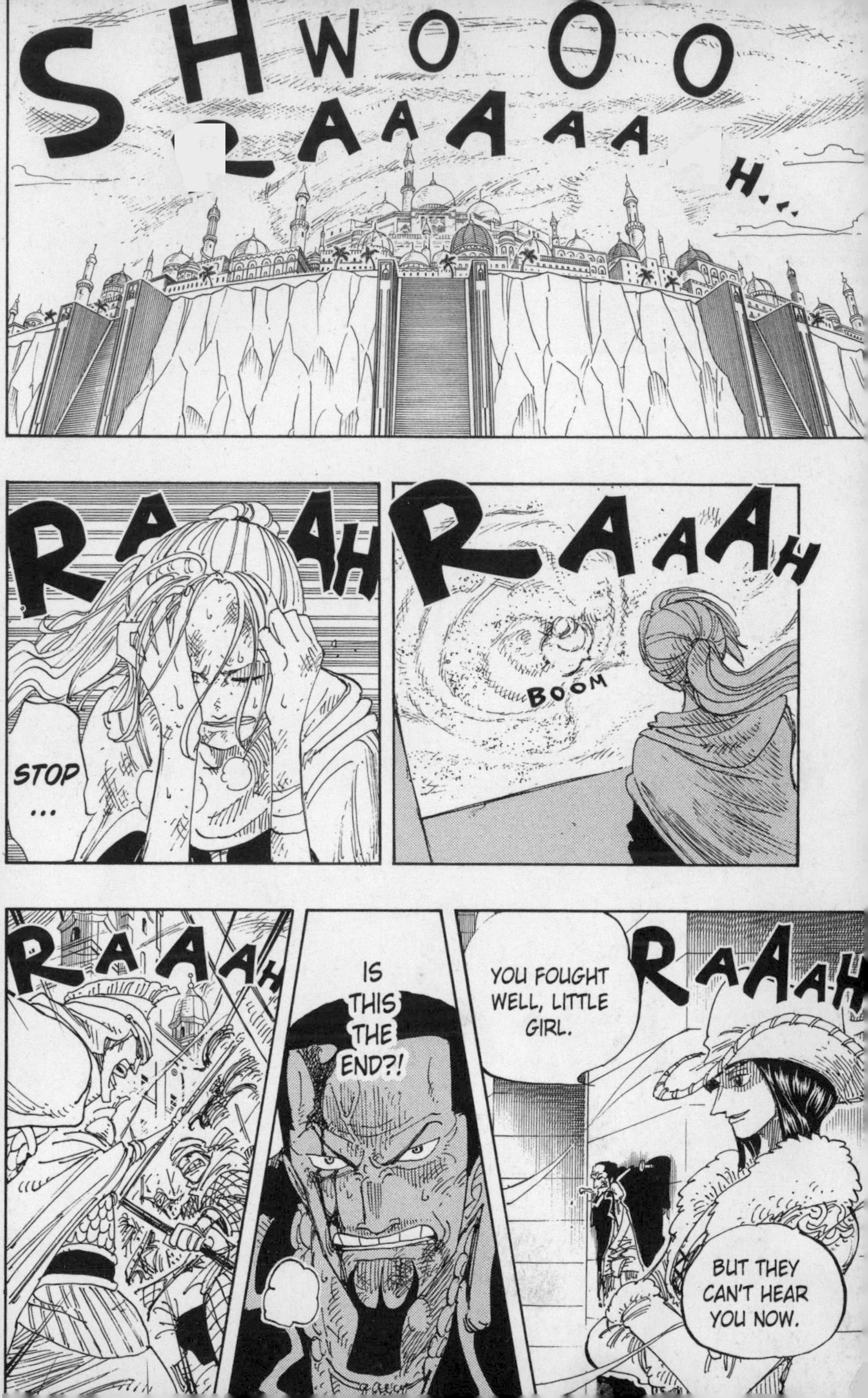
SHWOOO
RAAAAAH...
RAAAH
BOOM
RAAAH
STOP ...
RAAAH
YOU FOUGHT WELL, LITTLE GIRL.
BUT THEY CAN'T HEAR YOU NOW.
IS THIS THE END?!
RAAAH

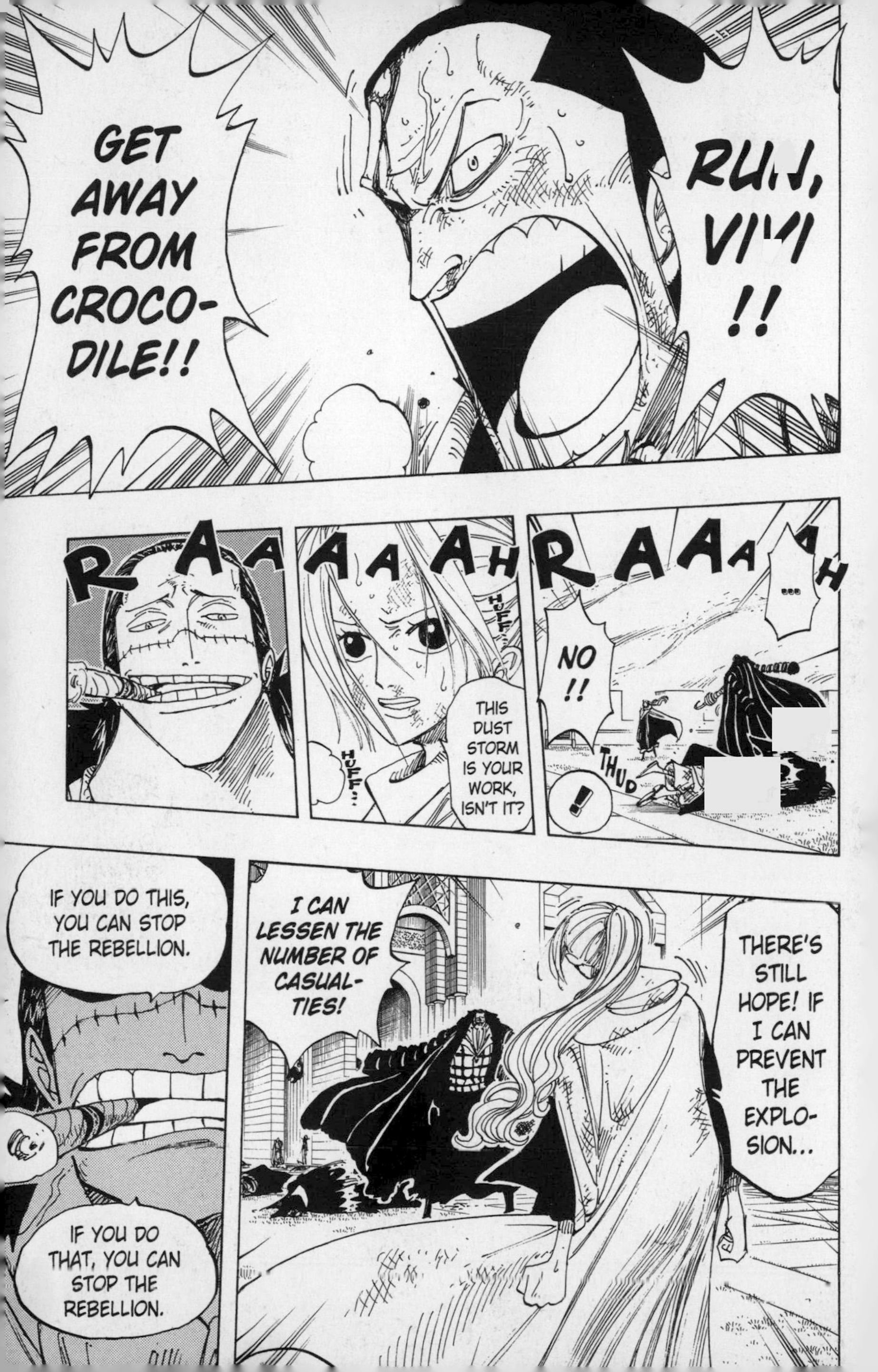
RUN, VIVI!!
GET AWAY FROM CROCODILE!!
RAAAAAHRAAAAAH
...
NO!!
THUD
!
HUFF
THIS DUST STORM IS YOUR WORK, ISN'T IT?
HUFF
THERE'S STILL HOPE! IF I CAN PREVENT THE EXPLOSION...
I CAN LESSEN THE NUMBER OF CASUALTIES!
IF YOU DO THIS, YOU CAN STOP THE REBELLION.
IF YOU DO THAT, YOU CAN STOP THE REBELLION.

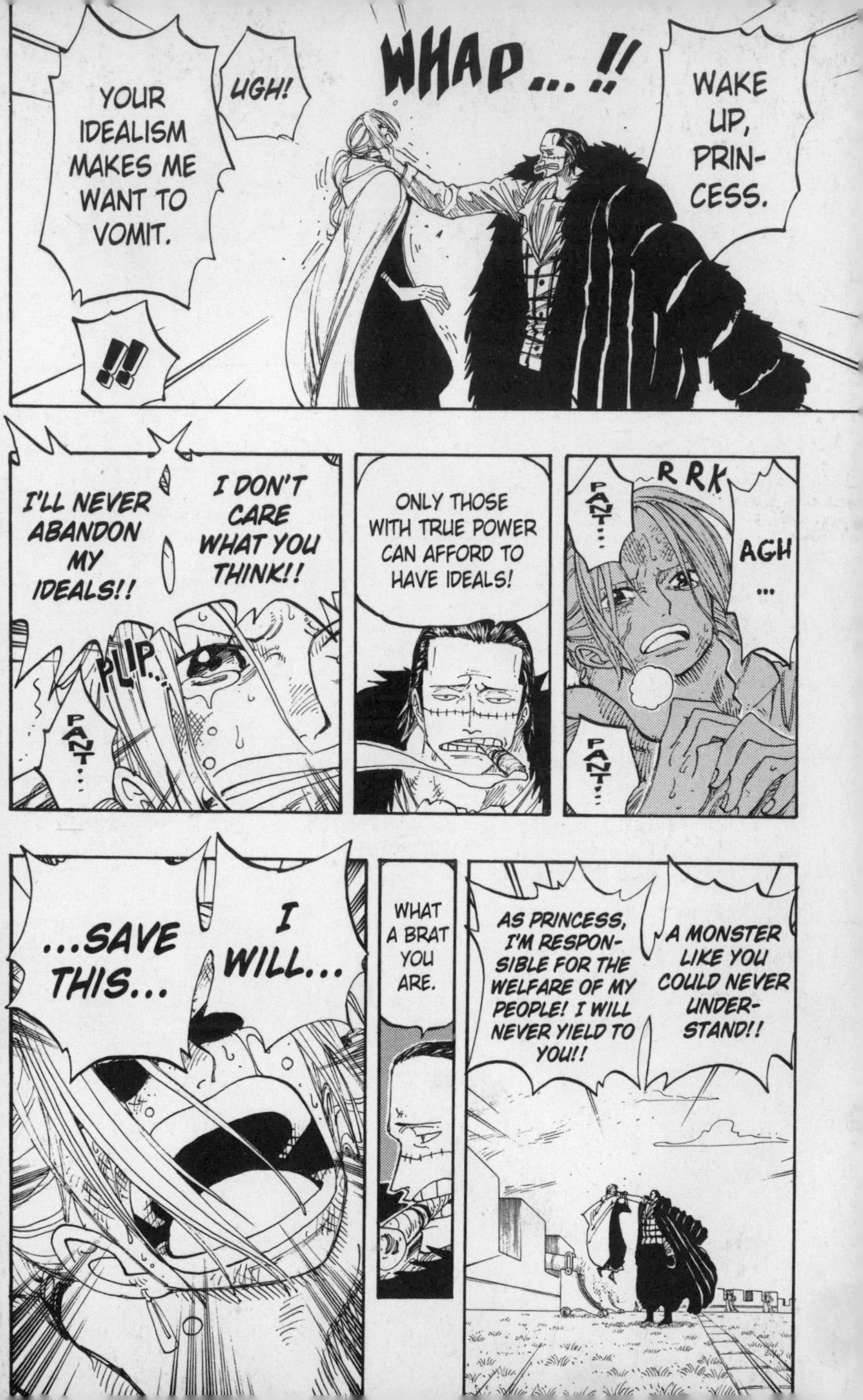
WAKE UP, PRIN-CESS.
WHAP...!!
UGH!
YOUR IDEALISM MAKES ME WANT TO VOMIT.
!!
RRK
PANT...
AGH...
PANT...
ONLY THOSE WITH TRUE POWER CAN AFFORD TO HAVE IDEALS!
I DON'T CARE WHAT YOU THINK!!
I'LL NEVER ABANDON MY IDEALS!!
PLIP...
PANT...
A MONSTER LIKE YOU COULD NEVER UNDER-STAND!!
AS PRINCESS, I'M RESPON-SIBLE FOR THE WELFARE OF MY PEOPLE! I WILL NEVER YIELD TO YOU!!
WHAT A BRAT YOU ARE.
I WILL...
...SAVE THIS...

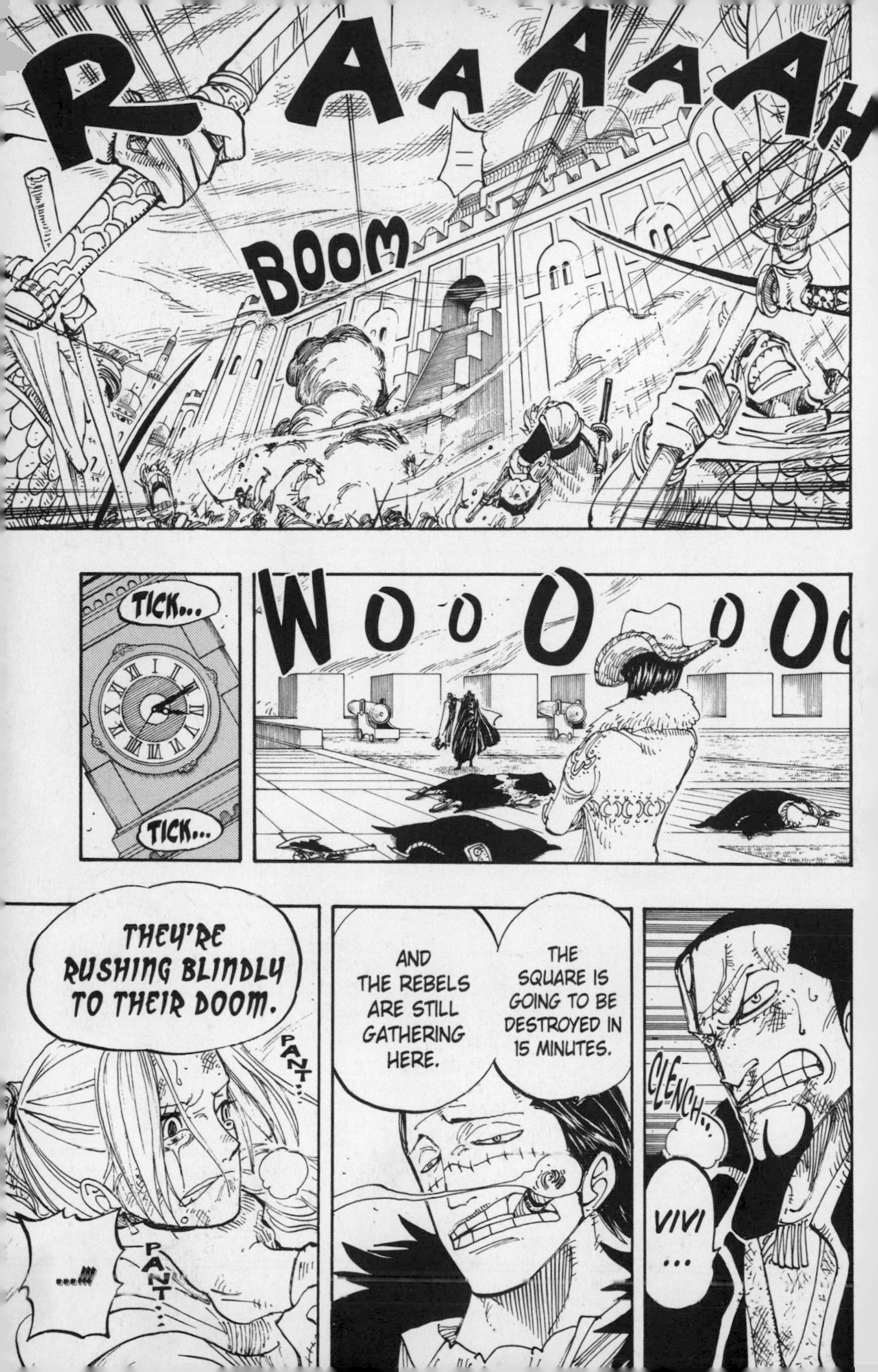
RAAAAAH
BOOM
WOOOOOO
TICK...
TICK...
CLENCH...
VIVI ...
THE SQUARE IS GOING TO BE DESTROYED IN 15 MINUTES.
AND THE REBELS ARE STILL GATHERING HERE.
THEY'RE RUSHING BLINDLY TO THEIR DOOM.
PANT...
PANT...
...!!!

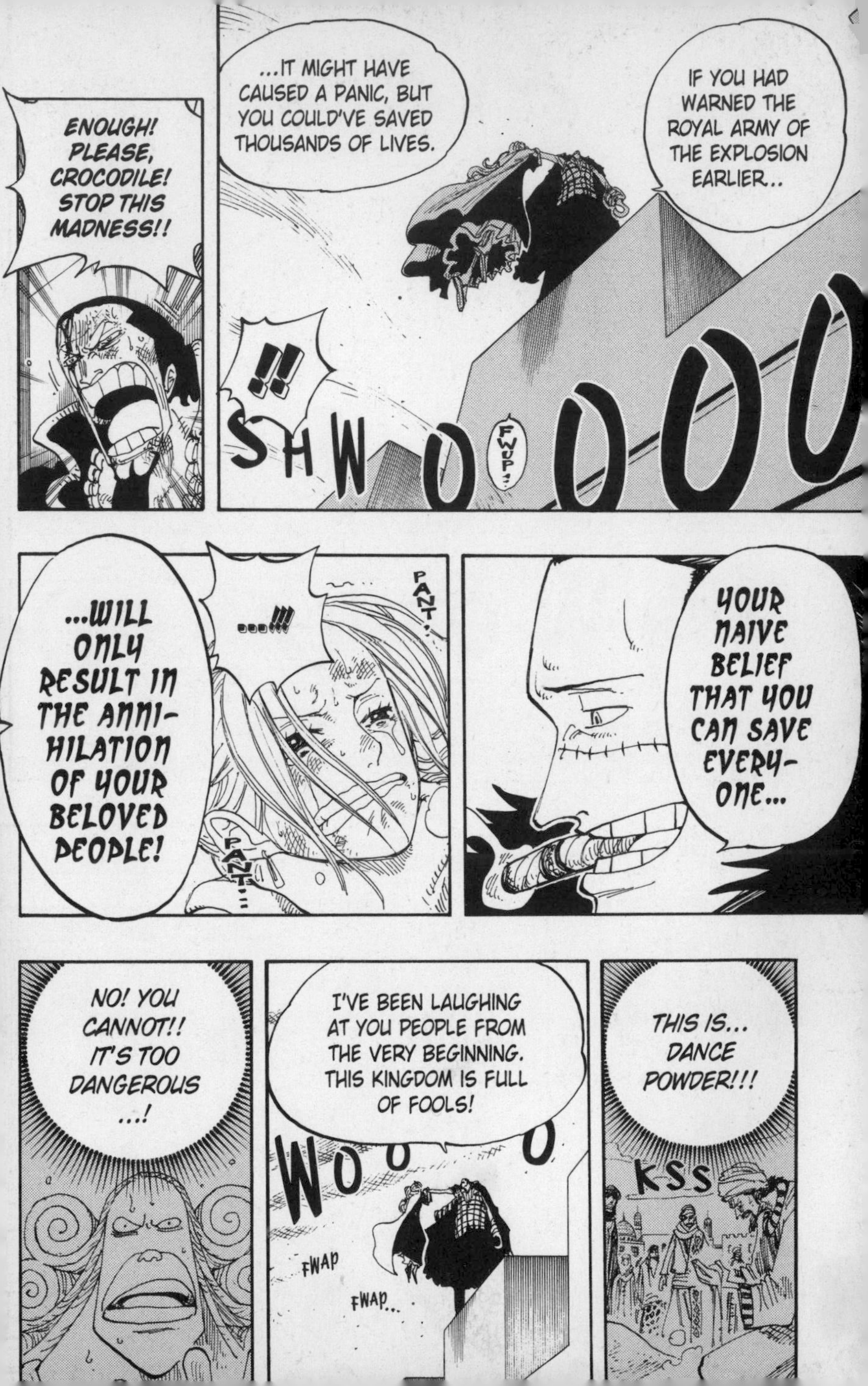
IF YOU HAD WARNED THE ROYAL ARMY OF THE EXPLOSION EARLIER...
...IT MIGHT HAVE CAUSED A PANIC, BUT YOU COULD'VE SAVED THOUSANDS OF LIVES.
!!
SHWOOOOOO
FWUP!
ENOUGH! PLEASE, CROCODILE! STOP THIS MADNESS!!
YOUR NAIVE BELIEF THAT YOU CAN SAVE EVERYONE...
PANT
...!!!
PANT...
...WILL ONLY RESULT IN THE ANNIHILATION OF YOUR BELOVED PEOPLE!
THIS IS... DANCE POWDER!!!
KSS
I'VE BEEN LAUGHING AT YOU PEOPLE FROM THE VERY BEGINNING. THIS KINGDOM IS FULL OF FOOLS!
WOOO
FWAP
FWAP...
NO! YOU CANNOT!! IT'S TOO DANGEROUS ...!

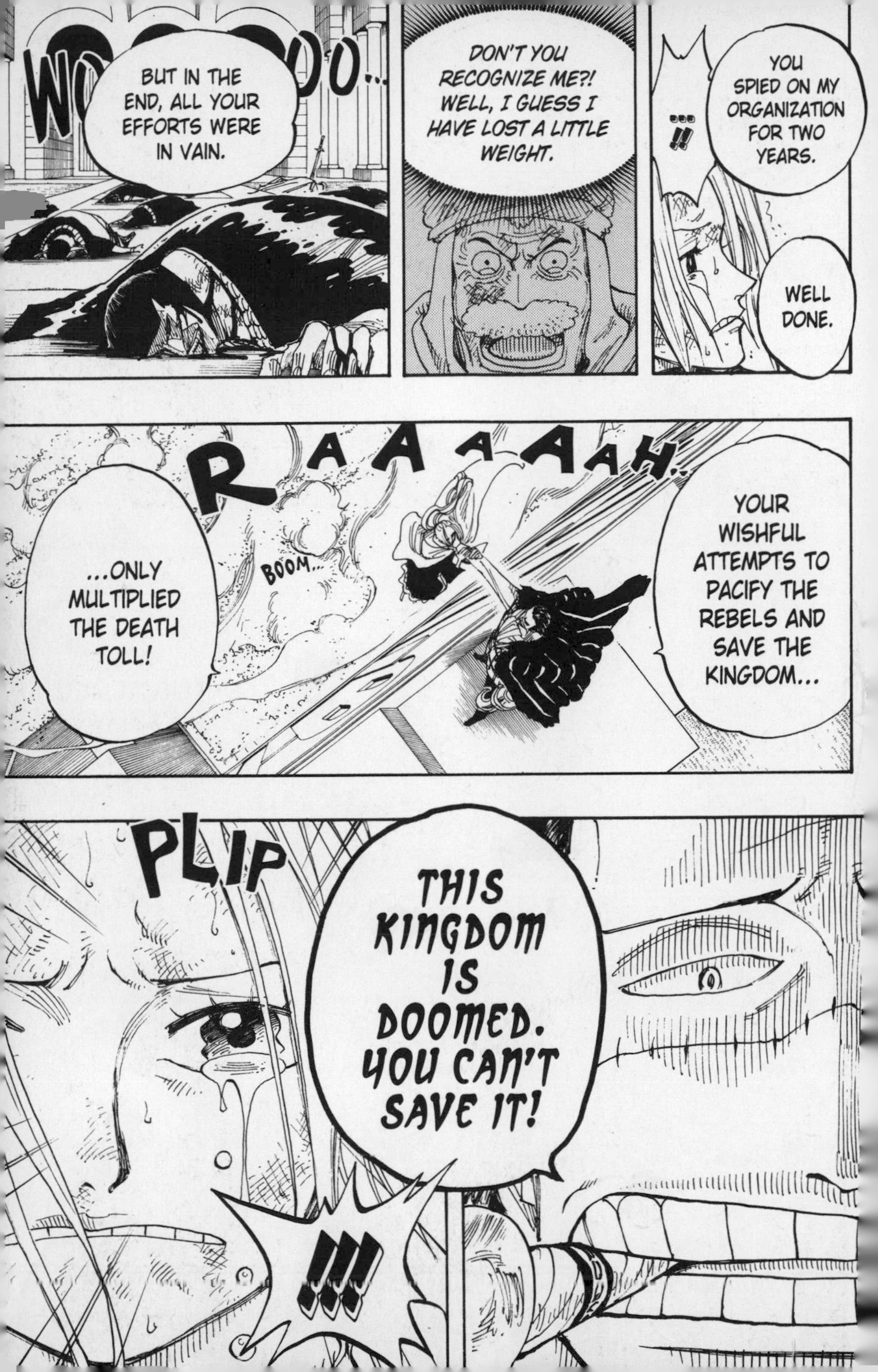

YOU SPIED ON MY ORGANIZATION FOR TWO YEARS.
...!!
WELL DONE.
DON'T YOU RECOGNIZE ME?! WELL, I GUESS I HAVE LOST A LITTLE WEIGHT.
BUT IN THE END, ALL YOUR EFFORTS WERE IN VAIN.
YOUR WISHFUL ATTEMPTS TO PACIFY THE REBELS AND SAVE THE KINGDOM...
RAAAAAH..
BOOM...
...ONLY MULTIPLIED THE DEATH TOLL!
PLIP
THIS KINGDOM IS DOOMED. YOU CAN'T SAVE IT!
!!!

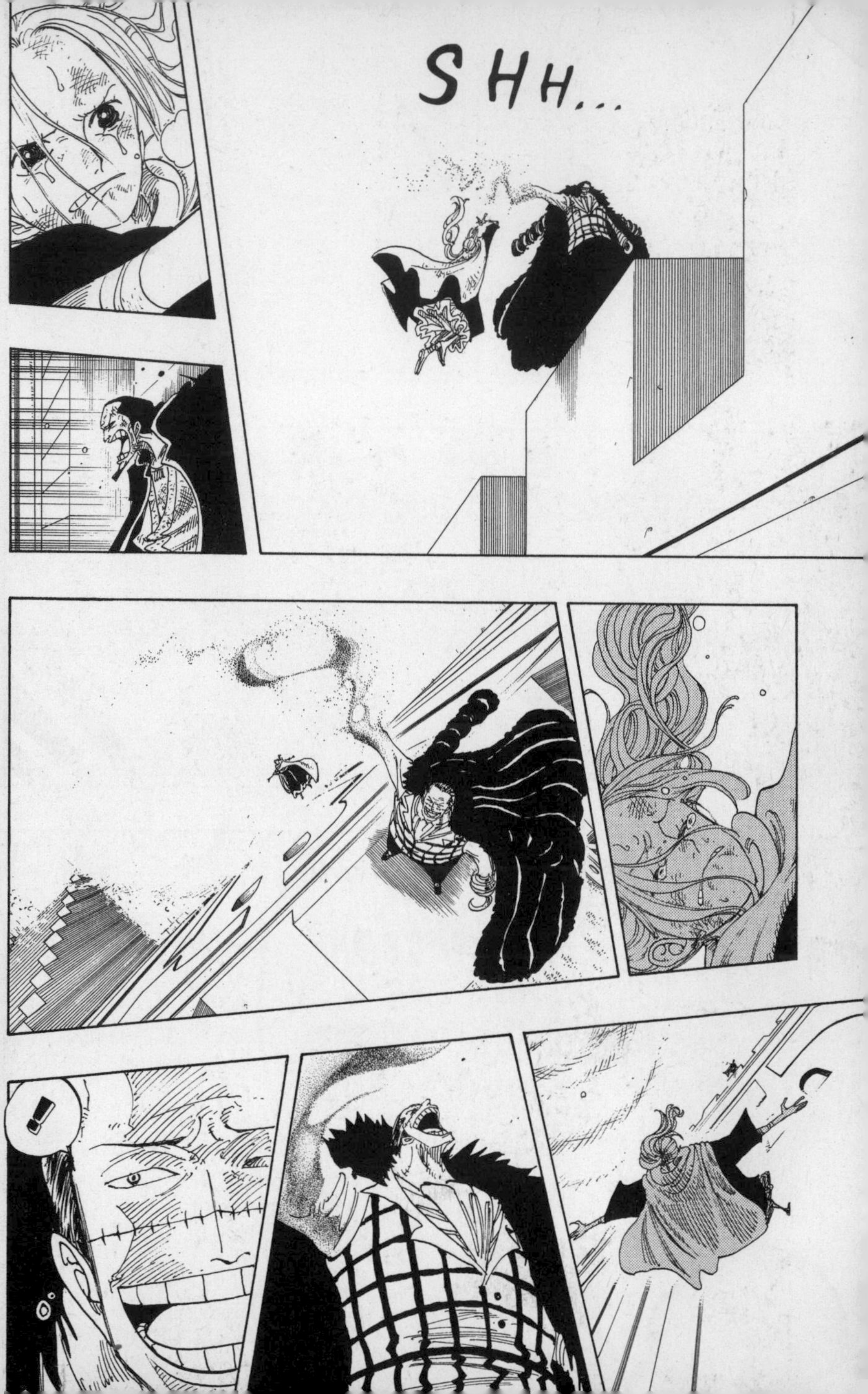

SHH...

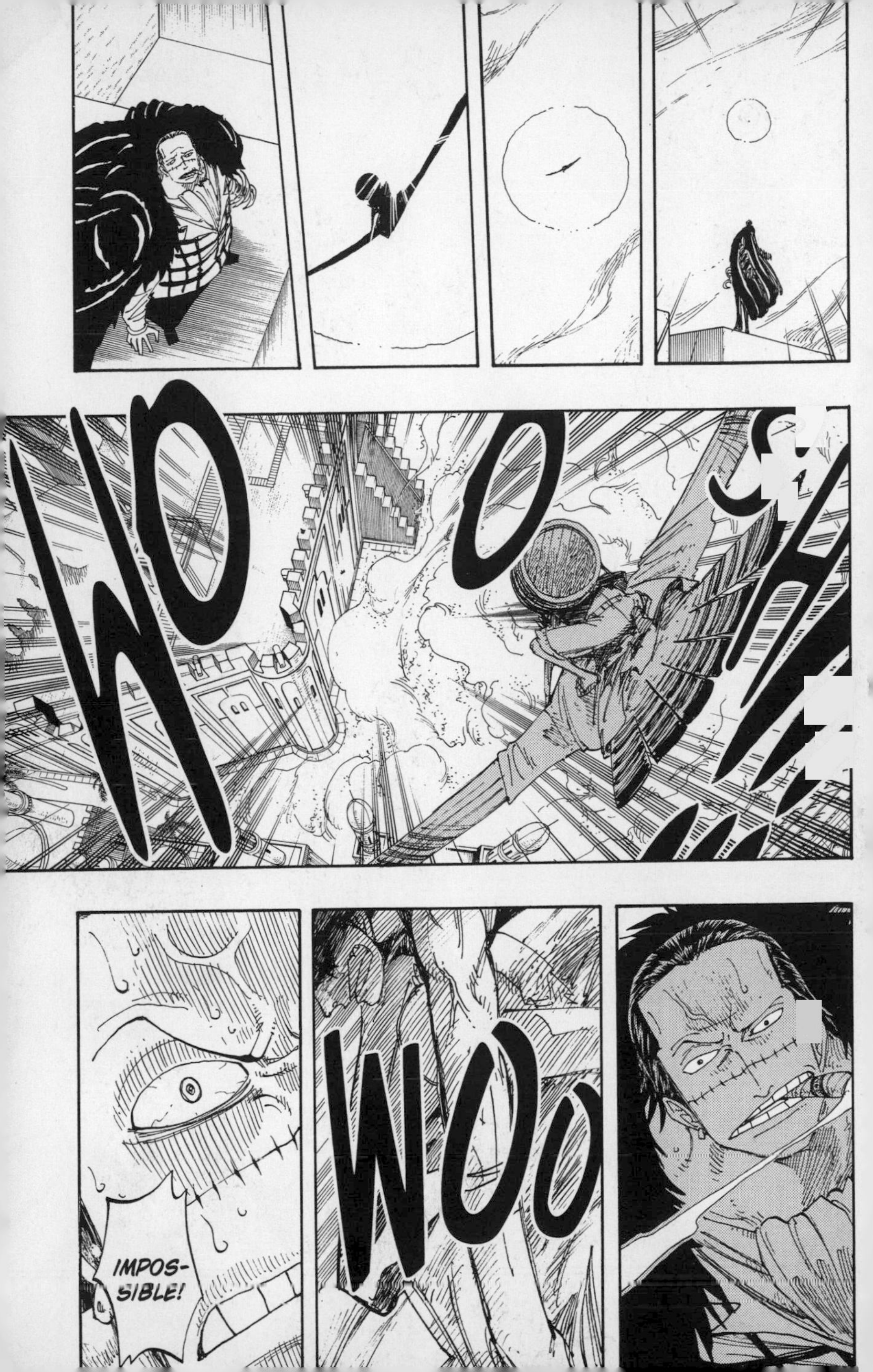
WHOOSH
WOO
IMPOS-
SIBLE!

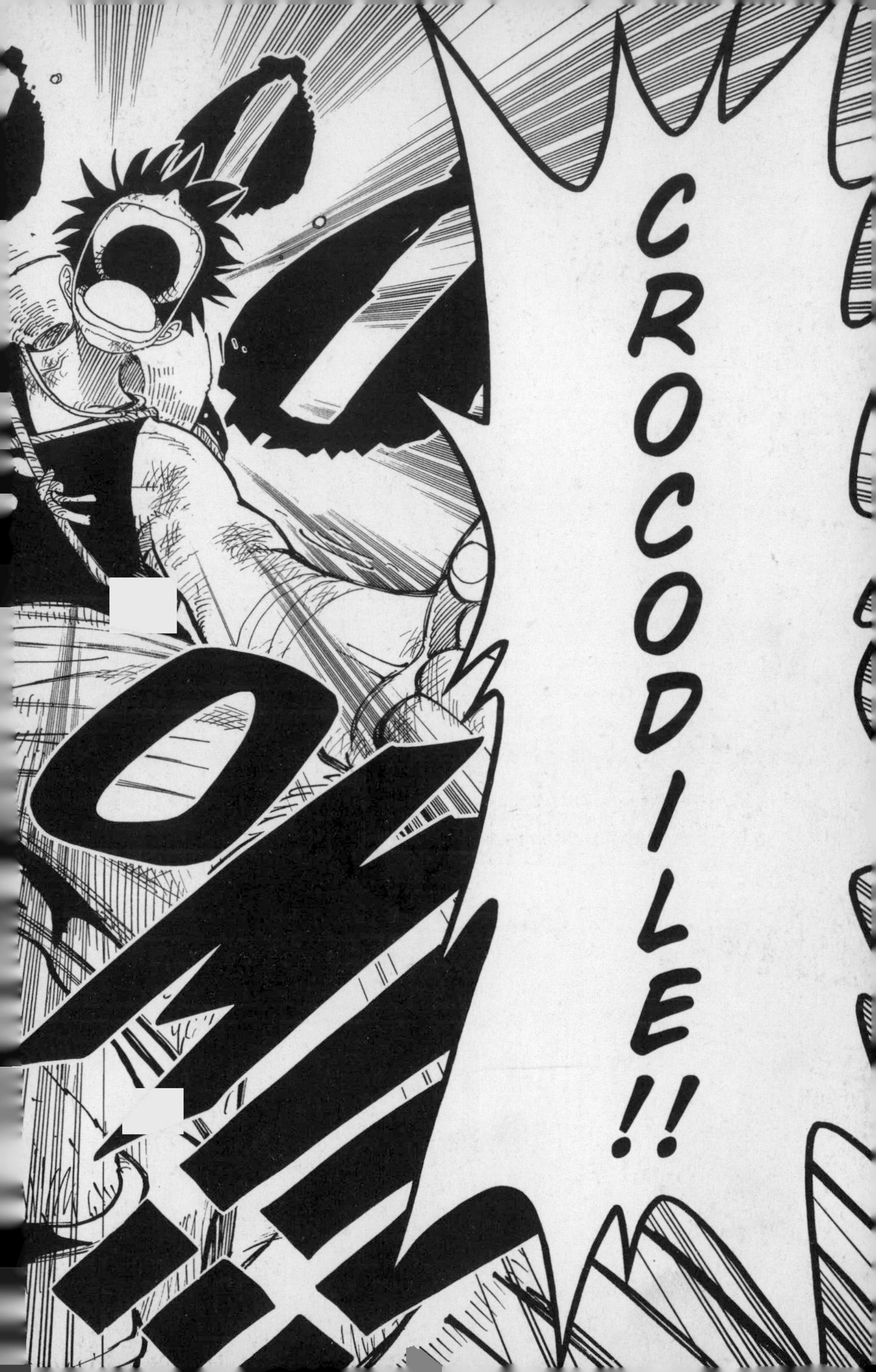
CROCODILE!!

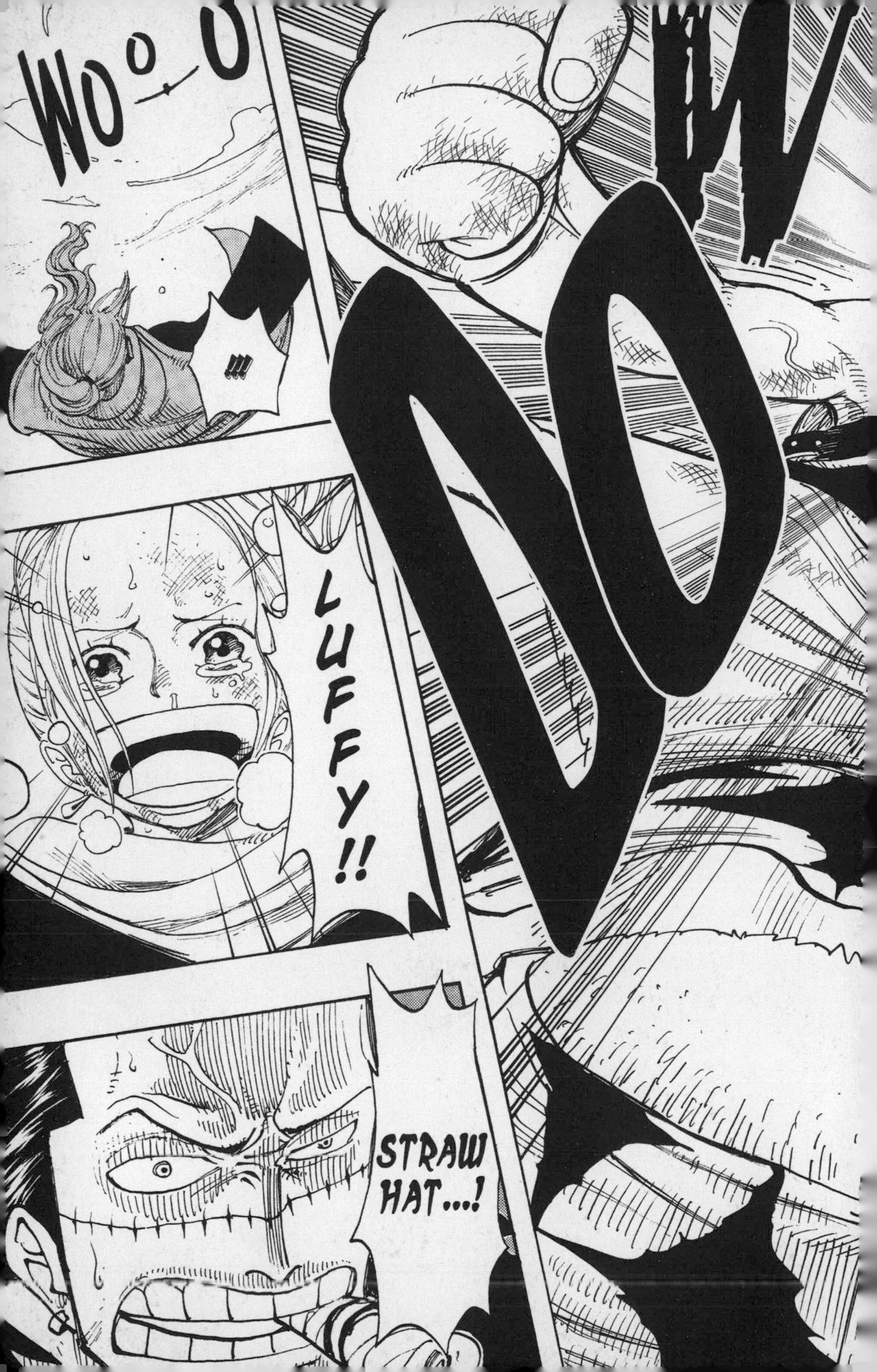
WOOO
!!!
LUFFY!!
STRAW HAT...!

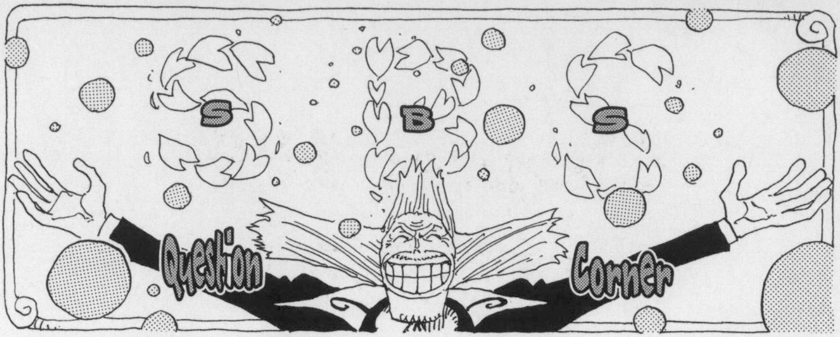
S
B
S
Question
Corner

Reader: Oda Sensei, something's been bothering me. What country are Luffy and the others from? In my sociology class we learned that Japanese pirates were called *wakô*. Is this a Japanese translation or something, or is "pirates" a special term used in this manga? Please tell me.

--Kuroman

Oda: Well, first of all, Luffy and his crew are not citizens of any country. And I won't make any conclusions about their ethnicity. As for *wakô*, let's see. Historically, *wakô* were pirates. *Wakô* mostly attacked in boats along the Korean peninsula and the Chinese mainland. Once in a while our history books mention "sending soldiers to Korea." These soldiers were actually pirates. They went there to pillage. They were bad guys. The *Murakami Suigun* ("Water Army") terrorized and controlled the Seto Inland Sea. They were pirates too. They had a real impact on Japanese history, though most people don't know much about them. I once researched the difference between the *wakô* and the *suigun*. Actually the *suigun* were sometimes called *wakô*, so there really wasn't much difference. In any case, there were lots of pirates in Japan.

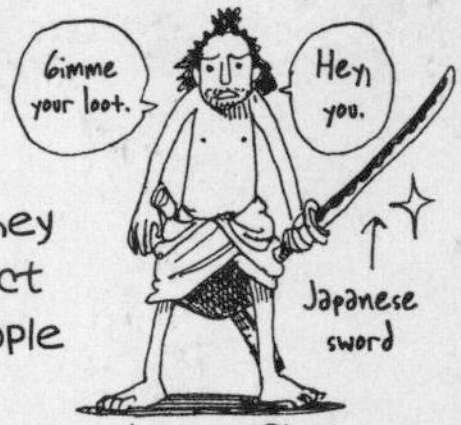
Hey, you.
Gimme your loot.
Japanese sword
Japanese Pirate (as I picture him)

Reader: What is the speed limit on the "Oh Come My Way" Way?

--Mr. Tsu Bon Curry

Oda: The speed limit is 300 fake eyelashes an hour.

# Chapter 199:
# HOPE!!

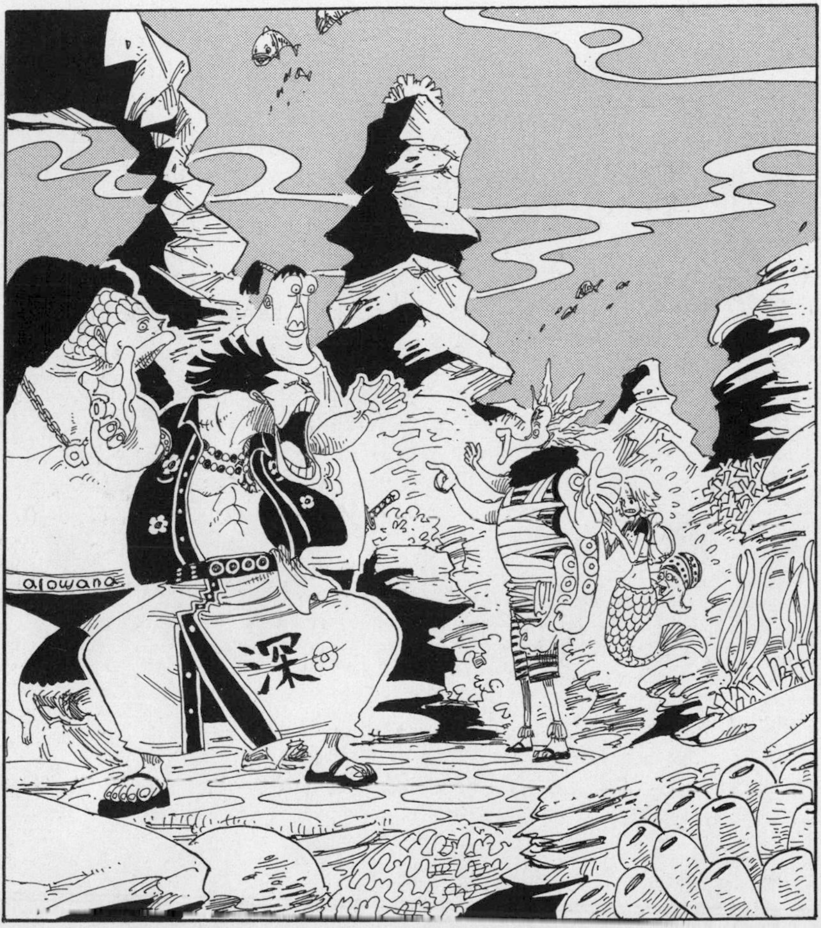
alowana
深

HACHI'S WALK ON THE SEAFLOOR, VOL. 15:
"A REUNION WITH OLD COMRADES"

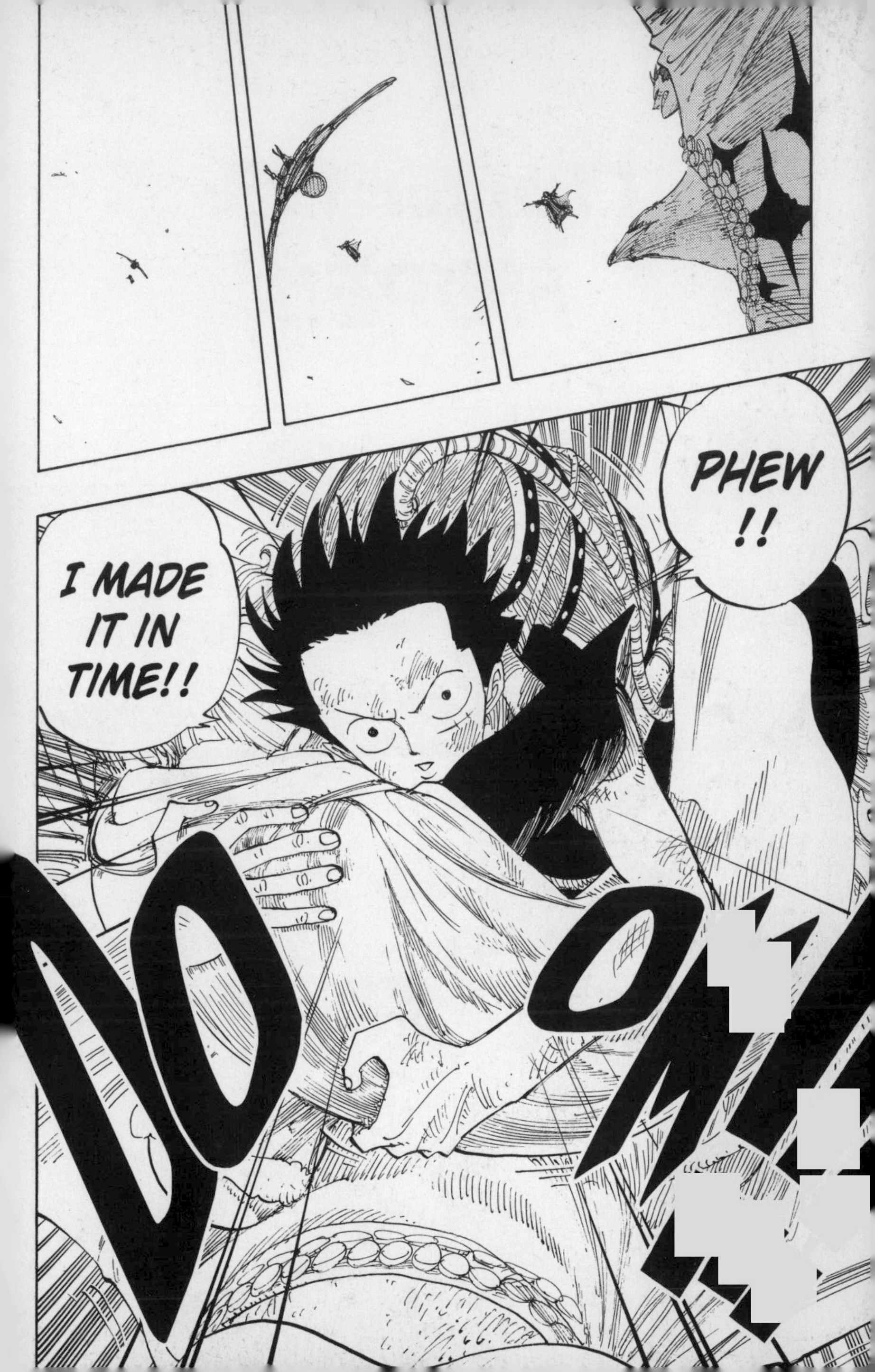
PHEW!!
I MADE IT IN TIME!!

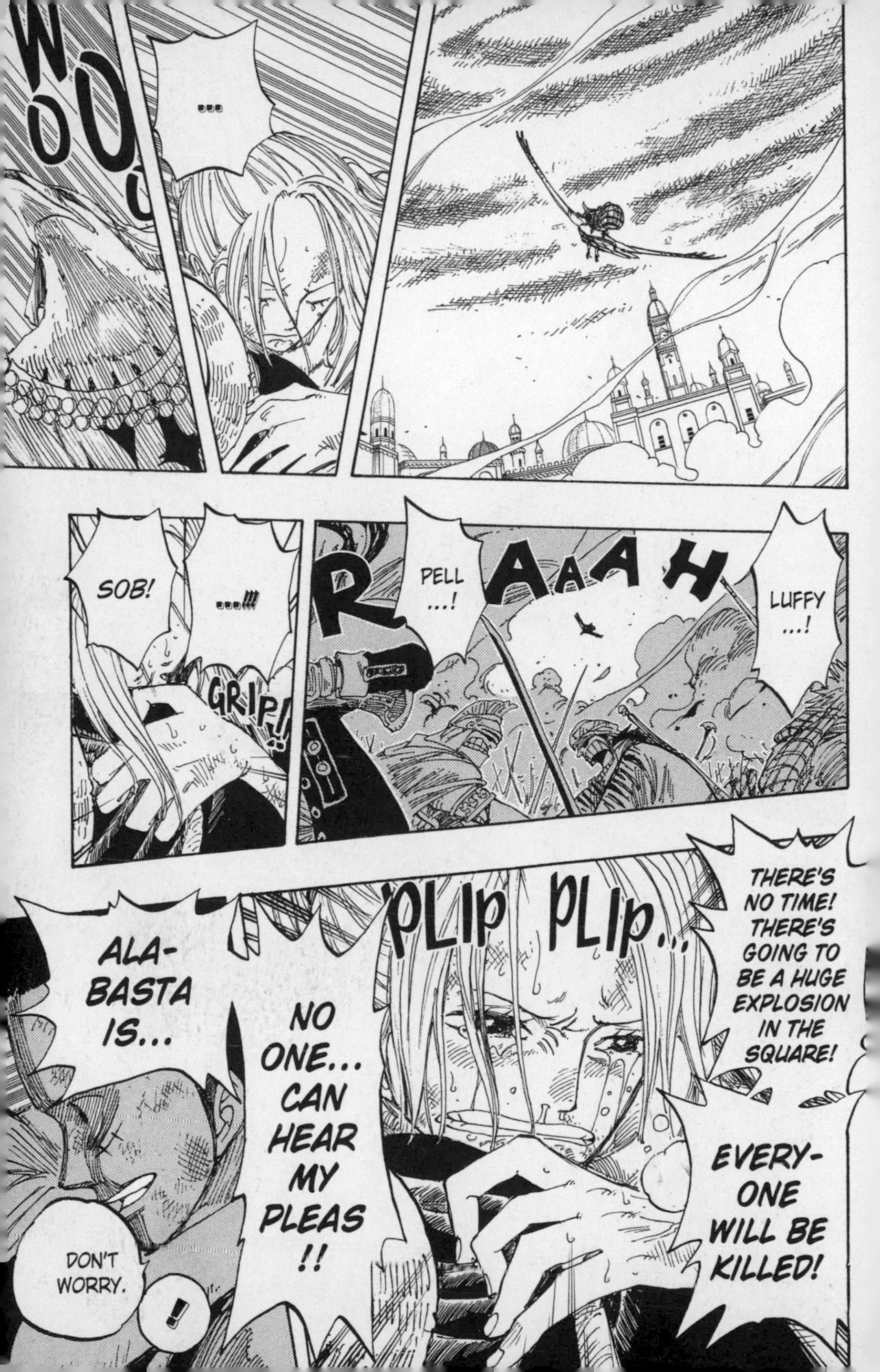
...
WOOO
LUFFY ...!
RAAAH
PELL ...!
...!!!
SOB!
GRIP!!
THERE'S NO TIME! THERE'S GOING TO BE A HUGE EXPLOSION IN THE SQUARE!
PLIP PLIP...
EVERYONE WILL BE KILLED!
NO ONE... CAN HEAR MY PLEAS!!
ALABASTA IS...
DON'T WORRY.
!

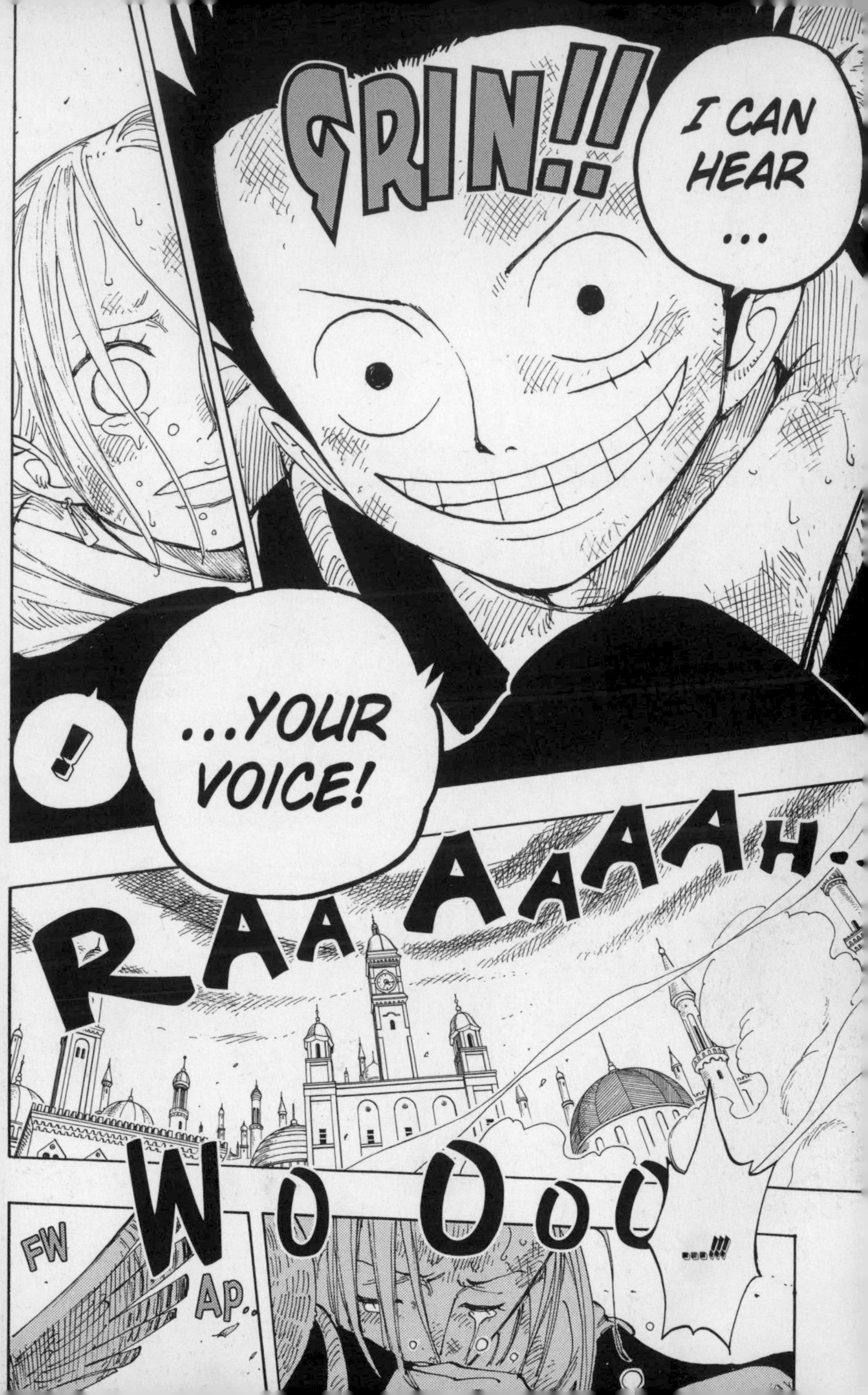
I CAN HEAR ...
GRIN!!
...YOUR VOICE!
!
RAAAAAAH...
WOOOO...!!!
FWAP..

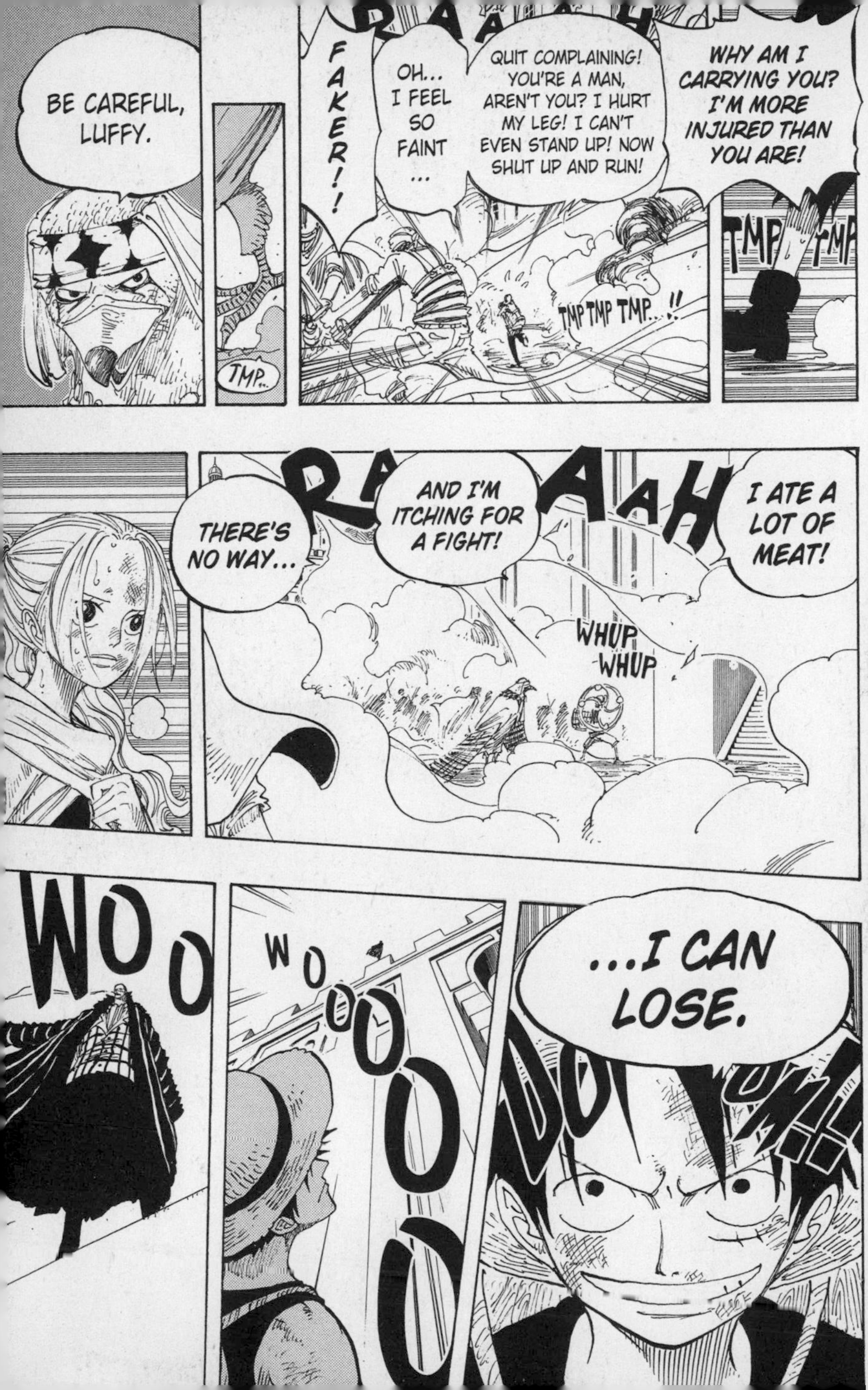
WHY AM I CARRYING YOU? I'M MORE INJURED THAN YOU ARE!
TMP TMP
QUIT COMPLAINING! YOU'RE A MAN, AREN'T YOU? I HURT MY LEG! I CAN'T EVEN STAND UP! NOW SHUT UP AND RUN!
OH... I FEEL SO FAINT ...
FAKER!!
TMP TMP TMP...!!
TMP...
BE CAREFUL, LUFFY.
I ATE A LOT OF MEAT!
RAAAH
AND I'M ITCHING FOR A FIGHT!
THERE'S NO WAY...
WHUP WHUP
...I CAN LOSE.
WOOOOOO
WOO

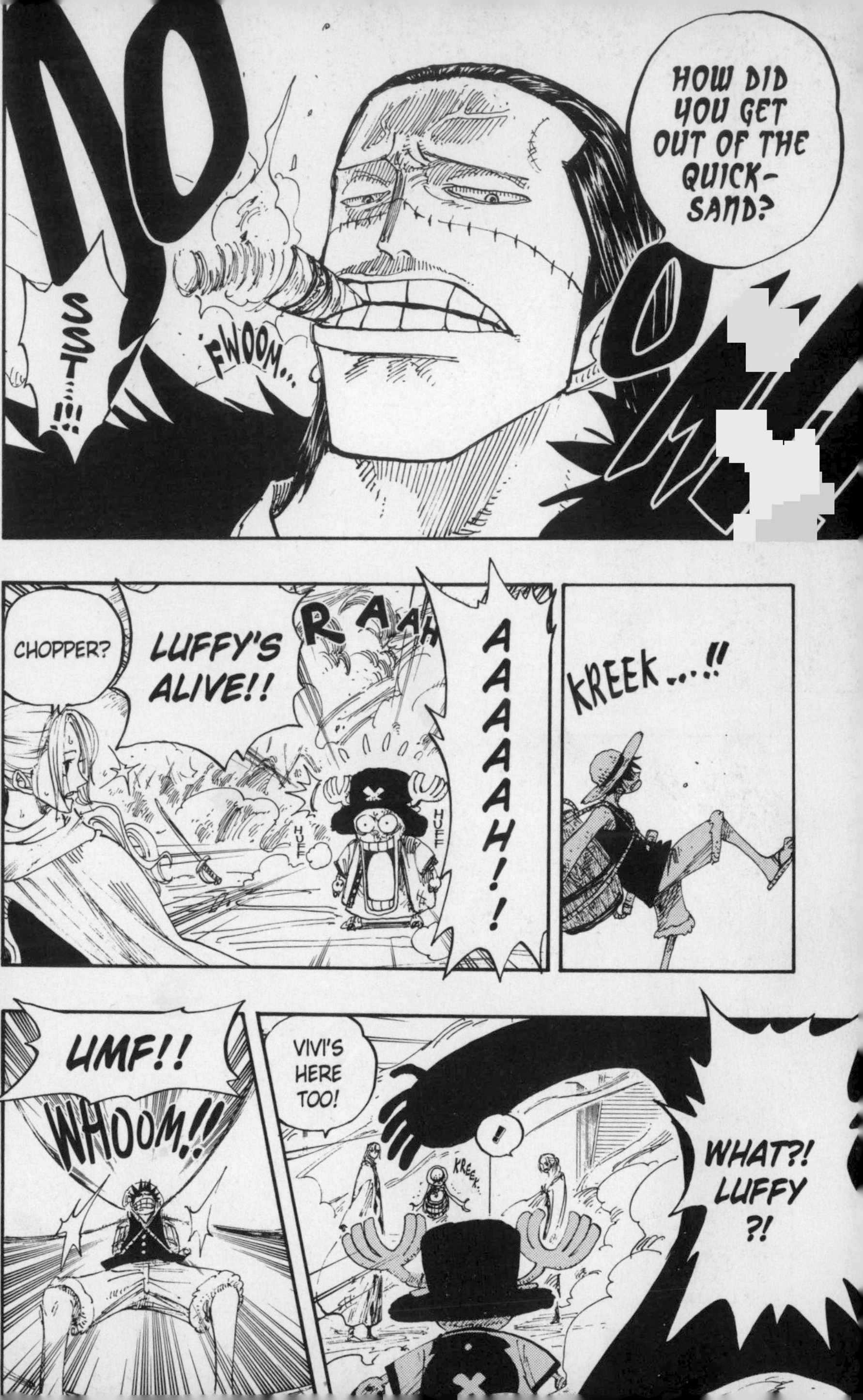

HOW DID YOU GET OUT OF THE QUICK-SAND?
FWOOM...
SST...!!!
KREEK...!!
RAAAAAAAAAH!!
LUFFY'S ALIVE!!
CHOPPER?
HUFF
HUFF
WHAT?! LUFFY?!
!
KREEK.
VIVI'S HERE TOO!
UMF!!
WHOOM!!

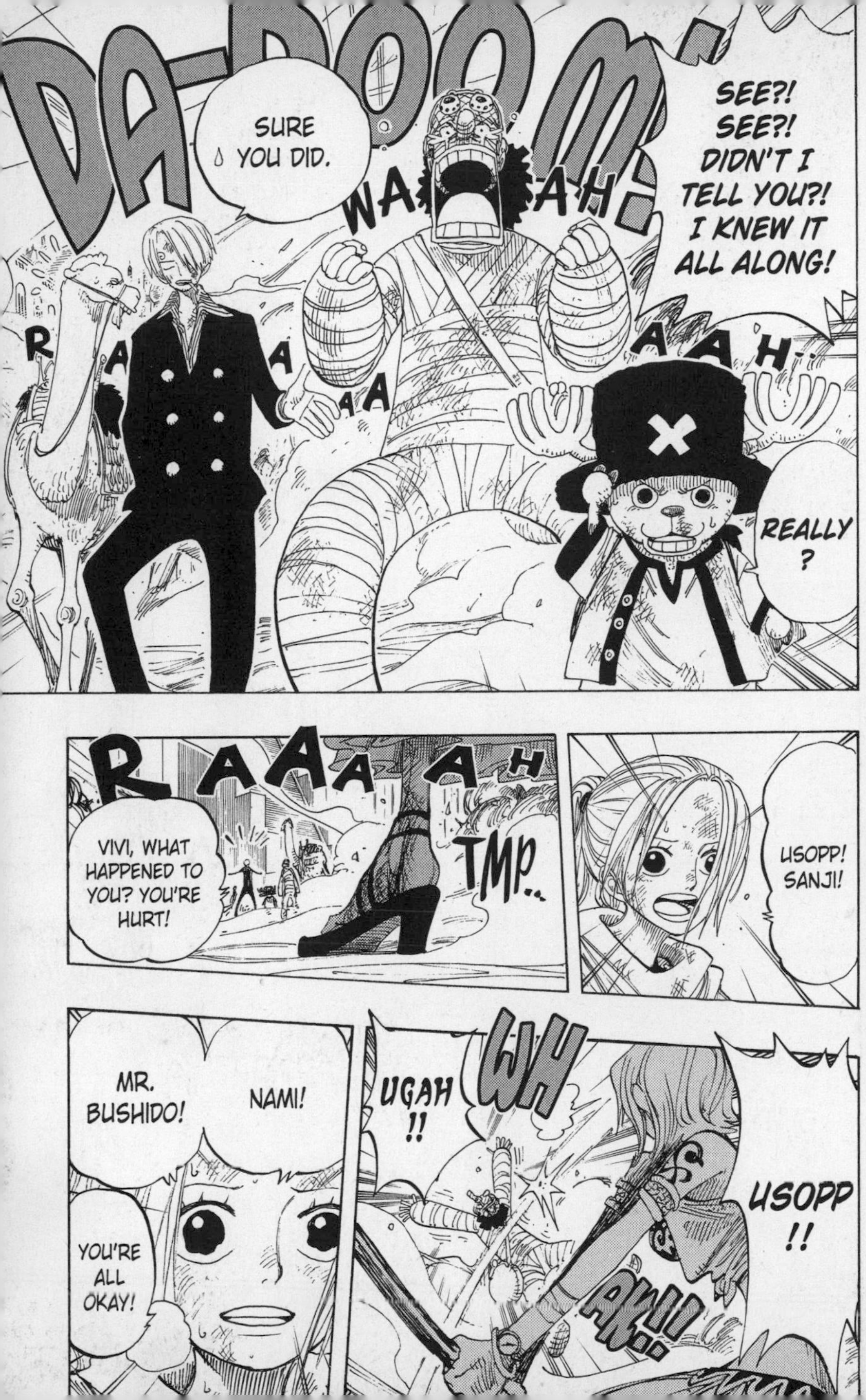
SEE?! SEE?! DIDN'T I TELL YOU?! I KNEW IT ALL ALONG!
DA-DOOM!
SURE YOU DID.
WAAH!
AAH..
REALLY ?
RAAAA
USOPP! SANJI!
RAAAAAH
TMP..
VIVI, WHAT HAPPENED TO YOU? YOU'RE HURT!
USOPP !!
WH
UGAH !!
AH!!
NAMI!
MR. BUSHIDO!
YOU'RE ALL OKAY!

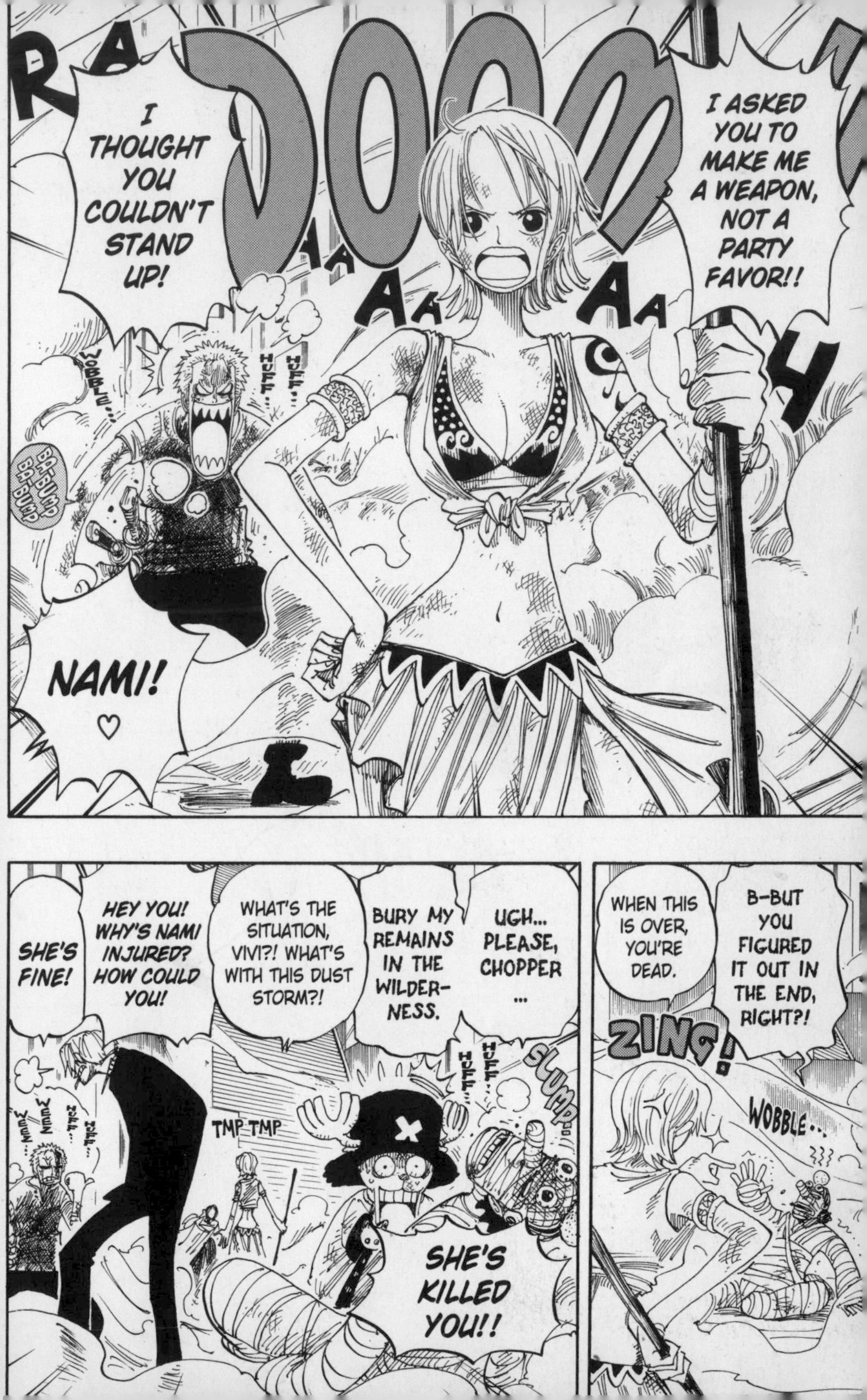
I ASKED YOU TO MAKE ME A WEAPON, NOT A PARTY FAVOR!!
I THOUGHT YOU COULDN'T STAND UP!
HUFF... HUFF...
WOBBLE...
BA-BUMP BA-BUMP
NAMI! ♡
B-BUT YOU FIGURED IT OUT IN THE END, RIGHT?!
WHEN THIS IS OVER, YOU'RE DEAD.
ZING!
WOBBLE...
UGH... PLEASE, CHOPPER...
BURY MY REMAINS IN THE WILDER-NESS.
WHAT'S THE SITUATION, VIVI?! WHAT'S WITH THIS DUST STORM?!
HEY YOU! WHY'S NAMI INJURED? HOW COULD YOU!
SHE'S FINE!
SLUMP...
HUFF... HUFF...
TMP TMP
WEEZ... WEEZ... HUFF... HUFF...
SHE'S KILLED YOU!!

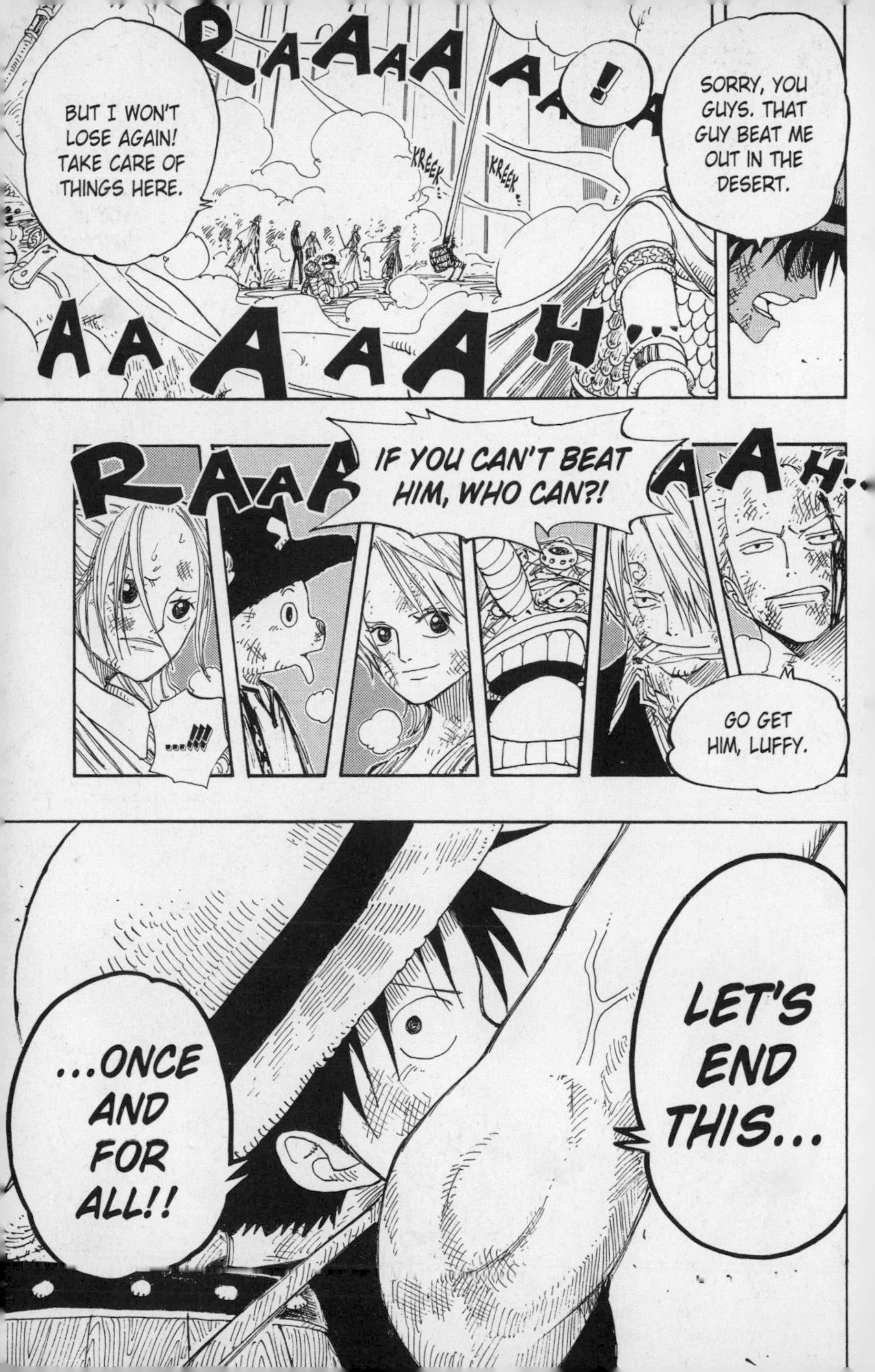
SORRY, YOU GUYS. THAT GUY BEAT ME OUT IN THE DESERT.
RAAAAAA!A
KREEK
KREEK
BUT I WON'T LOSE AGAIN! TAKE CARE OF THINGS HERE.
AAAAAAH...
RAAR
AAH...
IF YOU CAN'T BEAT HIM, WHO CAN?!
GO GET HIM, LUFFY.
...!!!
LET'S END THIS...
...ONCE AND FOR ALL!!

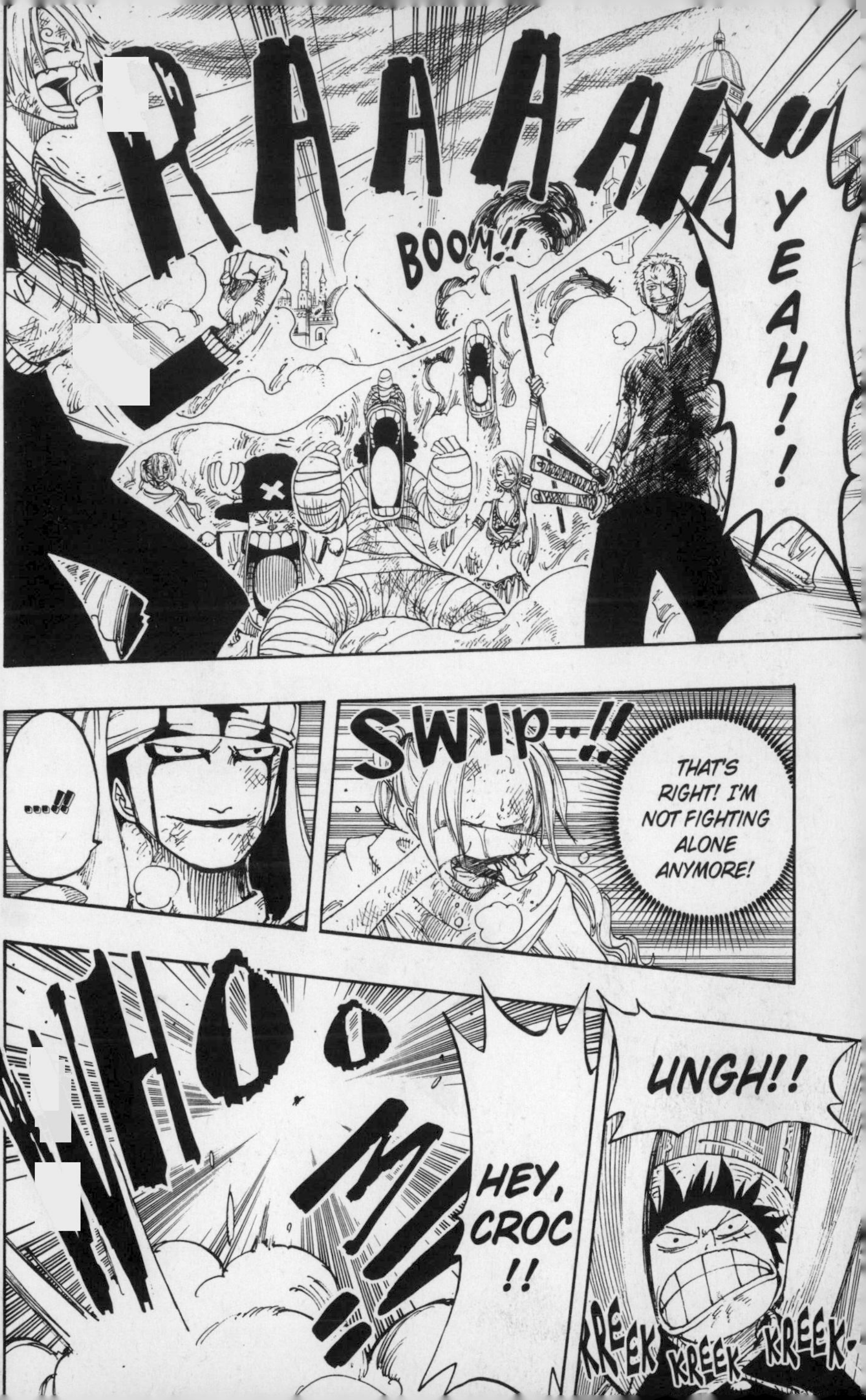
YEAH!!
RAAAAAH
BOOM..!!
SWIP..!!
THAT'S RIGHT! I'M NOT FIGHTING ALONE ANYMORE!
...!!
UNGH!!
KREEK KREEK KREEK
HEY, CROC!!
WHOOM..!!

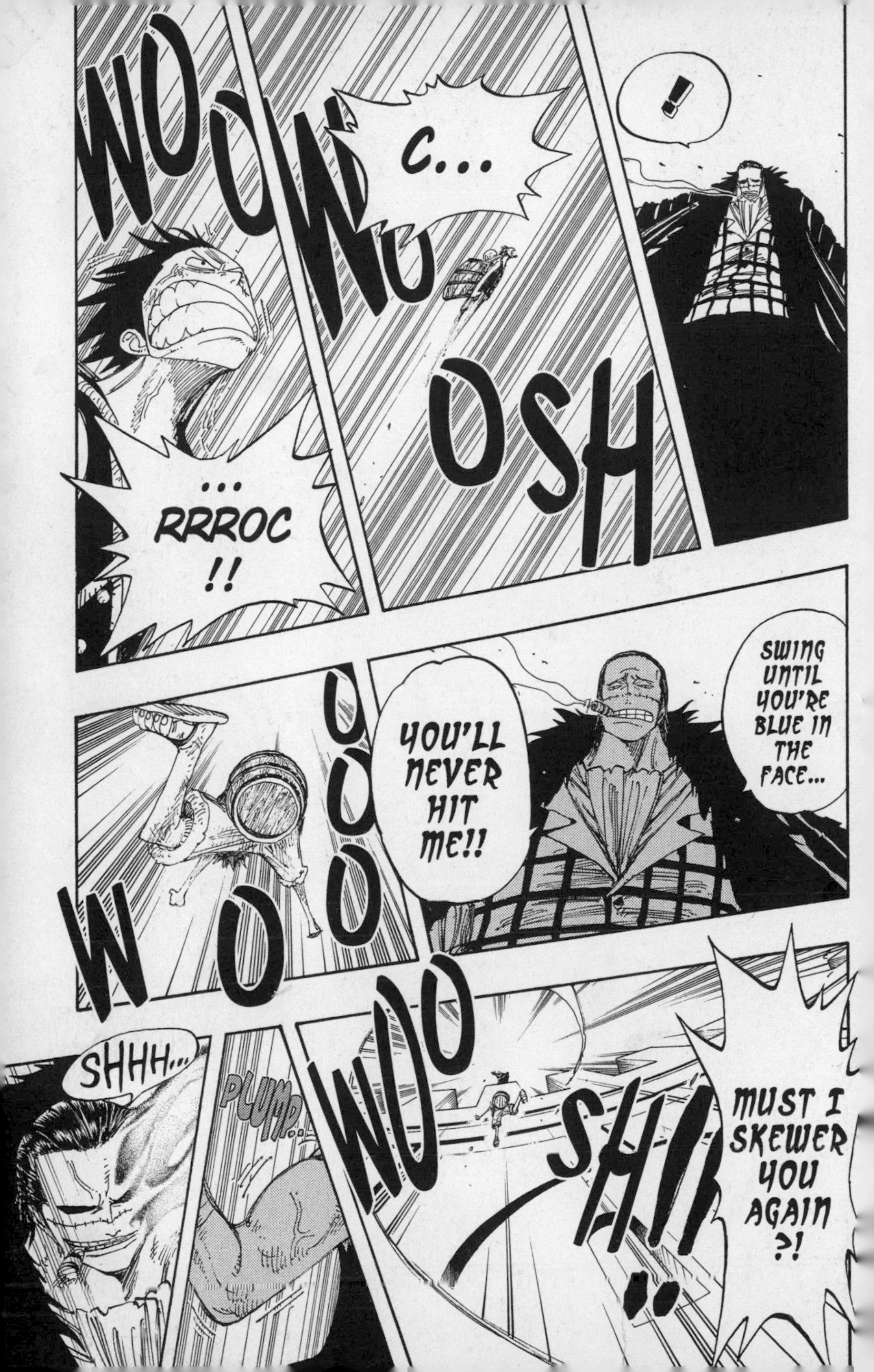
!
C...
WOOSH
...RRROC!!
SWING UNTIL YOU'RE BLUE IN THE FACE...
YOU'LL NEVER HIT ME!!
WOOOOO
MUST I SKEWER YOU AGAIN?!
WOOSH!!
PLUMP..
SHHH...

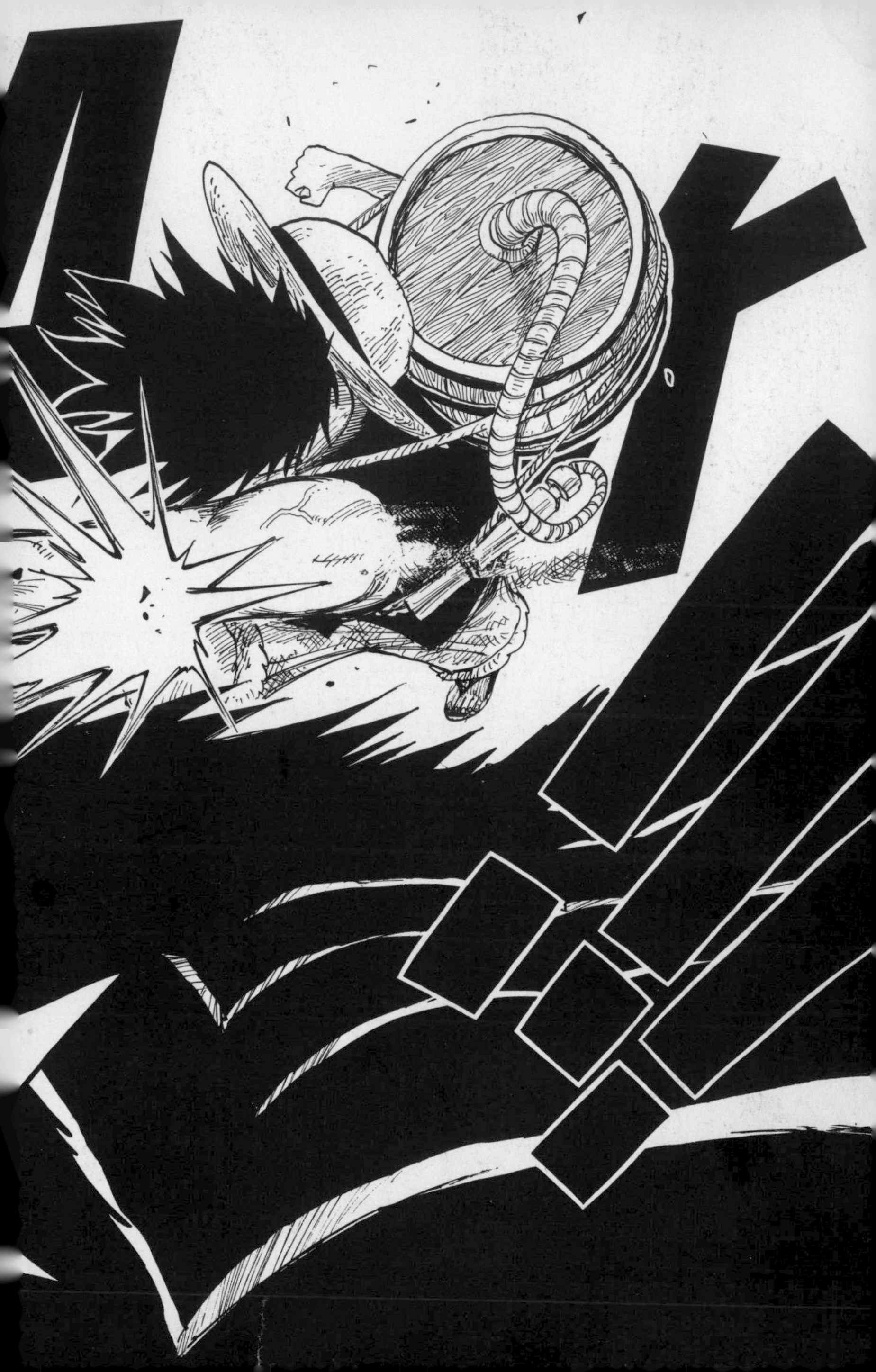

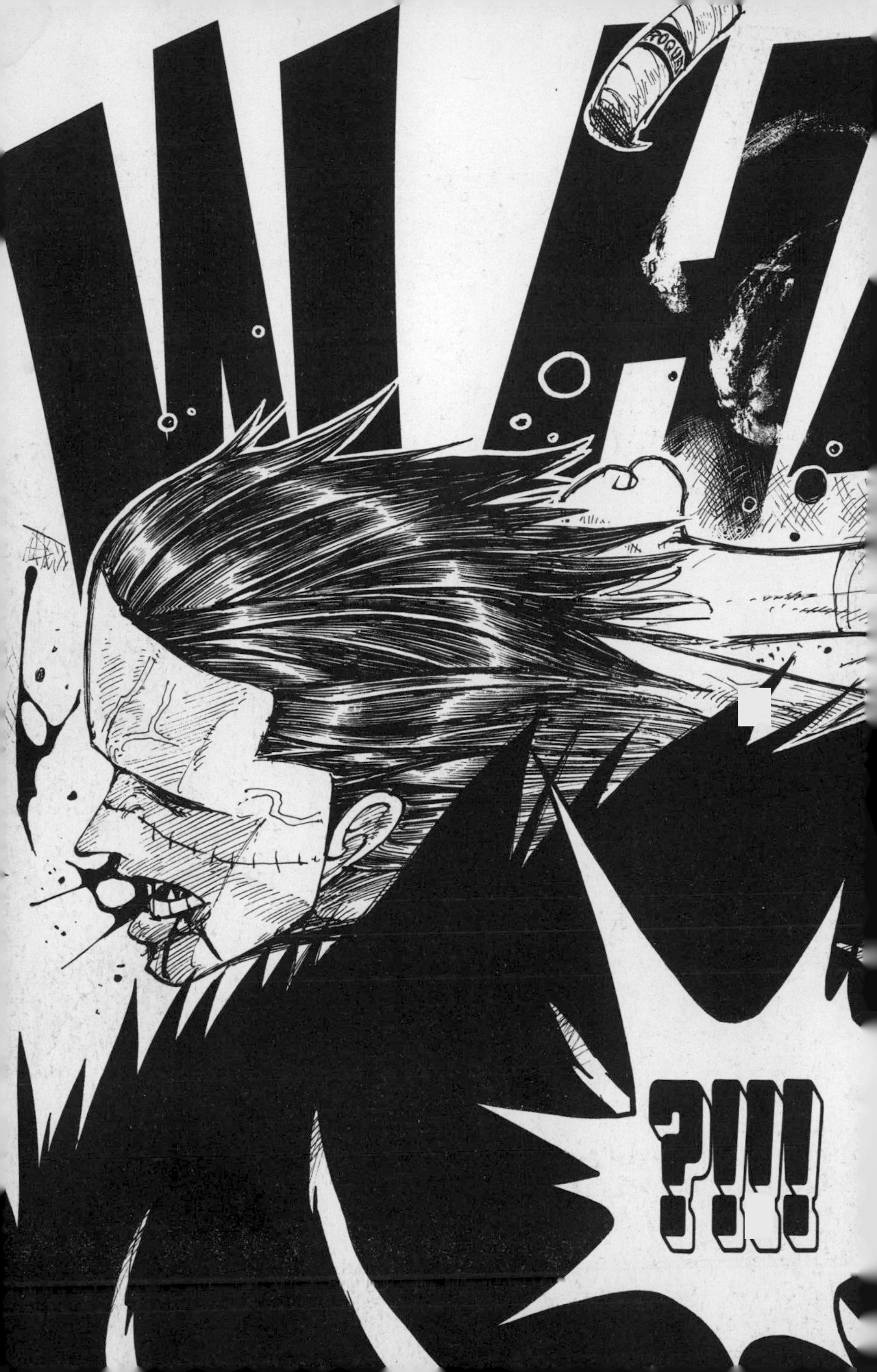
?!!!

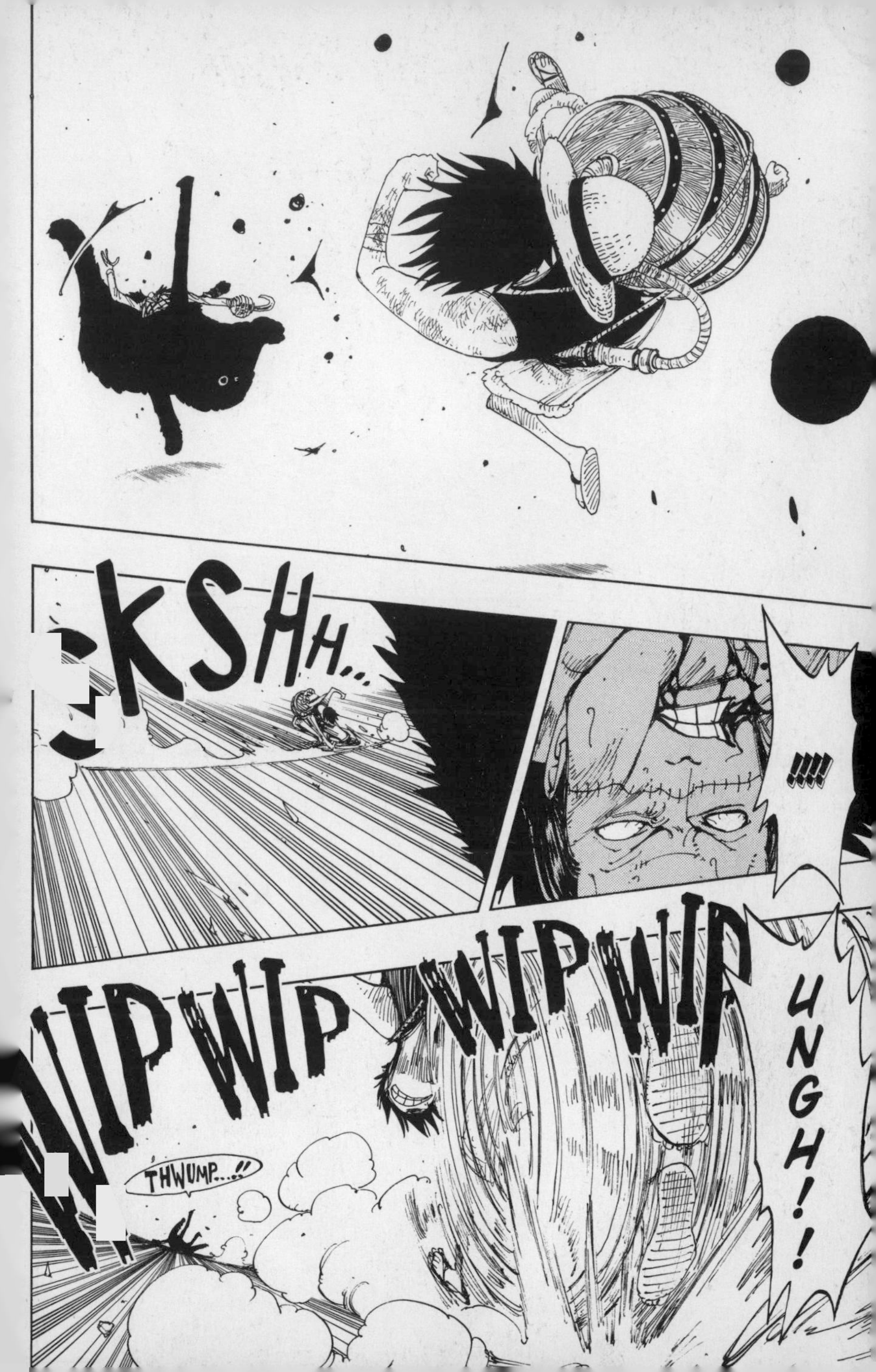
!!!!
KSHH...
UNGH!!!
WIP WIP WIP WIP
THWUMP...!!

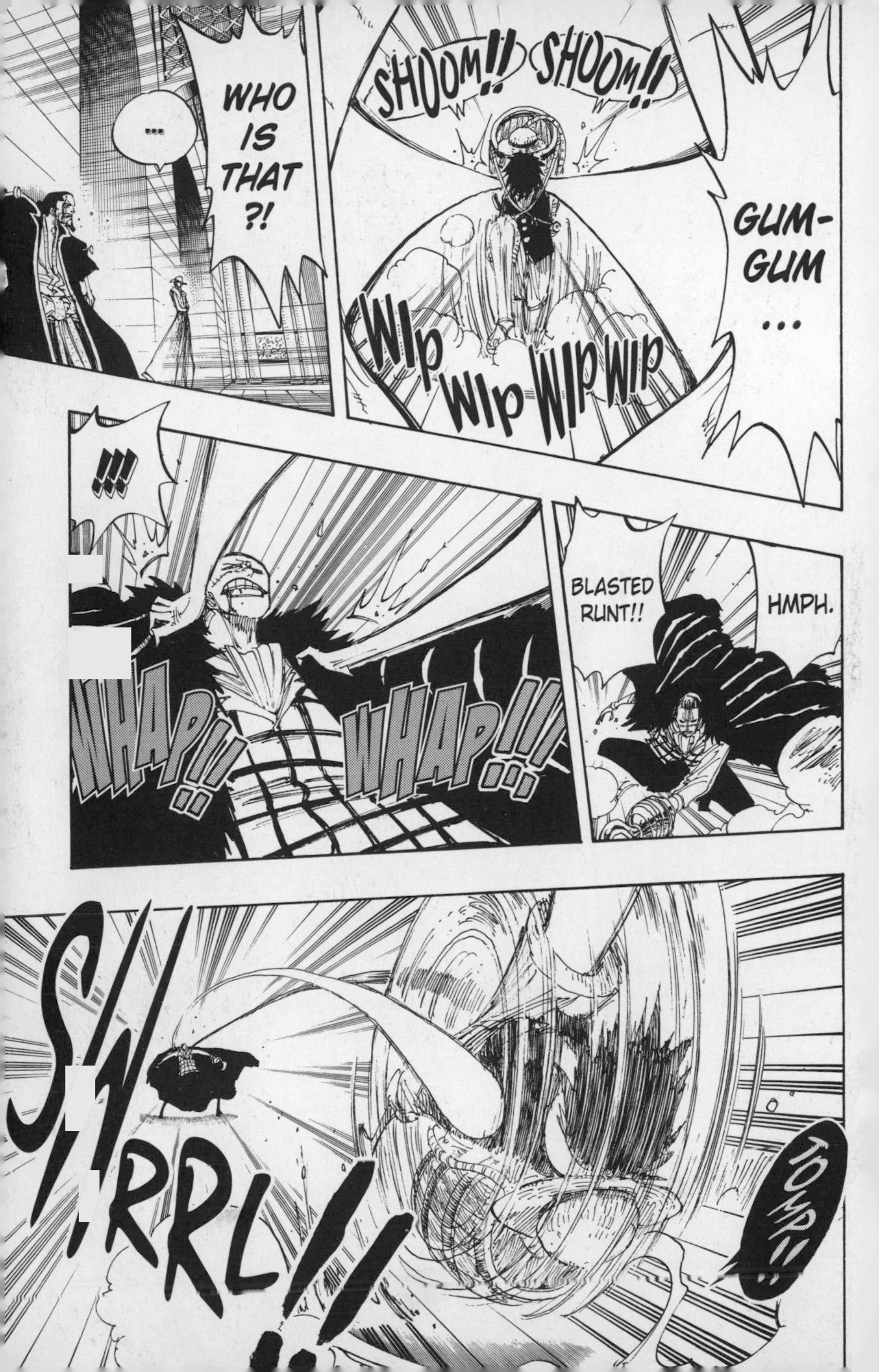
GUM-GUM...
SHOOM!! SHOOM!!
WIP WIP WIP WIP
WHO IS THAT?!
...
HMPH.
BLASTED RUNT!!
!!!
WHAP!!! WHAP!!!
TOMP!!
SWIRRL!!

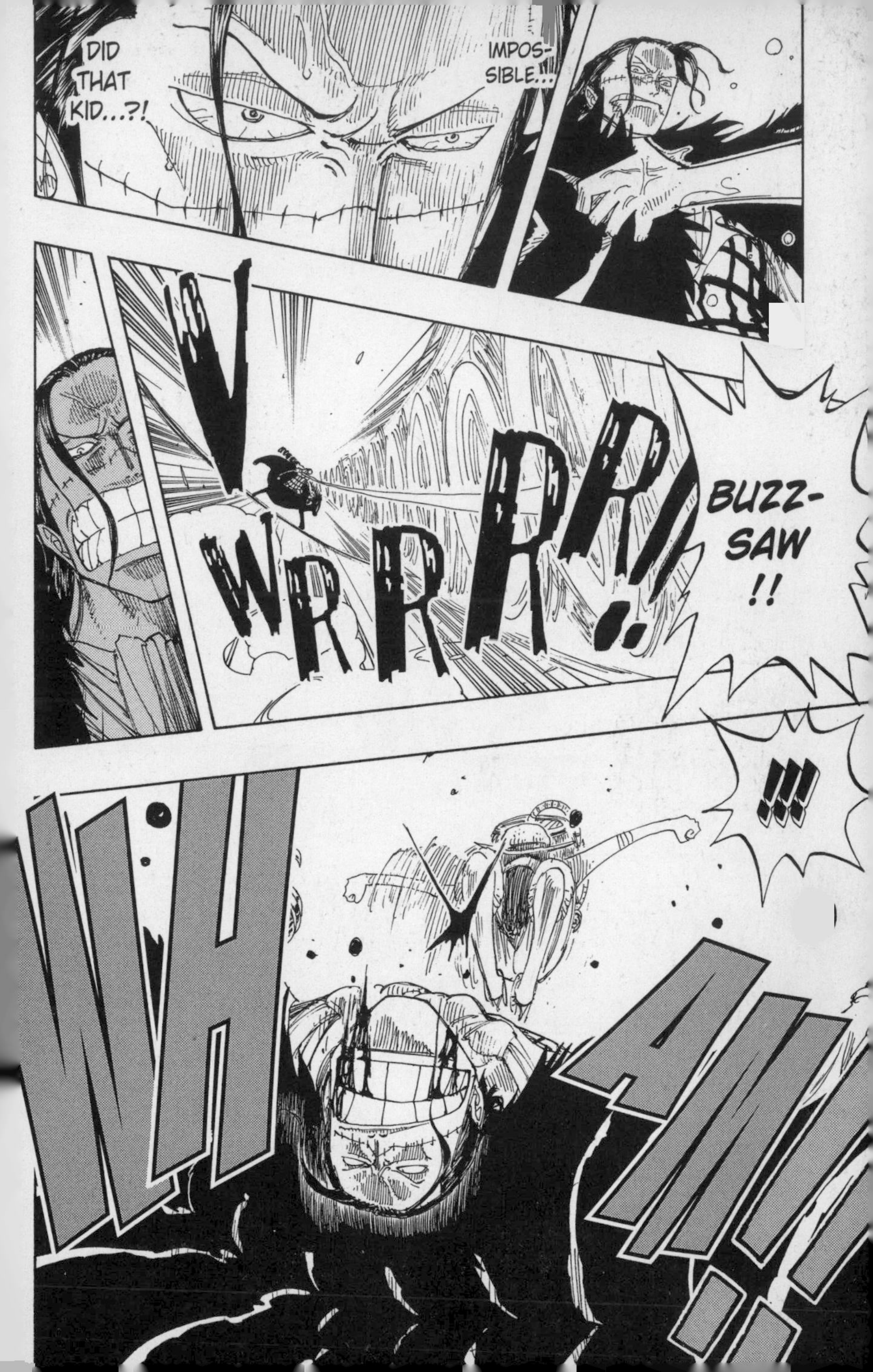
IMPOSSIBLE...
DID THAT KID...?!
BUZZ-SAW!!
VWRRRR!!
!!!
WHAM!!

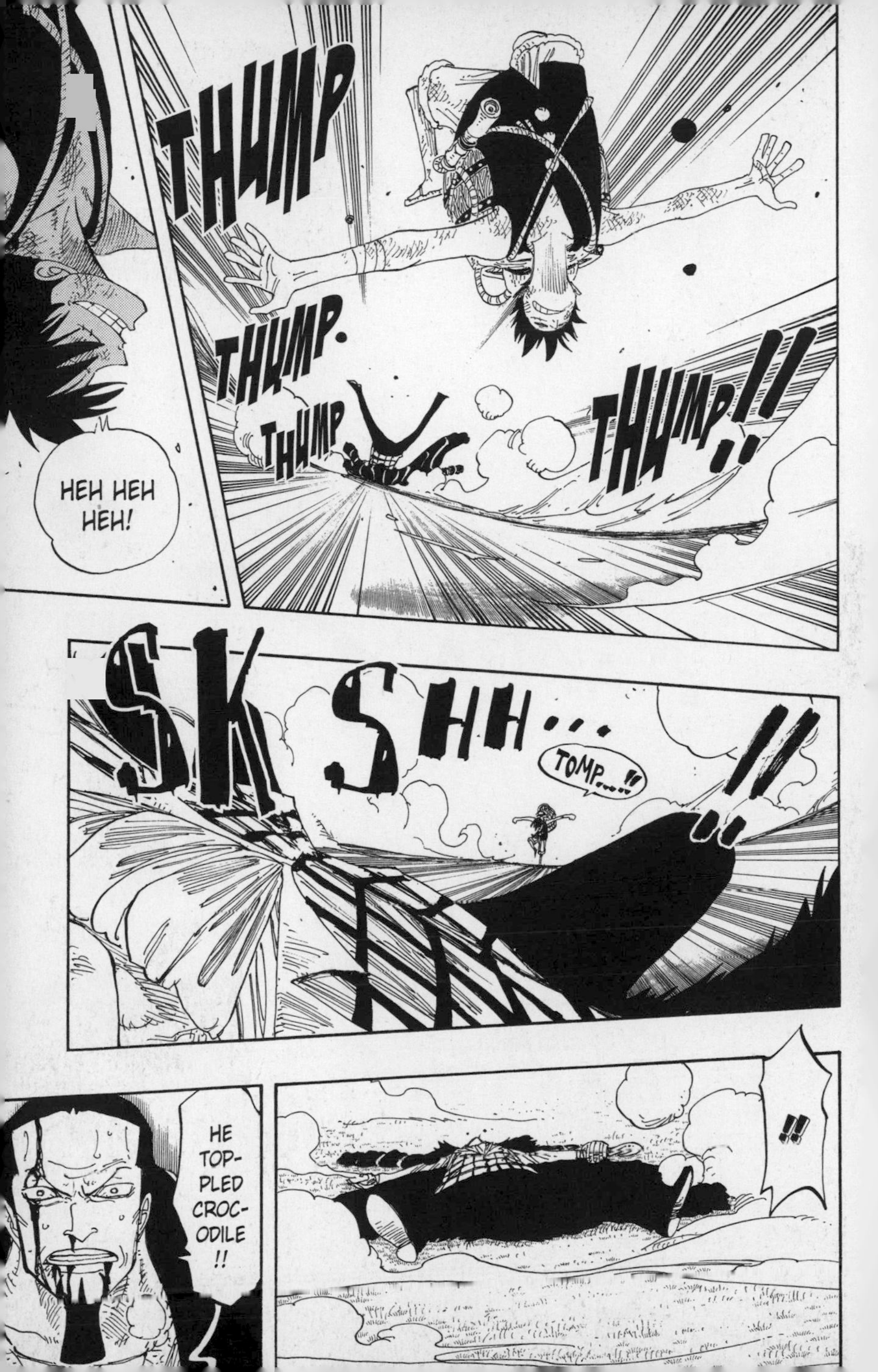
THUMP
THUMP.
THUMP
THUMP!!
HEH HEH HEH!
SKSHH...!!
TOMP...!!
!!
HE TOP-PLED CROC-ODILE!!

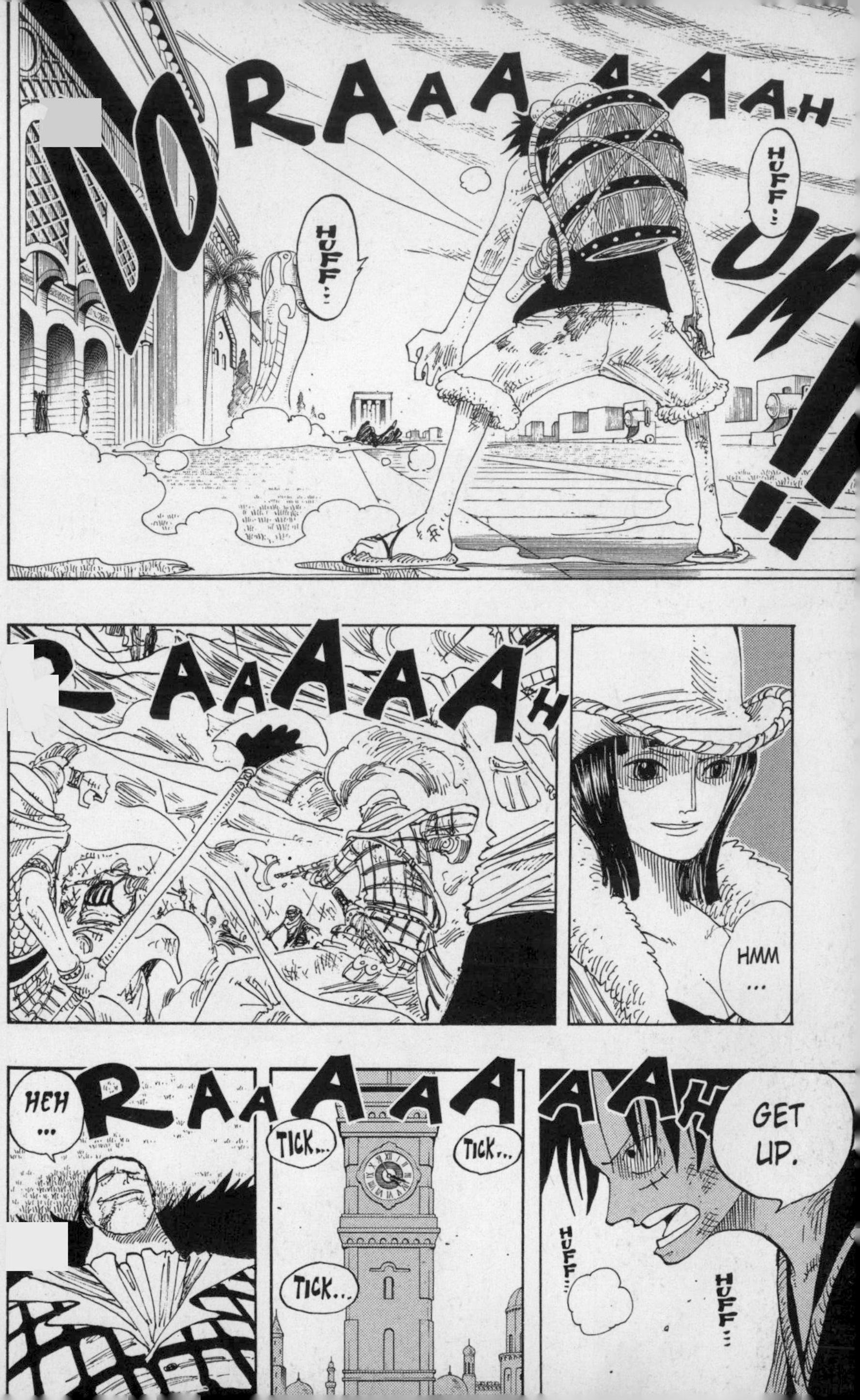
HUFF...
HUFF...
DORAAAAAAAH
HMM...
RAAAAAAH
GET UP.
HUFF...
HUFF...
TICK...
TICK...
TICK...
HEH...
RAAAAAAAAH

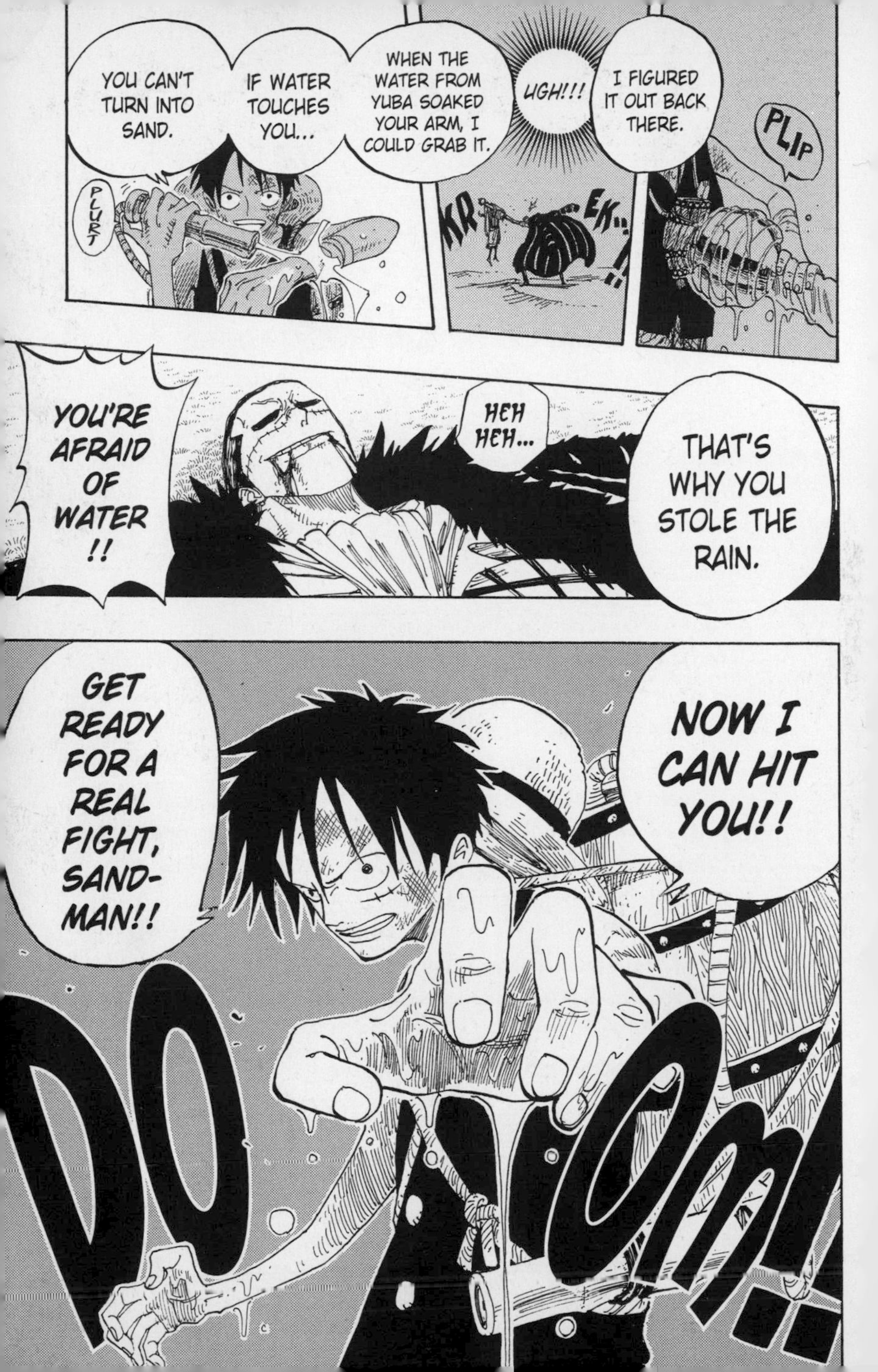

PLIP
I FIGURED IT OUT BACK THERE.
UGH!!!
KREEK..!!
WHEN THE WATER FROM YUBA SOAKED YOUR ARM, I COULD GRAB IT.
IF WATER TOUCHES YOU...
YOU CAN'T TURN INTO SAND.
PLURT
THAT'S WHY YOU STOLE THE RAIN.
HEH HEH...
YOU'RE AFRAID OF WATER!!
NOW I CAN HIT YOU!!
GET READY FOR A REAL FIGHT, SAND-MAN!!
DOOM!!

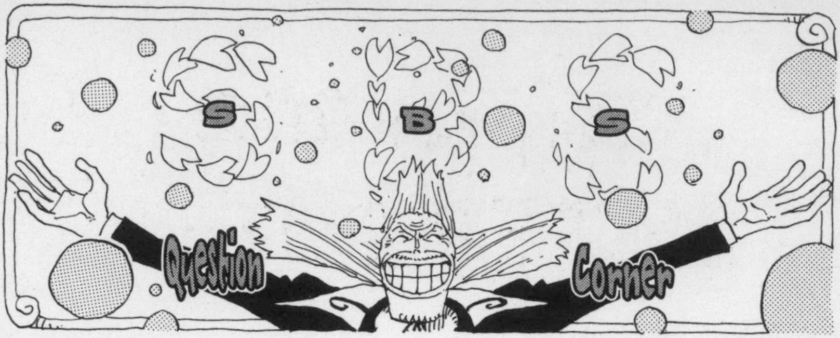
SBS
Question Corner

Reader: The town on the other side of the tunnel was very strange.

Oda: Okay, let's continue.

Reader: Hey, Mr. Bon Clay! Yeah, you! You brag about your dancing too much! Your *port de bras* stinks! Get it right! And your toe shoes aren't even tied properly! The ribbons go around your ankles… Your **ankles!** They should go two centimeters higher. And your Swan Arabesque--ha! You're not raising your leg correctly! You won't be ready to attempt an attitude turn for at least another hundred years.
Start over from the beginning! And shave your legs!
--Studied Ballet for Ten Years

Oda: Hmm… Well, I called him. Here he is.

Mr. 2: **This ain't no joke!! Shave my legs?! Never! If I shaved my legs, I'd be nothing! My leg hair is what makes me unique! Unless you're saying you want to get rid of me! Is that it?! Oh, and you say you studied ballet for ten years? Well, isn't that something?! But I've been studying my Oh Come My Way Karate for 20 years! Got any complaints?! If you do, I'll be happy to give you some free lessons! I'll twirl and twirl and twirl! Yes I will!**

Oda: Okay, enough of that ham-bone.

Reader: Hello, Oda Sensei! My name is Enari. Why does Vivi always pull on Usopp's nose?

Oda: Well… Let's say there's a pot in front of you. What part of it would you grab? You'd grab the handle, right? You'd grab the part that sticks out. I guess that's the reason. It's probably the easiest place to grab. Right? I guess it just works.

# Chapter 200:
# WATER LUFFY

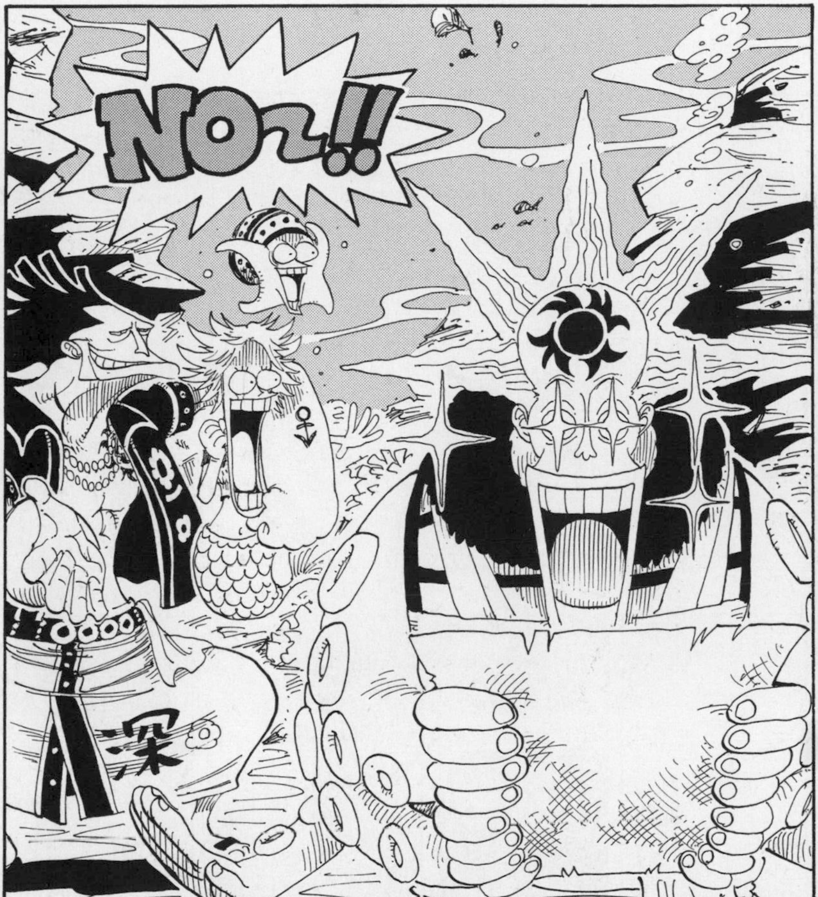
NOz!!
深

HACHI'S WALK ON THE SEAFLOOR, VOL. 16:
"CAMIE'S SURPRISE! A DEAL WITH THE FISH-MEN
FOR THE OCTOPUS FRITTER MAP"

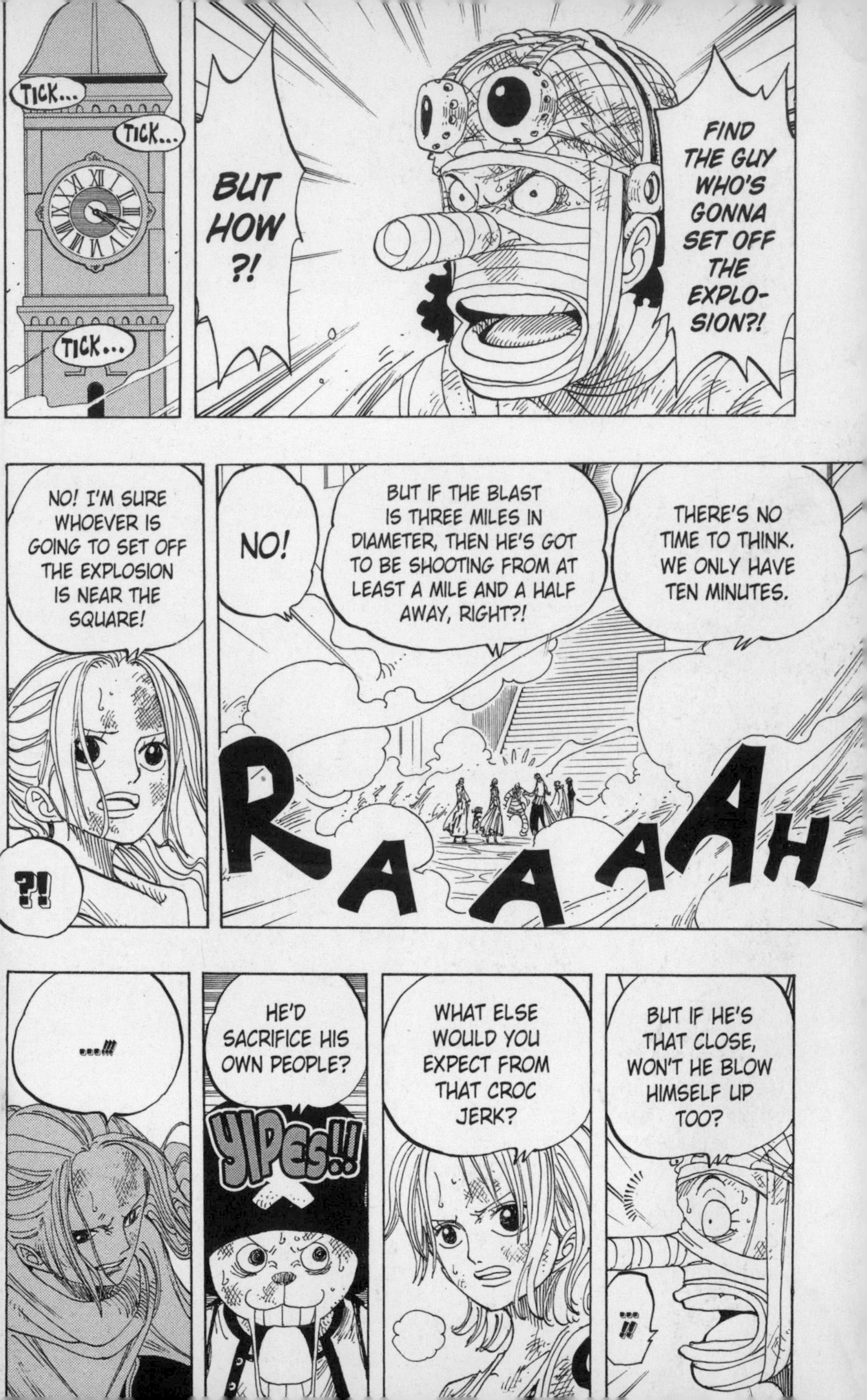
FIND THE GUY WHO'S GONNA SET OFF THE EXPLOSION?!
BUT HOW ?!
TICK...
TICK...
TICK...
THERE'S NO TIME TO THINK. WE ONLY HAVE TEN MINUTES.
BUT IF THE BLAST IS THREE MILES IN DIAMETER, THEN HE'S GOT TO BE SHOOTING FROM AT LEAST A MILE AND A HALF AWAY, RIGHT?!
NO!
RAAAAAH
NO! I'M SURE WHOEVER IS GOING TO SET OFF THE EXPLOSION IS NEAR THE SQUARE!
?!
BUT IF HE'S THAT CLOSE, WON'T HE BLOW HIMSELF UP TOO?
...!!
WHAT ELSE WOULD YOU EXPECT FROM THAT CROC JERK?
HE'D SACRIFICE HIS OWN PEOPLE?
YIPES!!!
...!!!

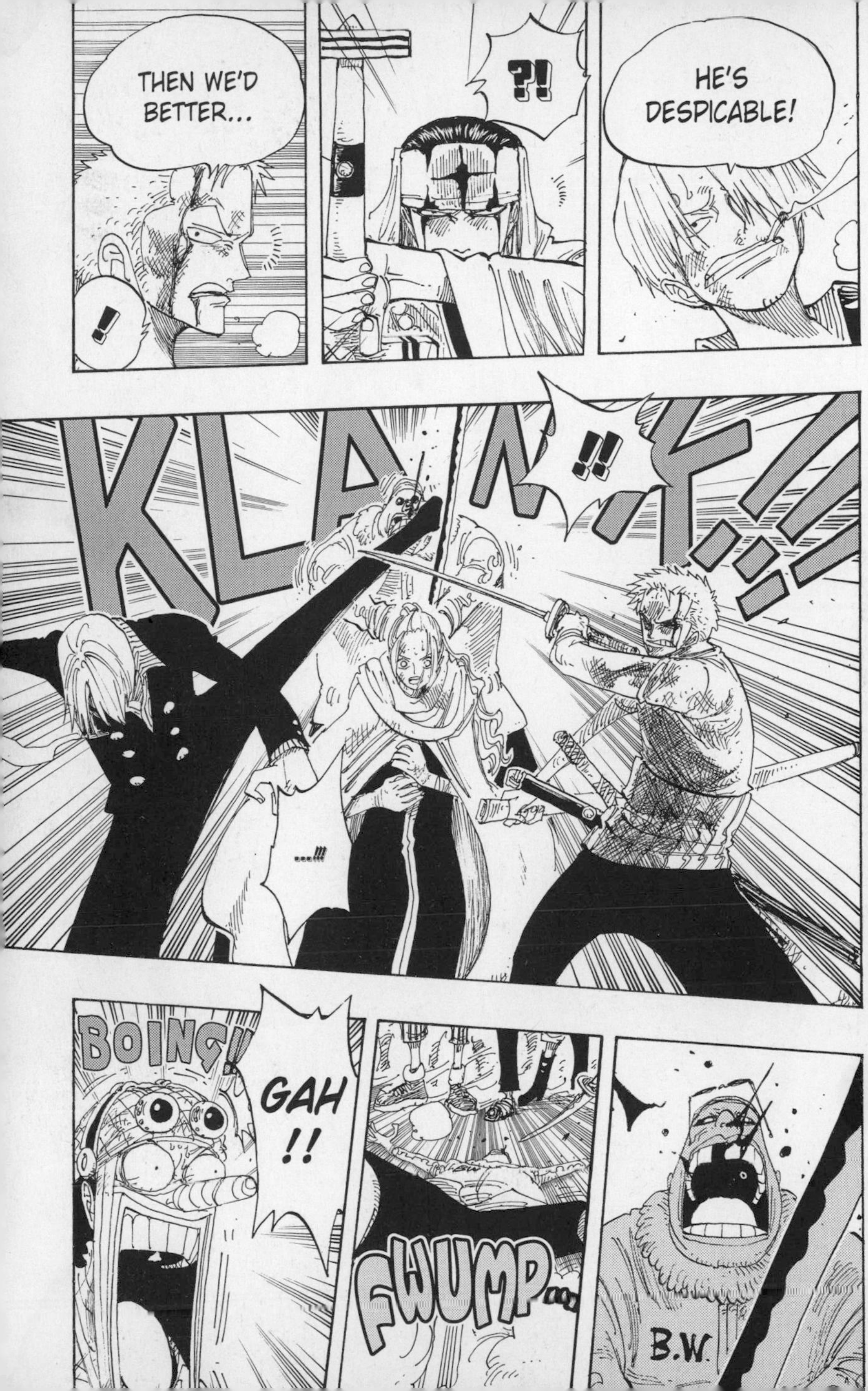
HE'S DESPICABLE!
?!
THEN WE'D BETTER...
!
KLANK!!
!!
...!!!
B.W.
FWUMP...
GAH !!
BOING!!

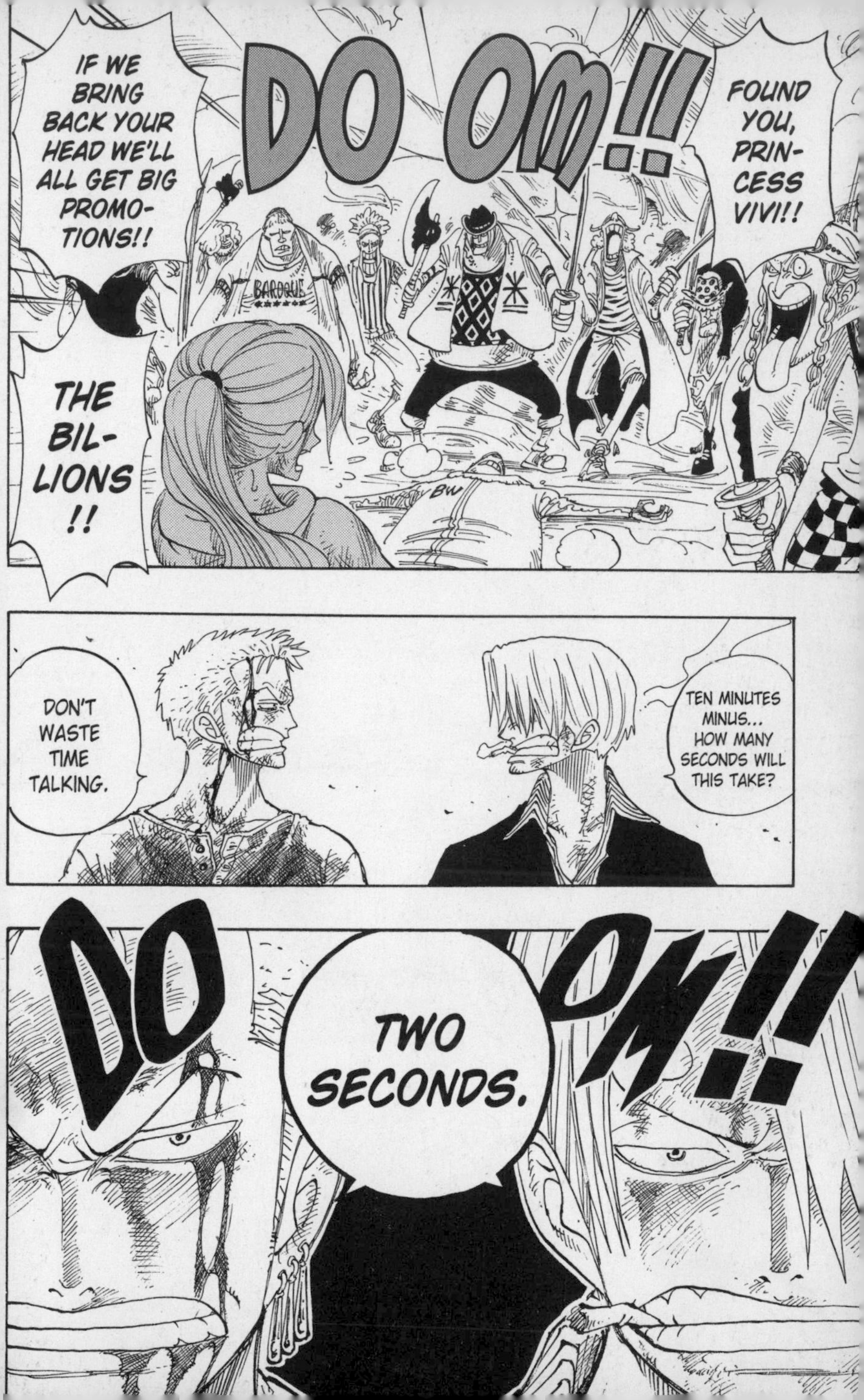
FOUND YOU, PRINCESS VIVI!!
DO OM!!
IF WE BRING BACK YOUR HEAD WE'LL ALL GET BIG PROMOTIONS!!
THE BILLIONS!!
BAROQUE
BW
TEN MINUTES MINUS... HOW MANY SECONDS WILL THIS TAKE?
DON'T WASTE TIME TALKING.
DO OM!!
TWO SECONDS.

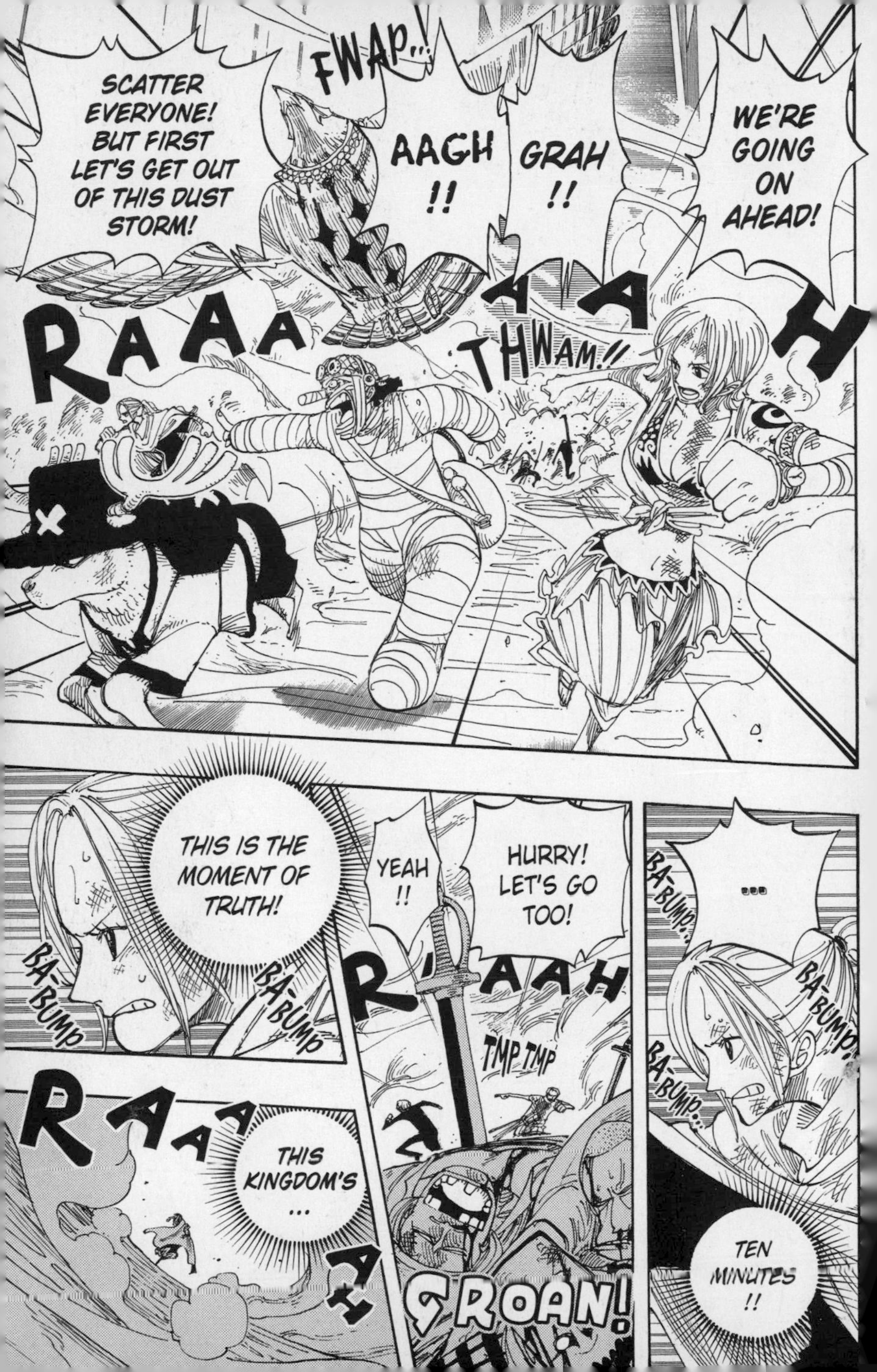
WE'RE GOING ON AHEAD!
GRAH !!
AAGH !!
FWAP..!
SCATTER EVERYONE! BUT FIRST LET'S GET OUT OF THIS DUST STORM!
RAAAAAAH
THWAM!!
...
BA-BUMP...
BA-BUMP...
BA-BUMP...
TEN MINUTES !!
HURRY! LET'S GO TOO!
YEAH !!
RAAAH
TMP TMP
GROAN!
THIS IS THE MOMENT OF TRUTH!
BA-BUMP
BA-BUMP
THIS KINGDOM'S ...
RAAAAH

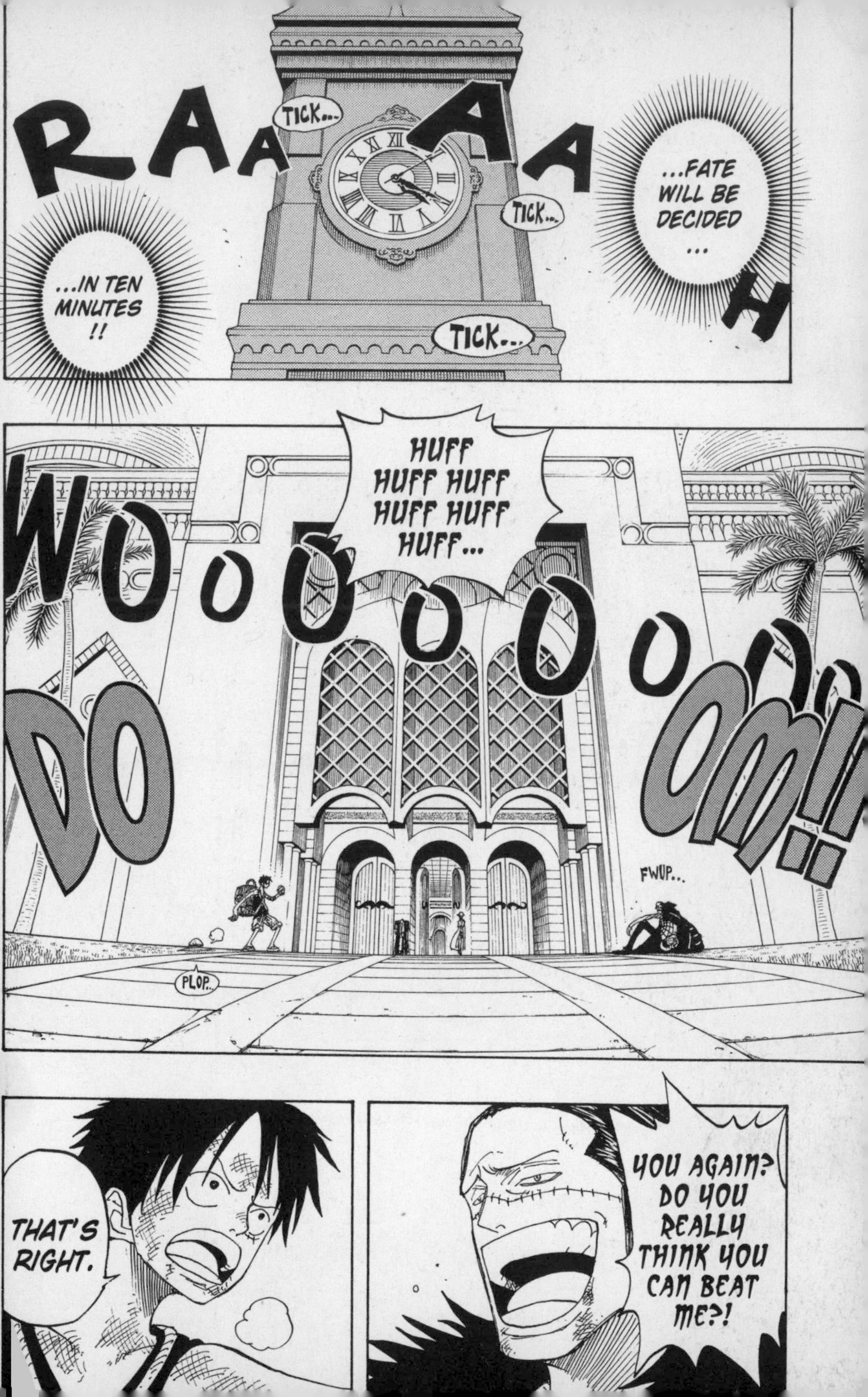
RAAAAH
TICK...
...FATE WILL BE DECIDED ...
TICK...
...IN TEN MINUTES !!
TICK...
HUFF HUFF HUFF HUFF HUFF HUFF...
WOOOOOOOO
DOOM!!
FWUP...
PLOP...
YOU AGAIN? DO YOU REALLY THINK YOU CAN BEAT ME?!
THAT'S RIGHT.

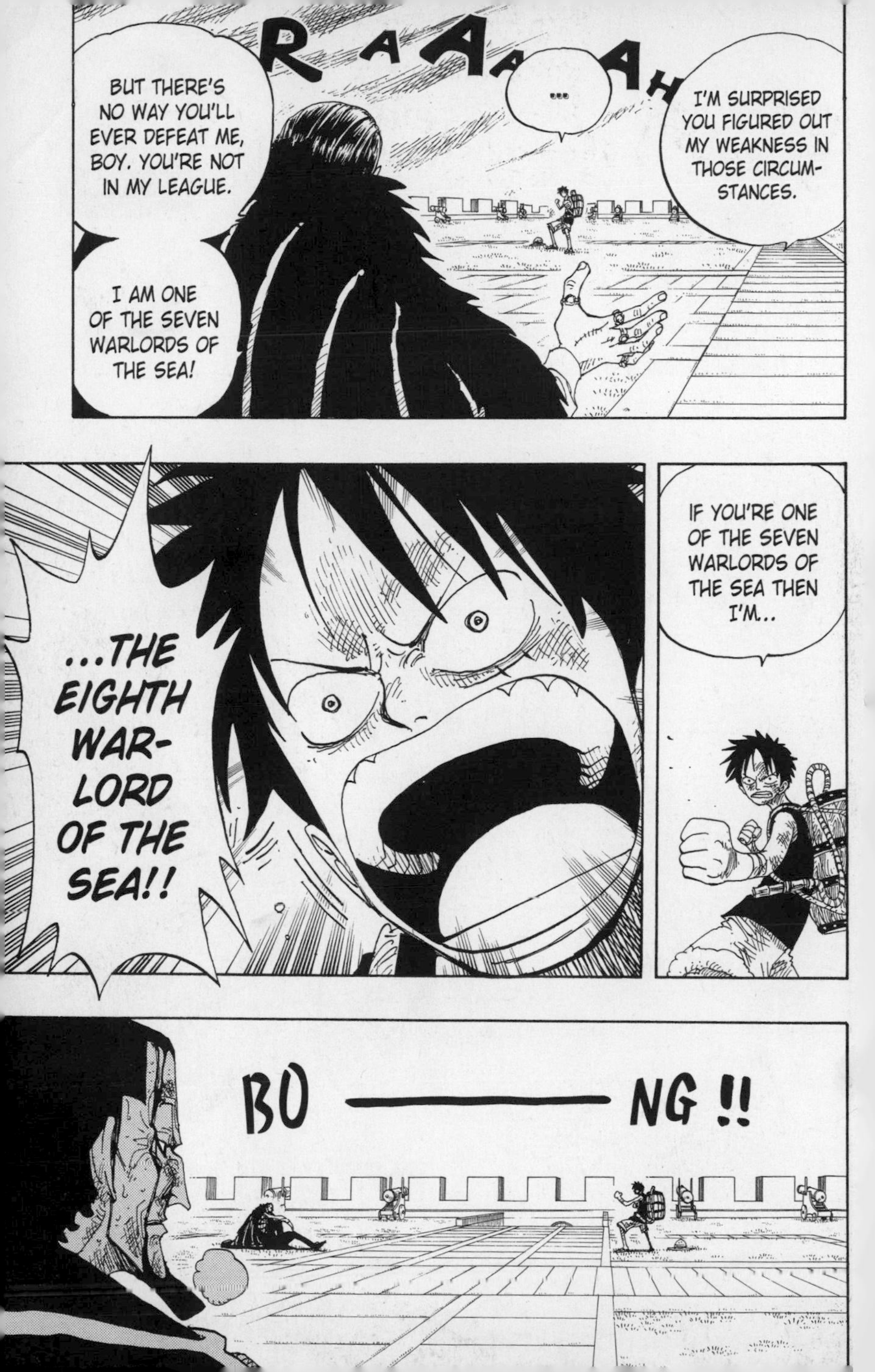

RAAAAH
I'M SURPRISED YOU FIGURED OUT MY WEAKNESS IN THOSE CIRCUM-STANCES.
...
BUT THERE'S NO WAY YOU'LL EVER DEFEAT ME, BOY. YOU'RE NOT IN MY LEAGUE.
I AM ONE OF THE SEVEN WARLORDS OF THE SEA!
IF YOU'RE ONE OF THE SEVEN WARLORDS OF THE SEA THEN I'M..
...THE EIGHTH WAR-LORD OF THE SEA!!
BO——NG!!

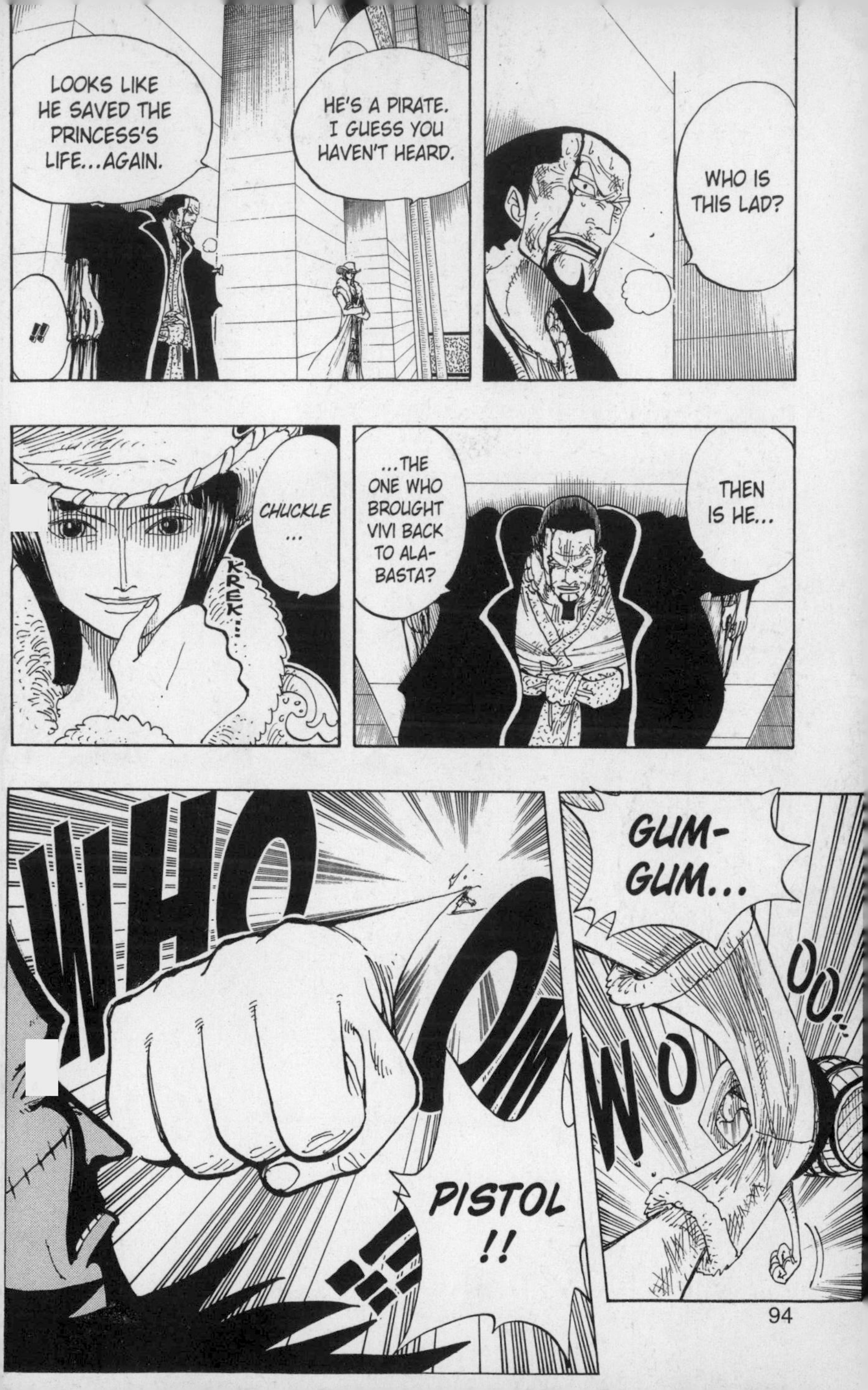
WHO IS THIS LAD?
HE'S A PIRATE. I GUESS YOU HAVEN'T HEARD.
LOOKS LIKE HE SAVED THE PRINCESS'S LIFE...AGAIN.
!!
THEN IS HE...
...THE ONE WHO BROUGHT VIVI BACK TO ALA-BASTA?
CHUCKLE...
KREK!!
GUM-GUM...
WOOO..
WHOOM
PISTOL!!

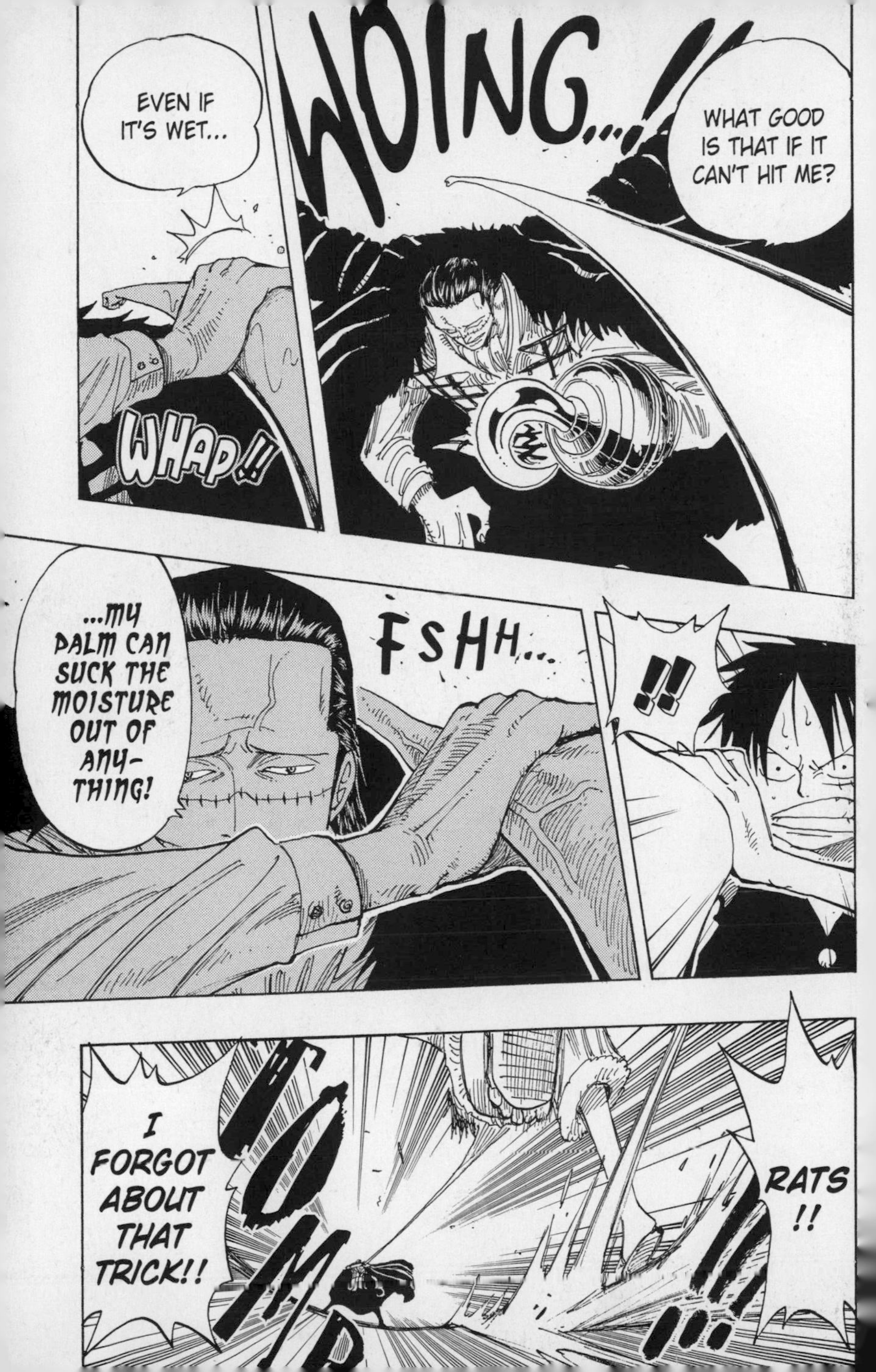
WHOING...!!
WHAT GOOD IS THAT IF IT CAN'T HIT ME?
EVEN IF IT'S WET...
WHAP!!
!!
...MY PALM CAN SUCK THE MOISTURE OUT OF ANY-THING!
FSHH...
RATS!!
I FORGOT ABOUT THAT TRICK!!

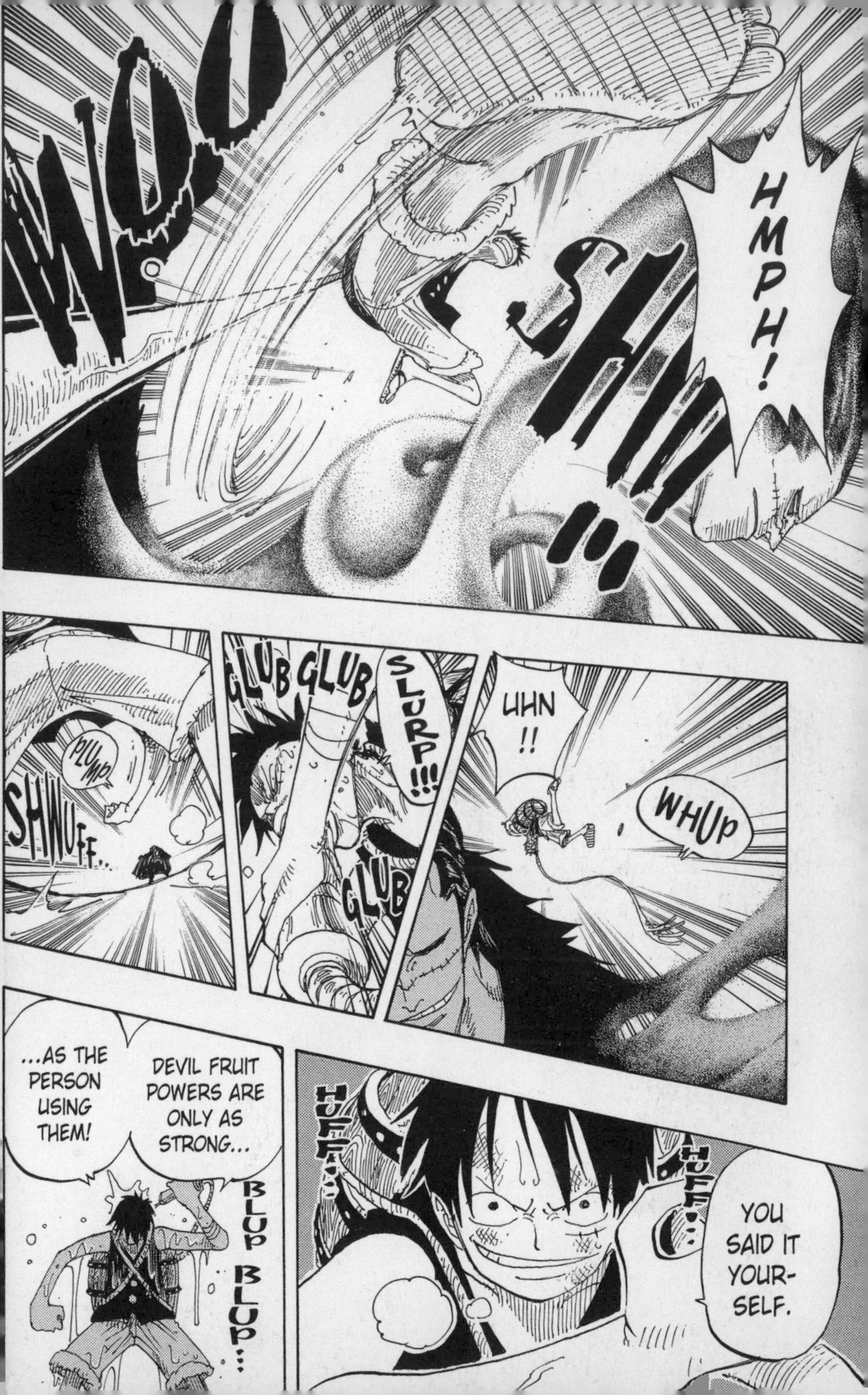
HMPH!
UHN !!
WHUP
GLUB GLUB
SLURP!!!
GLUB
PLUMP
SHWUFF...
HUFF...
HUFF...
YOU SAID IT YOURSELF.
DEVIL FRUIT POWERS ARE ONLY AS STRONG...
...AS THE PERSON USING THEM!
BLUP BLUP...

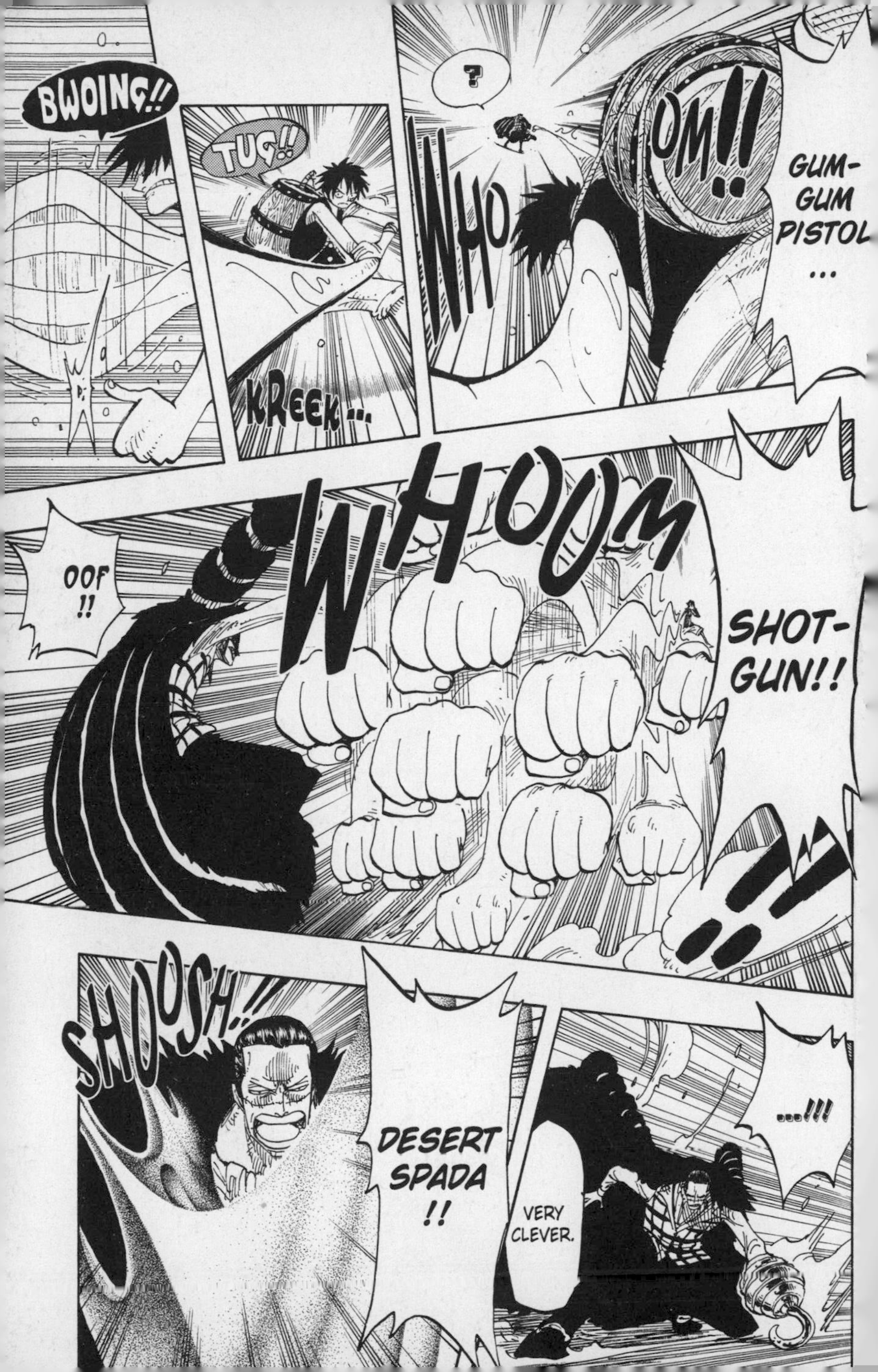

GUM-GUM PISTOL ...
WHOOM!!
?
TUG!!
KREEK...
BWOING!!
SHOT-GUN!!
WHOOM
OOF !!
...!!!
VERY CLEVER.
DESERT SPADA !!
SHOOSH!!

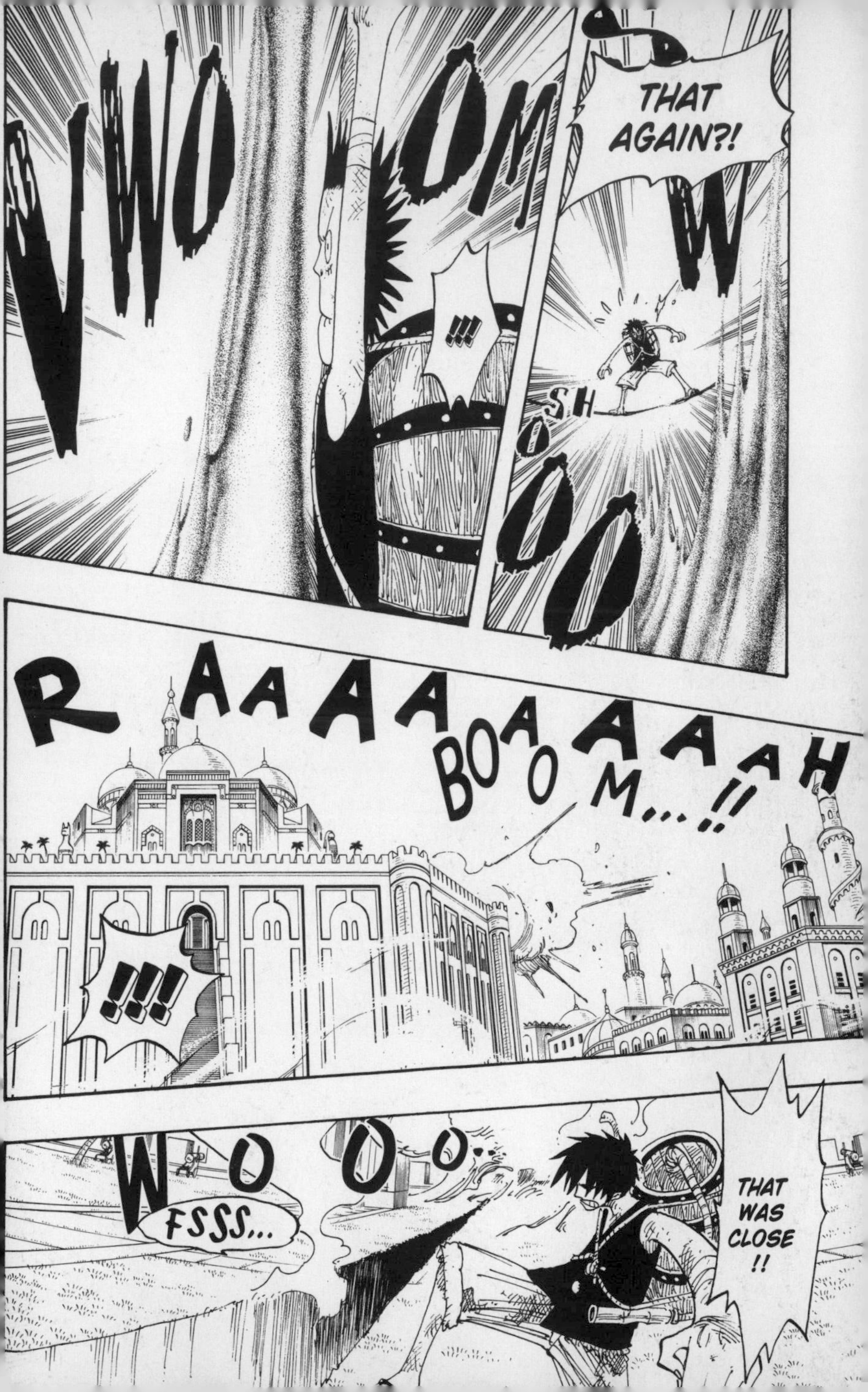
THAT AGAIN?!
W
SH
O
OOO
VWOOM
!!!
RAAAAAAAH
BOOOM...!!
!!!
THAT WAS CLOSE !!
WOOO
FSSS...

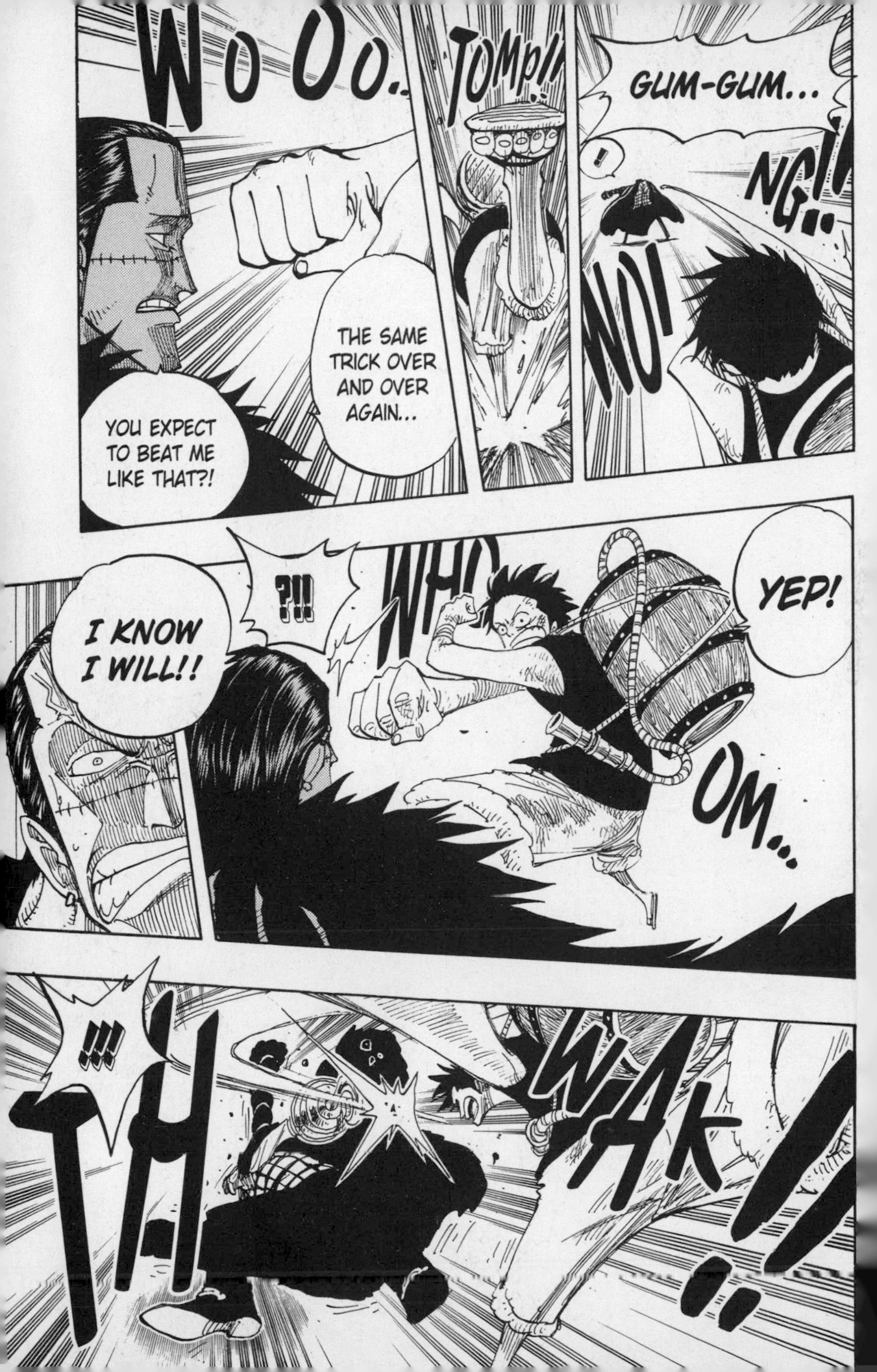
GUM-GUM...
!
NG!!
WOI
TOMP!!
WO OO..
THE SAME TRICK OVER AND OVER AGAIN...
YOU EXPECT TO BEAT ME LIKE THAT?!
YEP!
OM...
WHO
?!!
I KNOW I WILL!!
WAK!!
!!!
TH

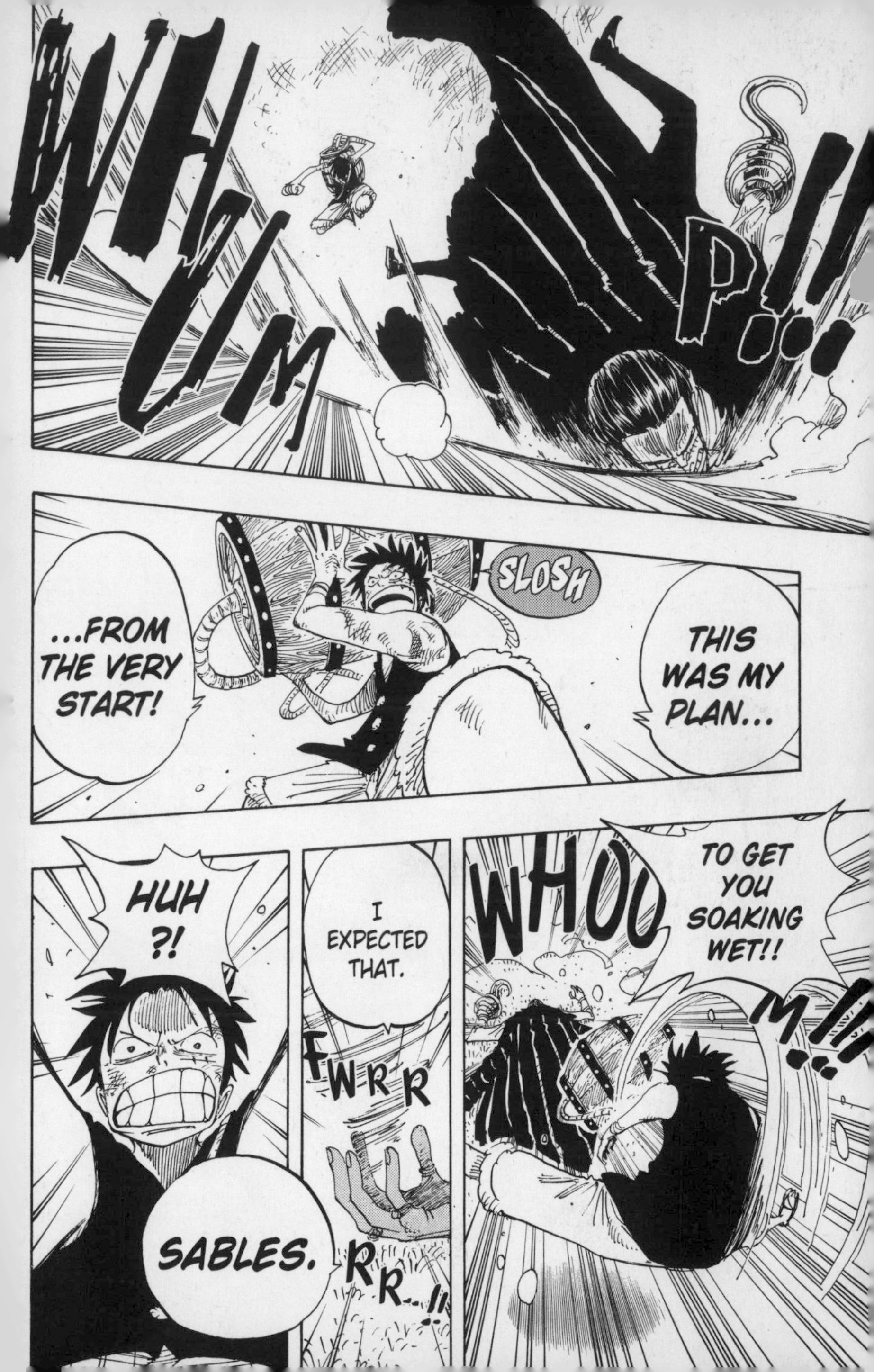
WHUMP!!
THIS WAS MY PLAN...
SLOSH
...FROM THE VERY START!
TO GET YOU SOAKING WET!!
WHOOMM!!!
I EXPECTED THAT.
FWRRRRR..!!
HUH?!
SABLES.

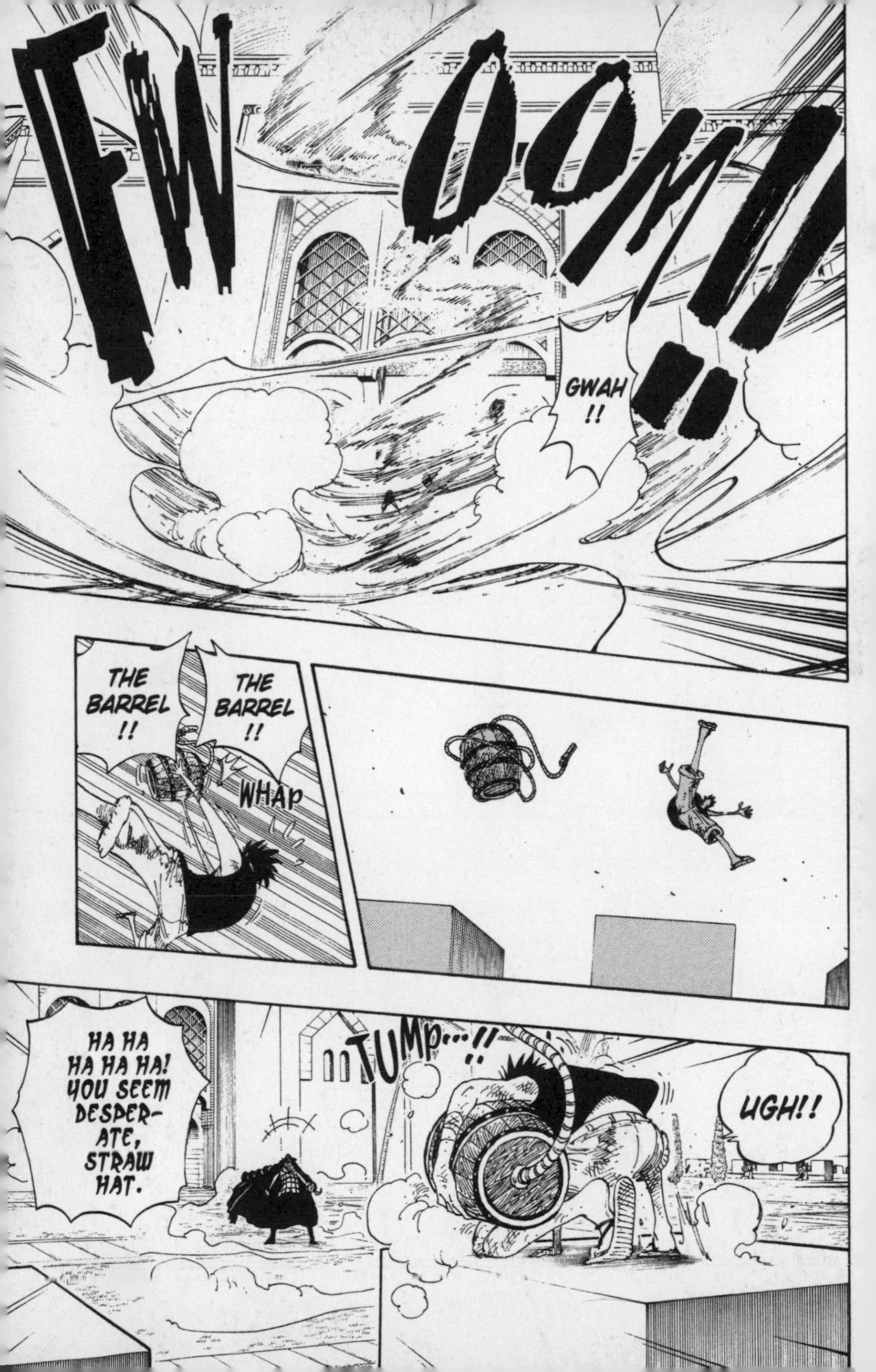
FWOOM!!
GWAH!!
THE BARREL!!
THE BARREL!!
WHAP
UGH!!
TUMP...!!
HA HA HA HA HA! YOU SEEM DESPERATE, STRAW HAT.

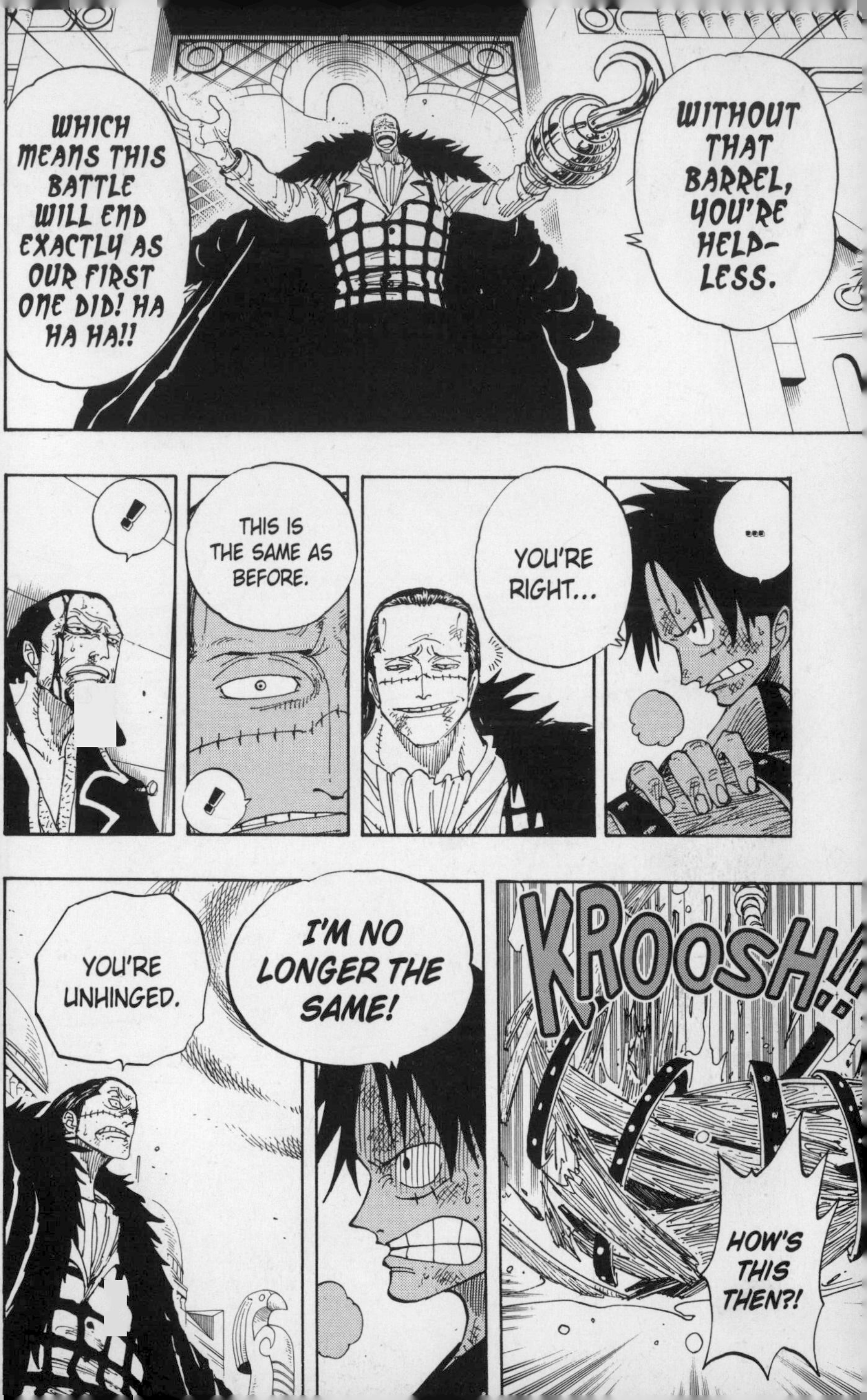
WITHOUT THAT BARREL, YOU'RE HELP-LESS.
WHICH MEANS THIS BATTLE WILL END EXACTLY AS OUR FIRST ONE DID! HA HA HA!!
...
YOU'RE RIGHT...
THIS IS THE SAME AS BEFORE.
!
!
KROOSH!!
HOW'S THIS THEN?!
I'M NO LONGER THE SAME!
YOU'RE UNHINGED.

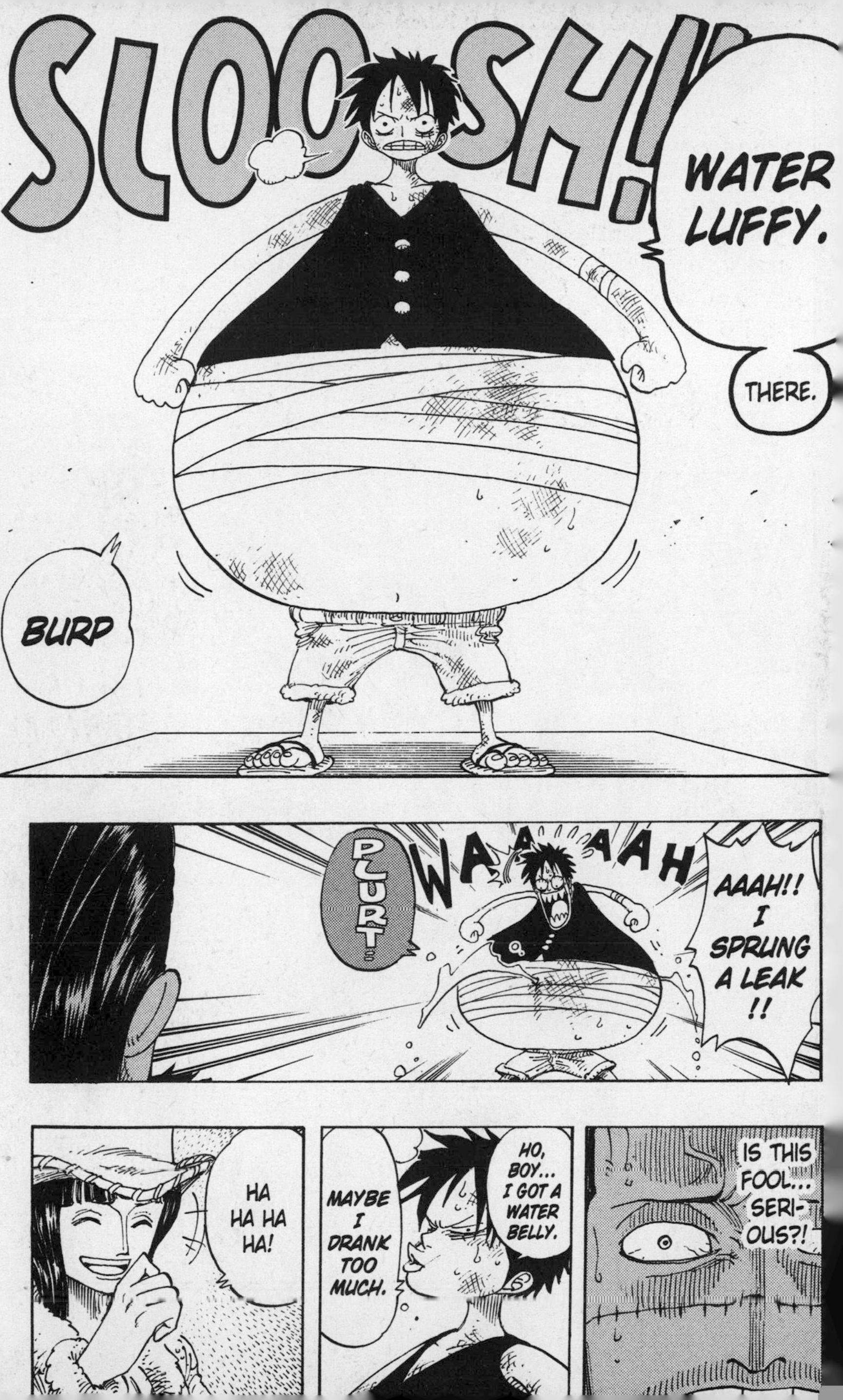
WATER LUFFY.
THERE.
SLOOSH!
BURP
AAAH!! I SPRUNG A LEAK!!
WAAAAAH
PLURT!
IS THIS FOOL... SERI-OUS?!
HO, BOY... I GOT A WATER BELLY.
MAYBE I DRANK TOO MUCH.
HA HA HA HA!

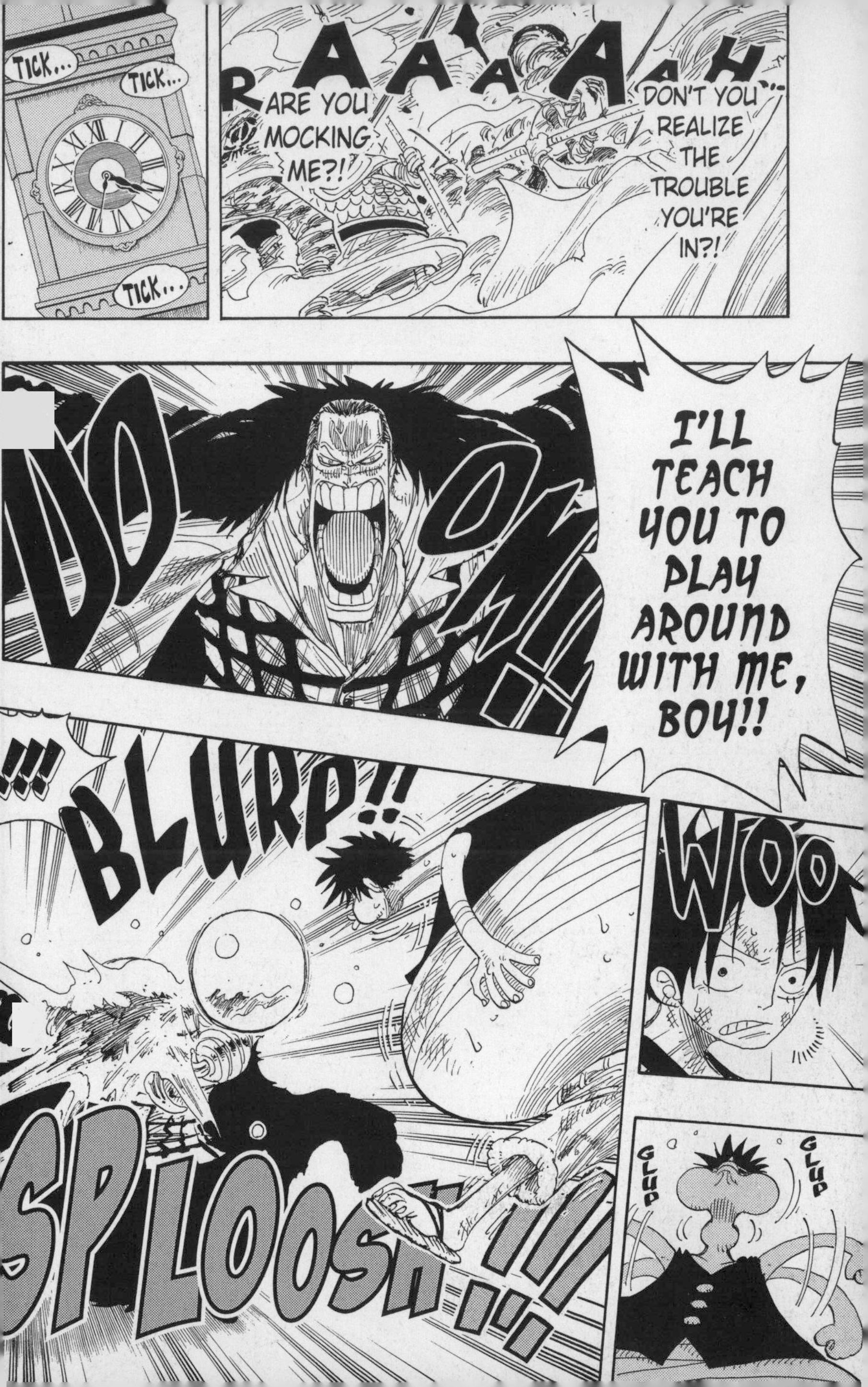
RAAAAAAH...
DON'T YOU REALIZE THE TROUBLE YOU'RE IN?!
ARE YOU MOCKING ME?!
TICK...
TICK...
TICK...
I'LL TEACH YOU TO PLAY AROUND WITH ME, BOY!!
DOOM!!
WOO
GLUP
GLUP
!!!
BLURP!!
SPLOOSH...!!!

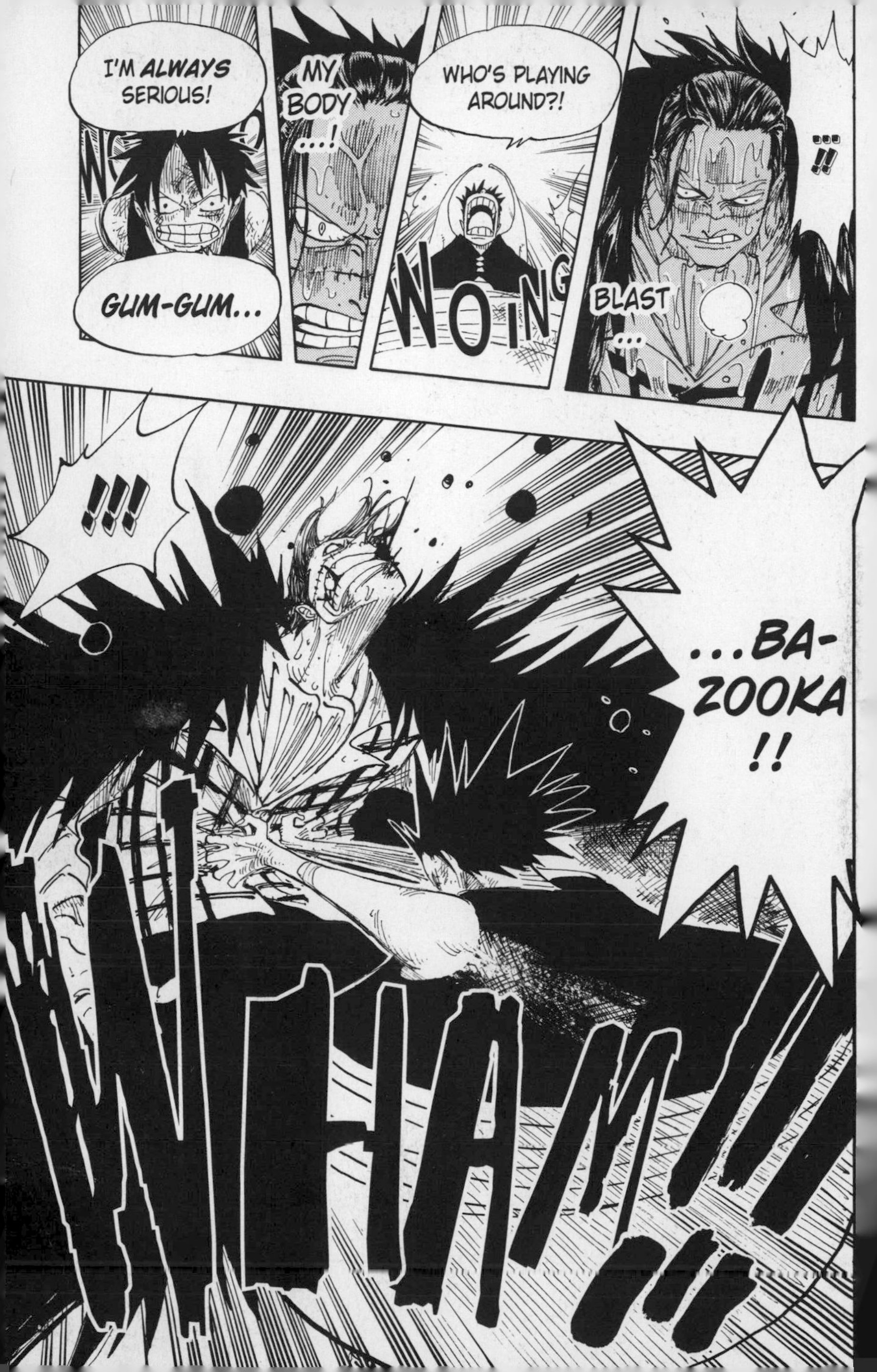
...!!
BLAST...
WHO'S PLAYING AROUND?!
WOING
MY BODY ...!
I'M ALWAYS SERIOUS!
GUM-GUM...
...BA-ZOOKA!!
!!!
WHAM!!

# Chapter 201: NICO ROBIN

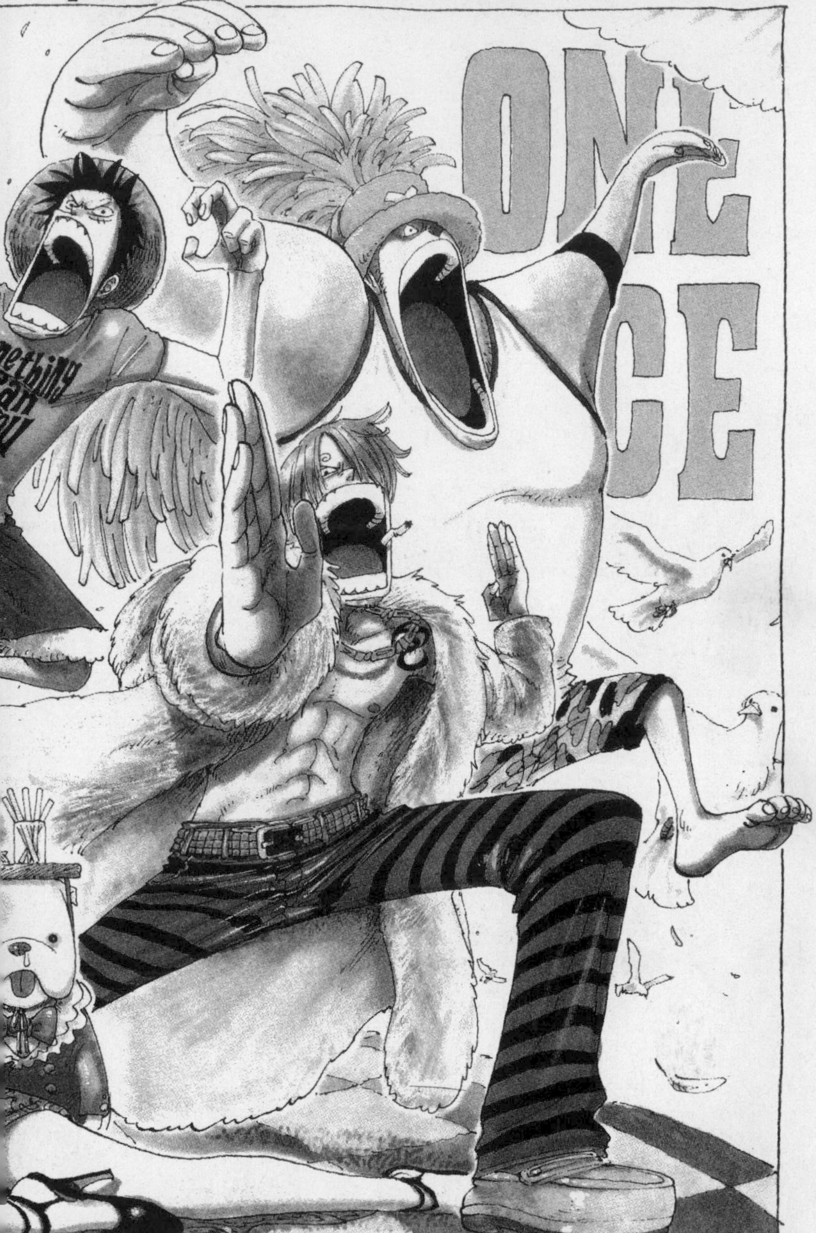

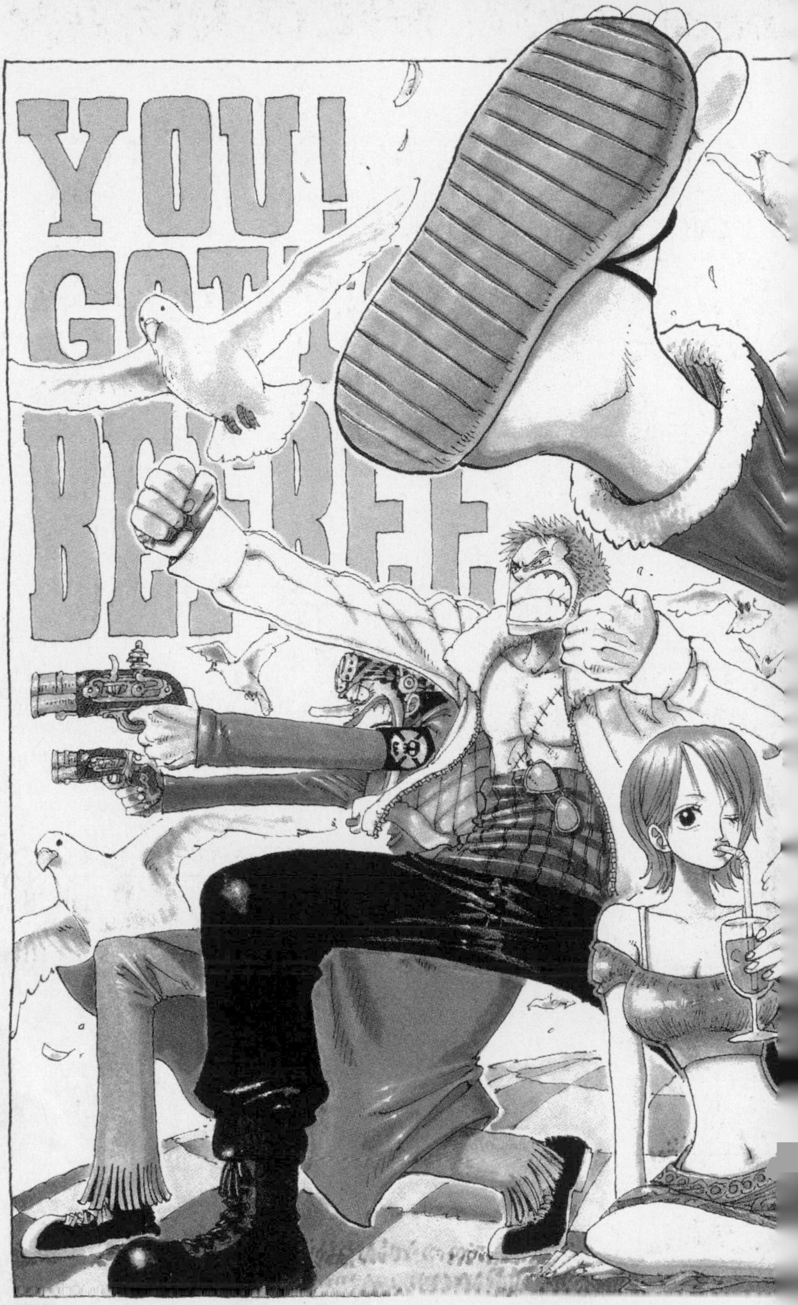
YOU!

READ THIS WAY

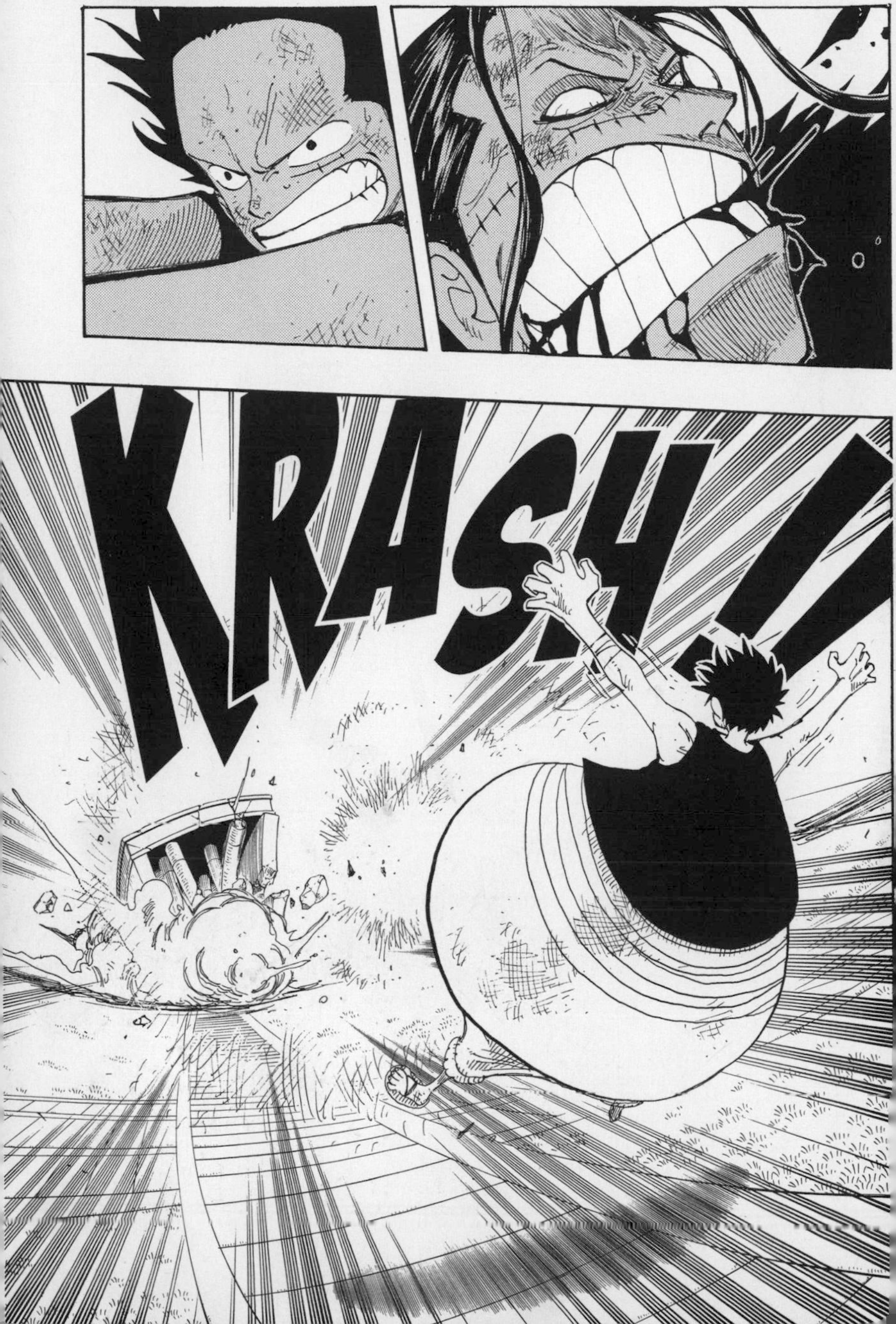
KRASH!!

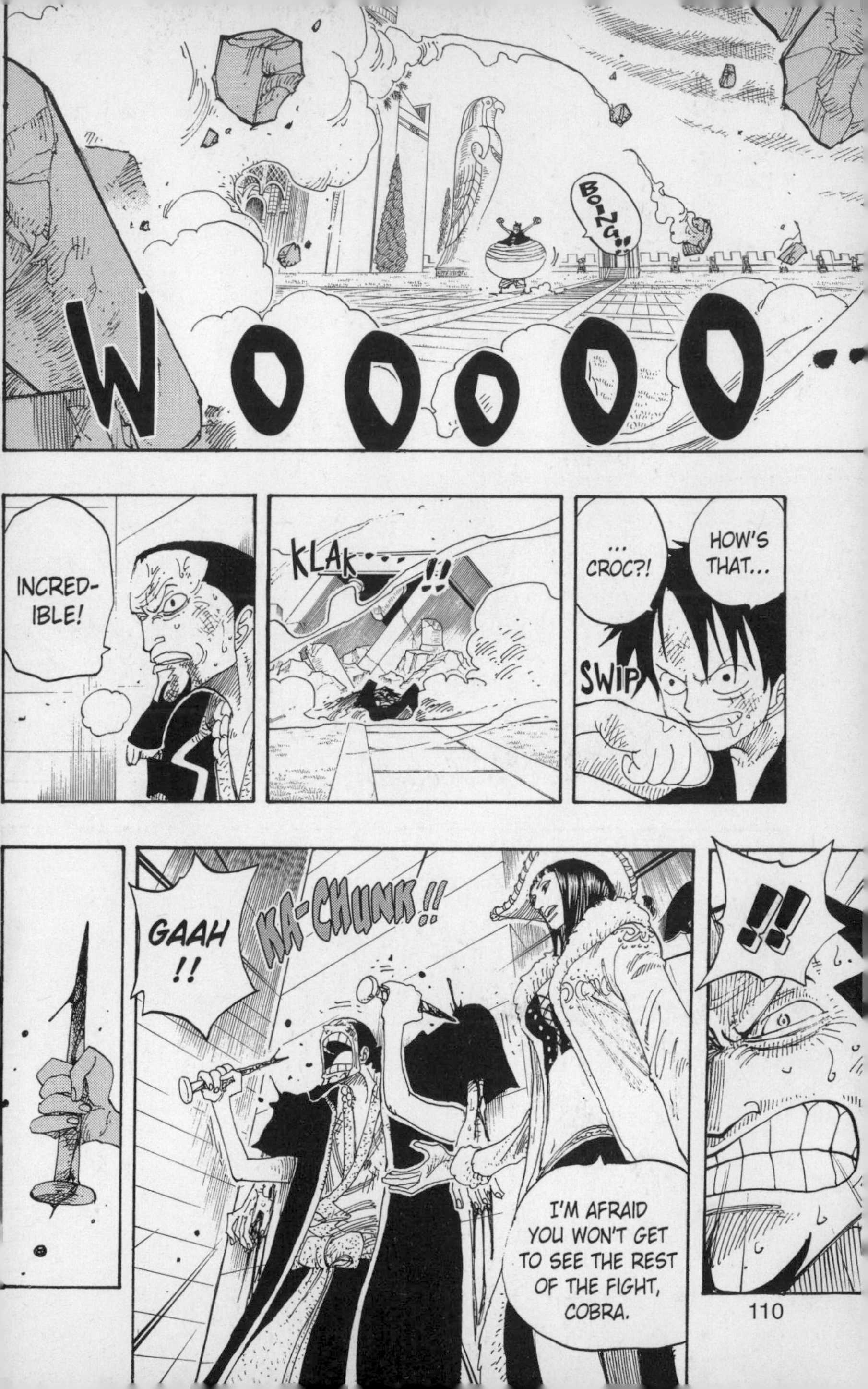
BOING!!
WOOOOO...
HOW'S THAT...
...CROC?!
SWIP
KLAK...!!
INCRED-IBLE!
!!
KA-CHUNK!!
GAAH!!
I'M AFRAID YOU WON'T GET TO SEE THE REST OF THE FIGHT, COBRA.

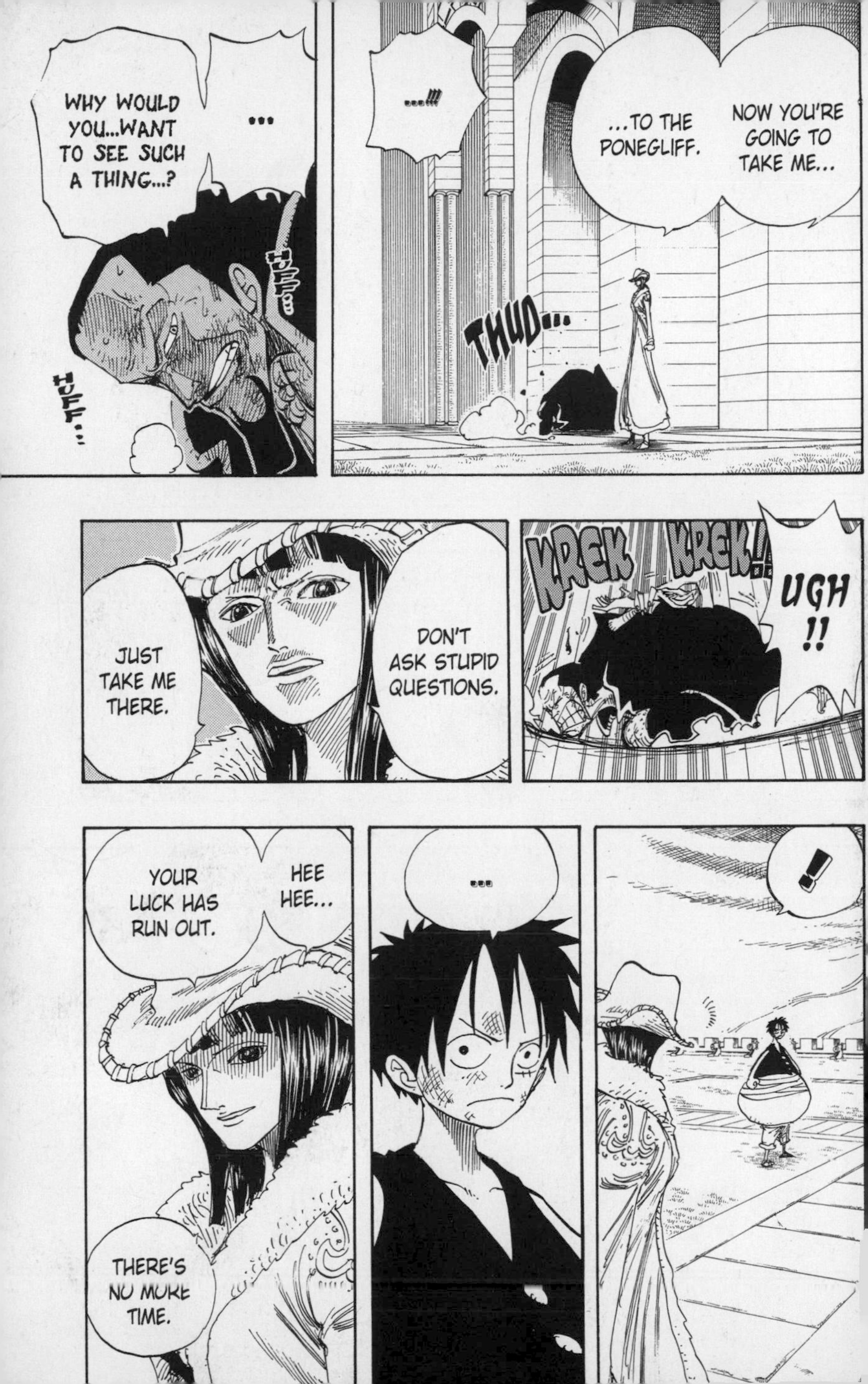
NOW YOU'RE GOING TO TAKE ME...
...TO THE PONEGLIFF.
...!!!
THUD...
...
WHY WOULD YOU...WANT TO SEE SUCH A THING...?
HUFF...
HUFF...
KREK KREK!!
UGH !!
DON'T ASK STUPID QUESTIONS.
JUST TAKE ME THERE.
!
...
HEE HEE...
YOUR LUCK HAS RUN OUT.
THERE'S NO MORE TIME.

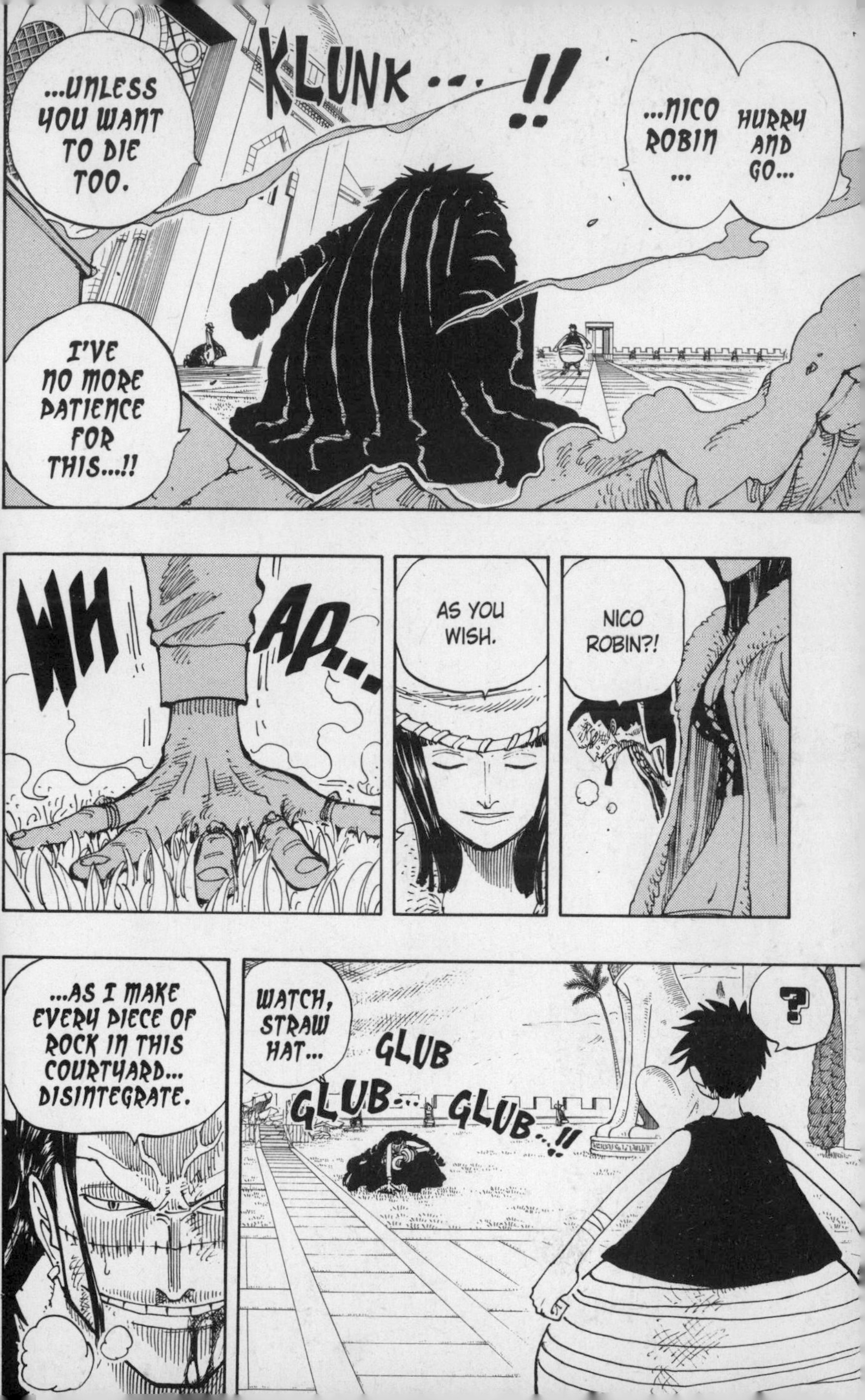
HURRY AND GO...
...NICO ROBIN ...
KLUNK...!!
...UNLESS YOU WANT TO DIE TOO.
I'VE NO MORE PATIENCE FOR THIS...!!
NICO ROBIN?!
AS YOU WISH.
WHAP...
?
WATCH, STRAW HAT...
GLUB GLUB... GLUB...!!
...AS I MAKE EVERY PIECE OF ROCK IN THIS COURTYARD... DISINTEGRATE.

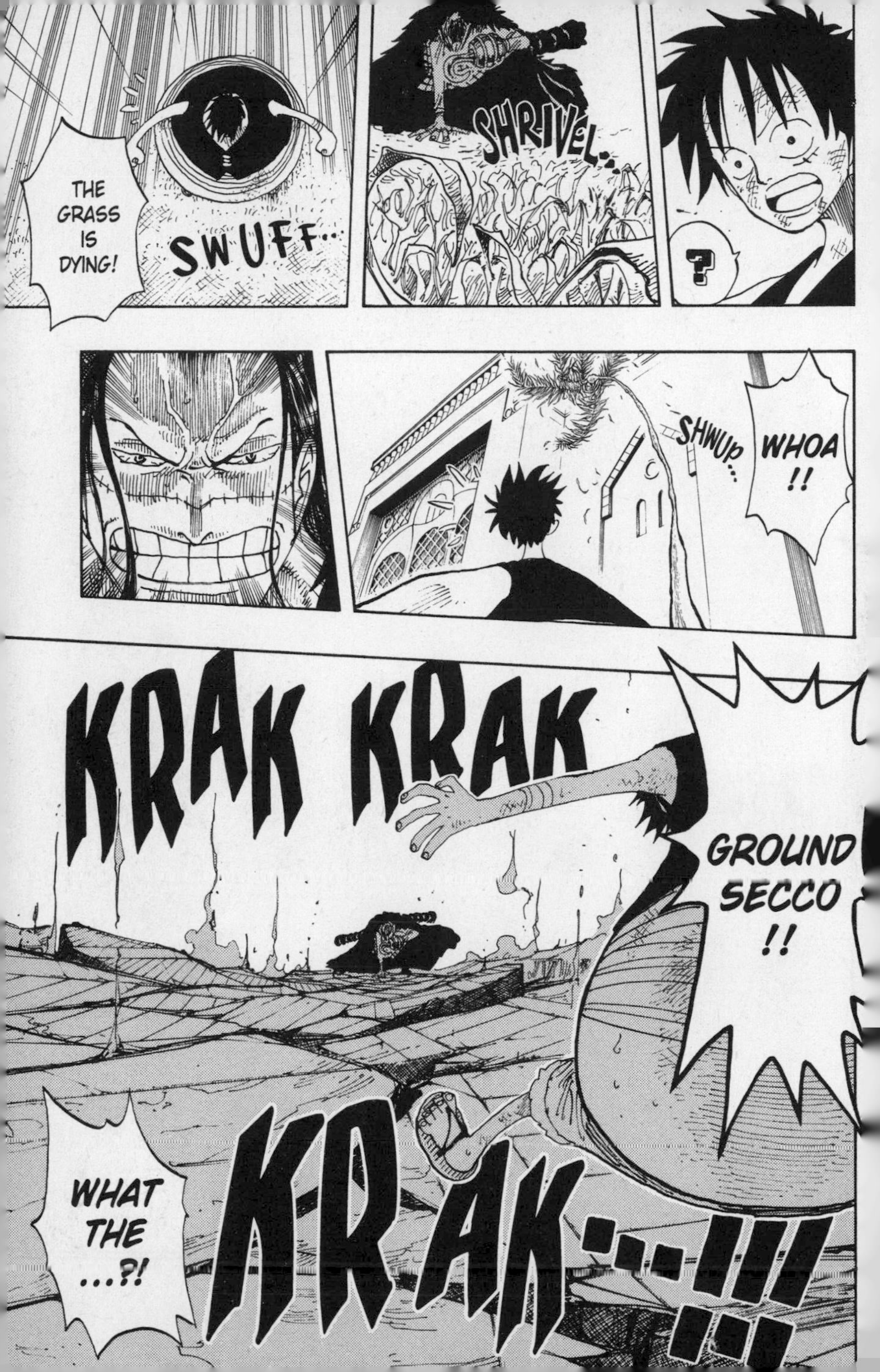
?
SHRIVEL...
SWUFF...
THE GRASS IS DYING!
WHOA!!
SHWUP...
GROUND SECCO!!
KRAK KRAK
KRAK...!!!
WHAT THE ...?!

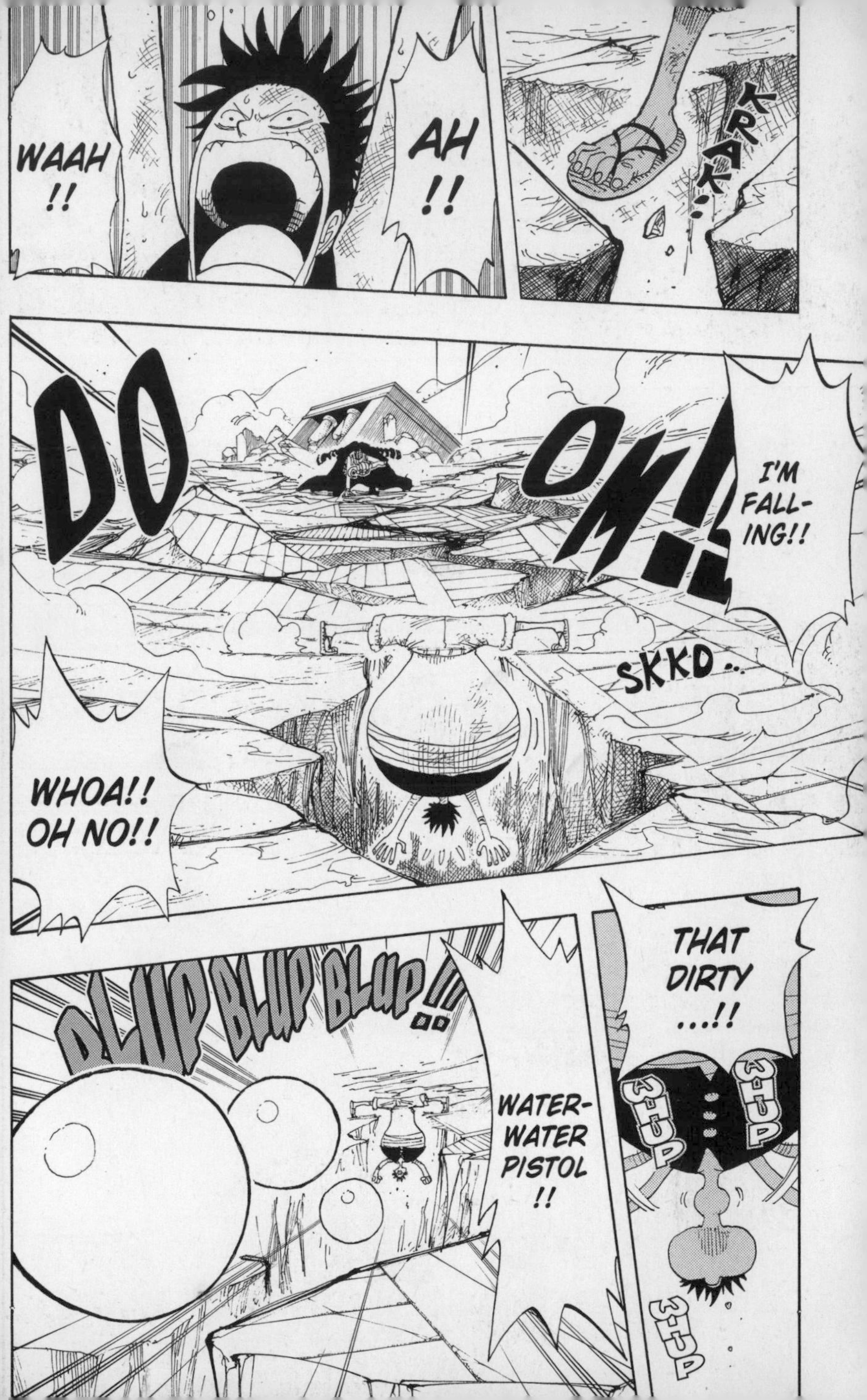
KRAK!
AH!!
WAAH!!
I'M FALLING!!
DOON!!
SKKD..
WHOA!! OH NO!!
THAT DIRTY ...!!
WHUP
WHUP
WHUP
BLUP BLUP BLUP!!!
WATER-WATER PISTOL!!

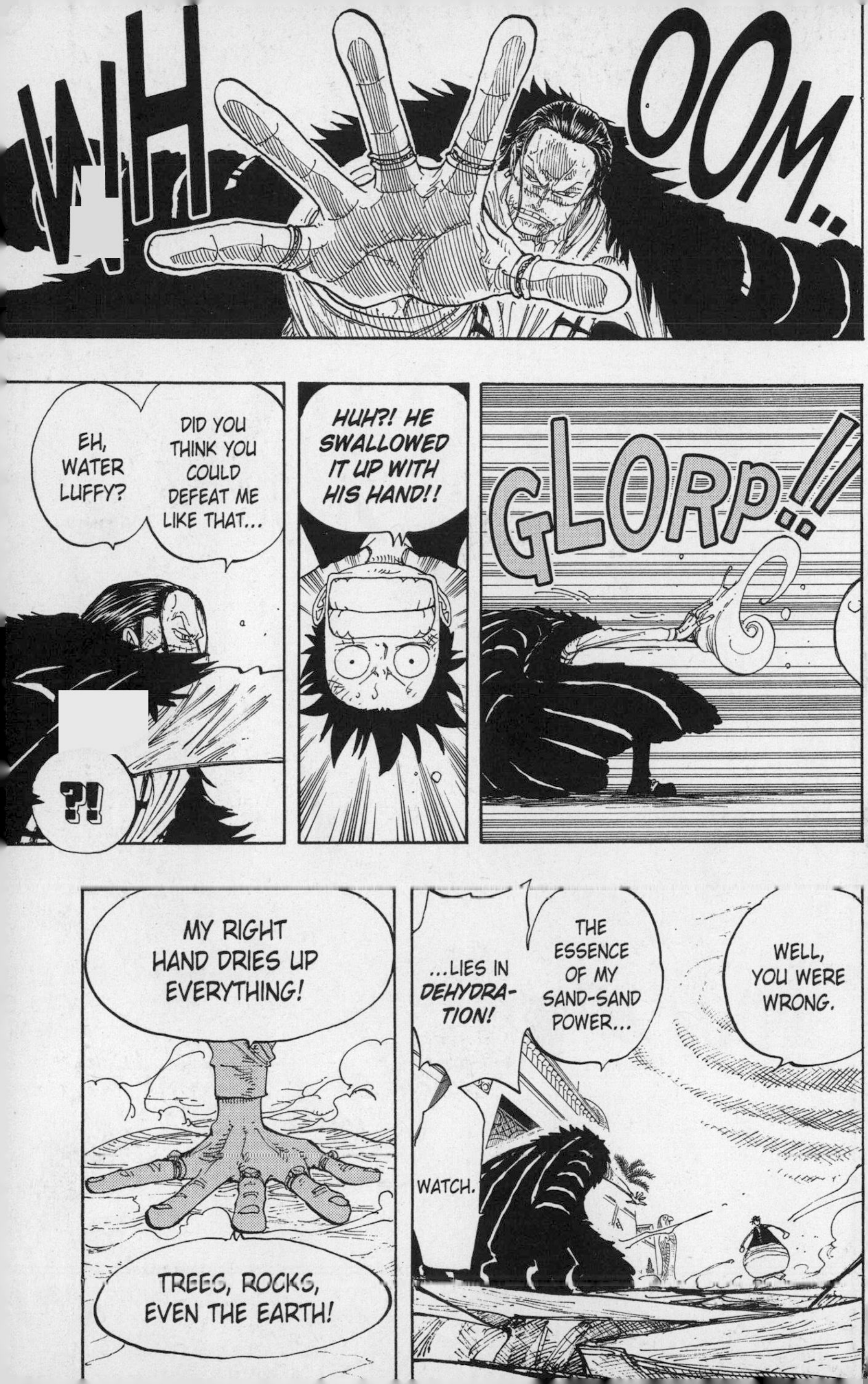

WHOOM..
GLORP!!
HUH?! HE SWALLOWED IT UP WITH HIS HAND!!
DID YOU THINK YOU COULD DEFEAT ME LIKE THAT...
EH, WATER LUFFY?
?!
WELL, YOU WERE WRONG.
THE ESSENCE OF MY SAND-SAND POWER...
...LIES IN DEHYDRATION!
WATCH.
MY RIGHT HAND DRIES UP EVERYTHING!
TREES, ROCKS, EVEN THE EARTH!

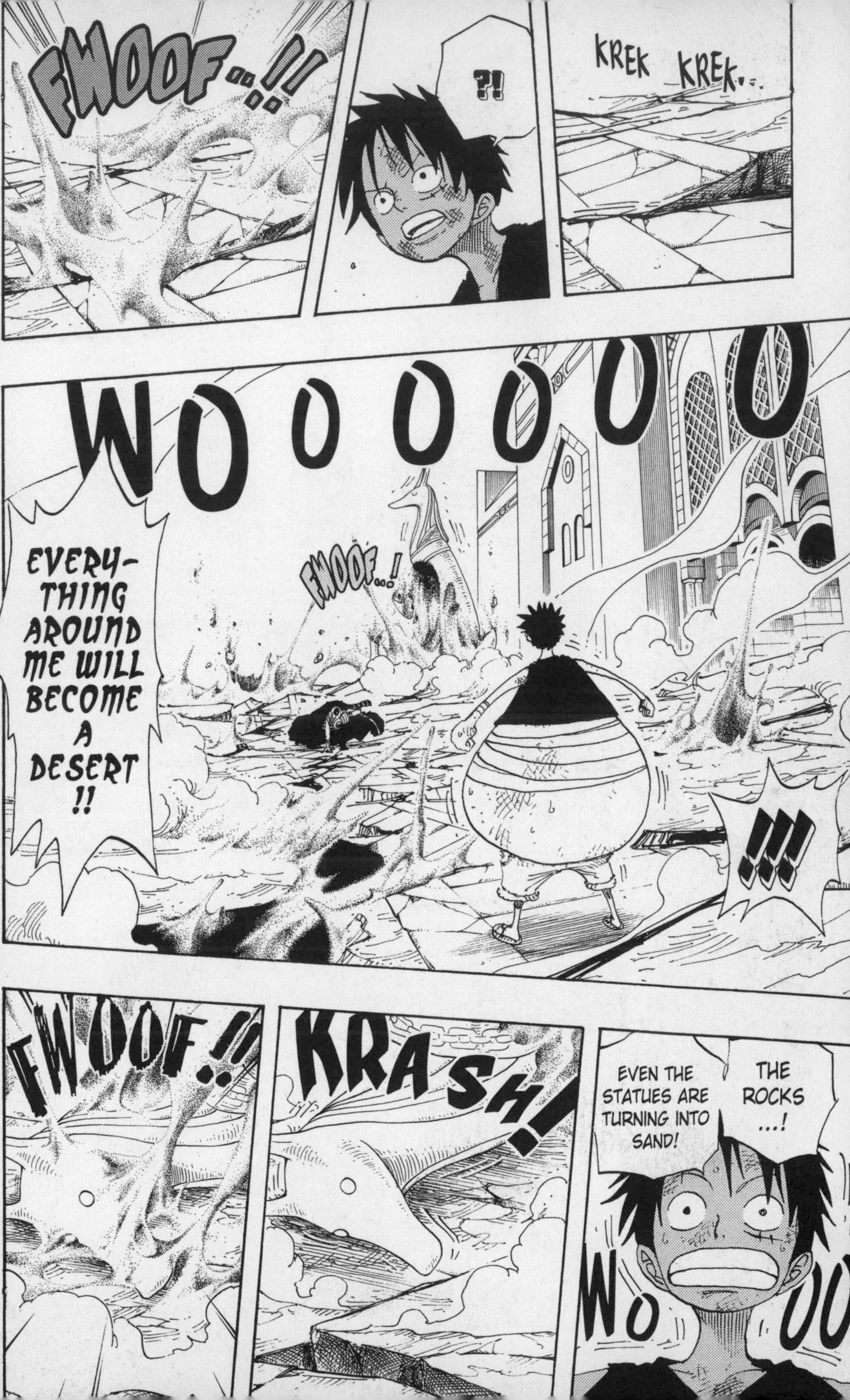

KREK KREK...
?!
FWOOF..!!
WOOOOOO
FWOOF..!
!!!
EVERY-THING AROUND ME WILL BECOME A DESERT !!
THE ROCKS ...!
EVEN THE STATUES ARE TURNING INTO SAND!
WOOO
KRASH!
FWOOF..!!

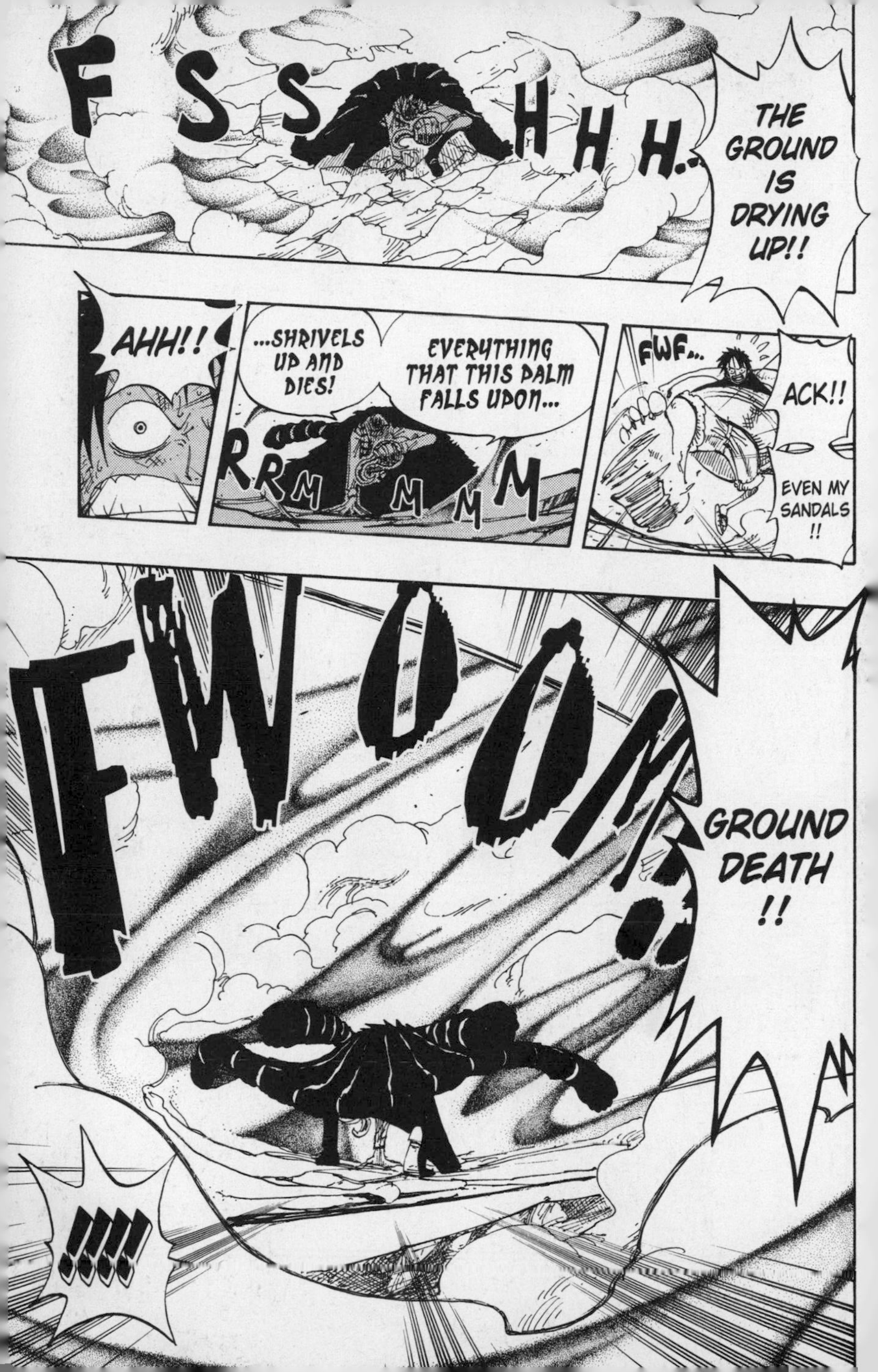
THE GROUND IS DRYING UP!!
FSSHHH..
FWF...
ACK!!
EVEN MY SANDALS!!
EVERYTHING THAT THIS PALM FALLS UPON...
...SHRIVELS UP AND DIES!
RRMMMM
AHH!!
GROUND DEATH!!
FWOOM..
!!!!

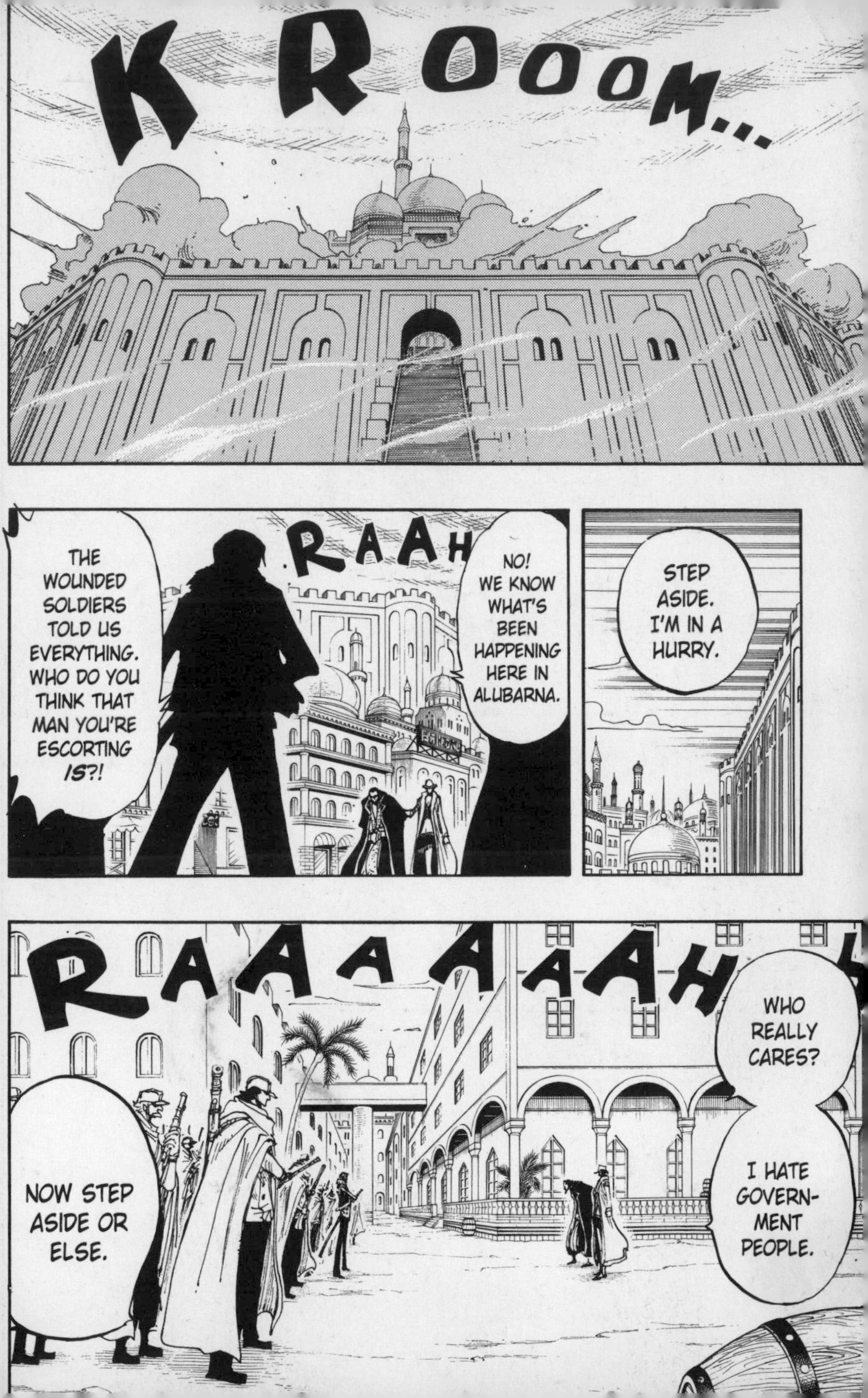
KROOOM...
STEP ASIDE. I'M IN A HURRY.
RAAH
NO! WE KNOW WHAT'S BEEN HAPPENING HERE IN ALUBARNA.
THE WOUNDED SOLDIERS TOLD US EVERYTHING. WHO DO YOU THINK THAT MAN YOU'RE ESCORTING *IS*?!
RAAAAAAH
WHO REALLY CARES?
I HATE GOVERNMENT PEOPLE.
NOW STEP ASIDE OR ELSE.

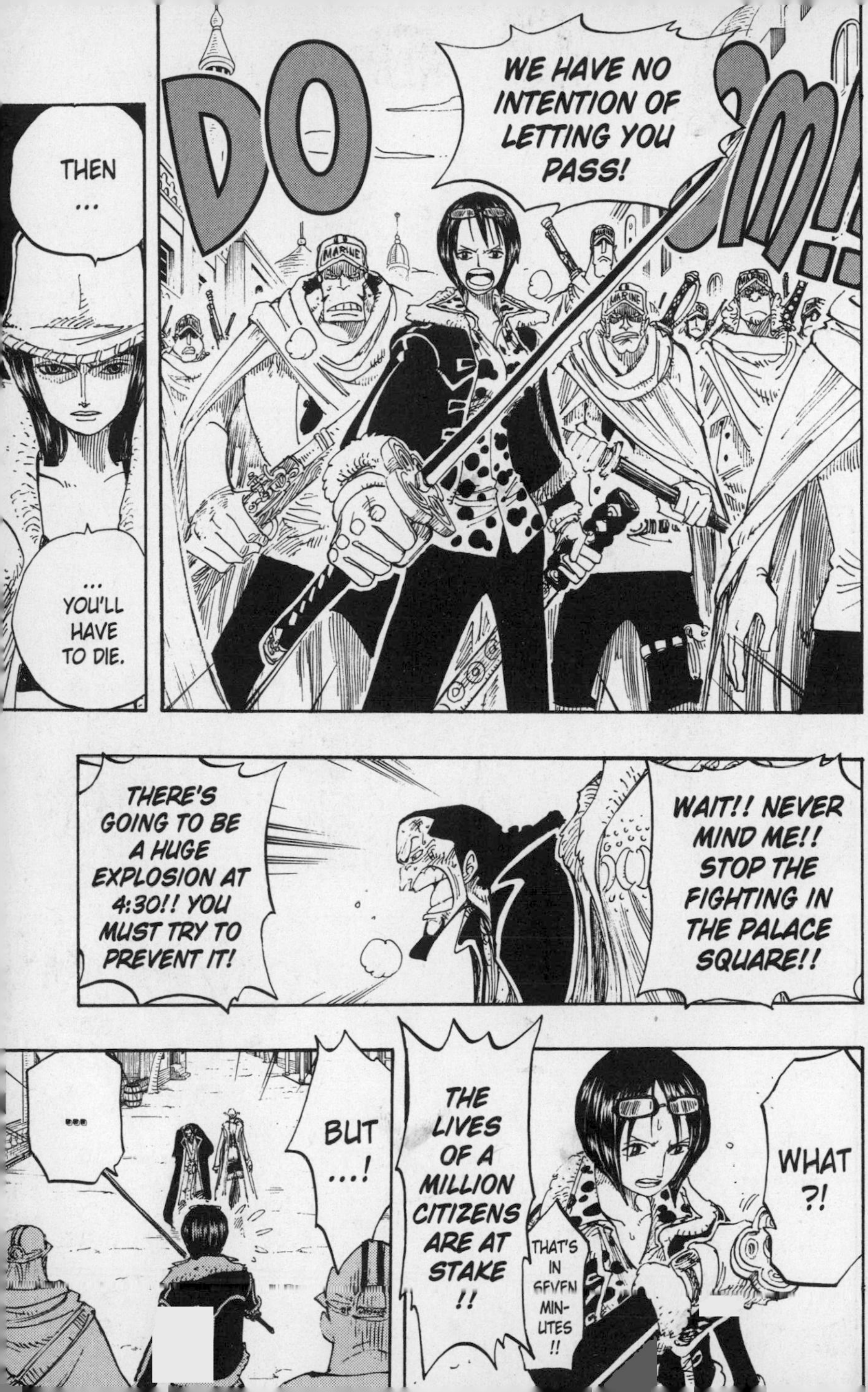
DOM!!
WE HAVE NO INTENTION OF LETTING YOU PASS!
THEN ...
... YOU'LL HAVE TO DIE.
WAIT!! NEVER MIND ME!! STOP THE FIGHTING IN THE PALACE SQUARE!!
THERE'S GOING TO BE A HUGE EXPLOSION AT 4:30!! YOU MUST TRY TO PREVENT IT!
WHAT ?!
THE LIVES OF A MILLION CITIZENS ARE AT STAKE !!
THAT'S IN SEVEN MIN-UTES !!
BUT ...!
...

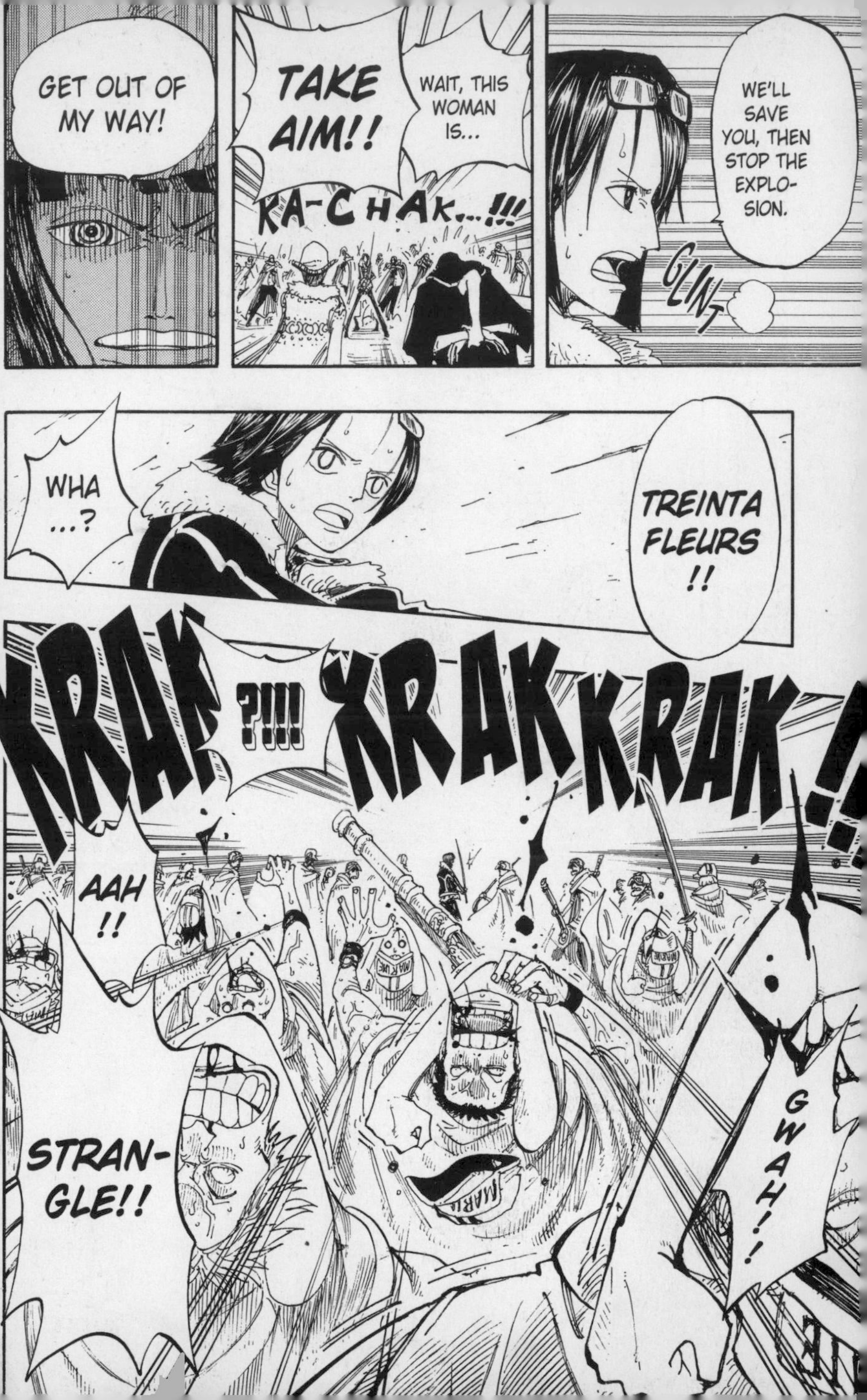
WE'LL SAVE YOU, THEN STOP THE EXPLO-SION.
GLINT
WAIT, THIS WOMAN IS...
TAKE AIM!!
KA-CHAK...!!!
GET OUT OF MY WAY!
TREINTA FLEURS!!
WHA...?
KRAK KRAK!!!
?!!!
KRAK
GWAH!!
AAH!!
STRAN-GLE!!

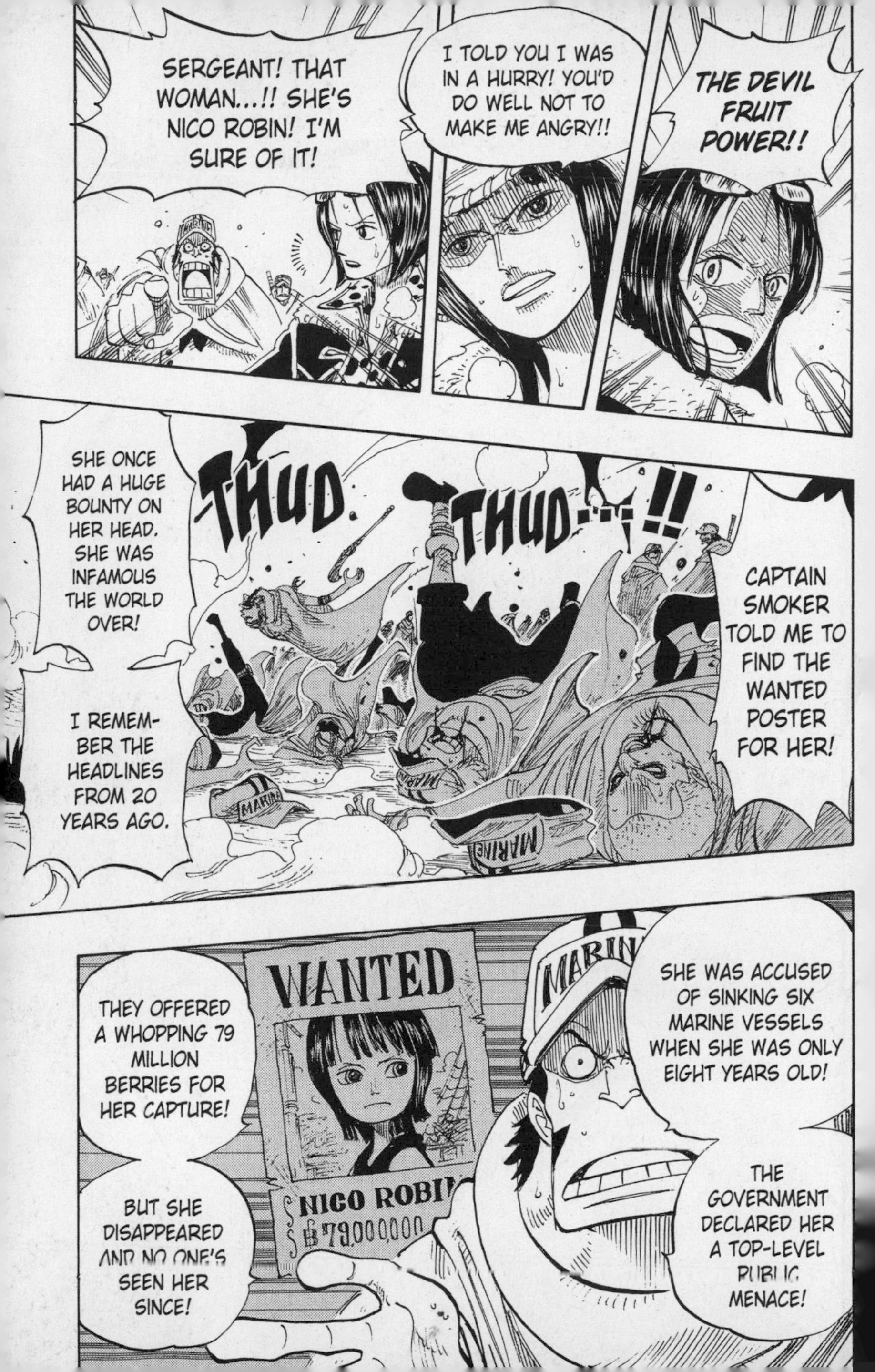
THE DEVIL FRUIT POWER!!
I TOLD YOU I WAS IN A HURRY! YOU'D DO WELL NOT TO MAKE ME ANGRY!!
SERGEANT! THAT WOMAN...!! SHE'S NICO ROBIN! I'M SURE OF IT!
THUD...!!
THUD
CAPTAIN SMOKER TOLD ME TO FIND THE WANTED POSTER FOR HER!
SHE ONCE HAD A HUGE BOUNTY ON HER HEAD. SHE WAS INFAMOUS THE WORLD OVER!
I REMEMBER THE HEADLINES FROM 20 YEARS AGO.
MARINE
SHE WAS ACCUSED OF SINKING SIX MARINE VESSELS WHEN SHE WAS ONLY EIGHT YEARS OLD!
THE GOVERNMENT DECLARED HER A TOP-LEVEL PUBLIC MENACE!
WANTED
NICO ROBI
฿79,000,000
THEY OFFERED A WHOPPING 79 MILLION BERRIES FOR HER CAPTURE!
BUT SHE DISAPPEARED AND NO ONE'S SEEN HER SINCE!

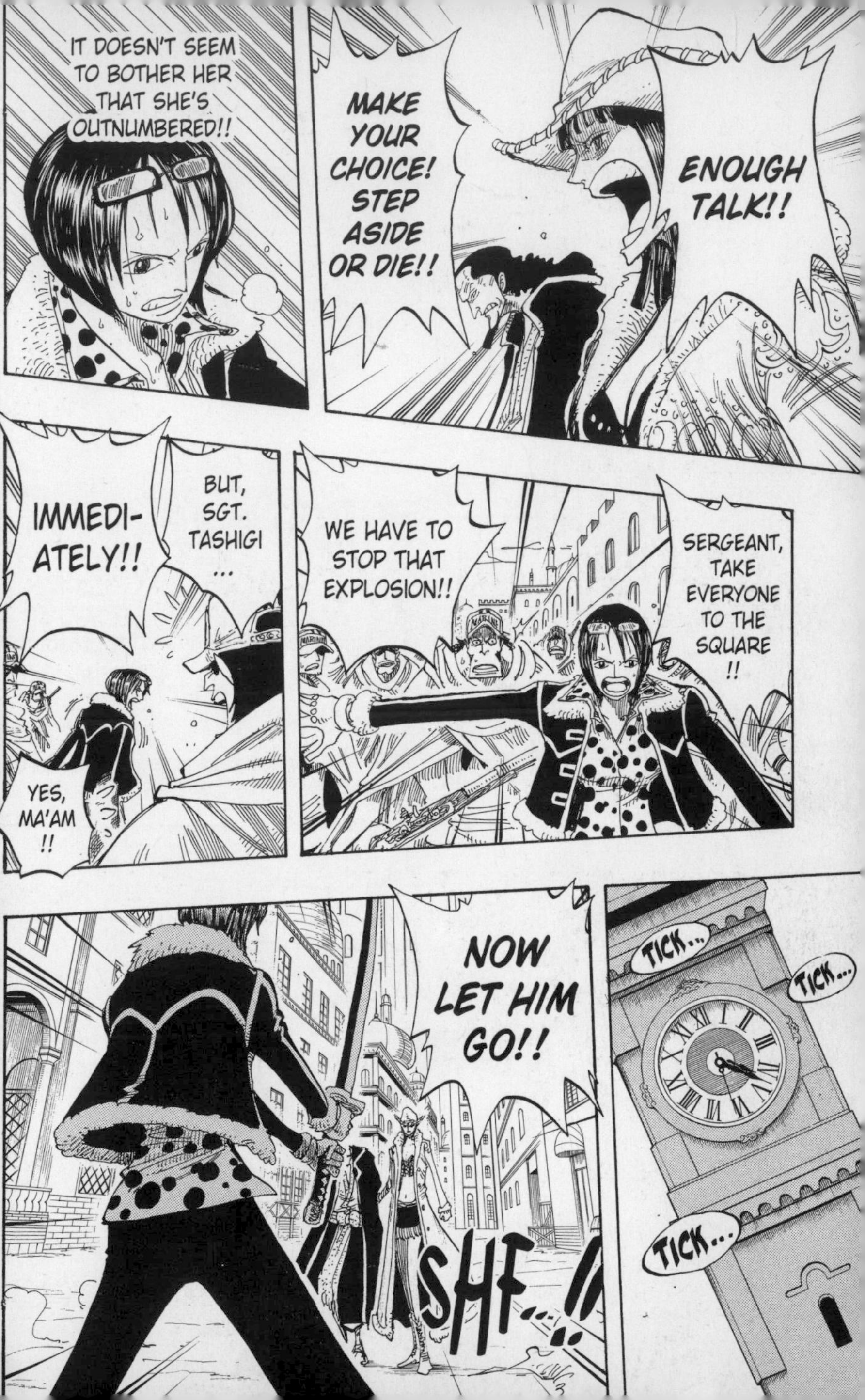
ENOUGH TALK!!
MAKE YOUR CHOICE! STEP ASIDE OR DIE!!
IT DOESN'T SEEM TO BOTHER HER THAT SHE'S OUTNUMBERED!!
SERGEANT, TAKE EVERYONE TO THE SQUARE!!
WE HAVE TO STOP THAT EXPLOSION!!
BUT, SGT. TASHIGI ...
IMMEDI-ATELY!!
YES, MA'AM!!
TICK...
TICK...
TICK...
NOW LET HIM GO!!
SHF..!!

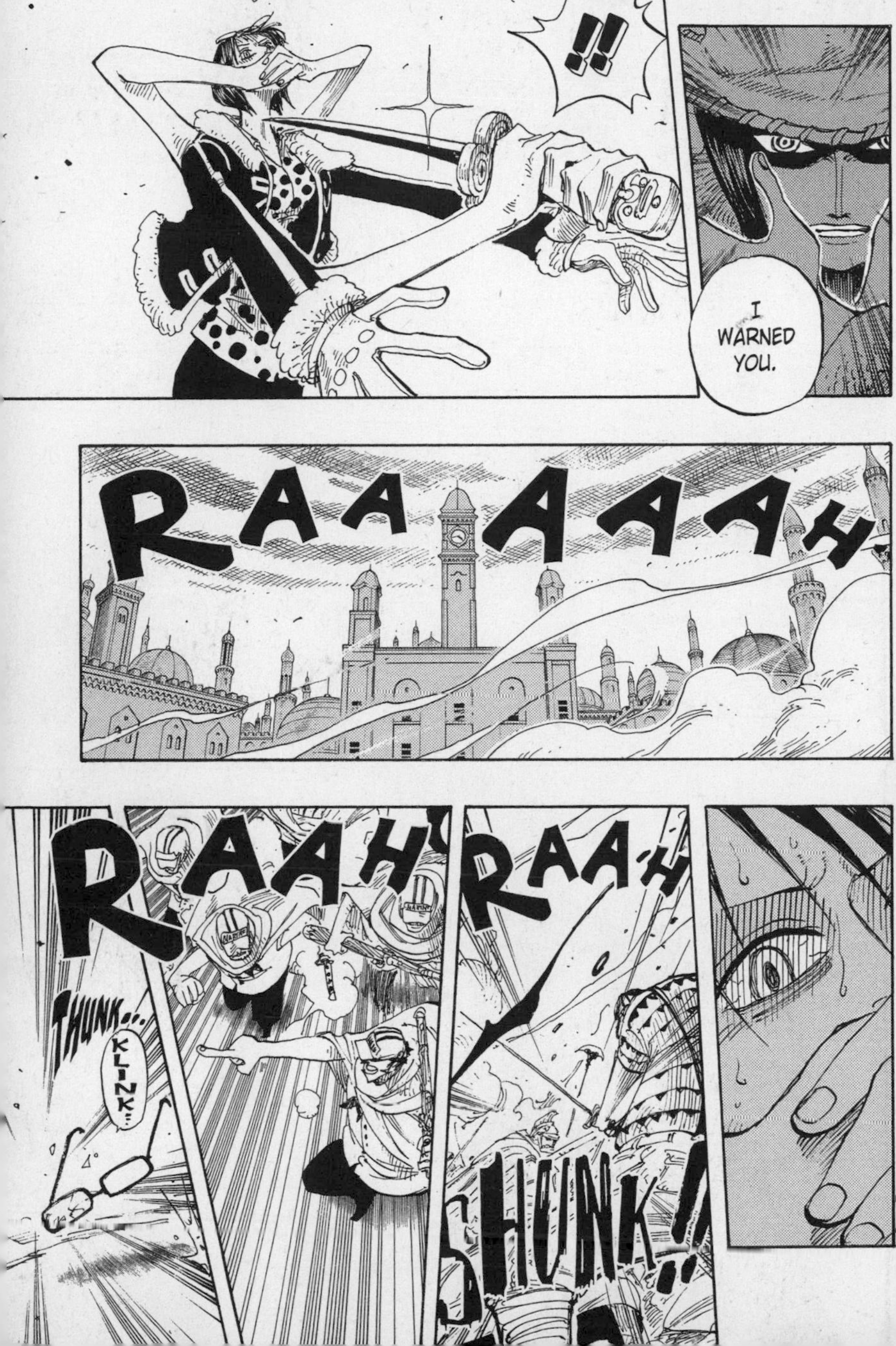
I WARNED YOU.
!!
RAAAAAH
RAAH
SHUNK!!
RAAH
THUNK...
KLINK...

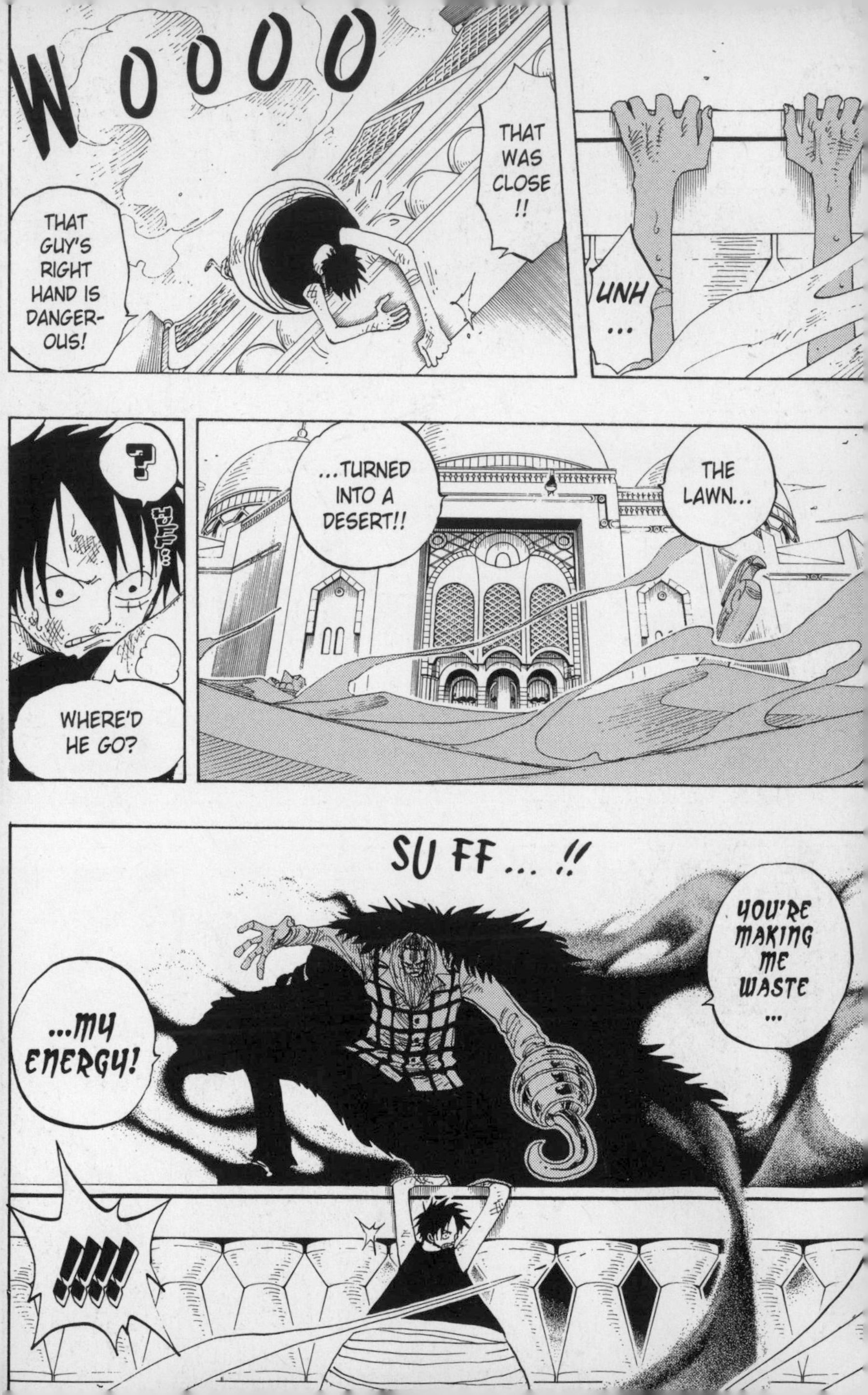
UNH ...
WOOOO
THAT WAS CLOSE !!
THAT GUY'S RIGHT HAND IS DANGER-OUS!
THE LAWN...
...TURNED INTO A DESERT!!
?
WHERE'D HE GO?
SU FF ... !!
YOU'RE MAKING ME WASTE ...
...MY ENERGY!
!!!!

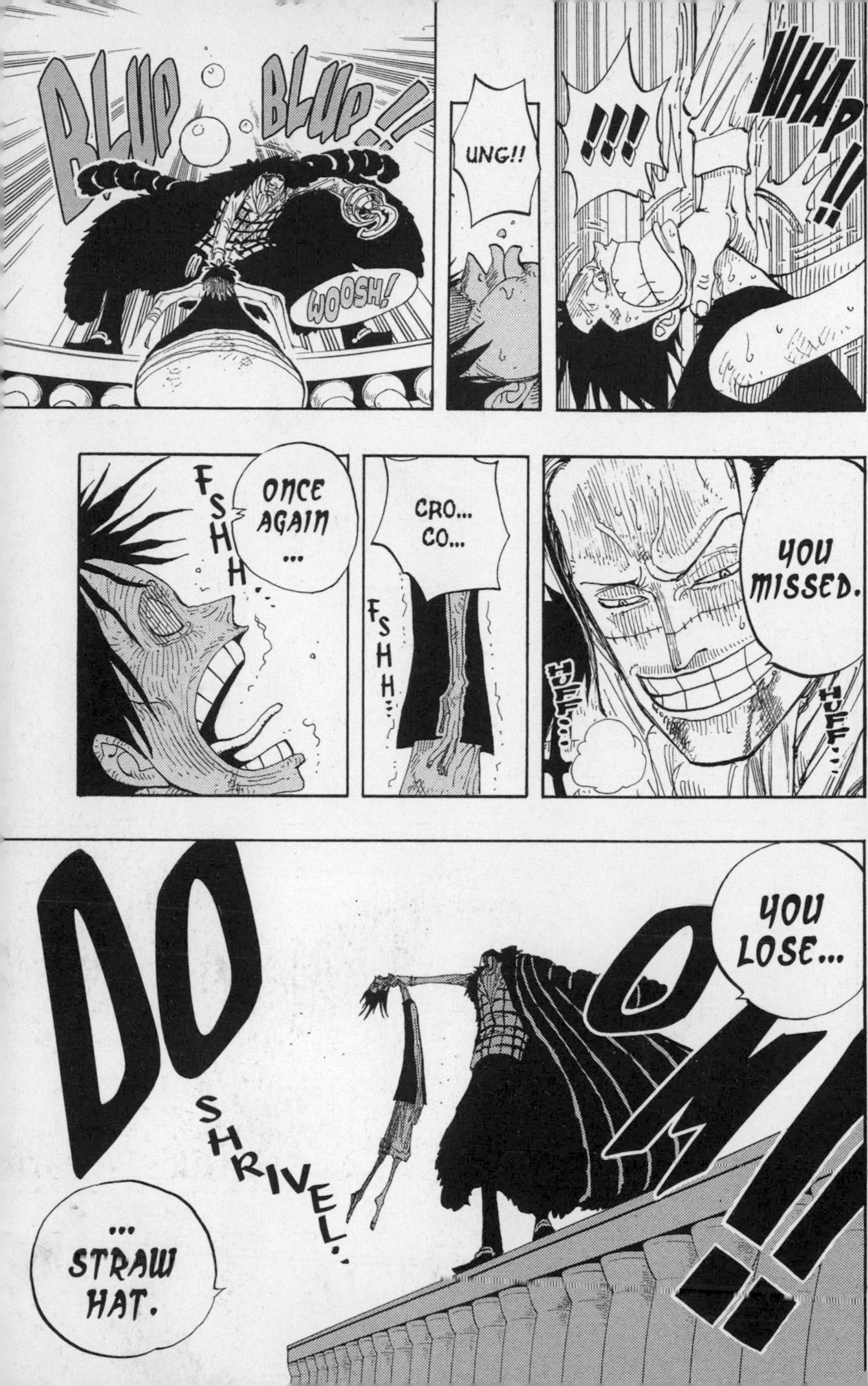
WHAP!!
!!!
UNG!!
BLUP BLUP!!
WOOSH!
YOU MISSED.
HUFF...
HUFF...
CRO... CO...
FSHH...
ONCE AGAIN ...
FSHH...
YOU LOSE...
DOOM!!
SHRIVEL..
... STRAW HAT.

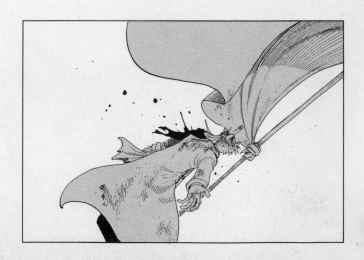

# Chapter 202:
# THE ROYAL MAUSOLEUM

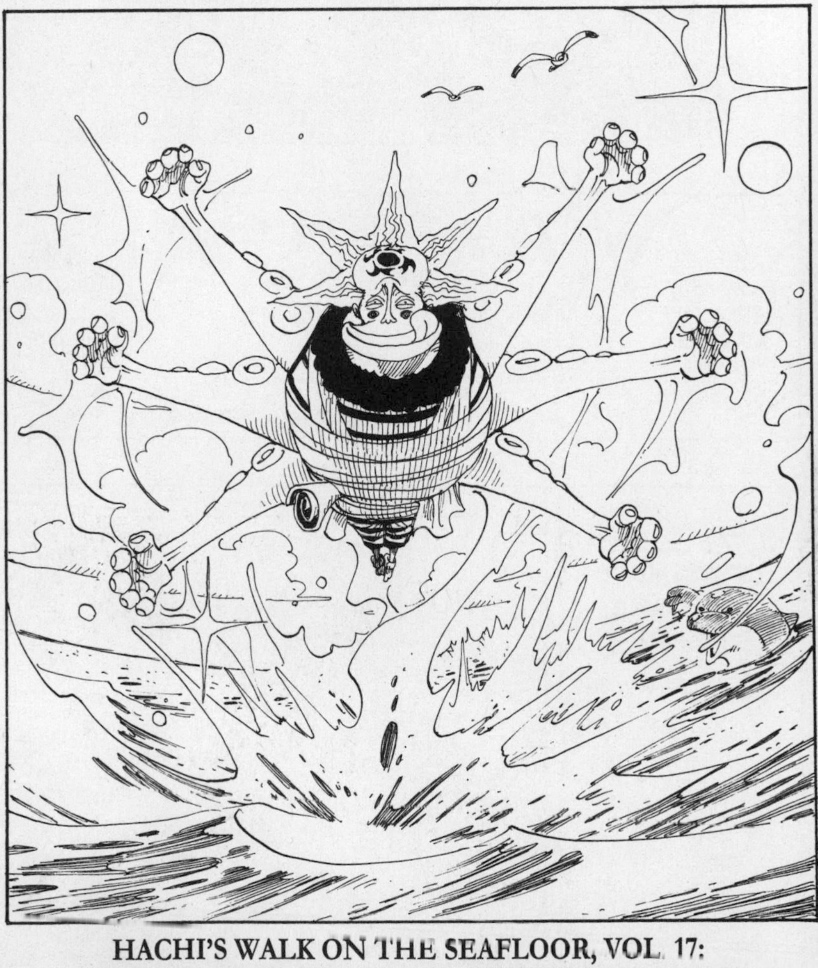

HACHI'S WALK ON THE SEAFLOOR, VOL. 17:
"IN SEARCH OF THE LEGENDARY SUPER-YUMMY OCTOPUS FRITTER RECIPE"

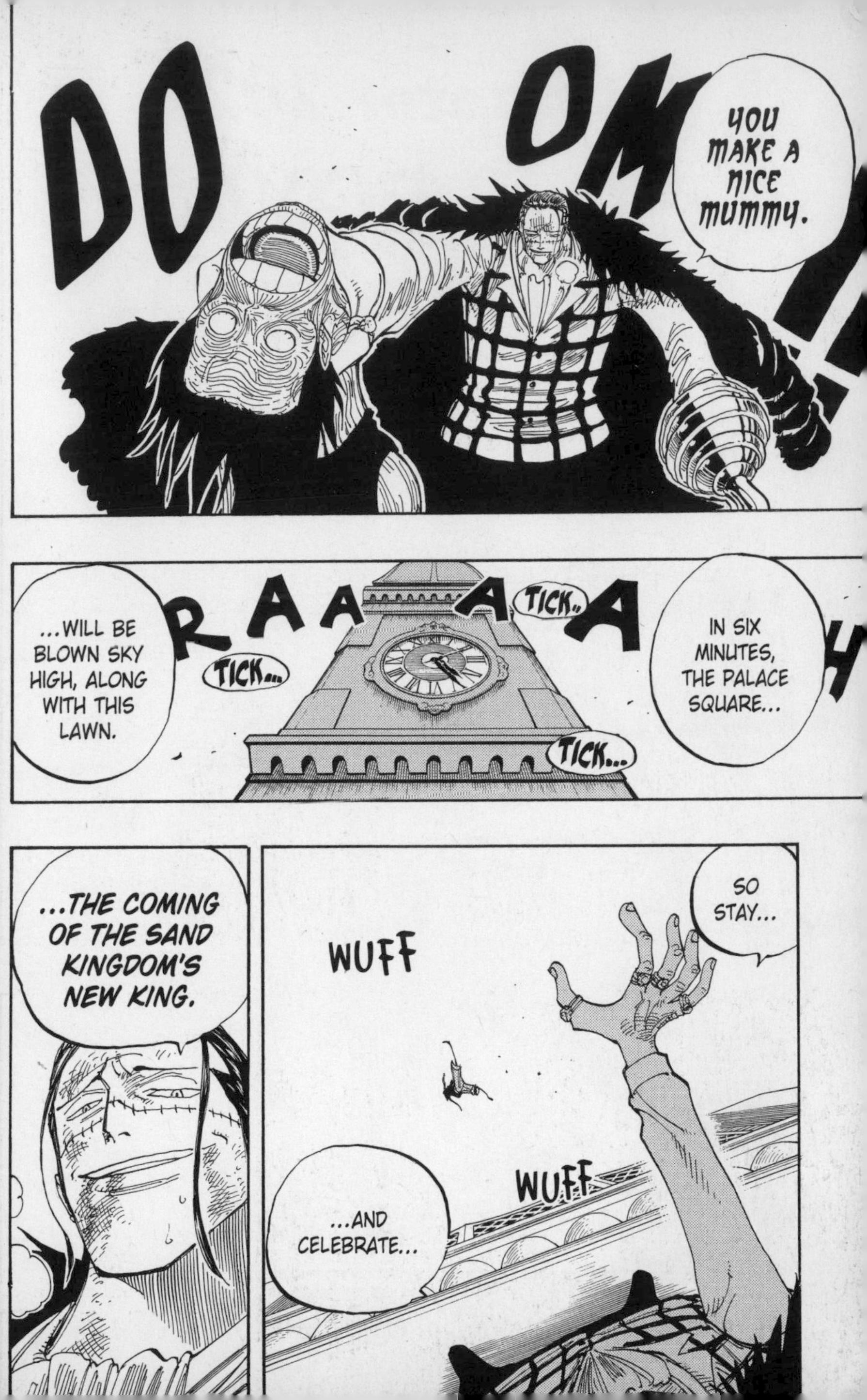
YOU MAKE A NICE MUMMY.
DOOM!!
IN SIX MINUTES, THE PALACE SQUARE...
...WILL BE BLOWN SKY HIGH, ALONG WITH THIS LAWN.
RAAAAH
TICK...
TICK..
TICK...
SO STAY...
WUFF
WUFF
...AND CELEBRATE...
...THE COMING OF THE SAND KINGDOM'S NEW KING.

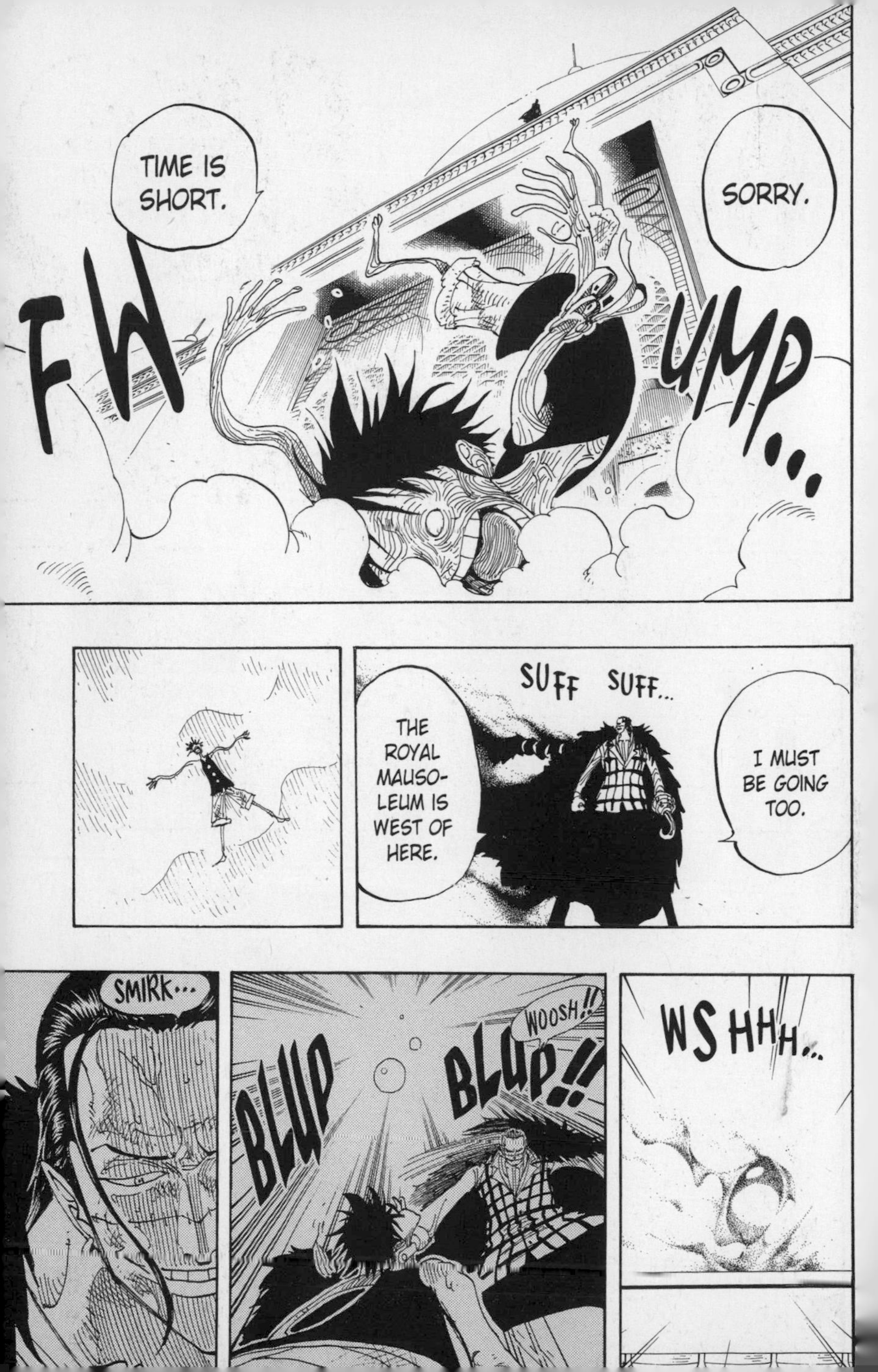
SORRY.
TIME IS SHORT.
FWUMP...
I MUST BE GOING TOO.
SUFF SUFF...
THE ROYAL MAUSOLEUM IS WEST OF HERE.
WSHHH...
WOOSH!!
BLUP
BLUP!!
SMIRK...

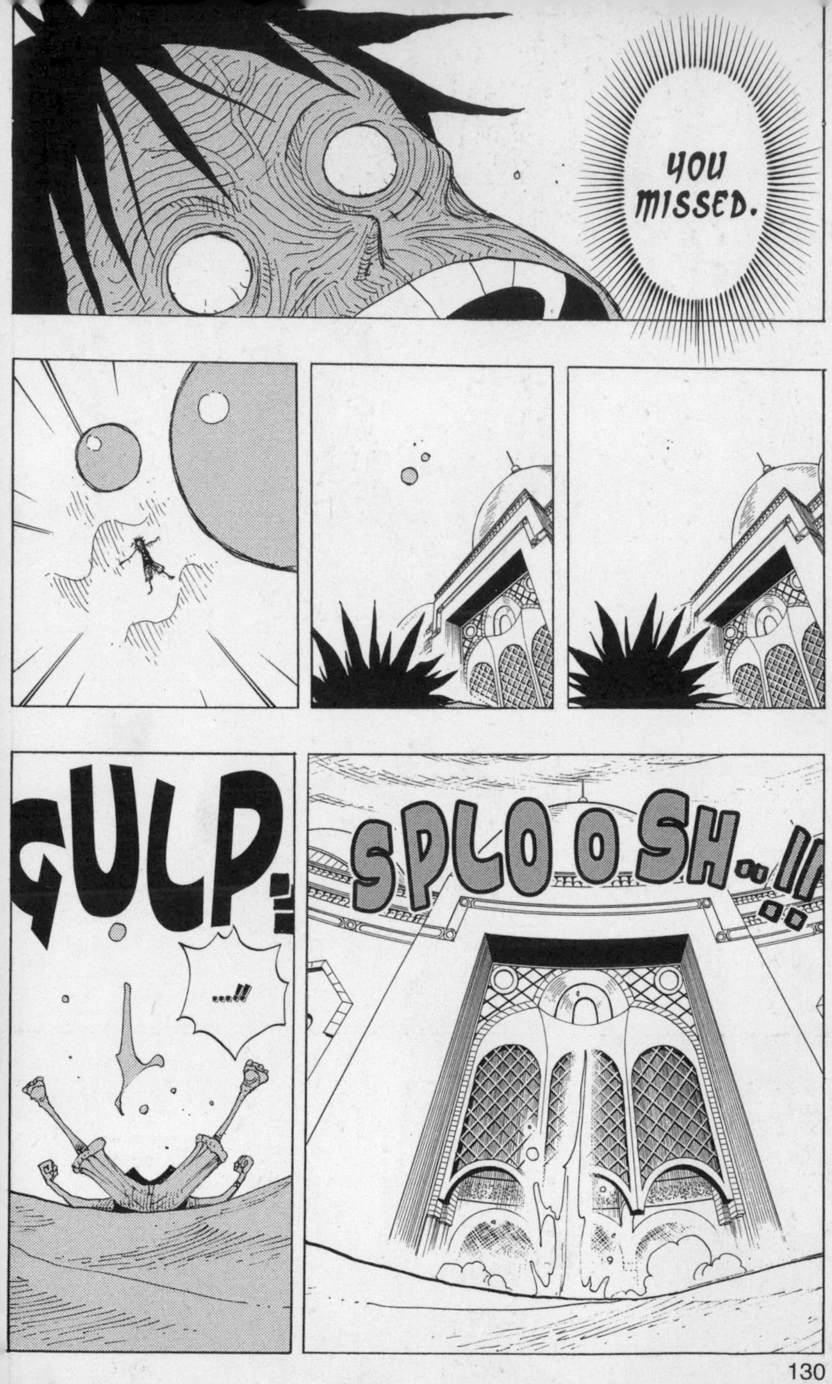
YOU MISSED.
SPLOOSH..!!
GULP.
...!!

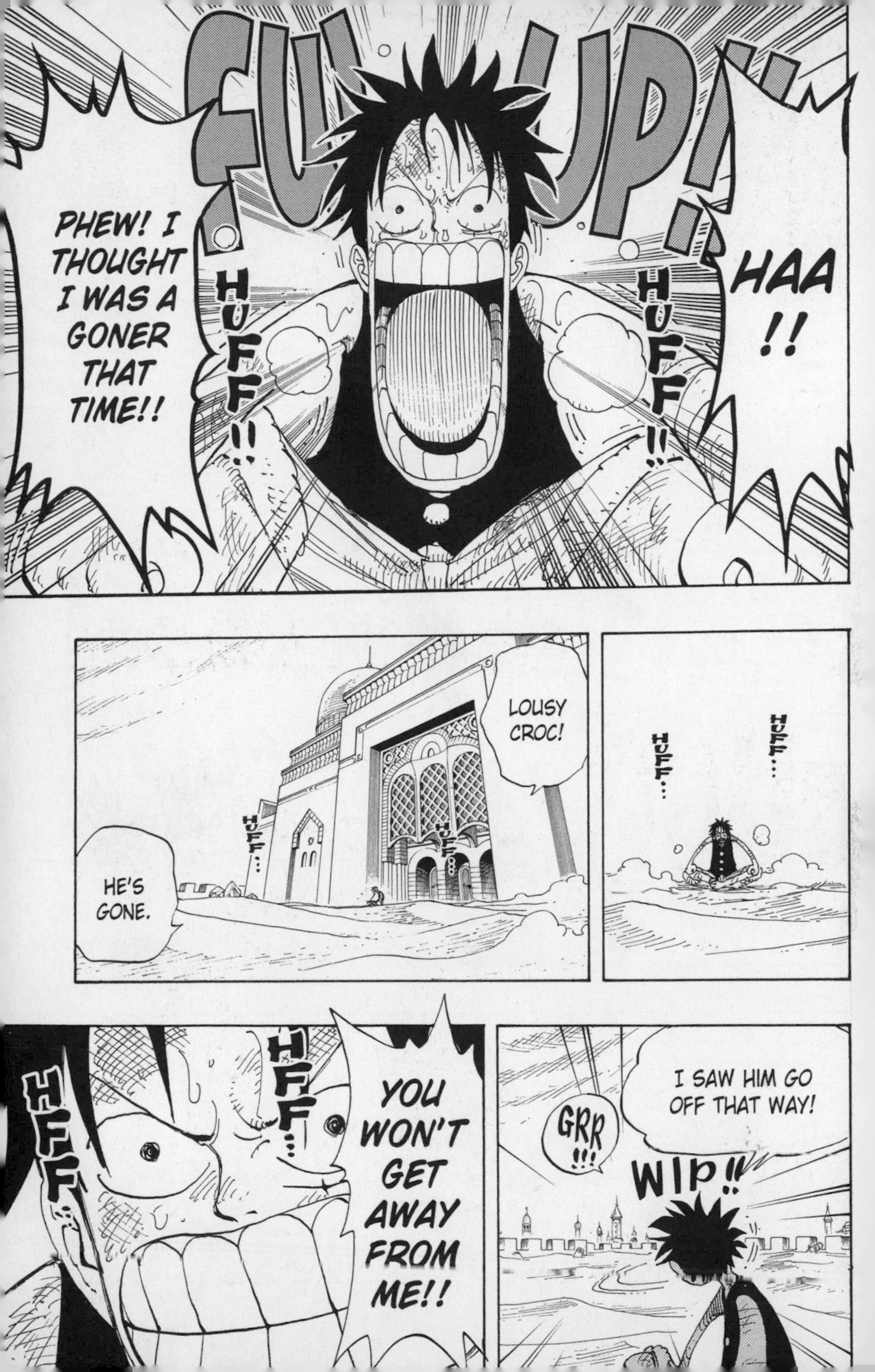
HAA !!
HUFF!!
HUFF!!
PHEW! I THOUGHT I WAS A GONER THAT TIME!!
HUFF...
HUFF...
LOUSY CROC!
HUFF...
HUFF...
HE'S GONE.
I SAW HIM GO OFF THAT WAY!
GRR!!!
WIP!!
YOU WON'T GET AWAY FROM ME!!
HFF...
HFF...

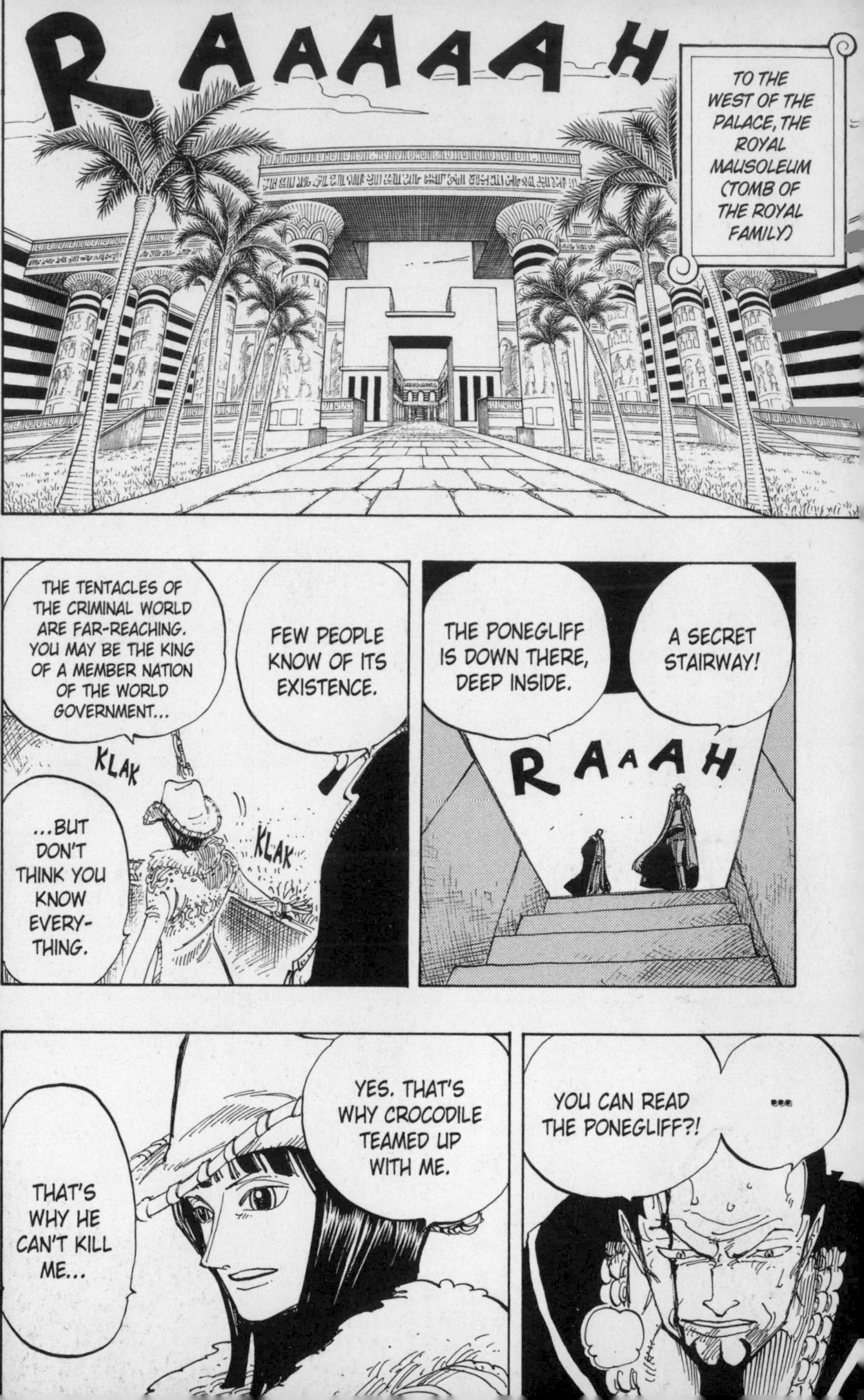
RAAAAH
TO THE WEST OF THE PALACE, THE ROYAL MAUSOLEUM (TOMB OF THE ROYAL FAMILY)
A SECRET STAIRWAY!
THE PONEGLIFF IS DOWN THERE, DEEP INSIDE.
RAAAH
FEW PEOPLE KNOW OF ITS EXISTENCE.
THE TENTACLES OF THE CRIMINAL WORLD ARE FAR-REACHING. YOU MAY BE THE KING OF A MEMBER NATION OF THE WORLD GOVERNMENT...
KLAK
KLAK
...BUT DON'T THINK YOU KNOW EVERY-THING.
...
YOU CAN READ THE PONEGLIFF?!
YES. THAT'S WHY CROCODILE TEAMED UP WITH ME.
THAT'S WHY HE CAN'T KILL ME...

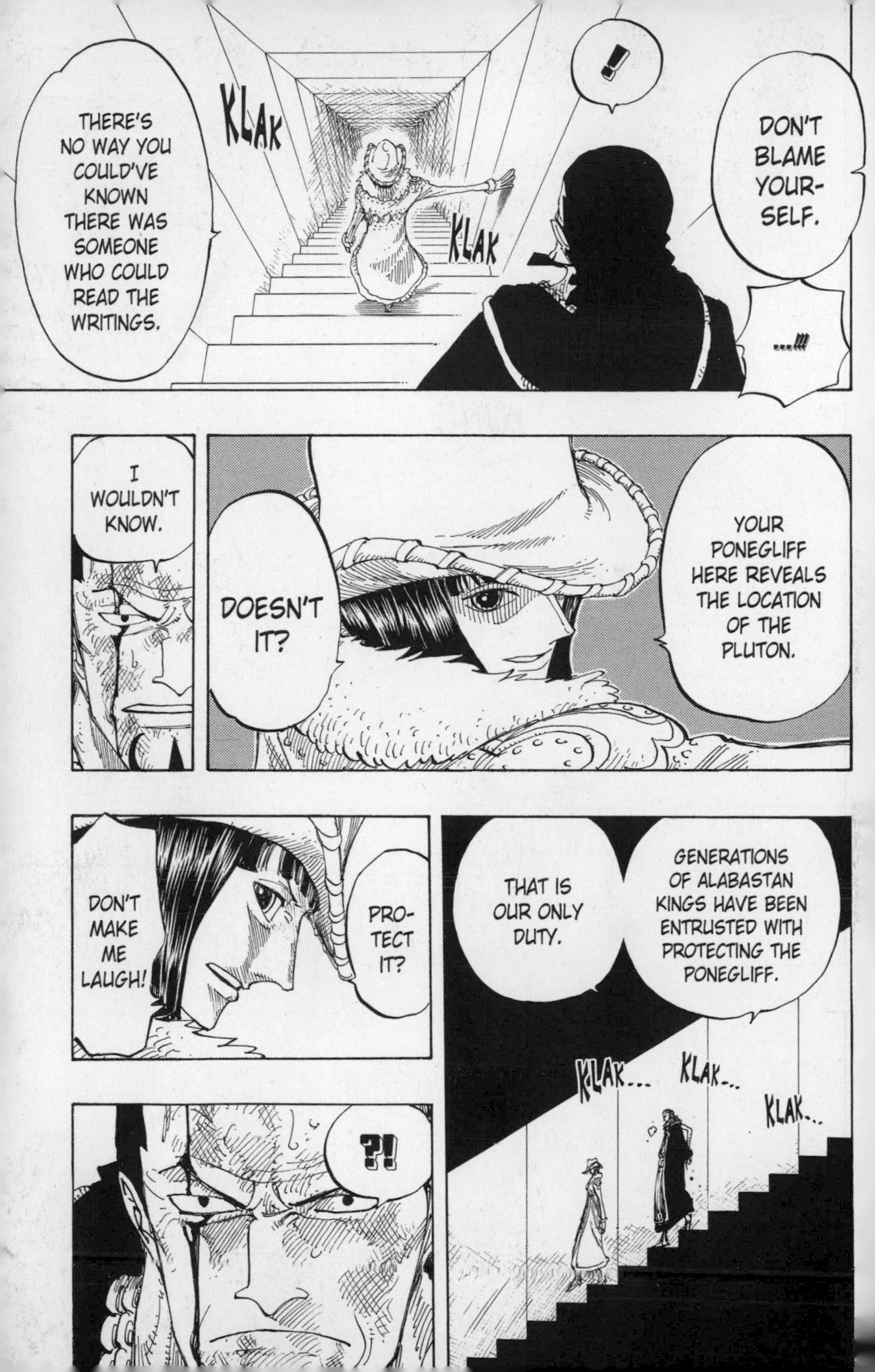
DON'T BLAME YOURSELF.
THERE'S NO WAY YOU COULD'VE KNOWN THERE WAS SOMEONE WHO COULD READ THE WRITINGS.
KLAK
KLAK
!
...!!!
YOUR PONEGLIFF HERE REVEALS THE LOCATION OF THE PLUTON.
DOESN'T IT?
I WOULDN'T KNOW.
GENERATIONS OF ALABASTAN KINGS HAVE BEEN ENTRUSTED WITH PROTECTING THE PONEGLIFF.
THAT IS OUR ONLY DUTY.
KLAK...
KLAK...
KLAK...
PRO-TECT IT?
DON'T MAKE ME LAUGH!
?!

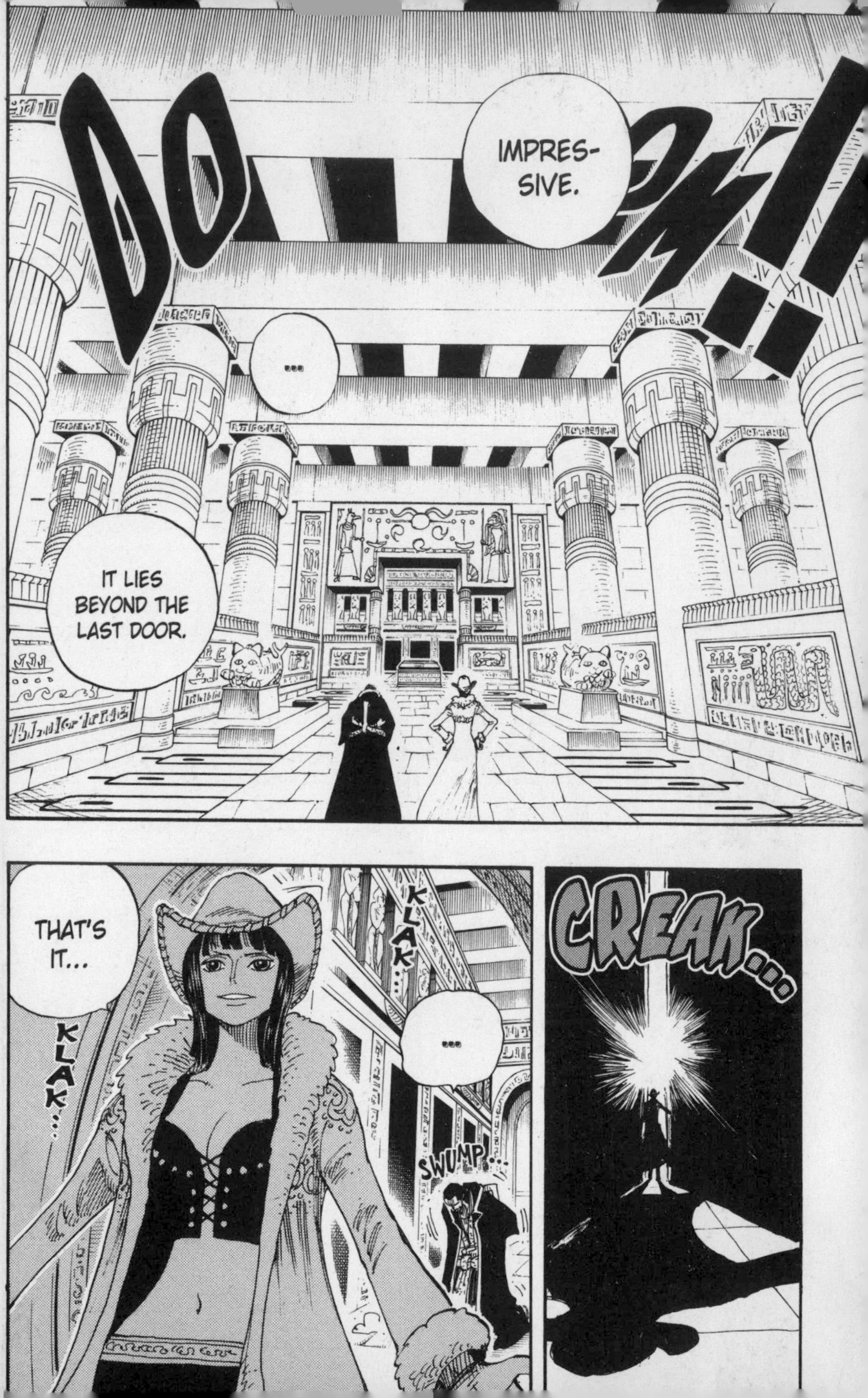
IMPRES-
SIVE.
DOOM!!
...
IT LIES BEYOND THE LAST DOOR.
CREAK...
KLAK...
...
THAT'S IT...
KLAK...
SWUMP...

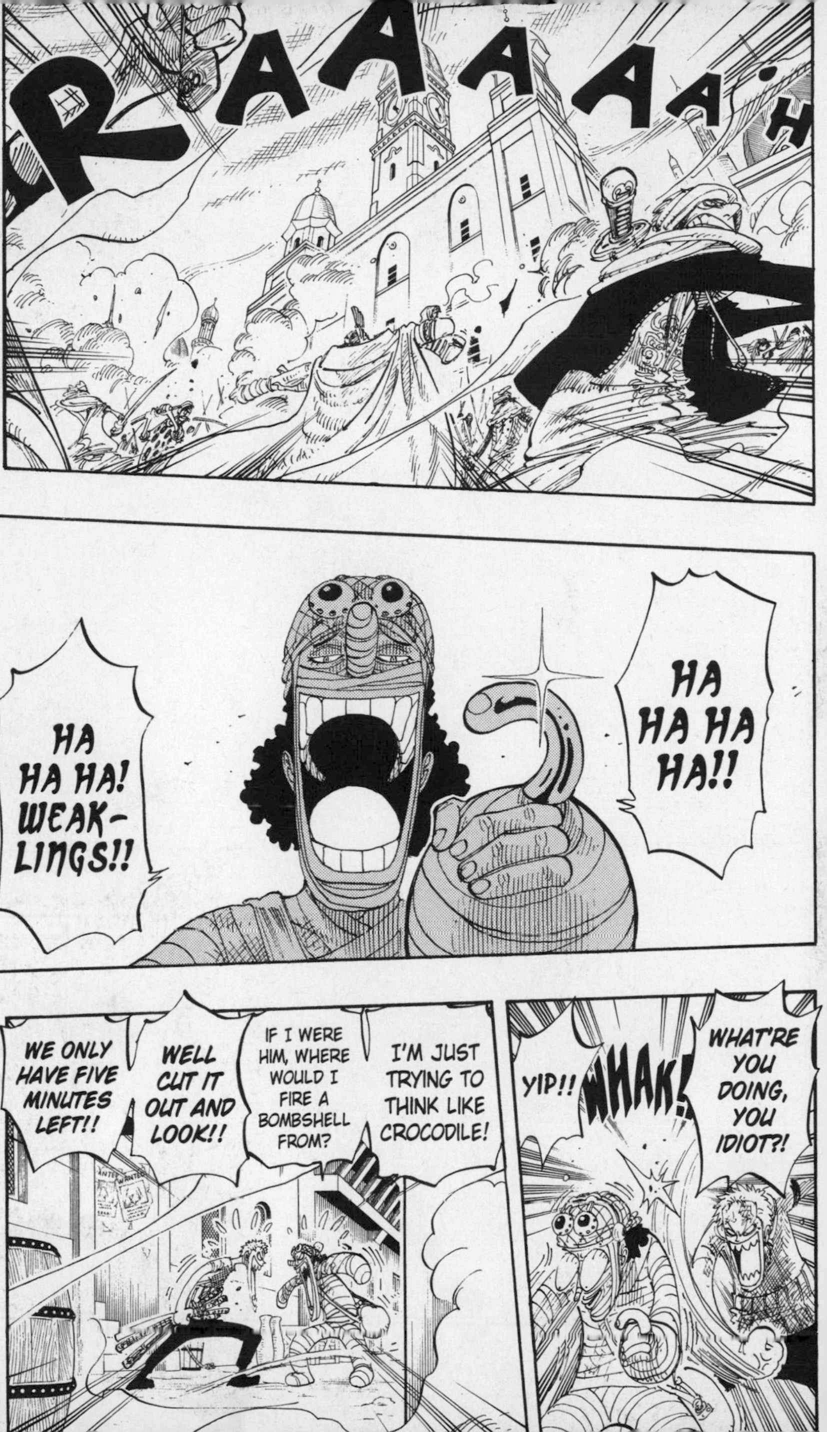
RAAAAAH
HA HA HA HA HA!!
HA HA HA! WEAK-LINGS!!
WHAT'RE YOU DOING, YOU IDIOT?!
WHAK!
YIP!!
I'M JUST TRYING TO THINK LIKE CROCODILE!
IF I WERE HIM, WHERE WOULD I FIRE A BOMBSHELL FROM?
WELL CUT IT OUT AND LOOK!!
WE ONLY HAVE FIVE MINUTES LEFT!!

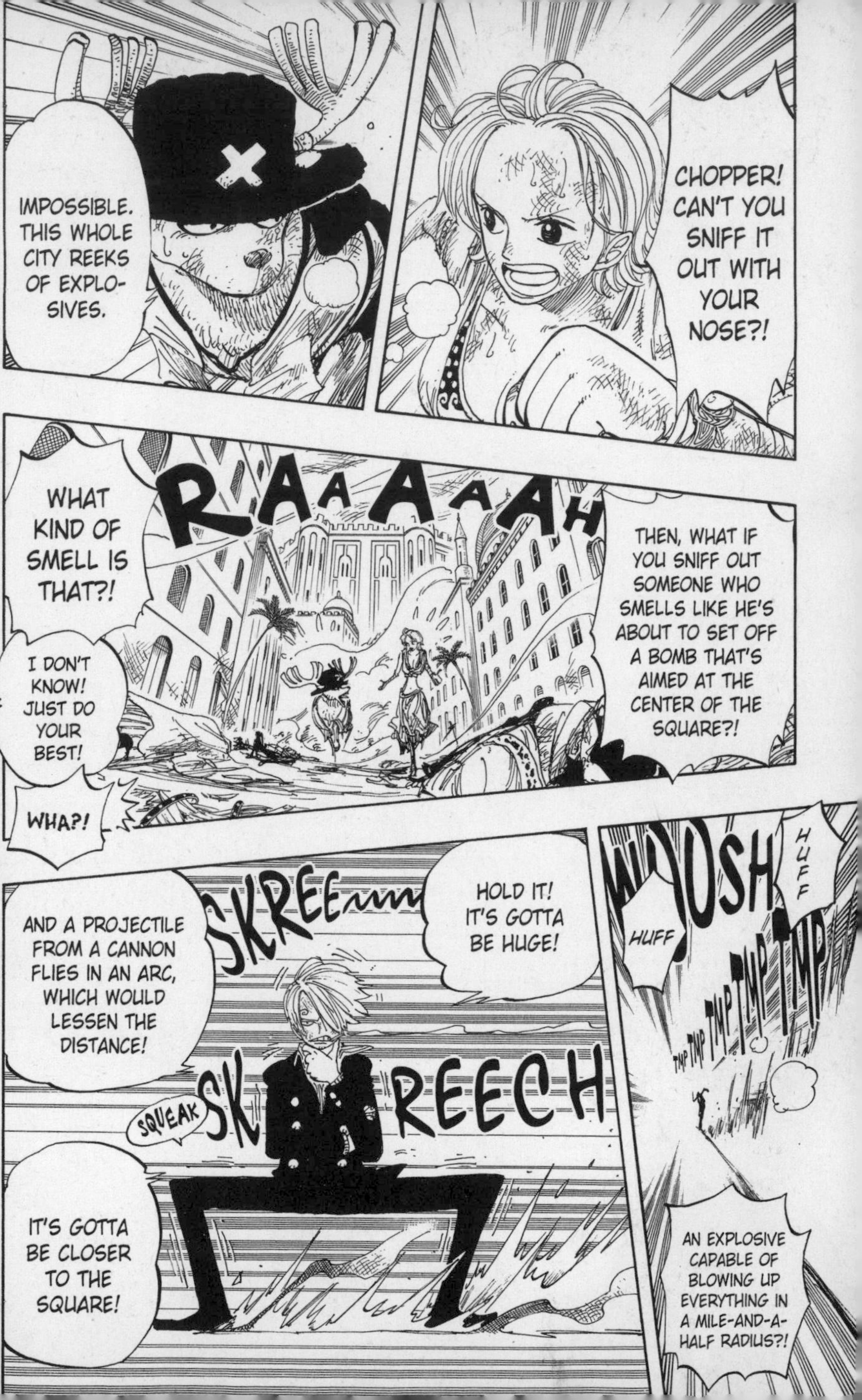
CHOPPER! CAN'T YOU SNIFF IT OUT WITH YOUR NOSE?!
IMPOSSIBLE. THIS WHOLE CITY REEKS OF EXPLOSIVES.
THEN, WHAT IF YOU SNIFF OUT SOMEONE WHO SMELLS LIKE HE'S ABOUT TO SET OFF A BOMB THAT'S AIMED AT THE CENTER OF THE SQUARE?!
RAAAAAH
WHAT KIND OF SMELL IS THAT?!
I DON'T KNOW! JUST DO YOUR BEST!
WHA?!
HUFF
HUFF
TMP TMP TMP TMP TMP TMP
AN EXPLOSIVE CAPABLE OF BLOWING UP EVERYTHING IN A MILE-AND-A-HALF RADIUS?!
HOLD IT! IT'S GOTTA BE HUGE!
SKREE
AND A PROJECTILE FROM A CANNON FLIES IN AN ARC, WHICH WOULD LESSEN THE DISTANCE!
SKREECH
SQUEAK
IT'S GOTTA BE CLOSER TO THE SQUARE!

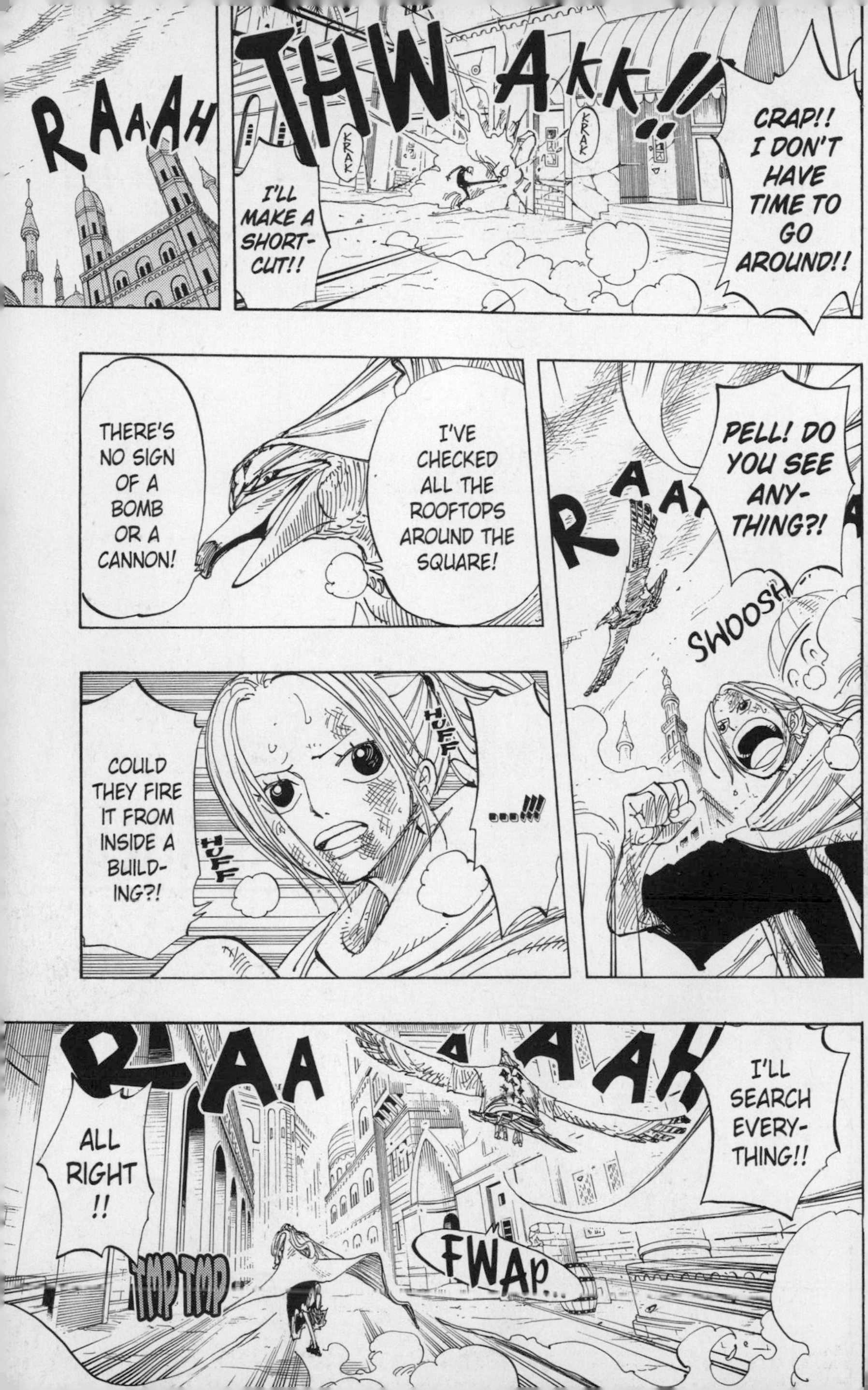
CRAP!! I DON'T HAVE TIME TO GO AROUND!!
THWAKK!!
KRAK
KRAK
I'LL MAKE A SHORT-CUT!!
RAAAH
PELL! DO YOU SEE ANY-THING?!
RAAA
SWOOSH
I'VE CHECKED ALL THE ROOFTOPS AROUND THE SQUARE!
THERE'S NO SIGN OF A BOMB OR A CANNON!
HUFF
...!!!
COULD THEY FIRE IT FROM INSIDE A BUILD-ING?!
HUFF
I'LL SEARCH EVERY-THING!!
RAAAAAH
FWAP
ALL RIGHT!!
TMP TMP

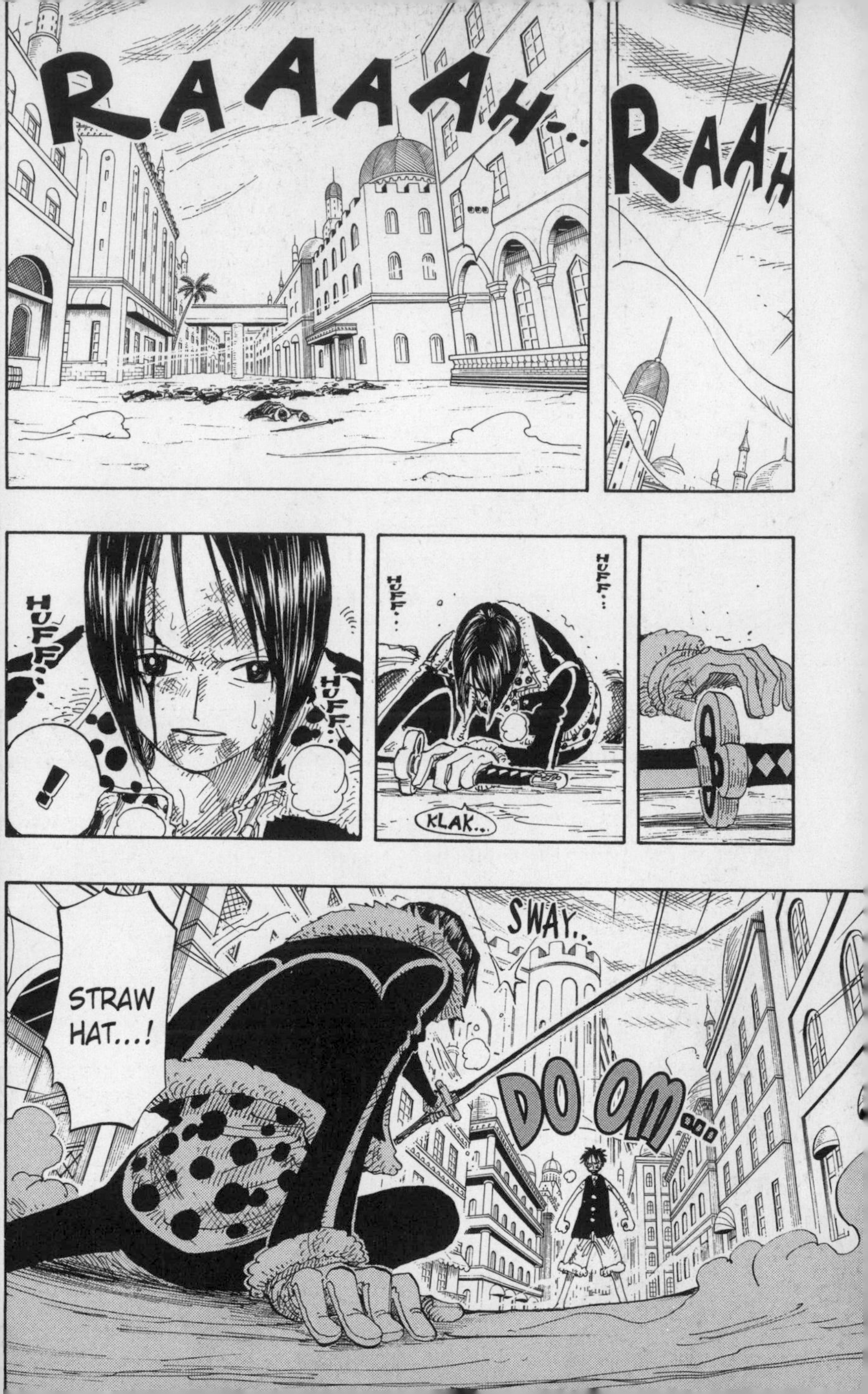
RAAH
RAAAAH...
HUFF...
HUFF...
KLAK...
HUFF...
HUFF...
!
SWAY...
STRAW HAT...!
DOOM...

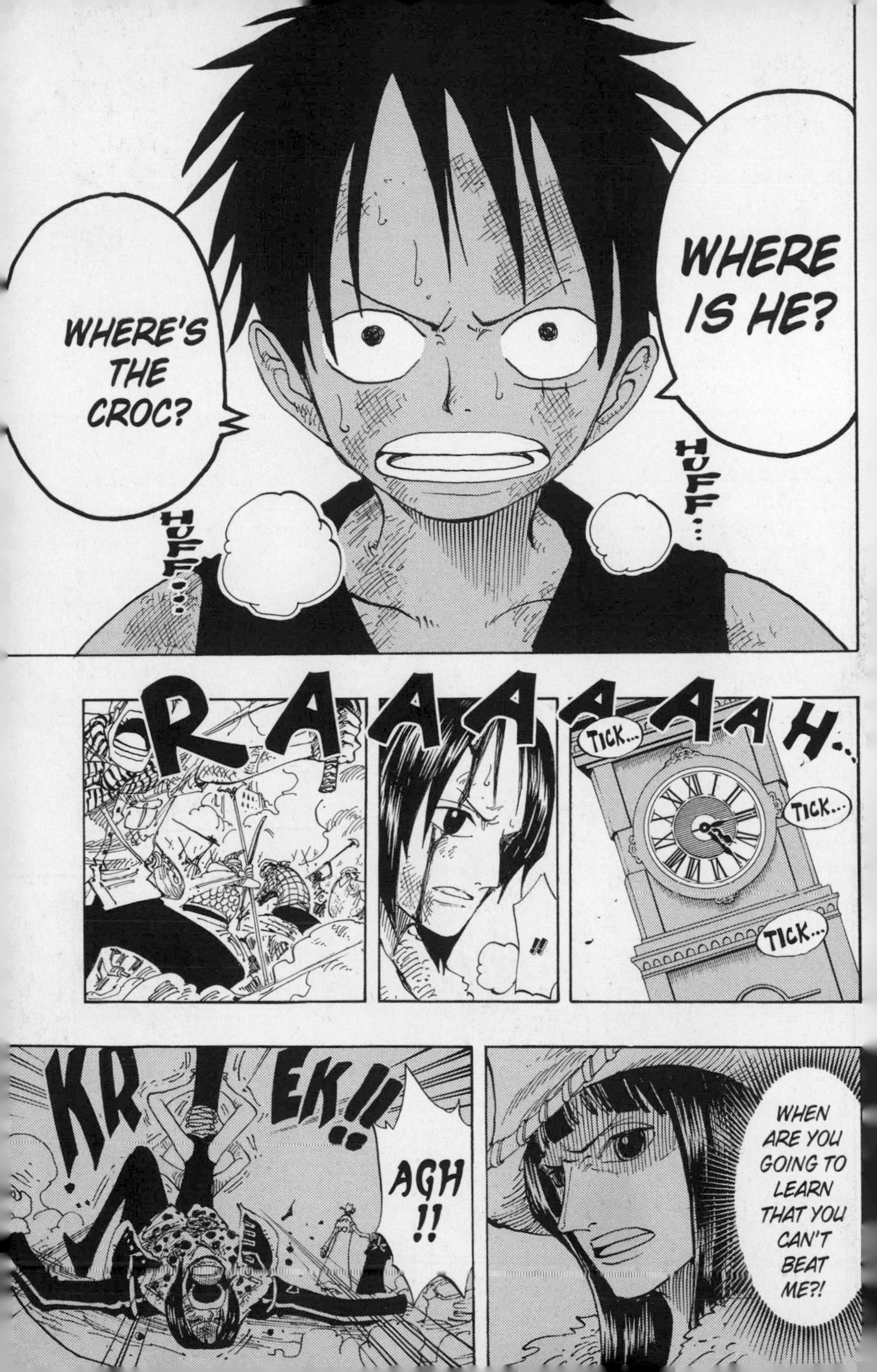
WHERE IS HE?
HUFF...
WHERE'S THE CROC?
HUFF...
RAAAAAH...
TICK...
TICK...
TICK...
!!
WHEN ARE YOU GOING TO LEARN THAT YOU CAN'T BEAT ME?!
KR EK!!
AGH !!

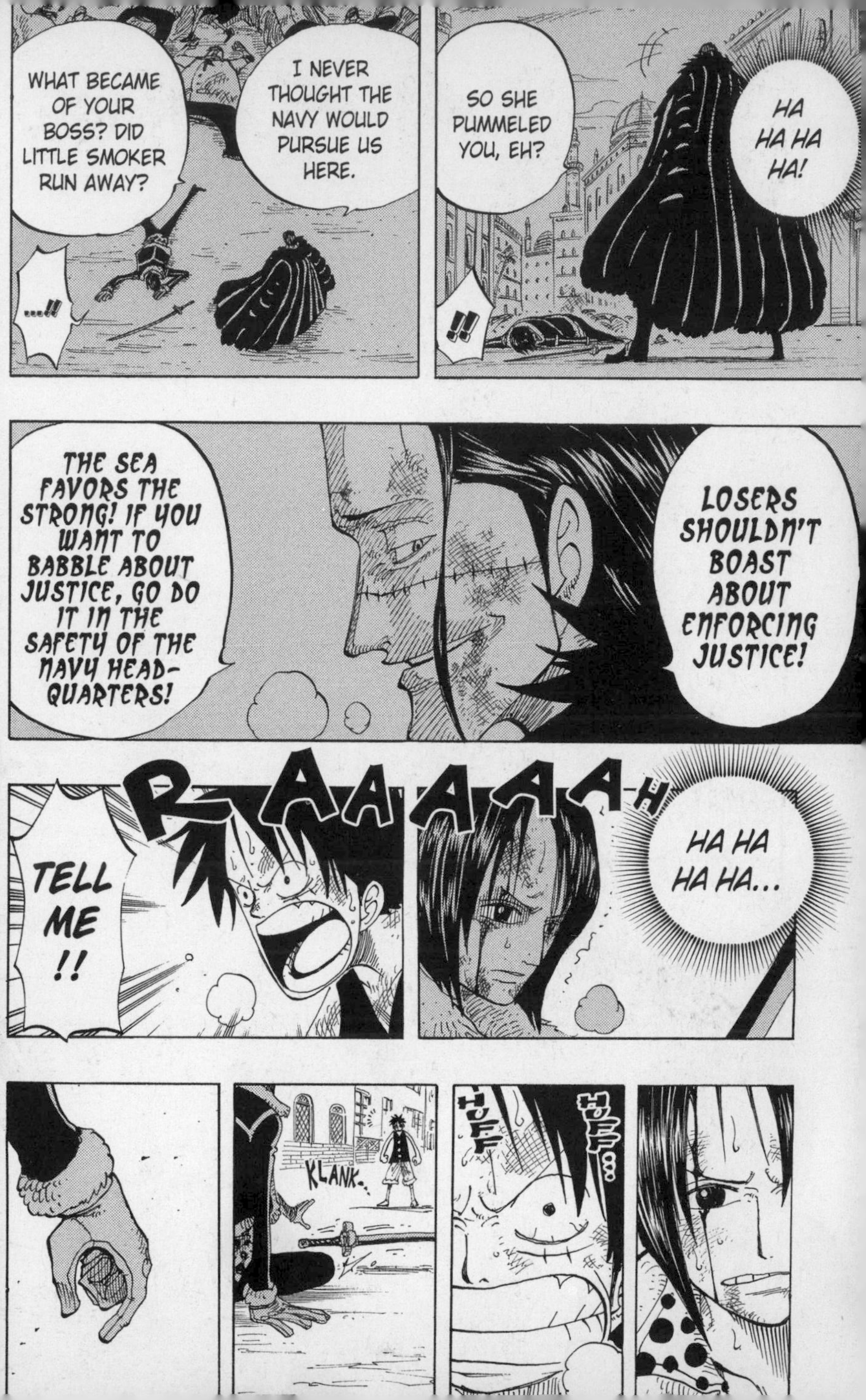
HA HA HA HA!
SO SHE PUMMELED YOU, EH?
!!
I NEVER THOUGHT THE NAVY WOULD PURSUE US HERE.
WHAT BECAME OF YOUR BOSS? DID LITTLE SMOKER RUN AWAY?
...!!
LOSERS SHOULDN'T BOAST ABOUT ENFORCING JUSTICE!
THE SEA FAVORS THE STRONG! IF YOU WANT TO BABBLE ABOUT JUSTICE, GO DO IT IN THE SAFETY OF THE NAVY HEAD-QUARTERS!
HA HA HA HA...
RAAAAAH
TELL ME !!
HUFF
HUFF...
KLANK...

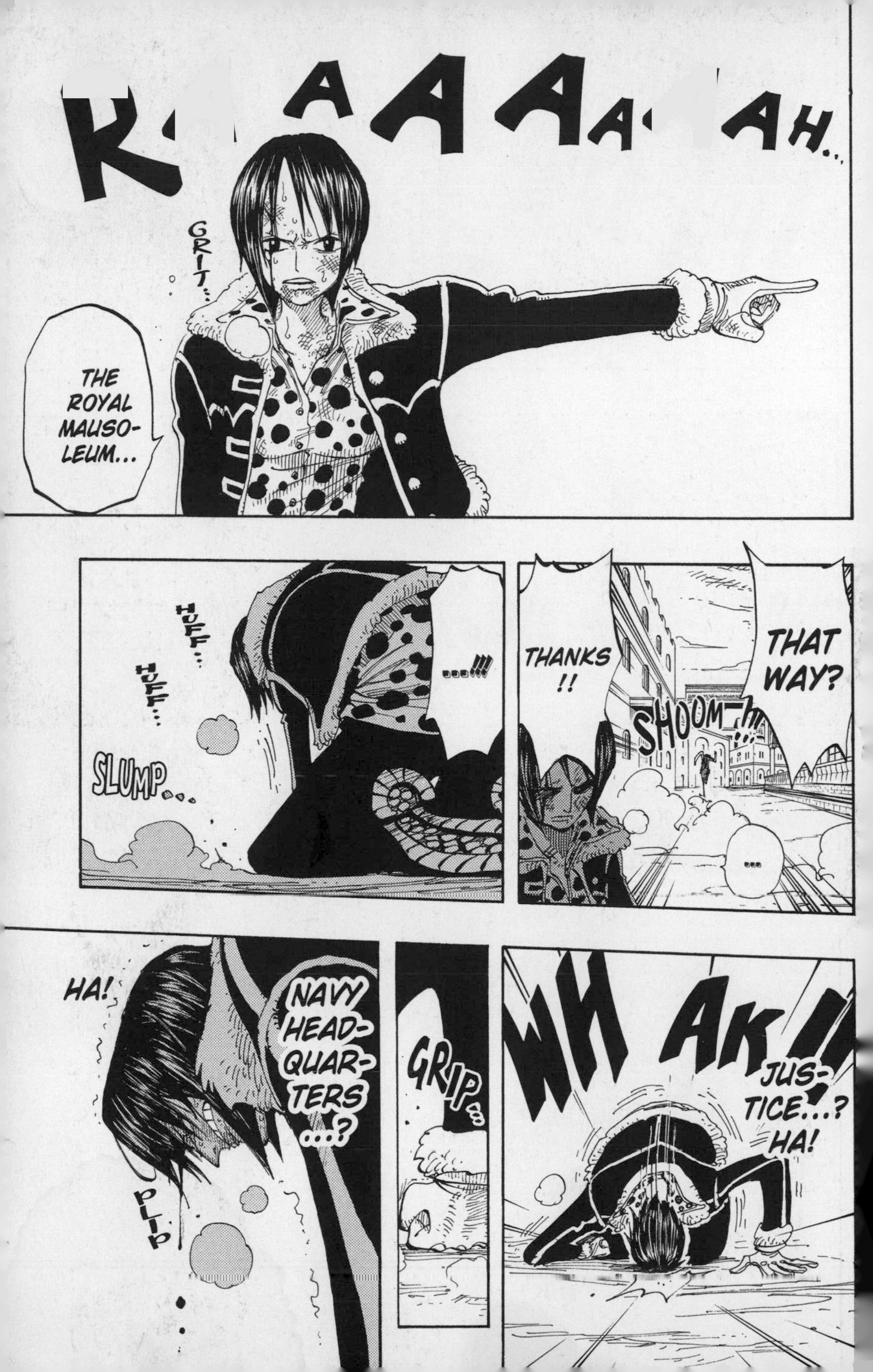

AAAAAH...
GRIT...
THE ROYAL MAUSOLEUM...
THAT WAY?
THANKS!!
SHOOM!!!
...
...!!!
HUFF...
HUFF...
SLUMP...
WHAK!!
JUSTICE...? HA!
GRIP...
NAVY HEADQUARTERS...?
HA!
PLIP

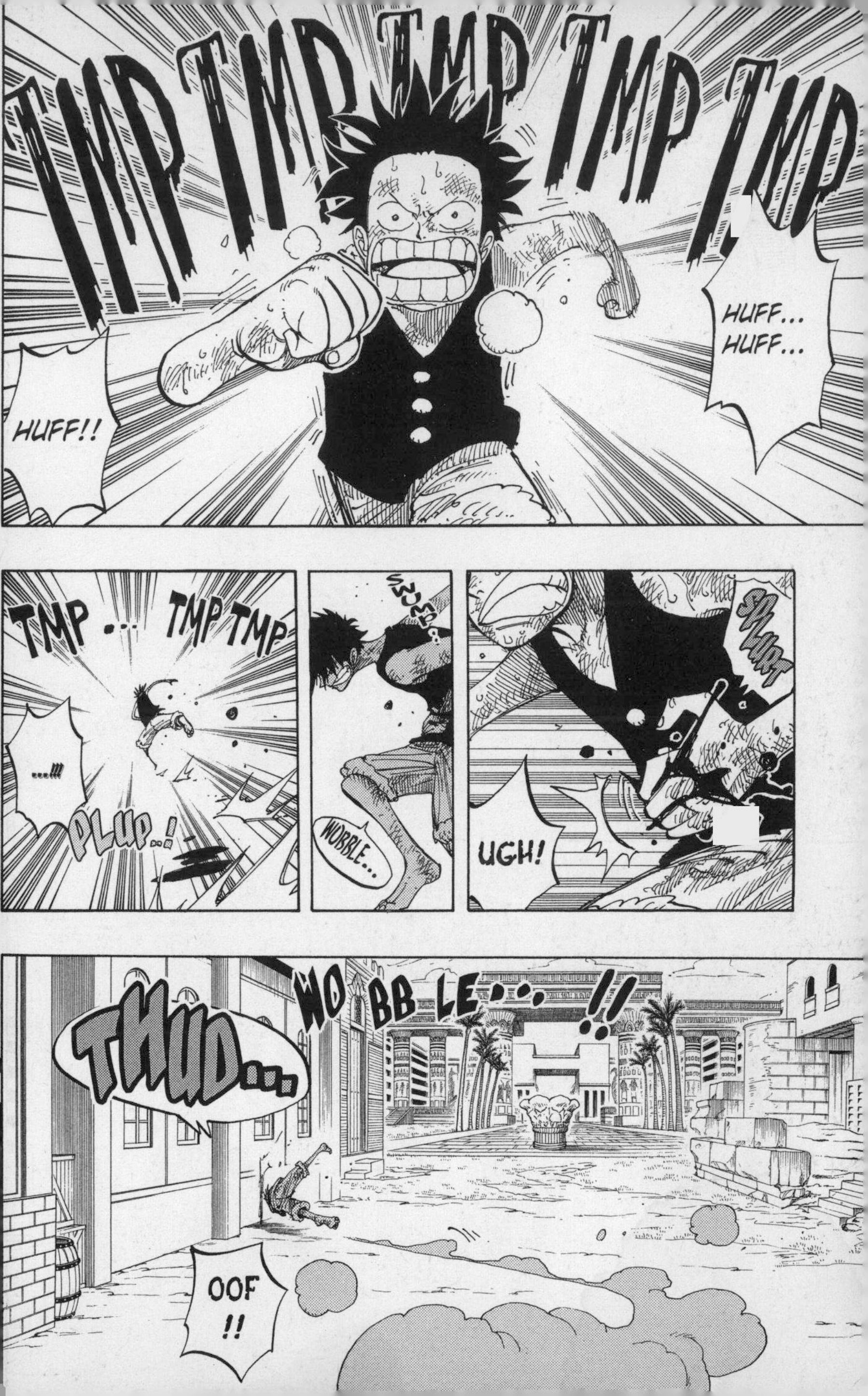
TMP TMP TMP TMP TMP TMP
HUFF... HUFF...
HUFF!!
SPLURT
UGH!
SWUMP..
WOBBLE...
TMP ... TMP TMP
...!!!
PLUP..!
WOBBLE..!!
THUD...
OOF !!

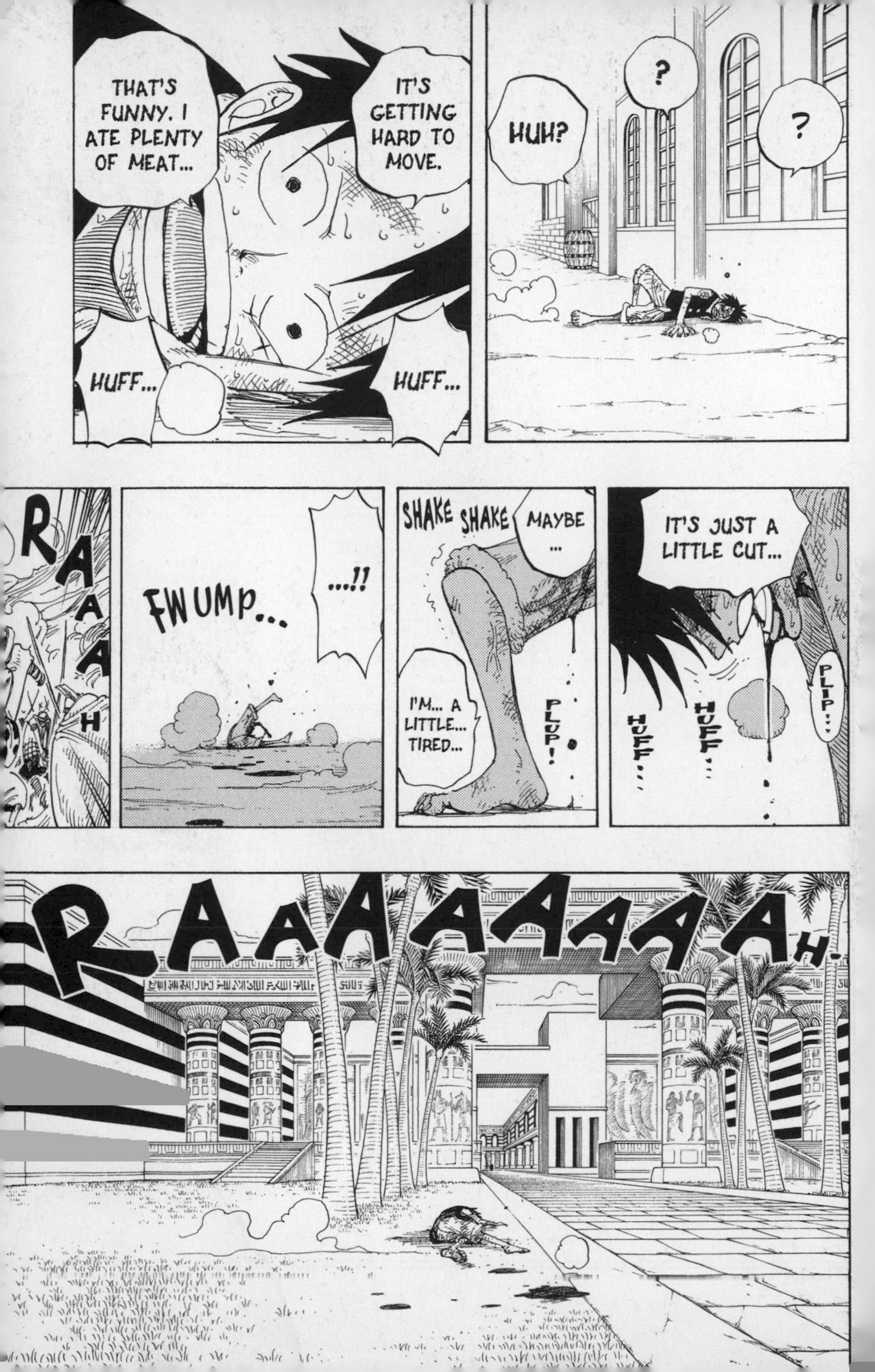
HUH?
?
?
IT'S GETTING HARD TO MOVE.
THAT'S FUNNY. I ATE PLENTY OF MEAT...
HUFF...
HUFF...
IT'S JUST A LITTLE CUT...
PLIP...
HUFF...
HUFF...
MAYBE...
SHAKE
SHAKE
PLUP!
I'M... A LITTLE... TIRED...
...!!
FWUMP...
RAAAH
RAAAAAAAAH

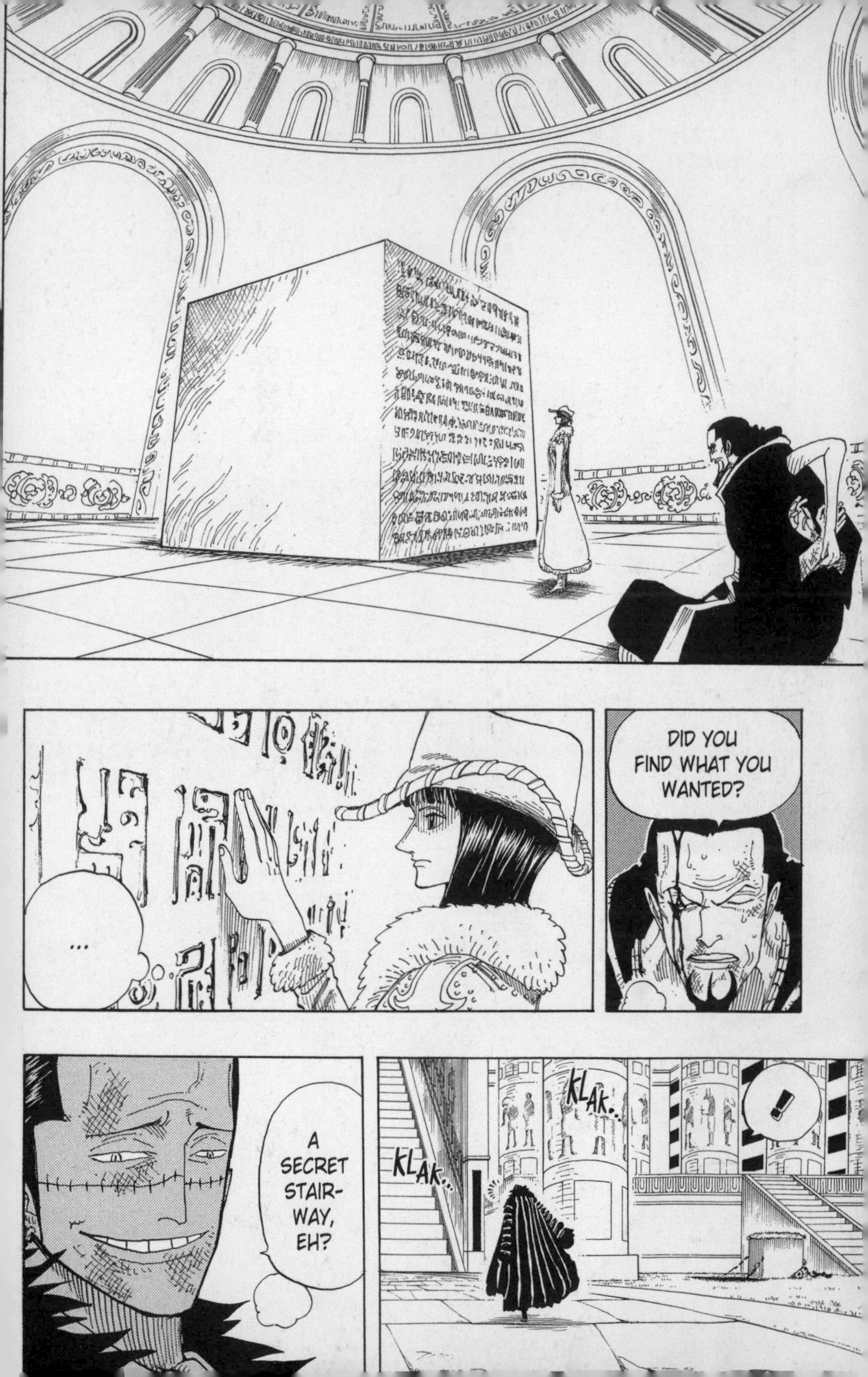
DID YOU FIND WHAT YOU WANTED?
...
!
KLAK...
KLAK...
A SECRET STAIR-WAY, EH?

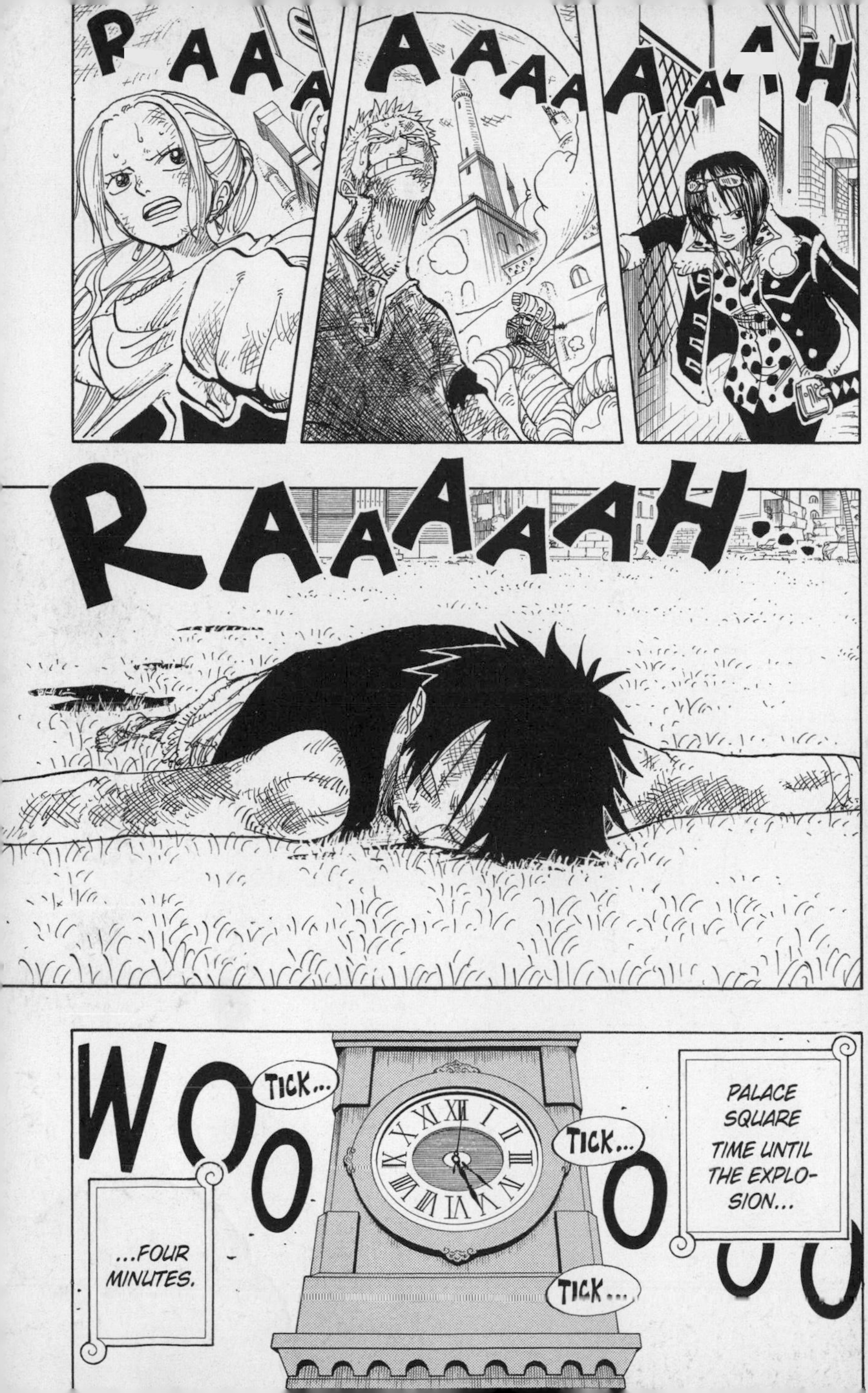
RAAAAAAAAAAAH
RAAAAAH
PALACE SQUARE
TIME UNTIL THE EXPLOSION...
TICK...
TICK...
TICK...
WOOOOOO
...FOUR MINUTES.

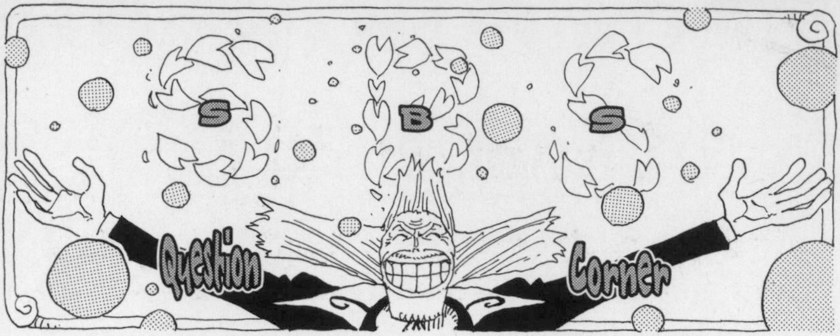
S B S
Question Corner

Reader: Found him! Fo!! Pa!! Pa!! Sa!! Also, Que!! Whe!! Do!! …Ack! (Translation) Panda Man!! It's Panda Man!! I saw Panda Man running away!! (Volume 20, page 60, first panel) Also, I have a question. Where does Panda Man live? Does Panda Man like to travel?

Oda: The last part was a little hard to make out. Are you all right there? Anyway, about Panda Man's residence—rumor has it that he's a very important person (on some islands anyway). Maybe that's why he's being pursued, and therefore needs to be on the run… Sorry, but if I say any more, I'll put myself in danger…
Oh no! It's them!! (Runs away)

Reader: Hello, Oda Sensei. I have a question for you! Because Chopper ate the Rumble Ball, he's able to perform seven transformations, right? But Chopper has already done more than seven. Why is that?

Oda: You're wrong there. There are only seven.

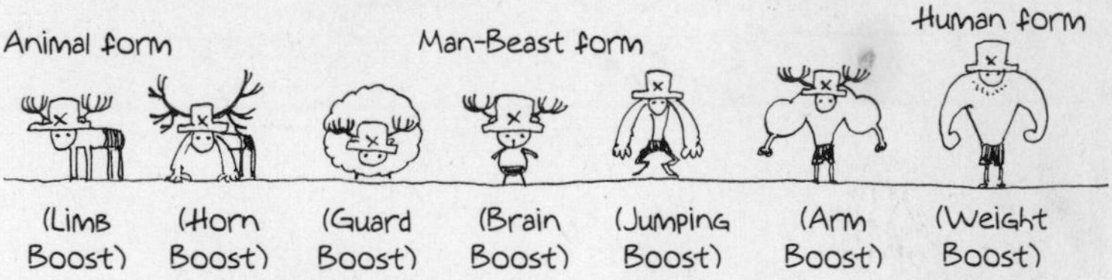
Animal form
Man-Beast form
Human form
(Limb Boost)
(Horn Boost)
(Guard Boost)
(Brain Boost)
(Jumping Boost)
(Arm Boost)
(Weight Boost)

↑ And there are the seven. His usual Animal form is "Limb Boost." His usual Man-Beast form is "Brain Boost," and his Human form is "Weight Boost." So the Rumble Ball allows him to do four transformations in addition to these three. I hope this clears that up.

# Chapter 203:
# CROCODILE-ISH

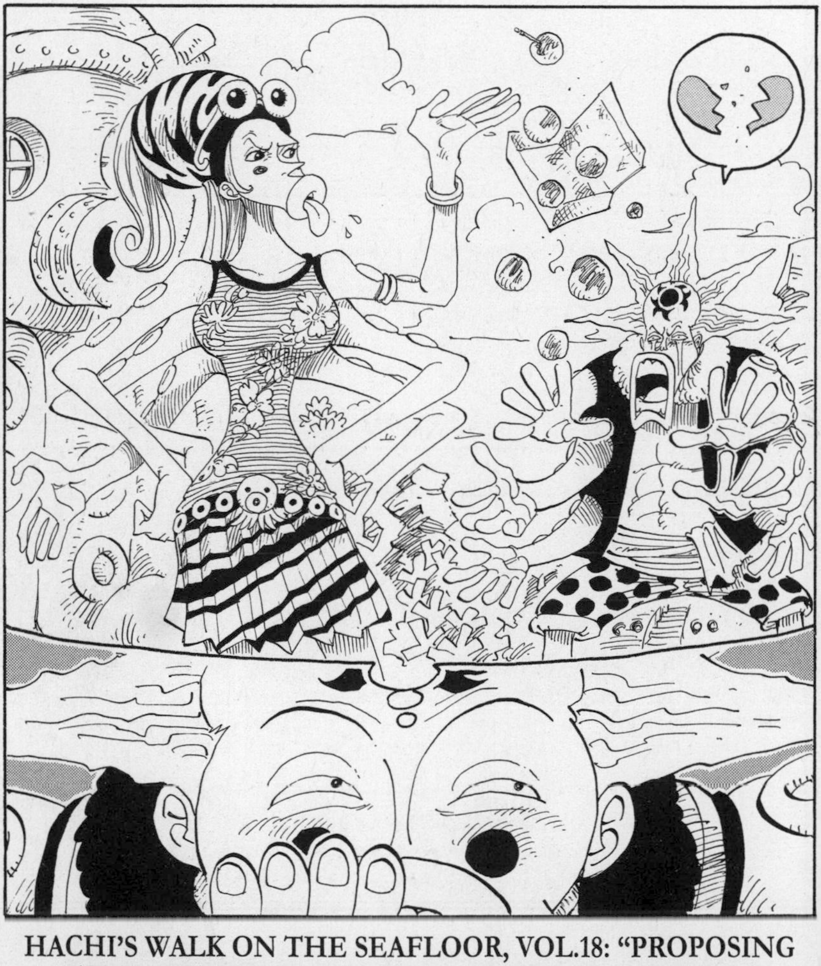

HACHI'S WALK ON THE SEAFLOOR, VOL.18: "PROPOSING TO MY BELOVED OCTOPAKO ONE MORE TIME ♡"

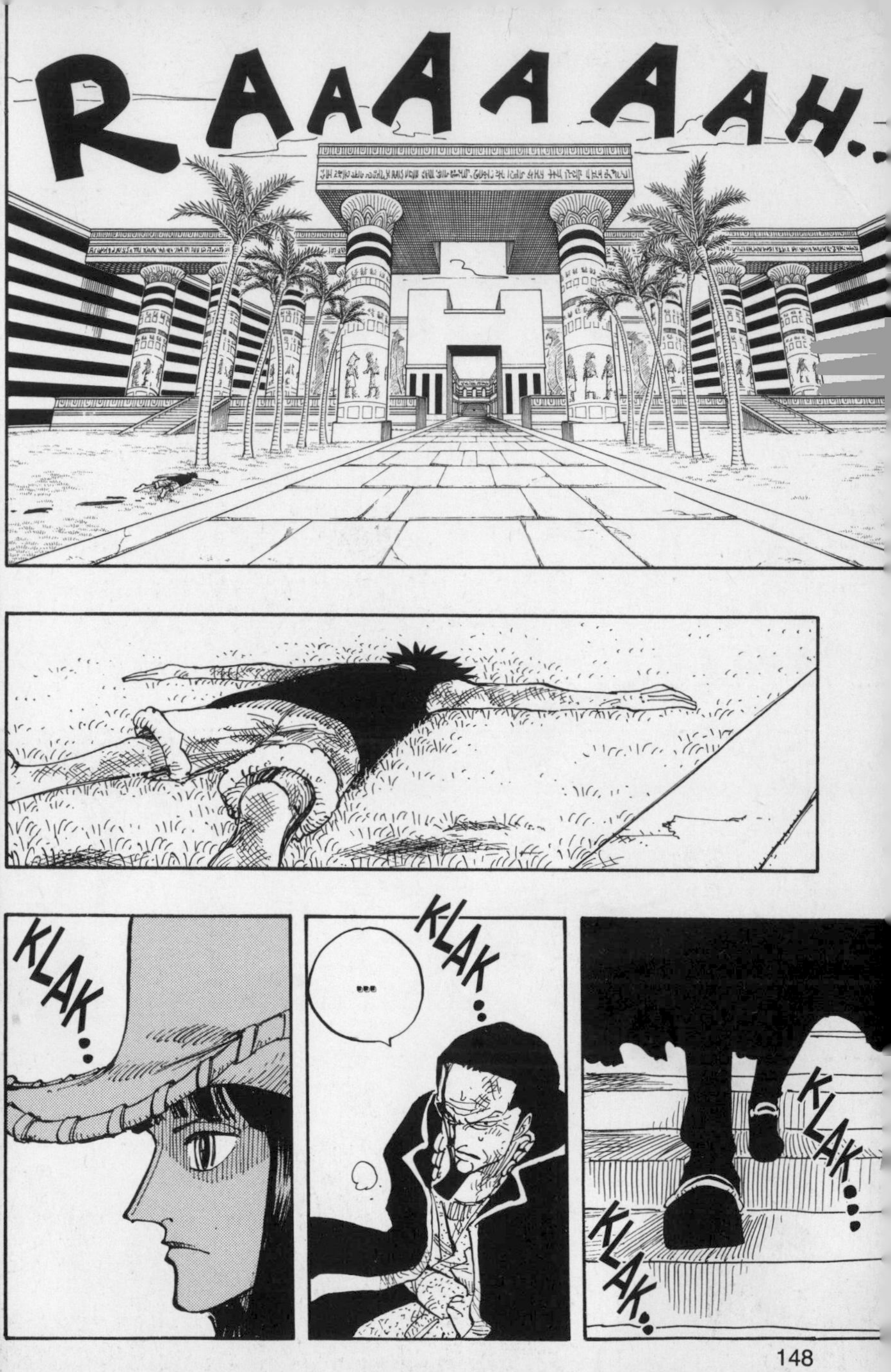
RAAAAAAH...
KLAK...
KLAK...
KLAK...
...
KLAK...

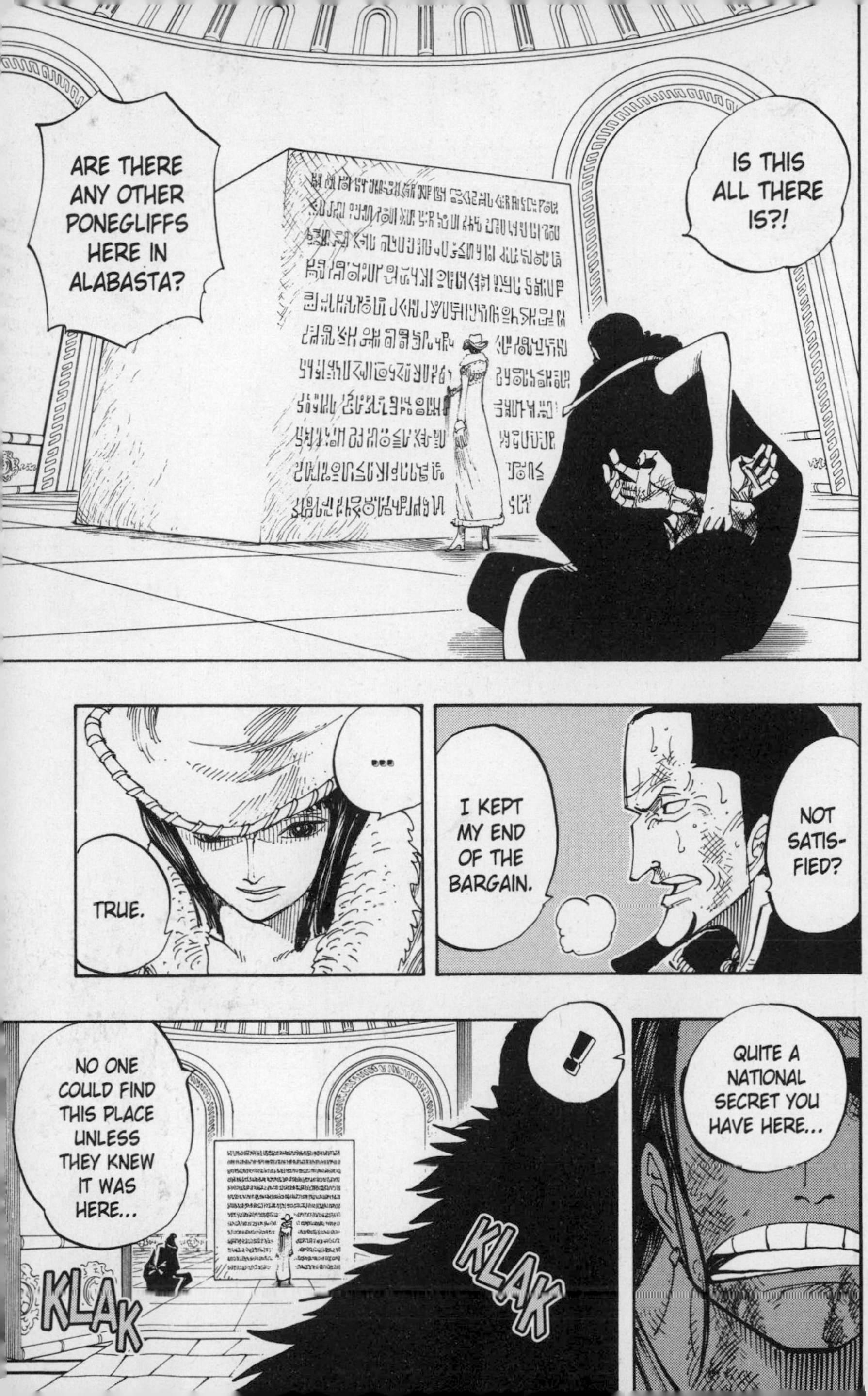
IS THIS ALL THERE IS?!
ARE THERE ANY OTHER PONEGLIFFS HERE IN ALABASTA?
NOT SATIS-FIED?
I KEPT MY END OF THE BARGAIN.
...
TRUE.
QUITE A NATIONAL SECRET YOU HAVE HERE...
!
NO ONE COULD FIND THIS PLACE UNLESS THEY KNEW IT WAS HERE...
KLAK
KLAK

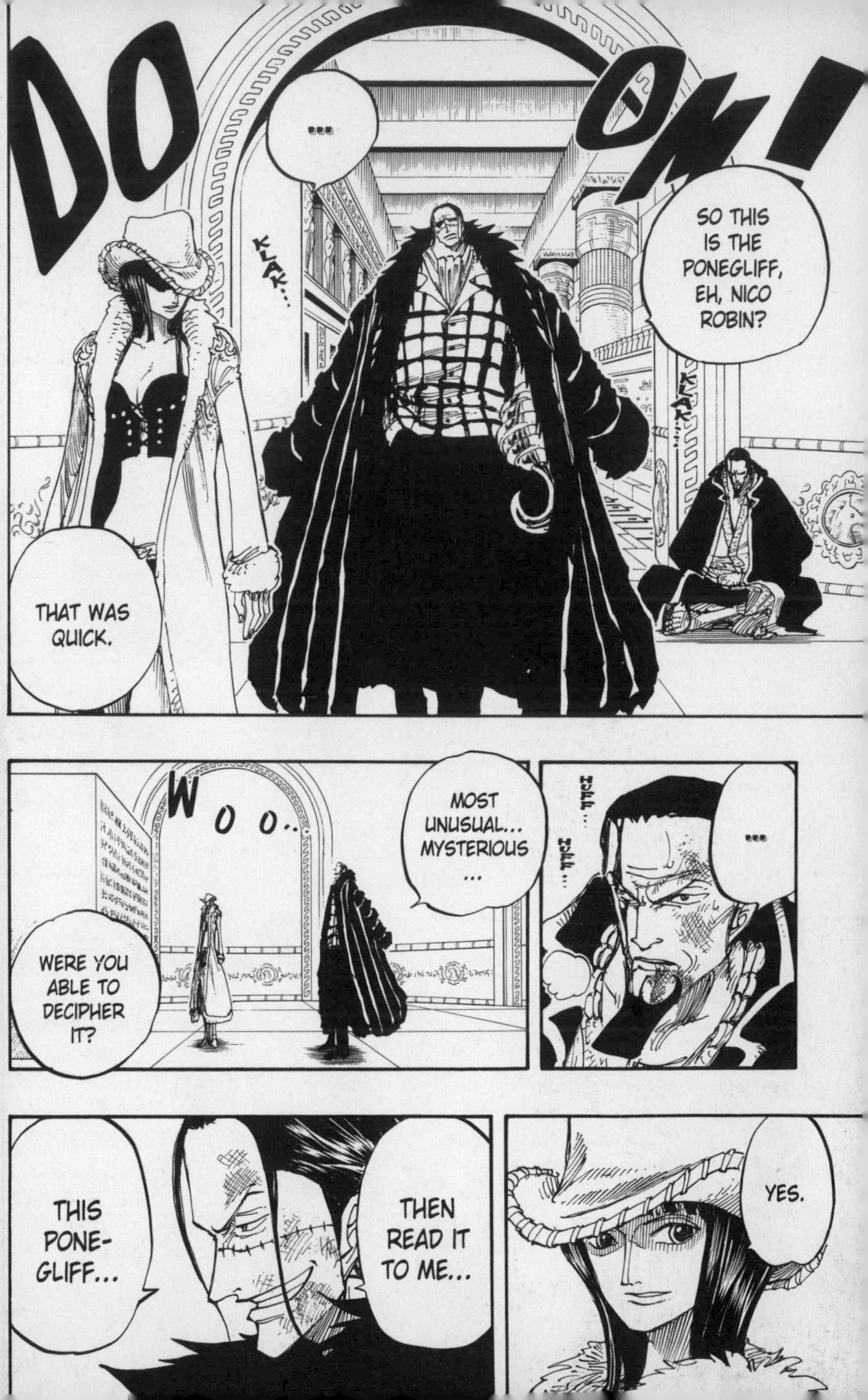
DO OM!
SO THIS IS THE PONEGLIFF, EH, NICO ROBIN?
KLAK...
KLAK...
...
THAT WAS QUICK.
HUFF... HUFF...
...
MOST UNUSUAL... MYSTERIOUS ...
WOO..
WERE YOU ABLE TO DECIPHER IT?
YES.
THIS PONE-GLIFF...
THEN READ IT TO ME...

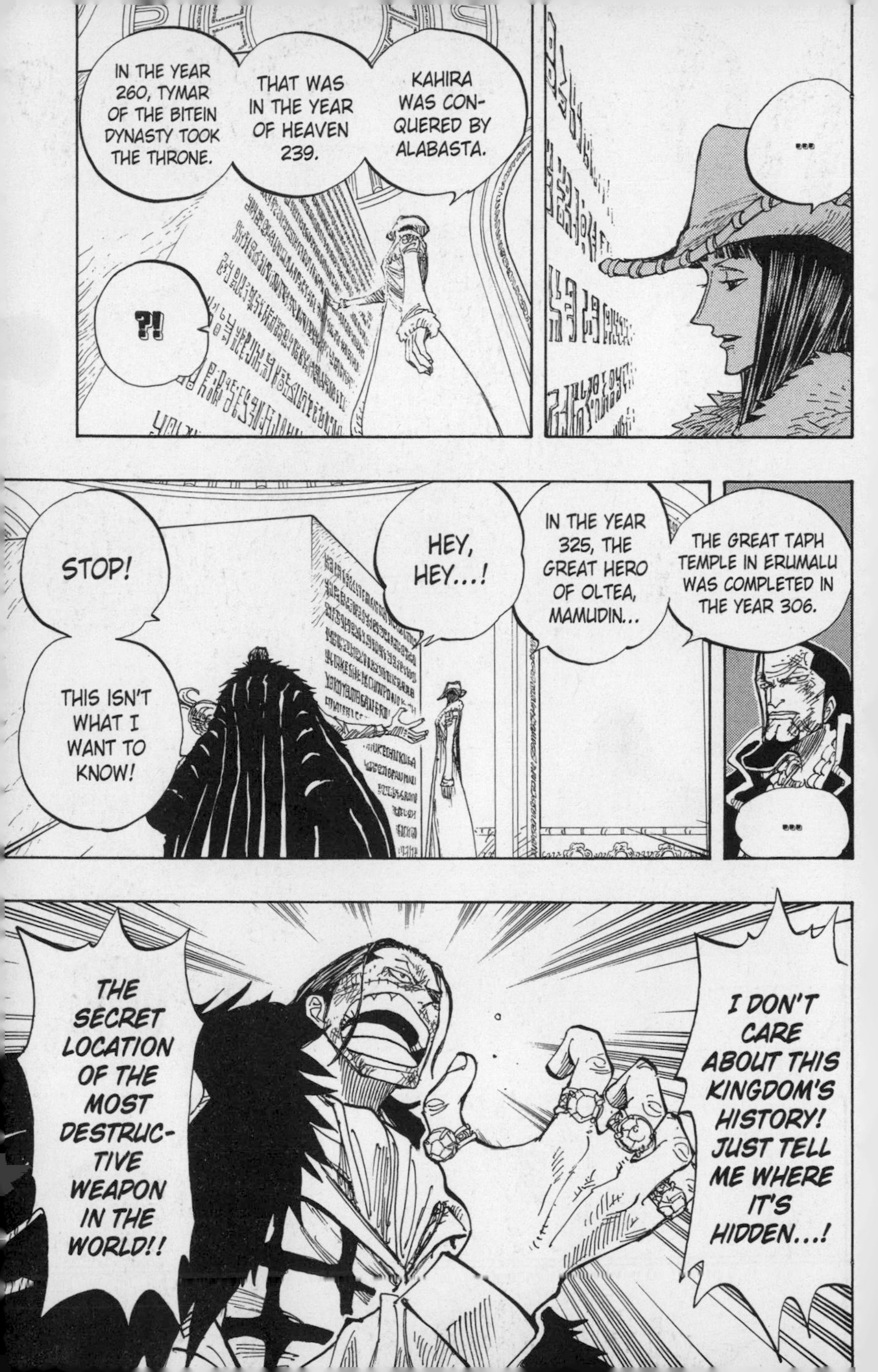
...
KAHIRA WAS CONQUERED BY ALABASTA.
THAT WAS IN THE YEAR OF HEAVEN 239.
IN THE YEAR 260, TYMAR OF THE BITEIN DYNASTY TOOK THE THRONE.
?!
...
THE GREAT TAPH TEMPLE IN ERUMALU WAS COMPLETED IN THE YEAR 306.
IN THE YEAR 325, THE GREAT HERO OF OLTEA, MAMUDIN...
HEY, HEY...!
STOP!
THIS ISN'T WHAT I WANT TO KNOW!
I DON'T CARE ABOUT THIS KINGDOM'S HISTORY! JUST TELL ME WHERE IT'S HIDDEN...!
THE SECRET LOCATION OF THE MOST DESTRUCTIVE WEAPON IN THE WORLD!!

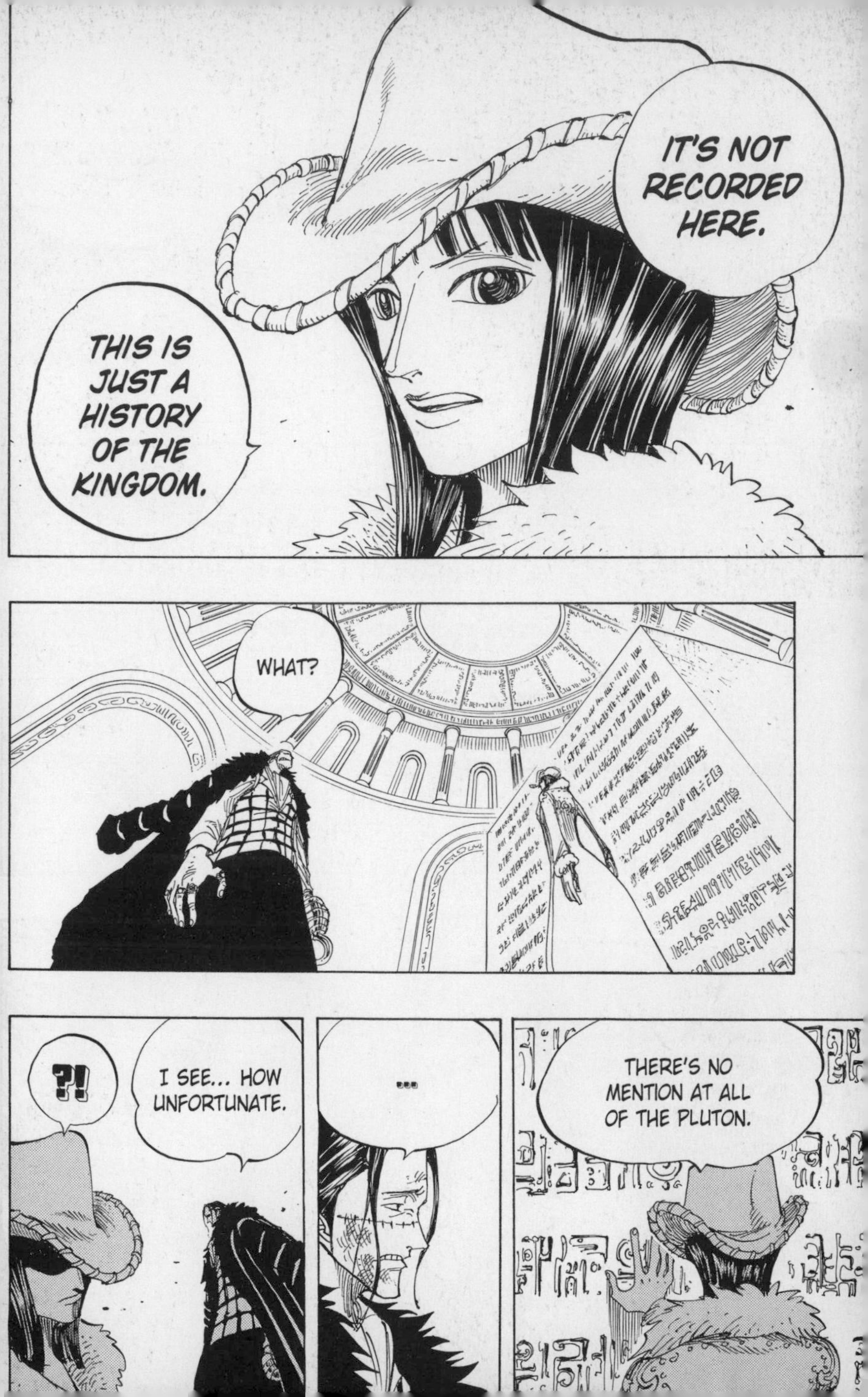
IT'S NOT RECORDED HERE.
THIS IS JUST A HISTORY OF THE KINGDOM.
WHAT?
THERE'S NO MENTION AT ALL OF THE PLUTON.
...
I SEE... HOW UNFORTUNATE.
?!

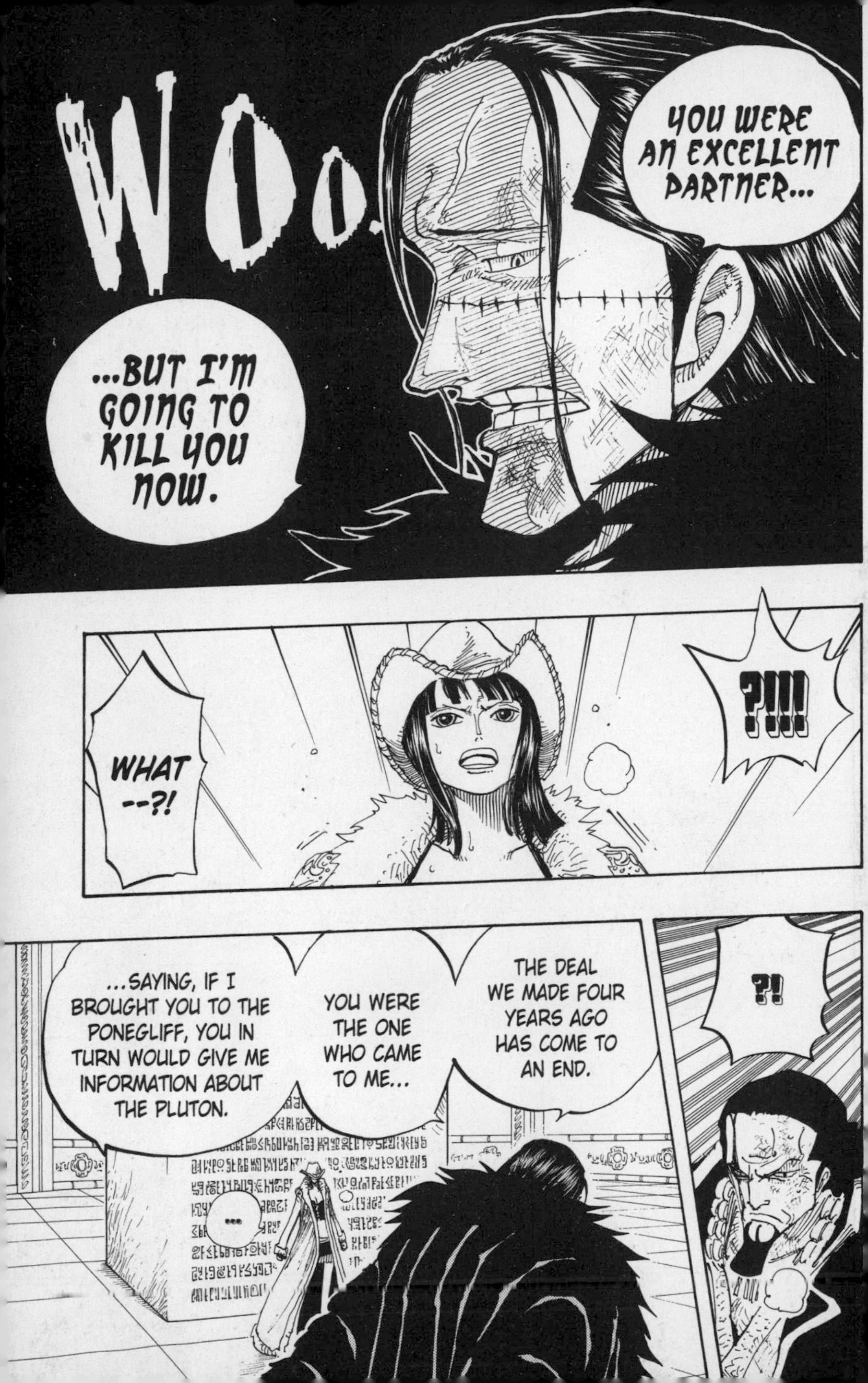
YOU WERE AN EXCELLENT PARTNER...
WOO.
...BUT I'M GOING TO KILL YOU NOW.
?!!!
WHAT --?!
?!
THE DEAL WE MADE FOUR YEARS AGO HAS COME TO AN END.
YOU WERE THE ONE WHO CAME TO ME...
...SAYING, IF I BROUGHT YOU TO THE PONEGLIFF, YOU IN TURN WOULD GIVE ME INFORMATION ABOUT THE PLUTON.
...

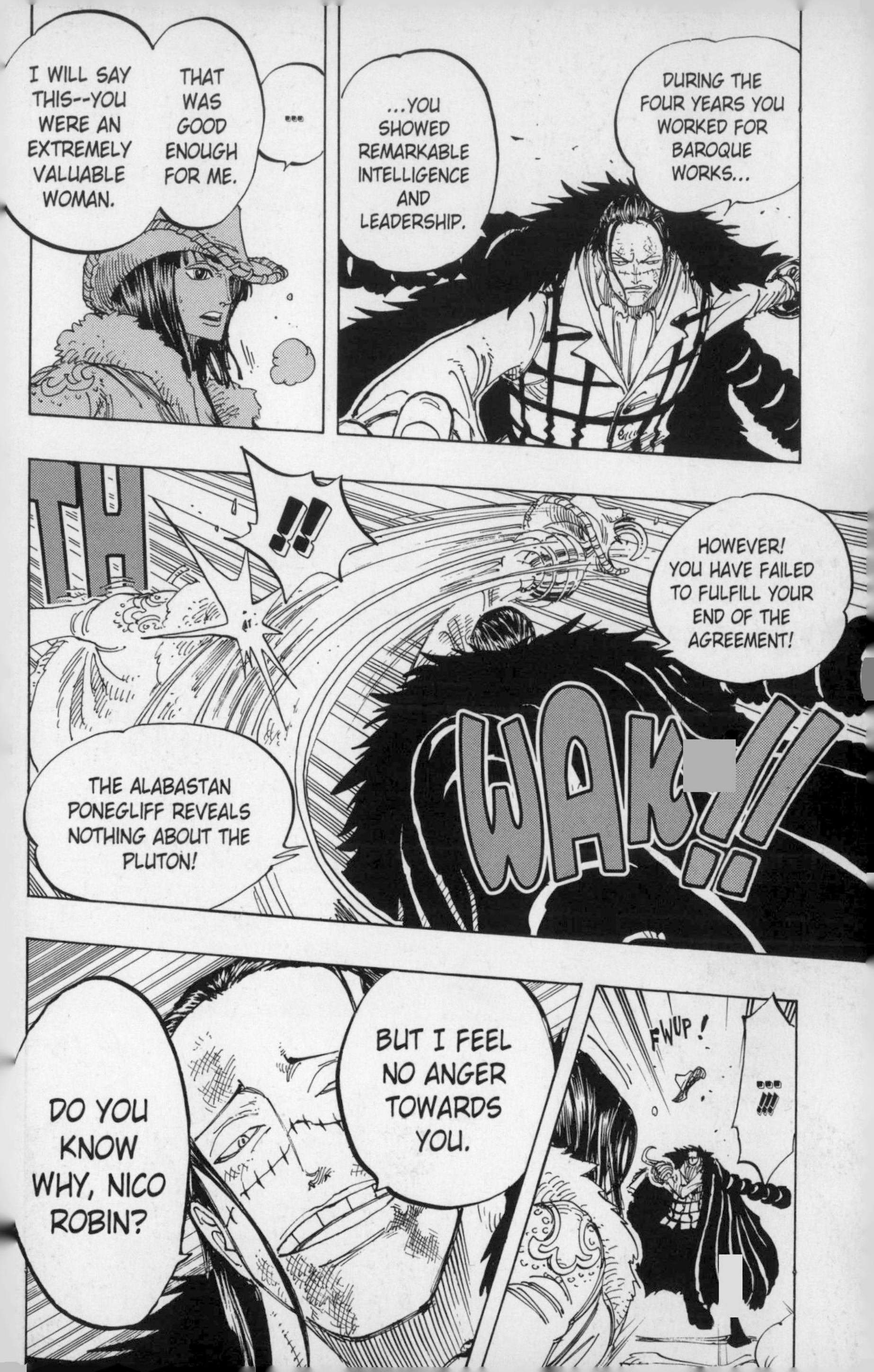
DURING THE FOUR YEARS YOU WORKED FOR BAROQUE WORKS...
...YOU SHOWED REMARKABLE INTELLIGENCE AND LEADERSHIP.
...
THAT WAS GOOD ENOUGH FOR ME.
I WILL SAY THIS--YOU WERE AN EXTREMELY VALUABLE WOMAN.
HOWEVER! YOU HAVE FAILED TO FULFILL YOUR END OF THE AGREEMENT!
!!
TH
WAK!!
THE ALABASTAN PONEGLIFF REVEALS NOTHING ABOUT THE PLUTON!
FWUP!
...!!!
BUT I FEEL NO ANGER TOWARDS YOU.
DO YOU KNOW WHY, NICO ROBIN?

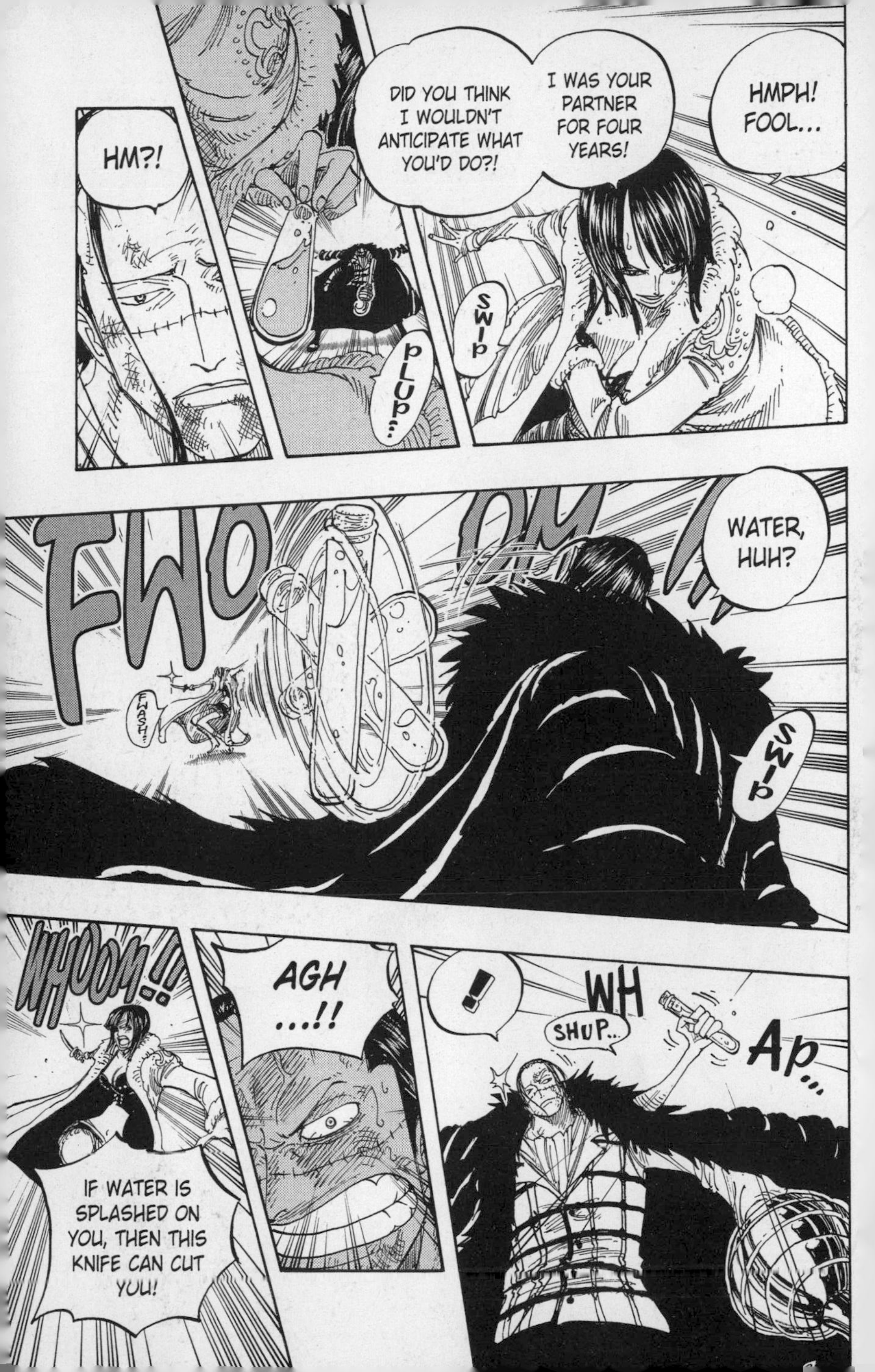
HMPH! FOOL...
I WAS YOUR PARTNER FOR FOUR YEARS!
DID YOU THINK I WOULDN'T ANTICIPATE WHAT YOU'D DO?!
SWIP
PLUP..
HM?!
WATER, HUH?
SWIP
FWO
OM
FWASH!
!
WH
SHUP...
Ap...
AGH ...!!
WHOOM!!
IF WATER IS SPLASHED ON YOU, THEN THIS KNIFE CAN CUT YOU!

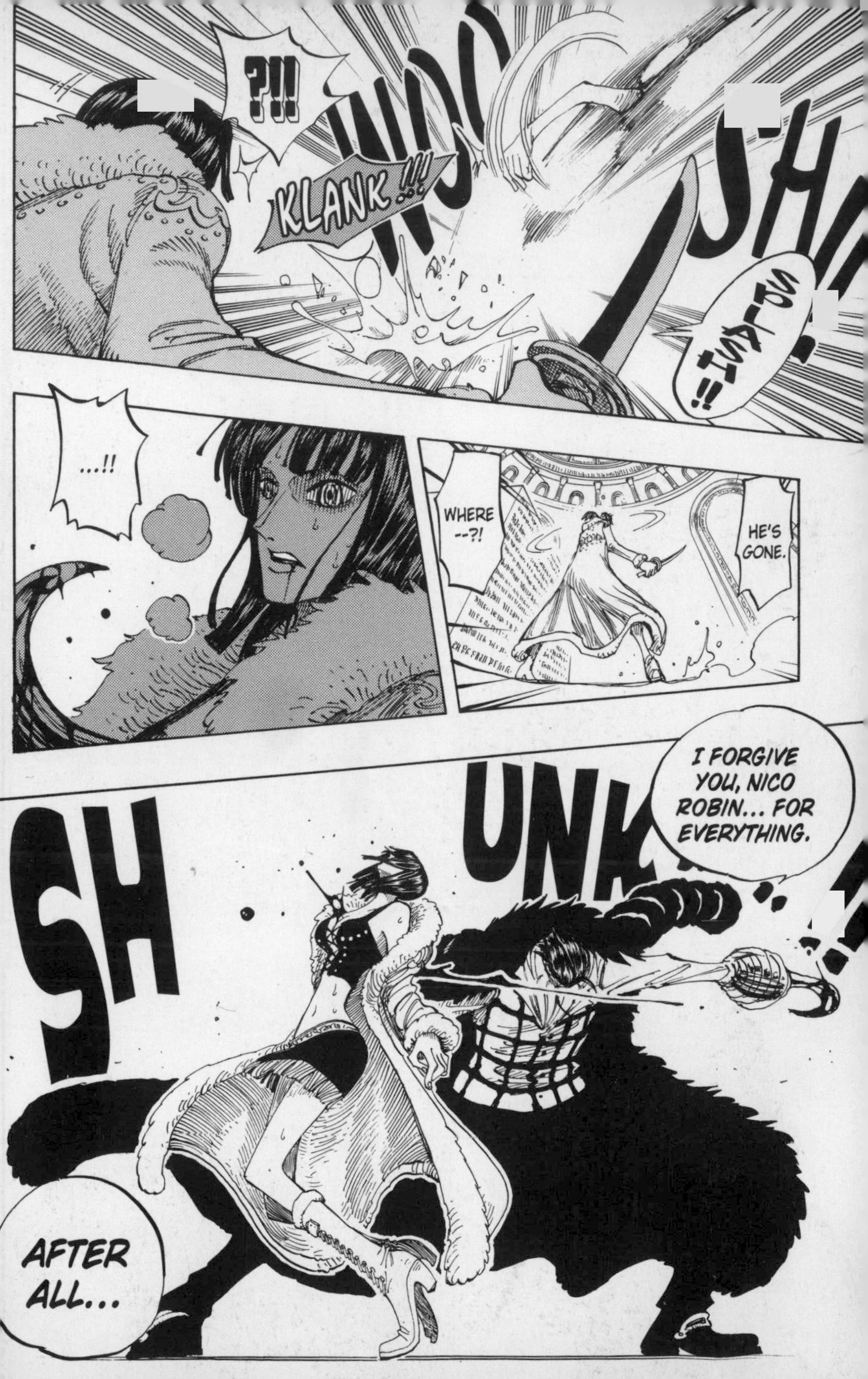
SPLASH!!
KLANK!!!
?!!
HE'S GONE.
WHERE --?!
...!!
I FORGIVE YOU, NICO ROBIN... FOR EVERYTHING.
SH
AFTER ALL...

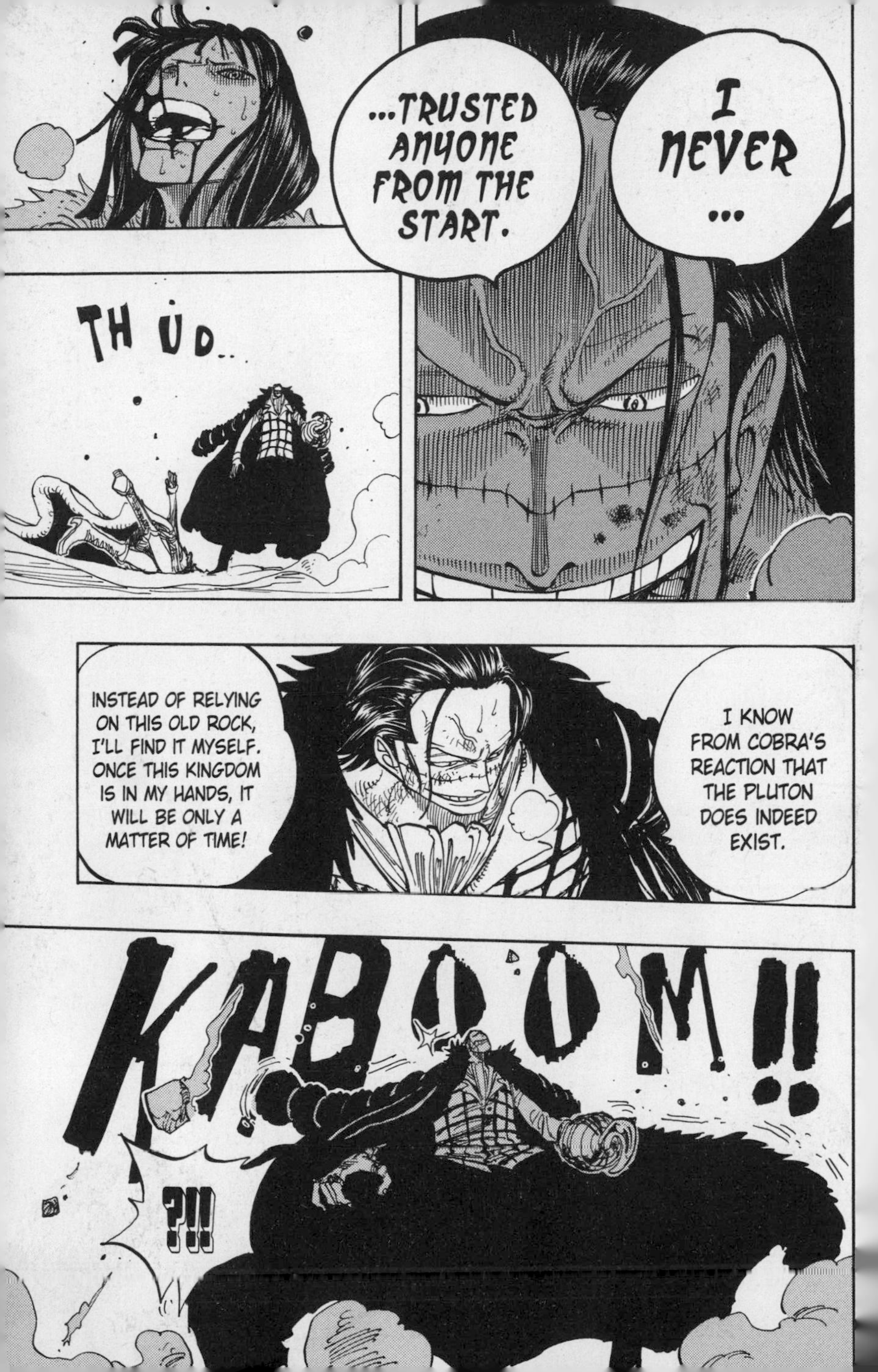
I NEVER ...
...TRUSTED ANYONE FROM THE START.
THUD..
I KNOW FROM COBRA'S REACTION THAT THE PLUTON DOES INDEED EXIST.
INSTEAD OF RELYING ON THIS OLD ROCK, I'LL FIND IT MYSELF. ONCE THIS KINGDOM IS IN MY HANDS, IT WILL BE ONLY A MATTER OF TIME!
KABOOM!!
?!!

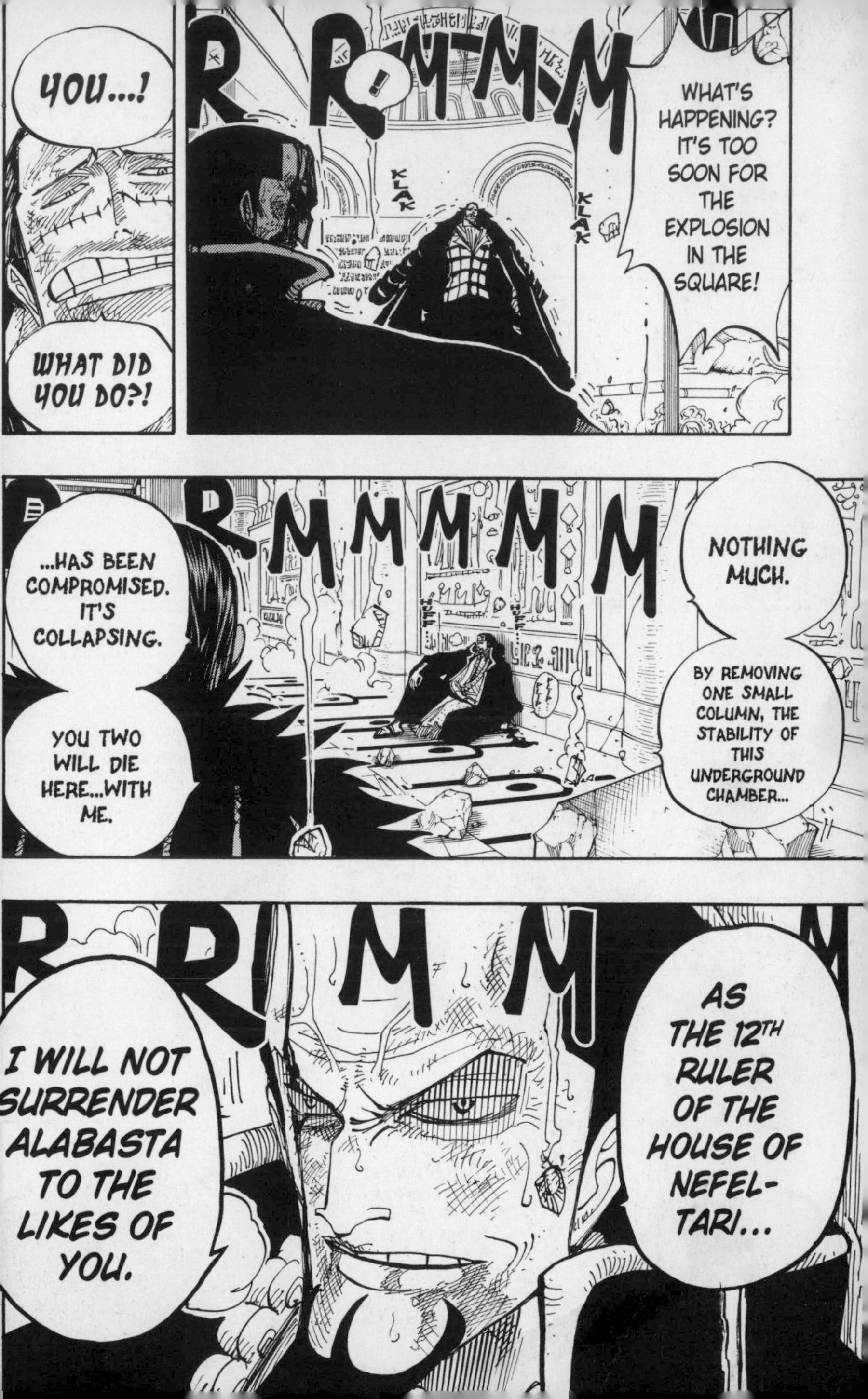
RRMMM
KLAK
KLAK
WHAT'S HAPPENING? IT'S TOO SOON FOR THE EXPLOSION IN THE SQUARE!
YOU...!
WHAT DID YOU DO?!
RRMMMMM
NOTHING MUCH.
BY REMOVING ONE SMALL COLUMN, THE STABILITY OF THIS UNDERGROUND CHAMBER...
HUFF
HUFF
...HAS BEEN COMPROMISED. IT'S COLLAPSING.
YOU TWO WILL DIE HERE...WITH ME.
RRMM
AS THE 12TH RULER OF THE HOUSE OF NEFEL-TARI...
I WILL NOT SURRENDER ALABASTA TO THE LIKES OF YOU.

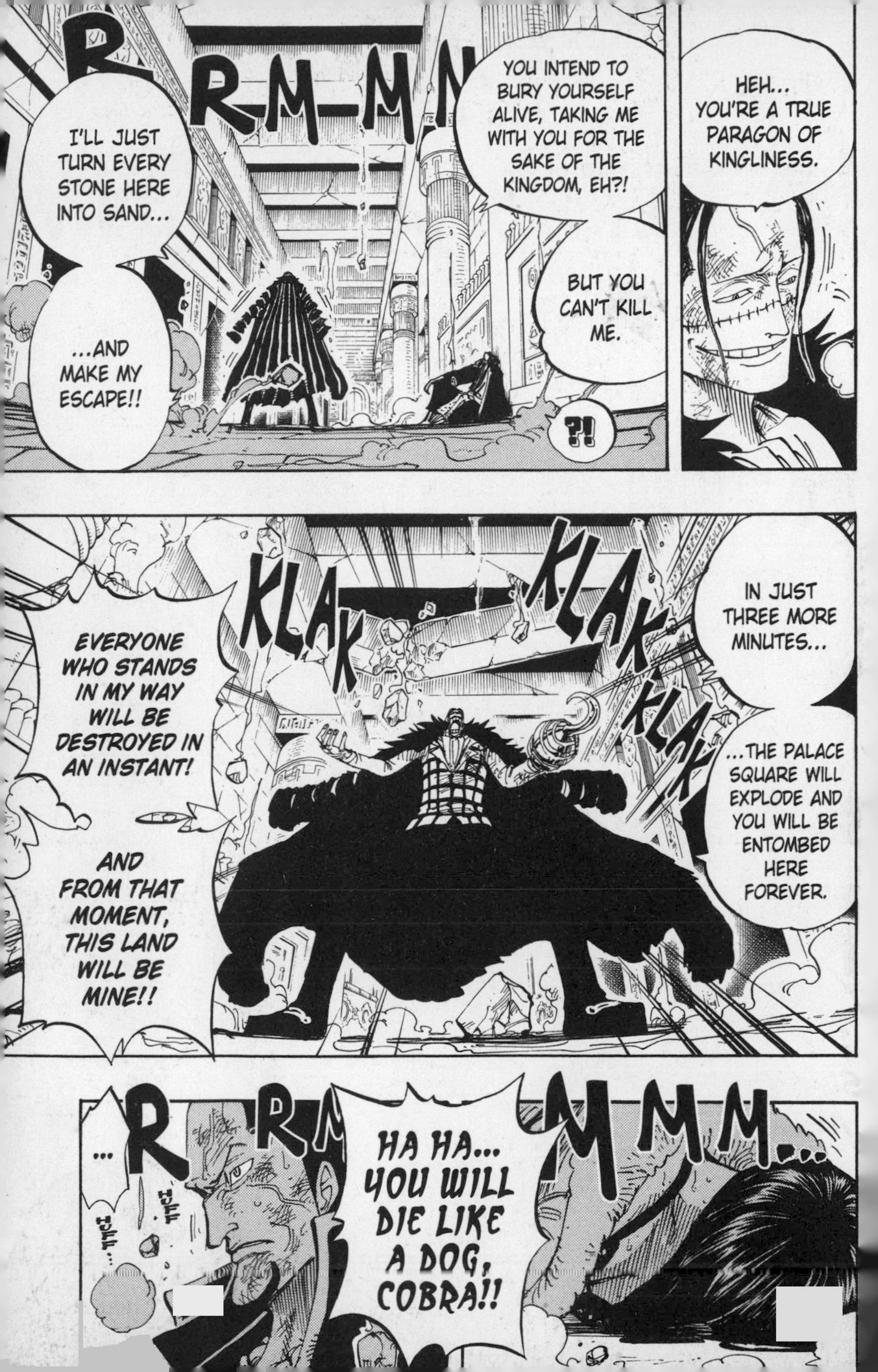
HEH... YOU'RE A TRUE PARAGON OF KINGLINESS.
YOU INTEND TO BURY YOURSELF ALIVE, TAKING ME WITH YOU FOR THE SAKE OF THE KINGDOM, EH?!
RRMMMN
BUT YOU CAN'T KILL ME.
?!
I'LL JUST TURN EVERY STONE HERE INTO SAND...
...AND MAKE MY ESCAPE!!
IN JUST THREE MORE MINUTES...
...THE PALACE SQUARE WILL EXPLODE AND YOU WILL BE ENTOMBED HERE FOREVER.
KLAK KLAK KLAK
KLAK
EVERYONE WHO STANDS IN MY WAY WILL BE DESTROYED IN AN INSTANT!
AND FROM THAT MOMENT, THIS LAND WILL BE MINE!!
RRRMMMM...
HA HA... YOU WILL DIE LIKE A DOG, COBRA!!
HUFF
HUFF...
...

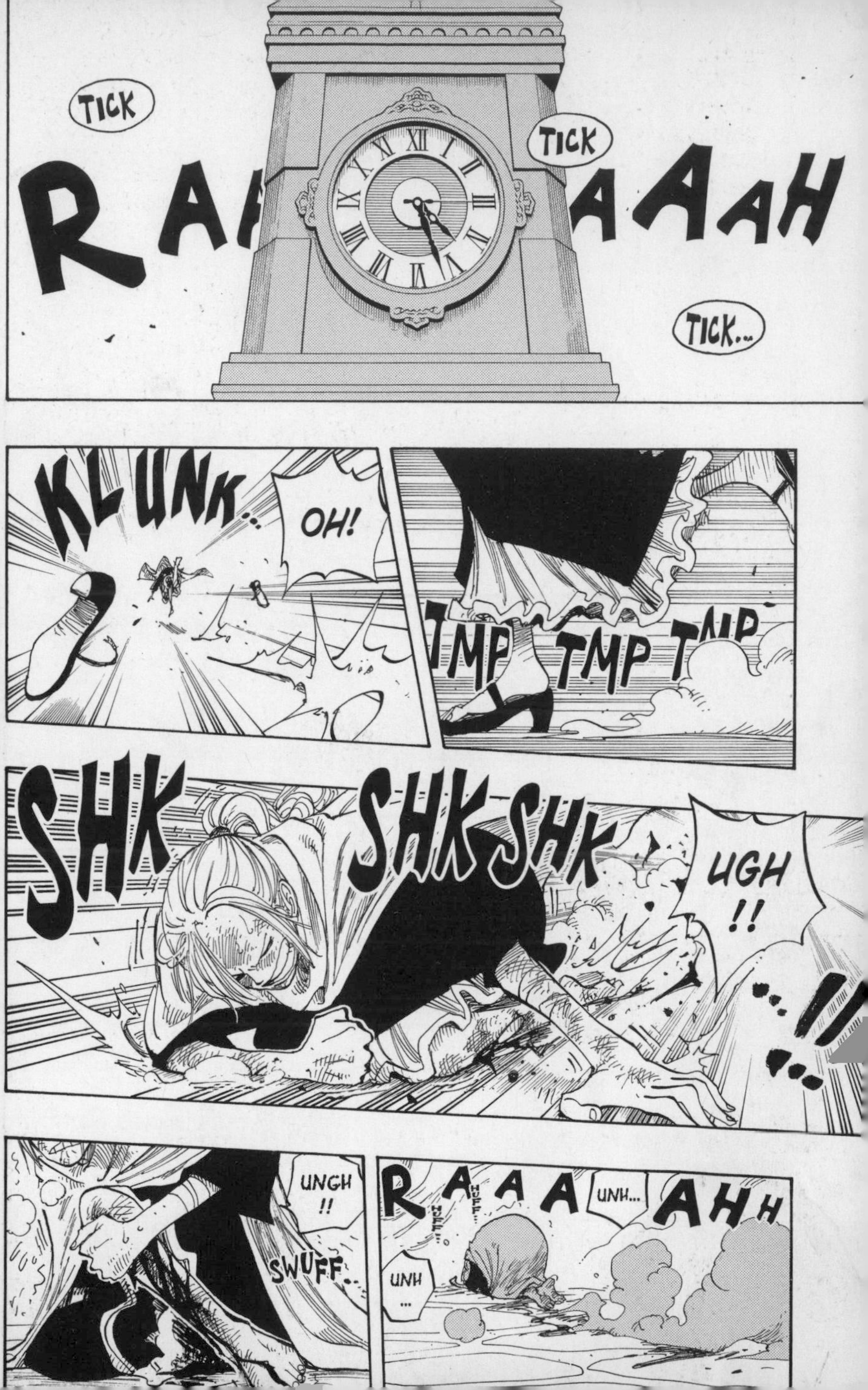

TICK
RAAAAAH
TICK
TICK...
TMP TMP TMP
KLUNK..
OH!
UGH!!
SHK SHK SHK
...!!...
RAAAAHH
UNH...
HUFF HUFF...
UNH...
UNGH!!
SWUFF...

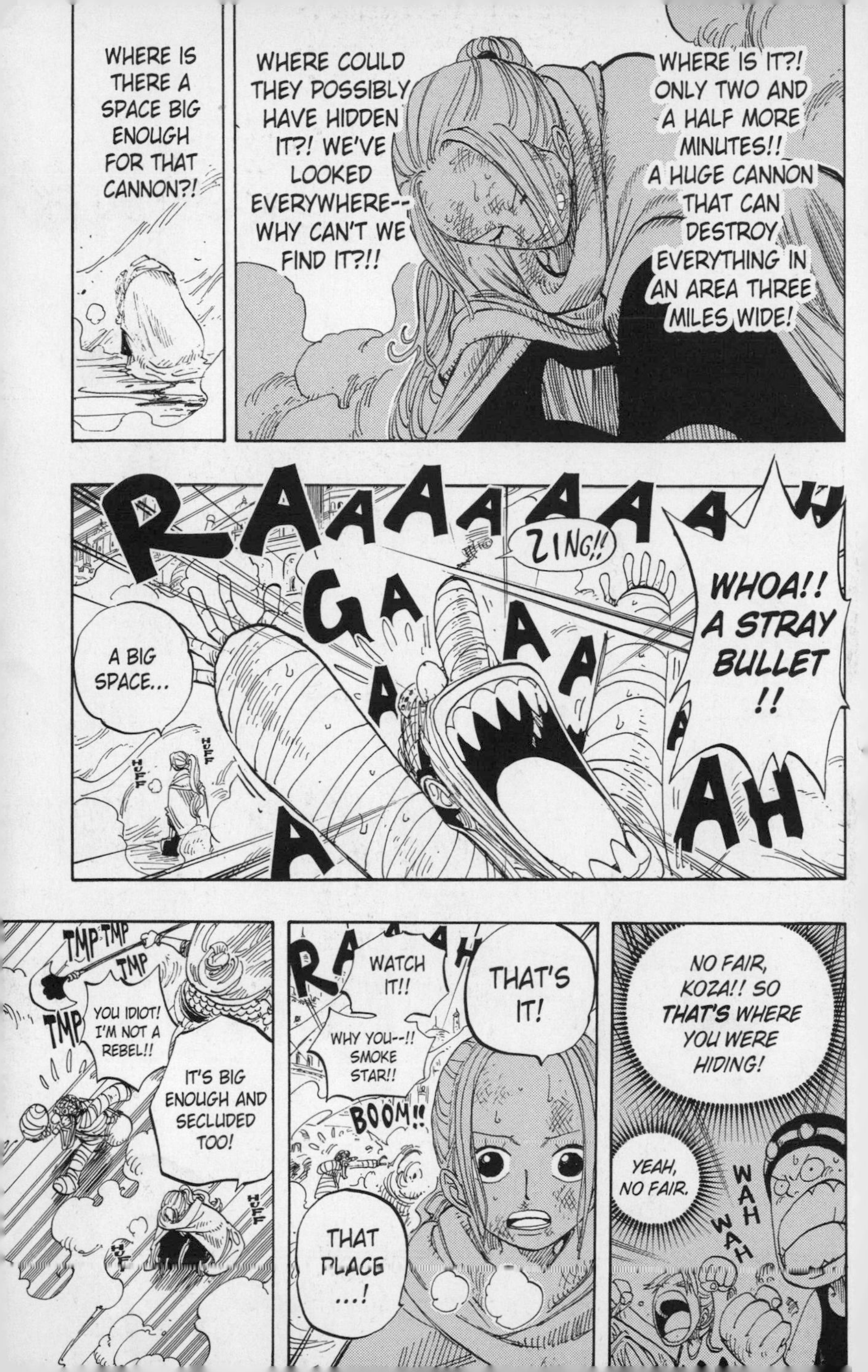
WHERE IS IT?! ONLY TWO AND A HALF MORE MINUTES!! A HUGE CANNON THAT CAN DESTROY EVERYTHING IN AN AREA THREE MILES WIDE!
WHERE COULD THEY POSSIBLY HAVE HIDDEN IT?! WE'VE LOOKED EVERYWHERE-- WHY CAN'T WE FIND IT?!!
WHERE IS THERE A SPACE BIG ENOUGH FOR THAT CANNON?!
RAAAAAAW
GAAAAAAAAH
ZING!!
WHOA!! A STRAY BULLET!!
A BIG SPACE...
HUFF HUFF
NO FAIR, KOZA!! SO THAT'S WHERE YOU WERE HIDING!
YEAH, NO FAIR.
WAH WAH WAH
THAT'S IT!
WATCH IT!!
WHY YOU--!! SMOKE STAR!!
BOOM!!
THAT PLACE ...!
TMP TMP TMP TMP
YOU IDIOT! I'M NOT A REBEL!!
IT'S BIG ENOUGH AND SECLUDED TOO!
HUFF HUFF

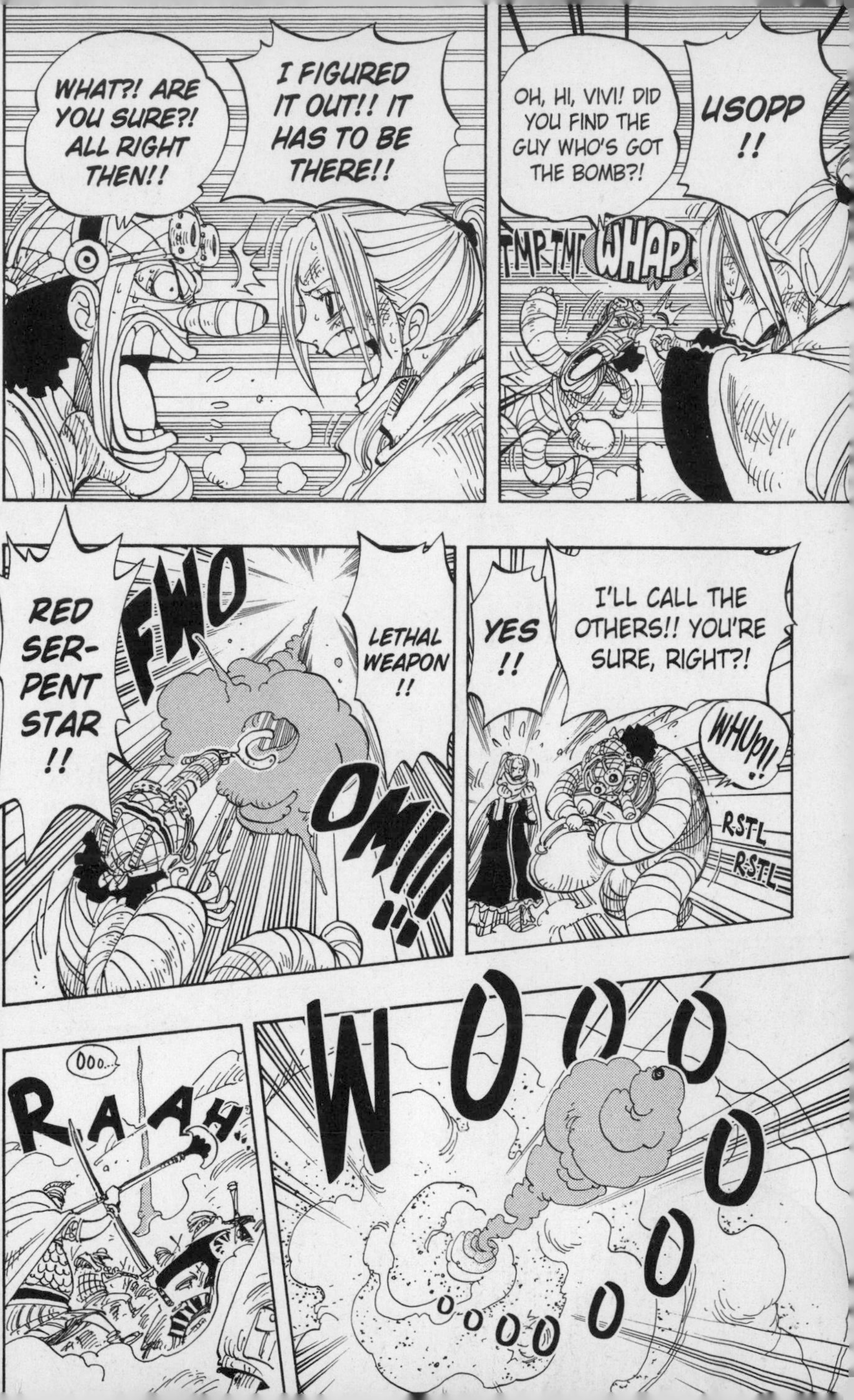
USOPP !!
OH, HI, VIVI! DID YOU FIND THE GUY WHO'S GOT THE BOMB?!
TMP TMP
WHAP!
I FIGURED IT OUT!! IT HAS TO BE THERE!!
WHAT?! ARE YOU SURE?! ALL RIGHT THEN!!
I'LL CALL THE OTHERS!! YOU'RE SURE, RIGHT?!
YES !!
WHUP!!
R-S-T-L
R-S-T-L
LETHAL WEAPON !!
FWO
OM!!!!
RED SER-PENT STAR !!
WOOOOOOOOOOOOO
Ooo...
RAAH.

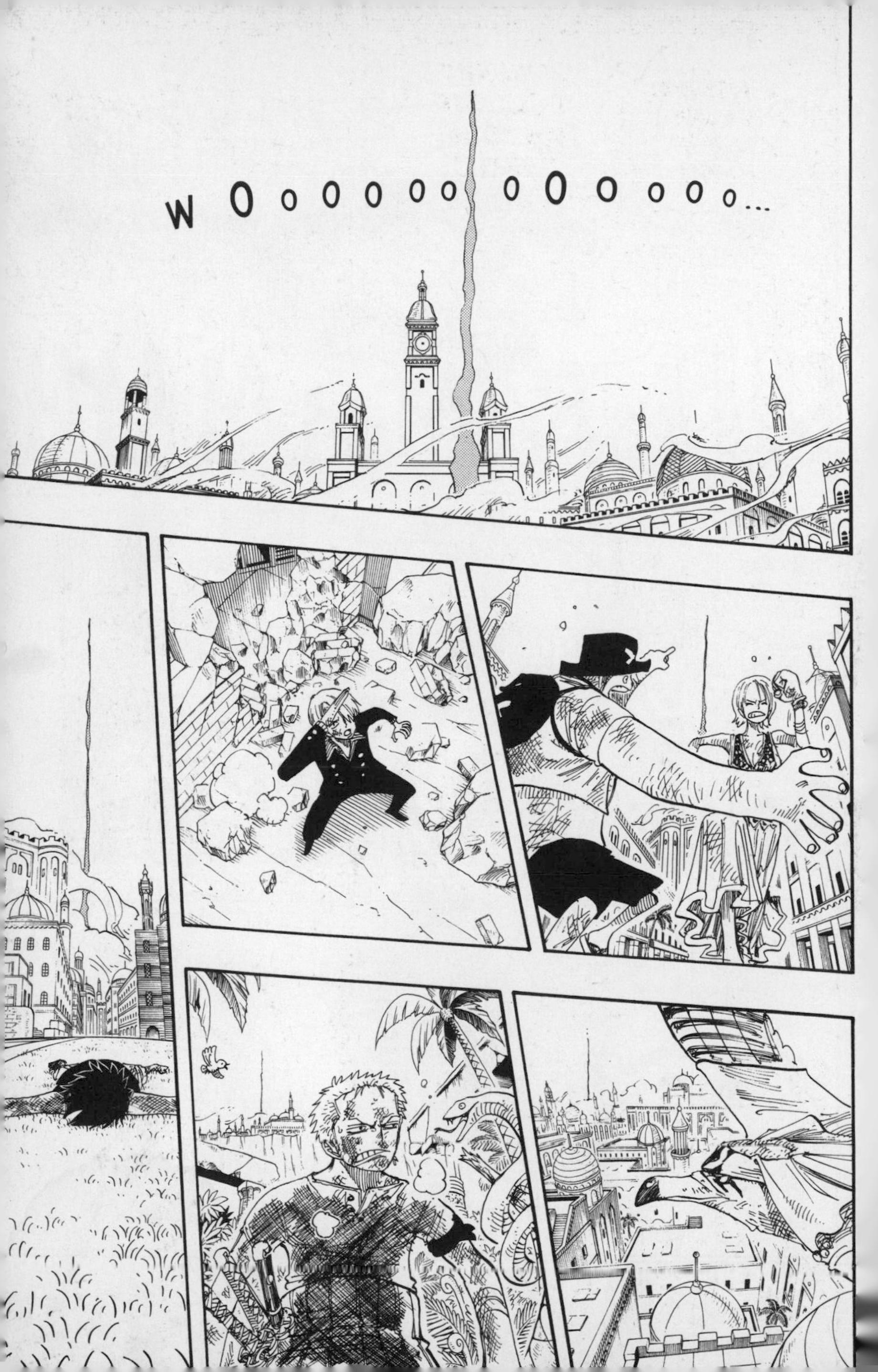
WOoooooo oOoooo...

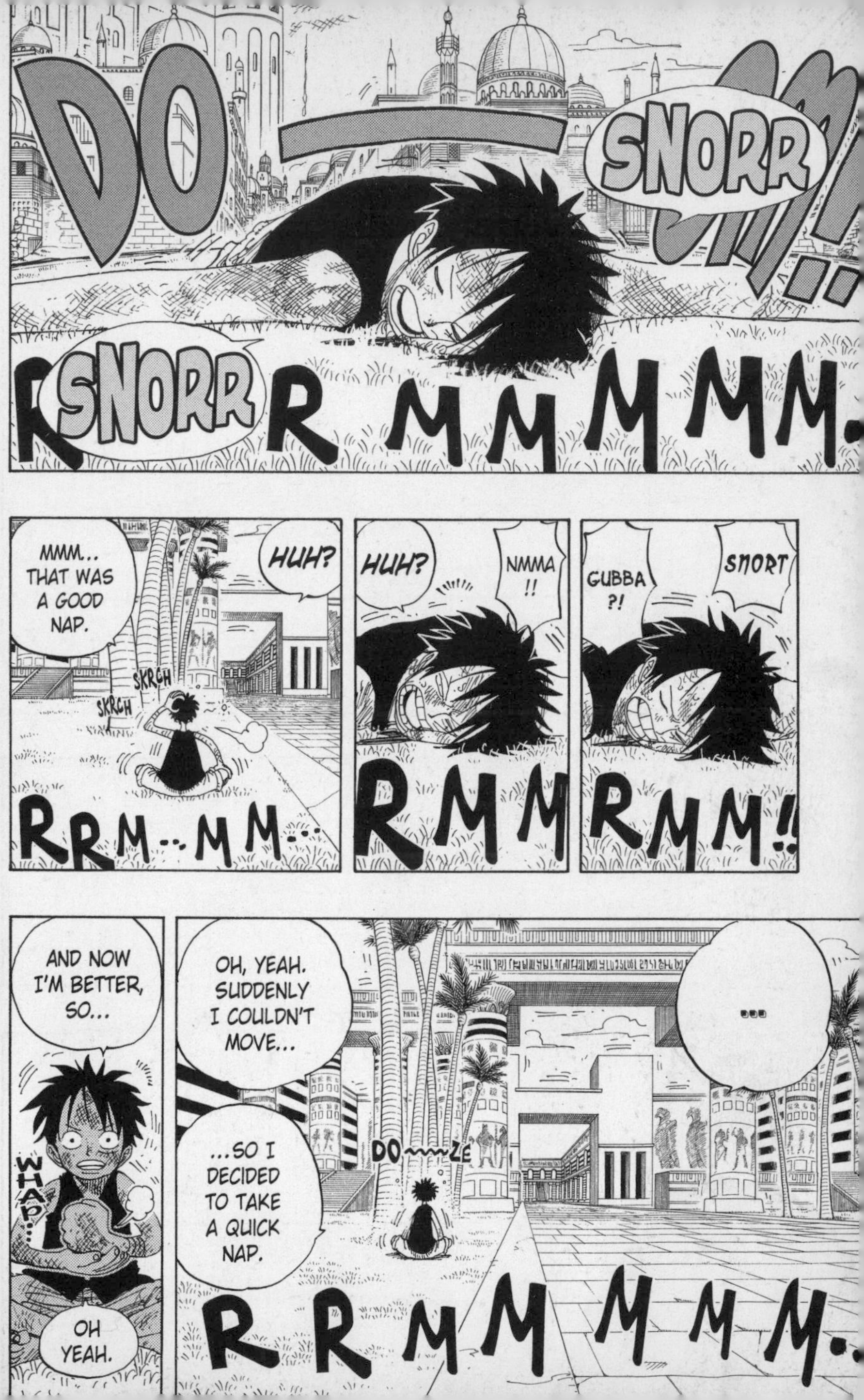
SNORR
DO—OM!!
RSNORR
RRMMMM...
SNORT
GUBBA ?!
RMM!!
NMMA !!
HUH?
RMM
HUH?
MMM... THAT WAS A GOOD NAP.
SKRCH
SKRCH
RRM.. MM...
...
OH, YEAH. SUDDENLY I COULDN'T MOVE...
...SO I DECIDED TO TAKE A QUICK NAP.
DO~~ZE
RRMMMMM...
AND NOW I'M BETTER, SO...
WHAP...
OH YEAH.

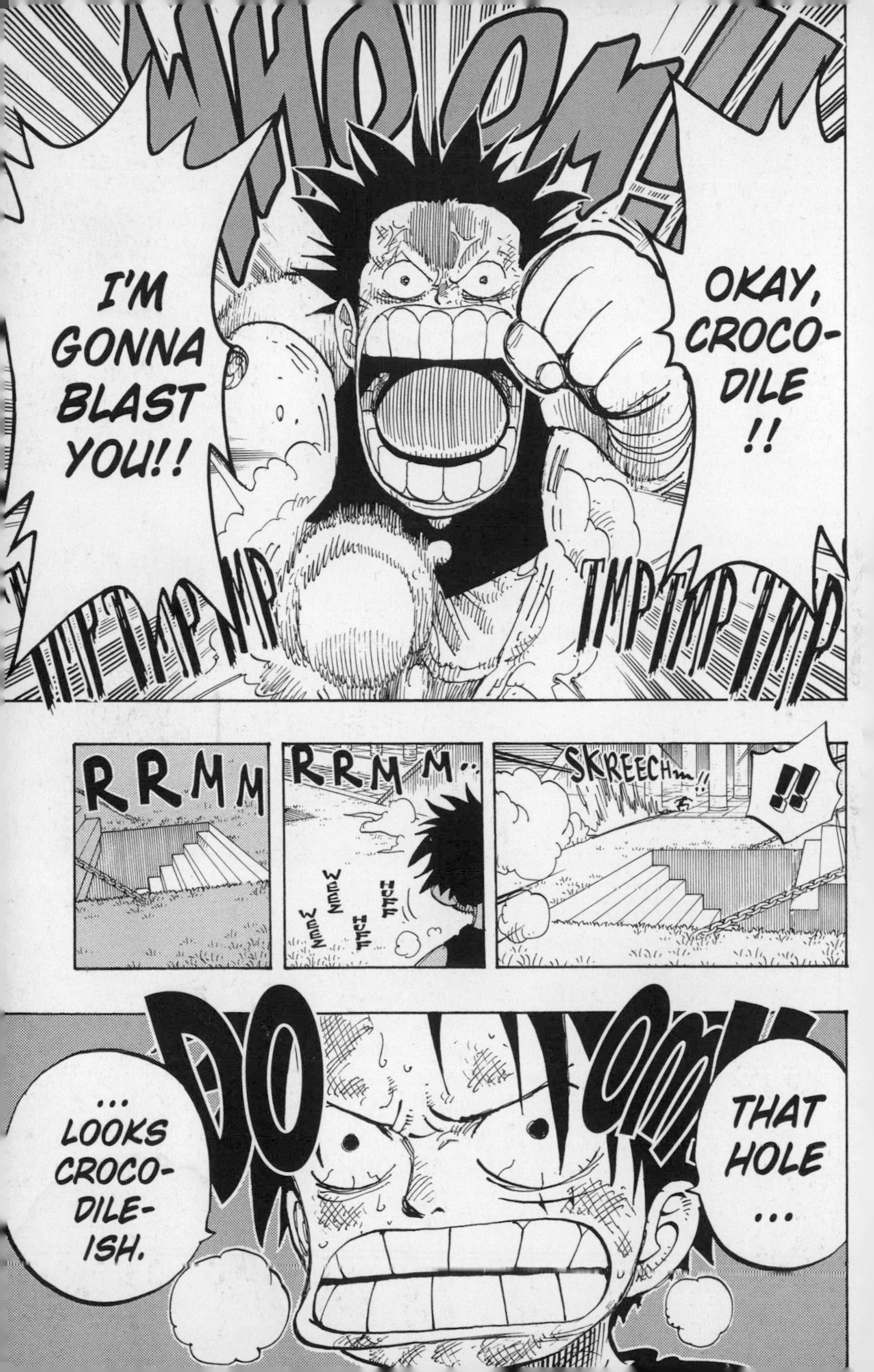
WHOOM
OKAY, CROCO-DILE!!
I'M GONNA BLAST YOU!!
TMP TMP TMP
TMP TMP TMP
SKREECH!!
!!
RRMM..
HUFF HUFF
WEEZ WEEZ
RRMM
THAT HOLE ...
... LOOKS CROCO-DILE-ISH.

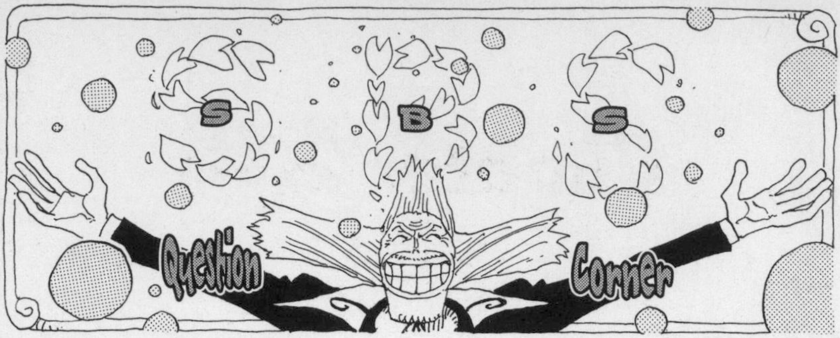
S B S
Question Corner

Reader: *Ding-dong.* Hi, Oda Sensei! You always seem awfully busy, so today, eighth-grader Meg is going to help you with your illustrations.♡ Eighth-grader Meg got an A in Art class, plus she's an aspiring manga artist!

splat (the sound of ink dropping) Oops. Sorry.♡
I'll be leaving now…♡♡

--Eighth-grader Meg

Oda: **What do you think you're doing?! Hey, you!! Get back here!!**
C'mon.. You could at least... white out that inkblot. (pathetic)

Reader: In Volume 19, upon close inspection, it seems that Chopper is pulling at the mouth of the mysterious Crab Mover in order to make it move faster. Why is that? Please tell meeee!!

--Moomin

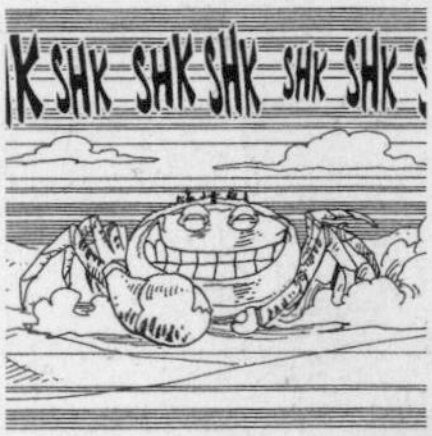
SHK SHK SHK SHK SHK

Oda: You're right. Crab Movers are very hard to control, so if you want it to go right, you tug at the right side of its mouth, and if you want to go left, you tug at the left side. In Crab Mover language, it would be a "right smirk" and a "left smirk." If you want to go slow, you give a little tug on both sides--doing a "right half-smirk" or a "left half-smirk." And if the rider happens to make a lame joke, the Crab Mover's face will cramp up making it impossible to control. So you have to be careful.

Reader: Mr. Oda, can you explain what the "ran" in "Gakuran"* means?

Oda: **I dunno.** Huh... Maybe it's the "ran" in "RANou" (egg yolk). Hmm... I know! It's "ran" as in "RANpaku" (egg white)! How's that?

*"Gakuran" is a boy's school uniform. "Gaku" means school and "ran(da)" means clothing. --Editor

# Chapter 204:
# RED

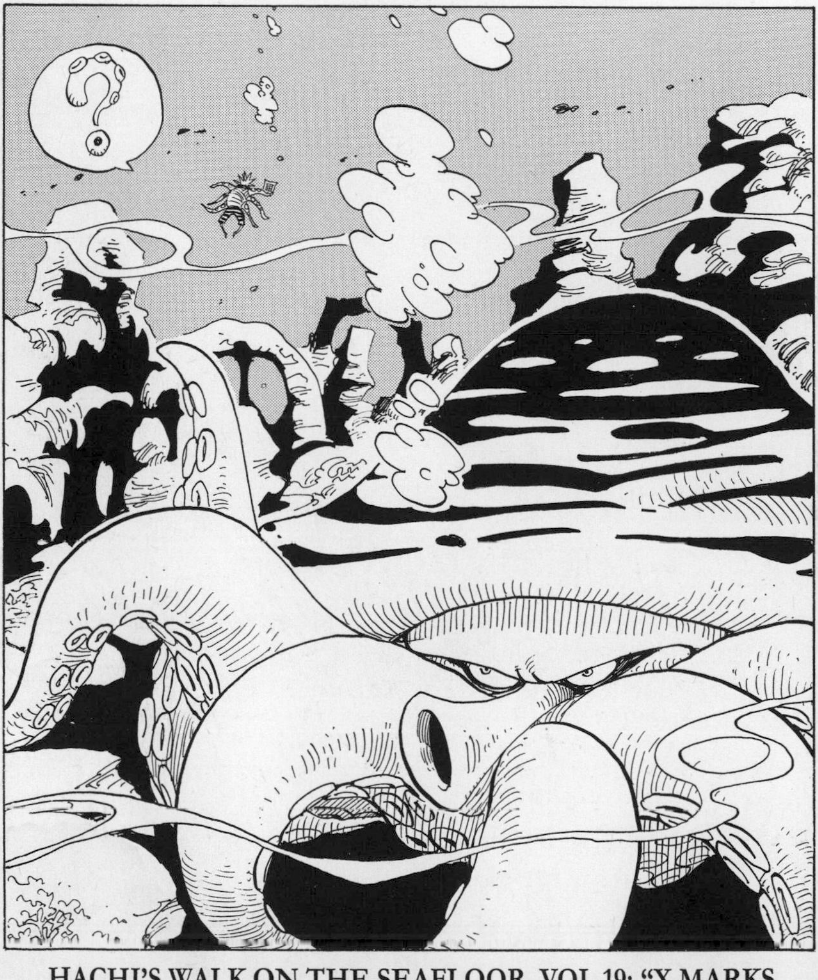

HACHI'S WALK ON THE SEAFLOOR, VOL.19: "X MARKS THE SPOT WHERE THE GREAT OCTOMASH LIVES"

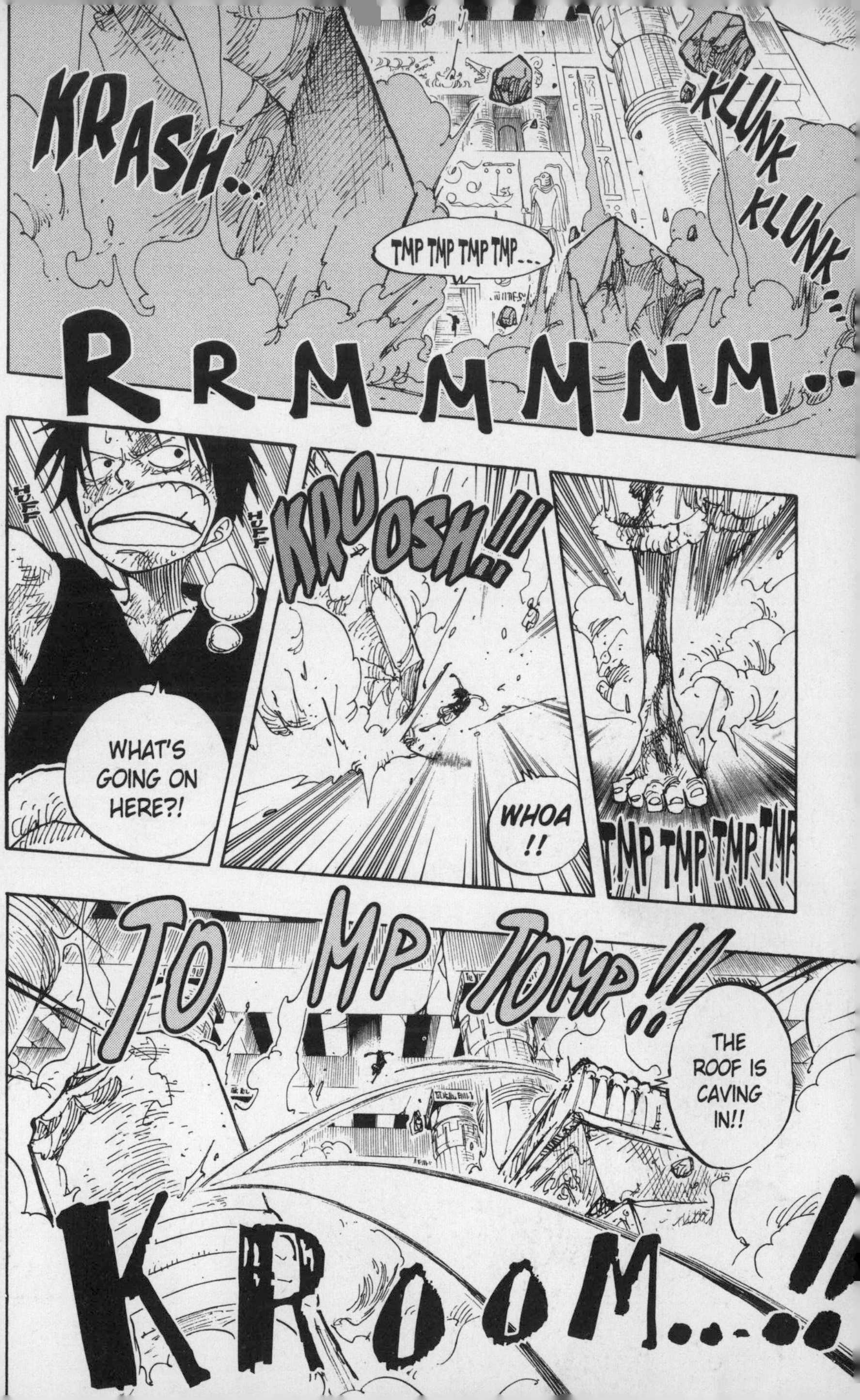
KLUNK KLUNK...
KRASH...
TMP TMP TMP TMP...
RRMMMMMM...
TMP TMP TMP TMP
KROOSH!!
WHOA!!
HUFF HUFF
WHAT'S GOING ON HERE?!
TOMP TOMP!!
THE ROOF IS CAVING IN!!
KROOM...!!

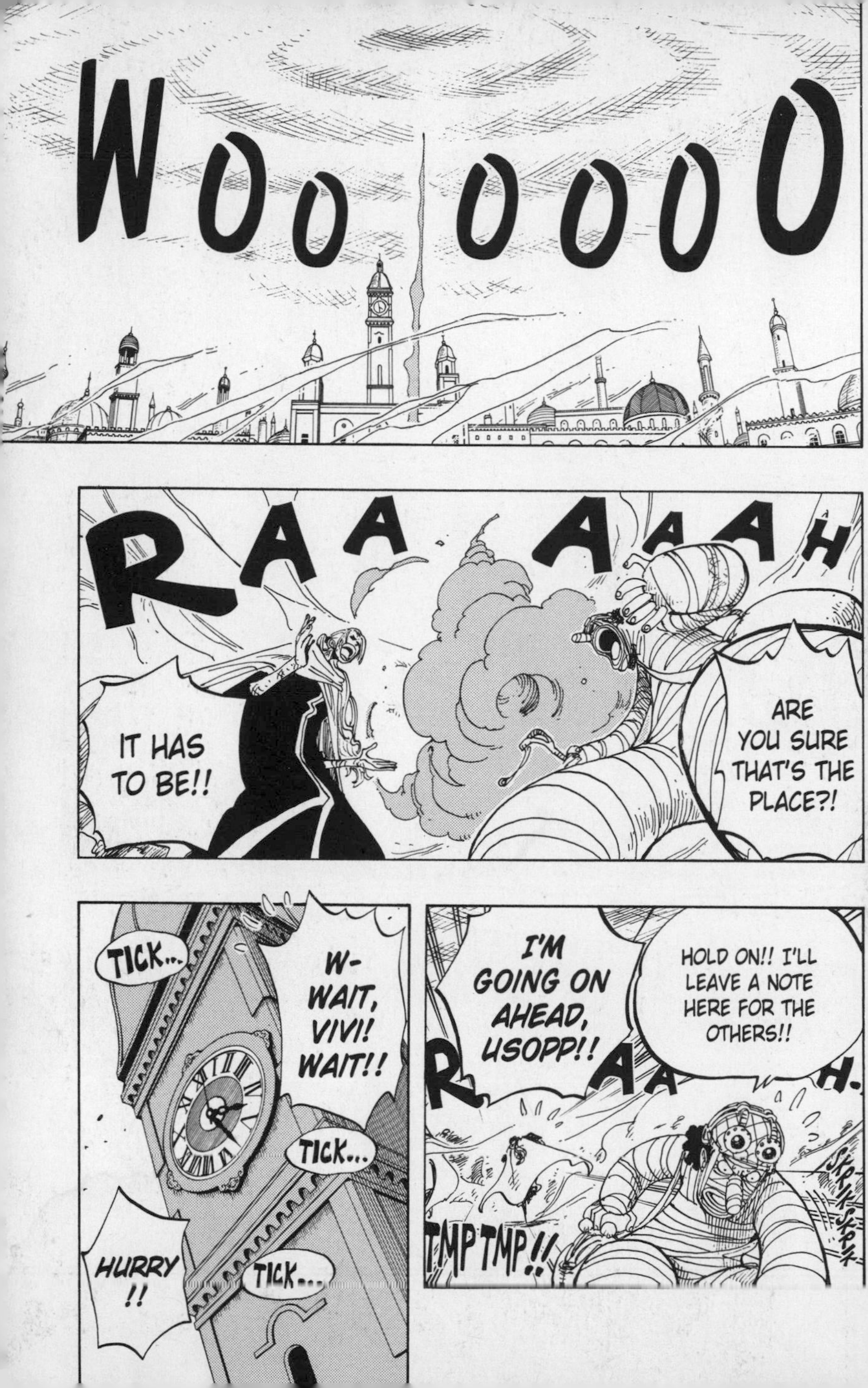
WOOOOOO
RAAAAAH
ARE YOU SURE THAT'S THE PLACE?!
IT HAS TO BE!!
HOLD ON!! I'LL LEAVE A NOTE HERE FOR THE OTHERS!!
I'M GOING ON AHEAD, USOPP!!
RAAAH-
SKRIK SKRIK
TMP TMP!!
W-WAIT, VIVI! WAIT!!
TICK...
TICK...
HURRY!!
TICK...

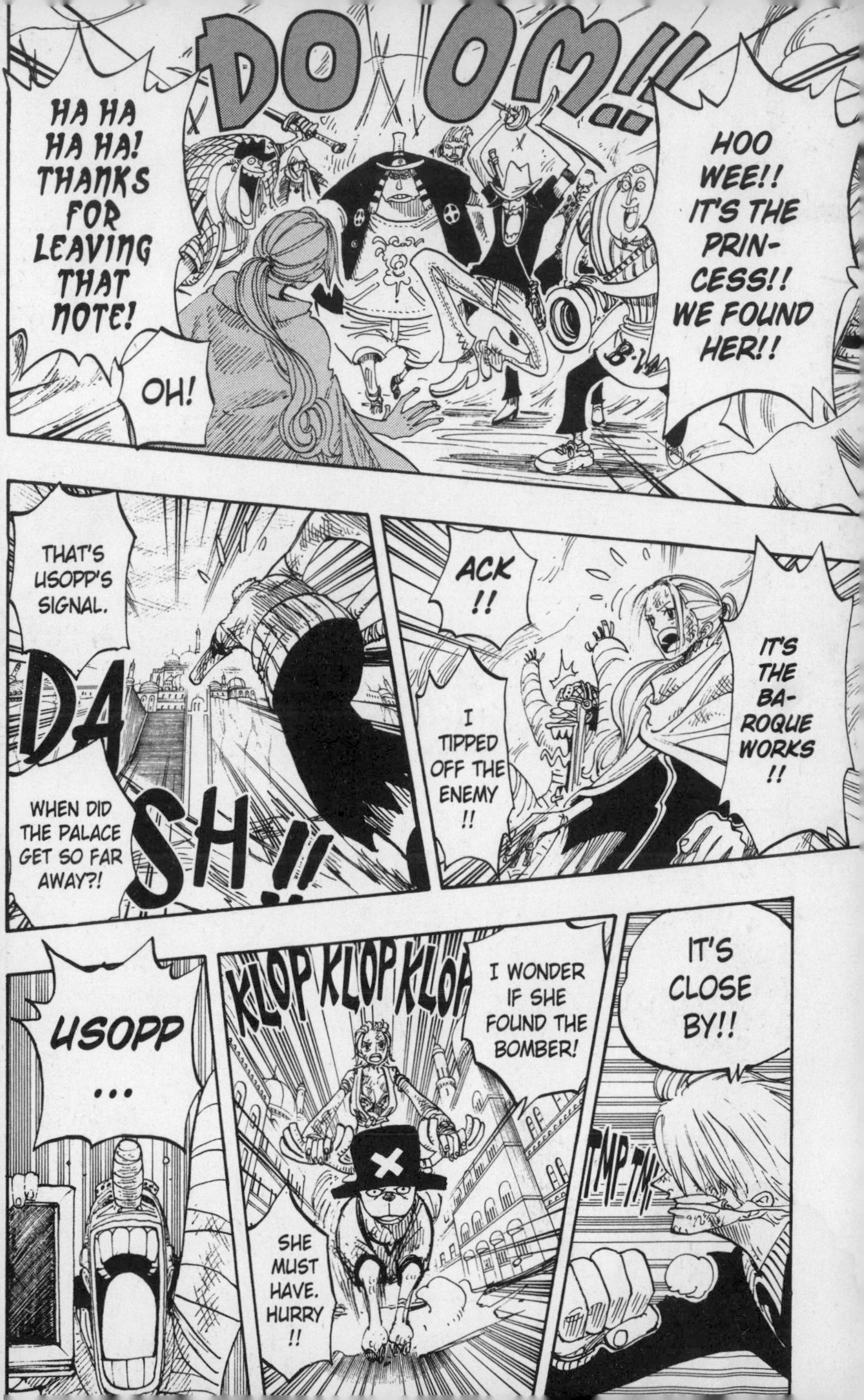
DOOM!!
HOO WEE!! IT'S THE PRIN-CESS!! WE FOUND HER!!
HA HA HA HA! THANKS FOR LEAVING THAT NOTE!
OH!
IT'S THE BA-ROQUE WORKS!!
ACK!!
I TIPPED OFF THE ENEMY!!
THAT'S USOPP'S SIGNAL.
DASH!!
WHEN DID THE PALACE GET SO FAR AWAY?!
IT'S CLOSE BY!!
TMP TM
KLOP KLOP KLOP
I WONDER IF SHE FOUND THE BOMBER!
SHE MUST HAVE. HURRY!!
USOPP ...

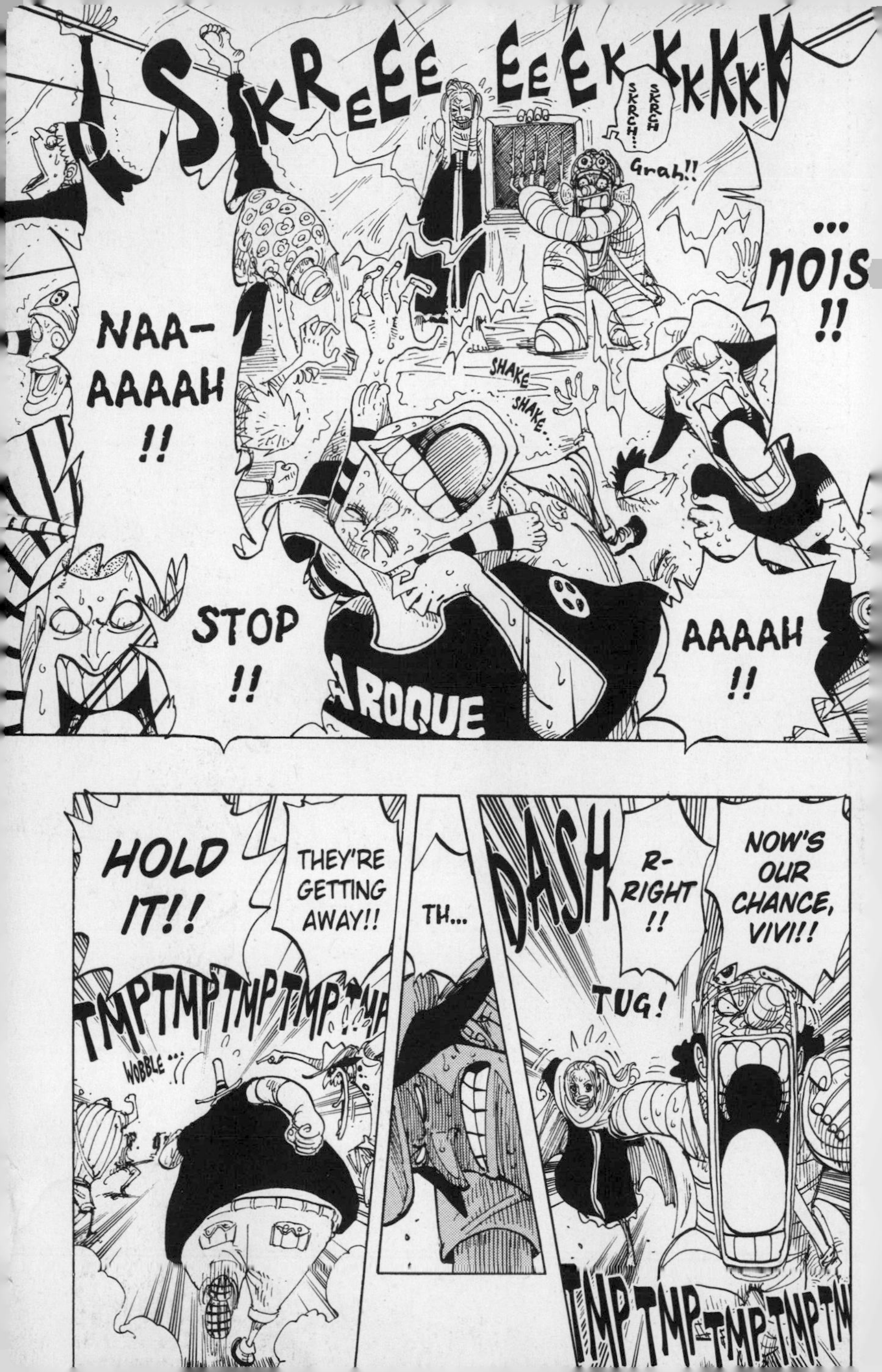
...noïs !!
SKREEEEEEEKKKKKK
SKRCH SKRCH...
Grah!!
NAA-AAAAH!!
SHAKE SHAKE...
AAAAH!!
STOP!!
AROQUE
NOW'S OUR CHANCE, VIVI!!
R-RIGHT!!
DASH
TUG!
TMP TMP TMP TMPTM
TH...
THEY'RE GETTING AWAY!!
HOLD IT!!
TMPTMPTMPTMPTM
WOBBLE...

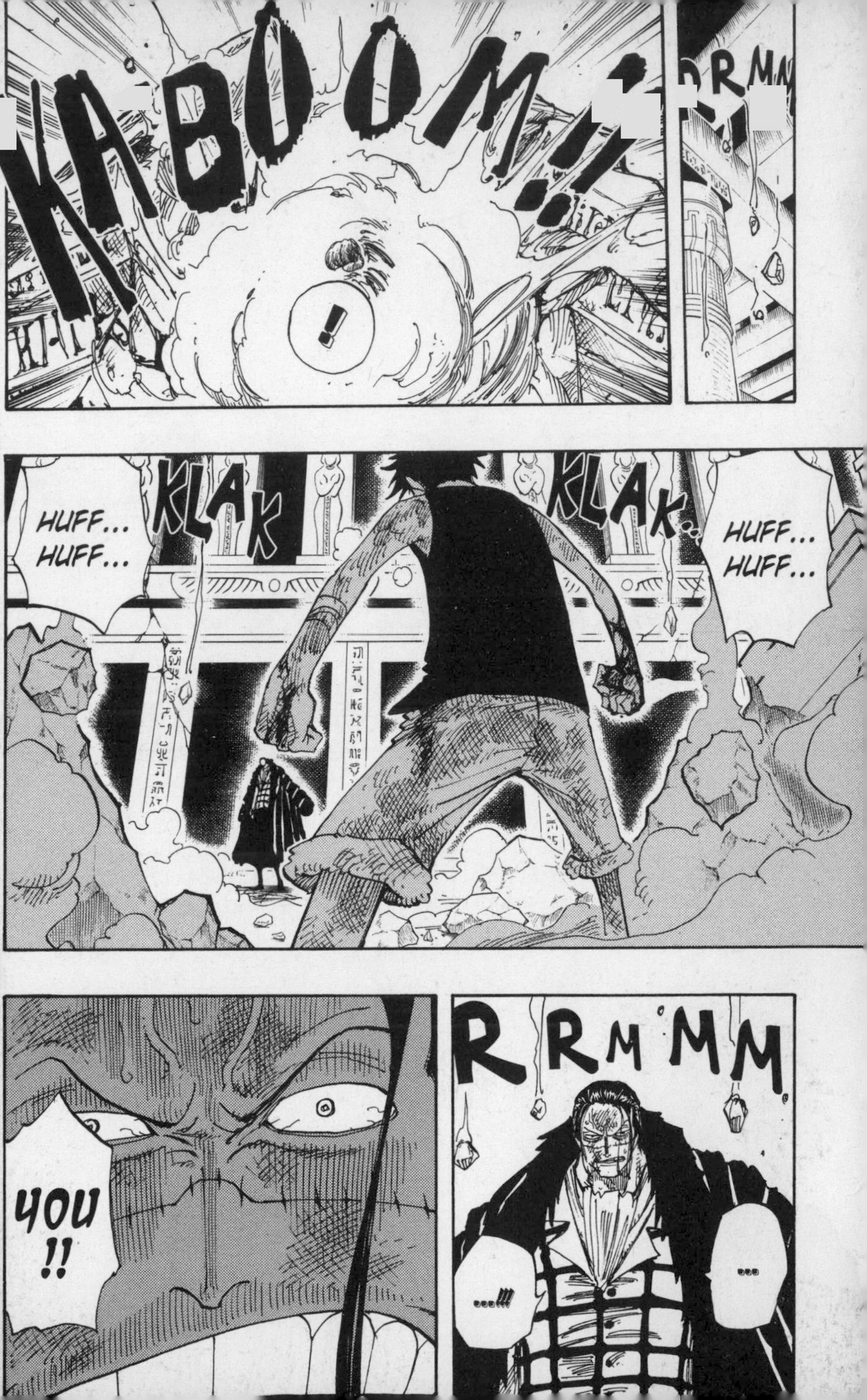
RRMM
KA-BOOM!!
!
HUFF... HUFF...
KLAK...
KLAK
HUFF... HUFF...
RRMMM
...
...!!!
YOU!!

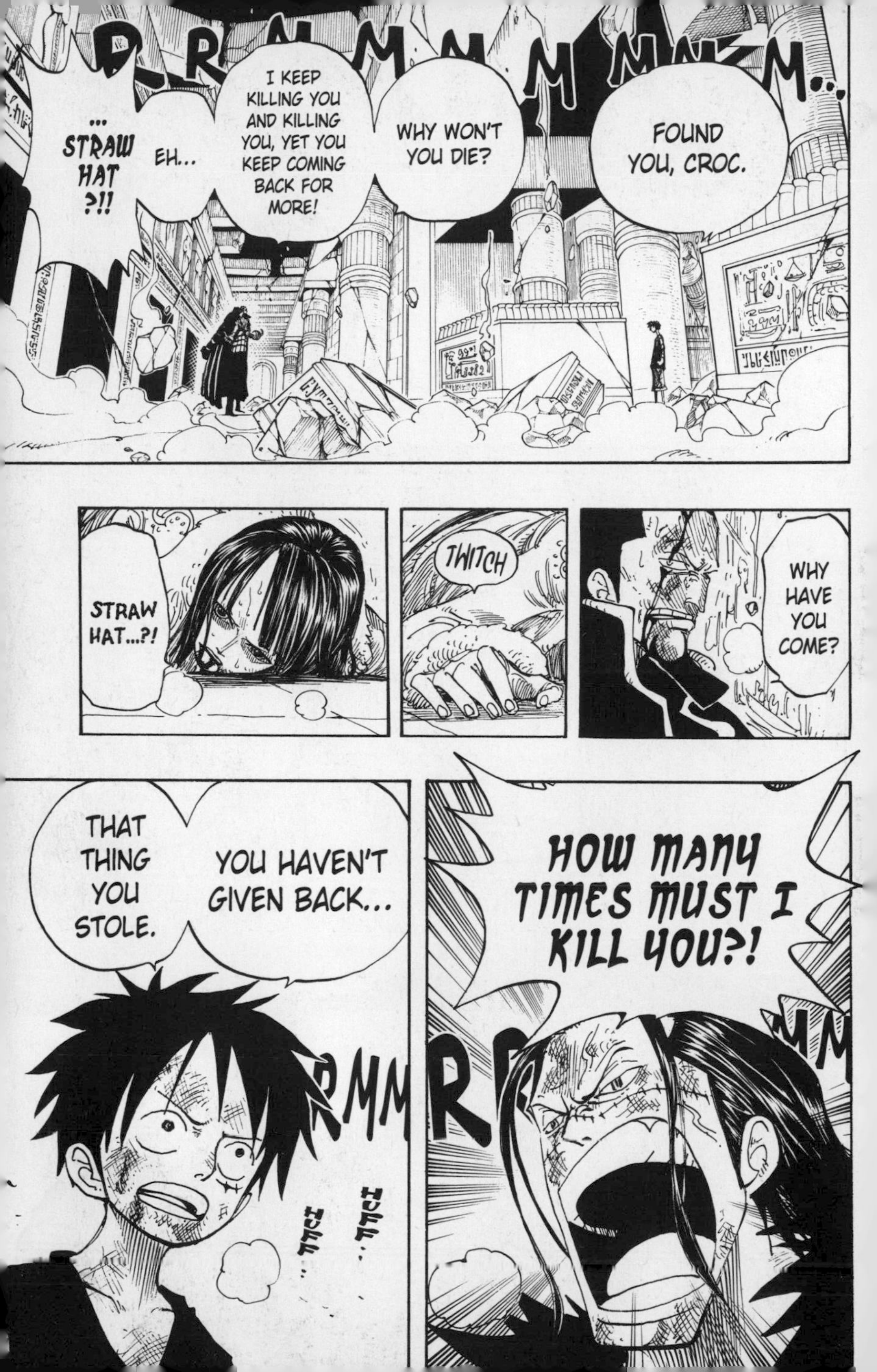
FOUND YOU, CROC.
WHY WON'T YOU DIE?
I KEEP KILLING YOU AND KILLING YOU, YET YOU KEEP COMING BACK FOR MORE!
EH...
... STRAW HAT ?!!
WHY HAVE YOU COME?
TWITCH
STRAW HAT...?!
HOW MANY TIMES MUST I KILL YOU?!
YOU HAVEN'T GIVEN BACK...
THAT THING YOU STOLE.
HUFF..
HUFF..

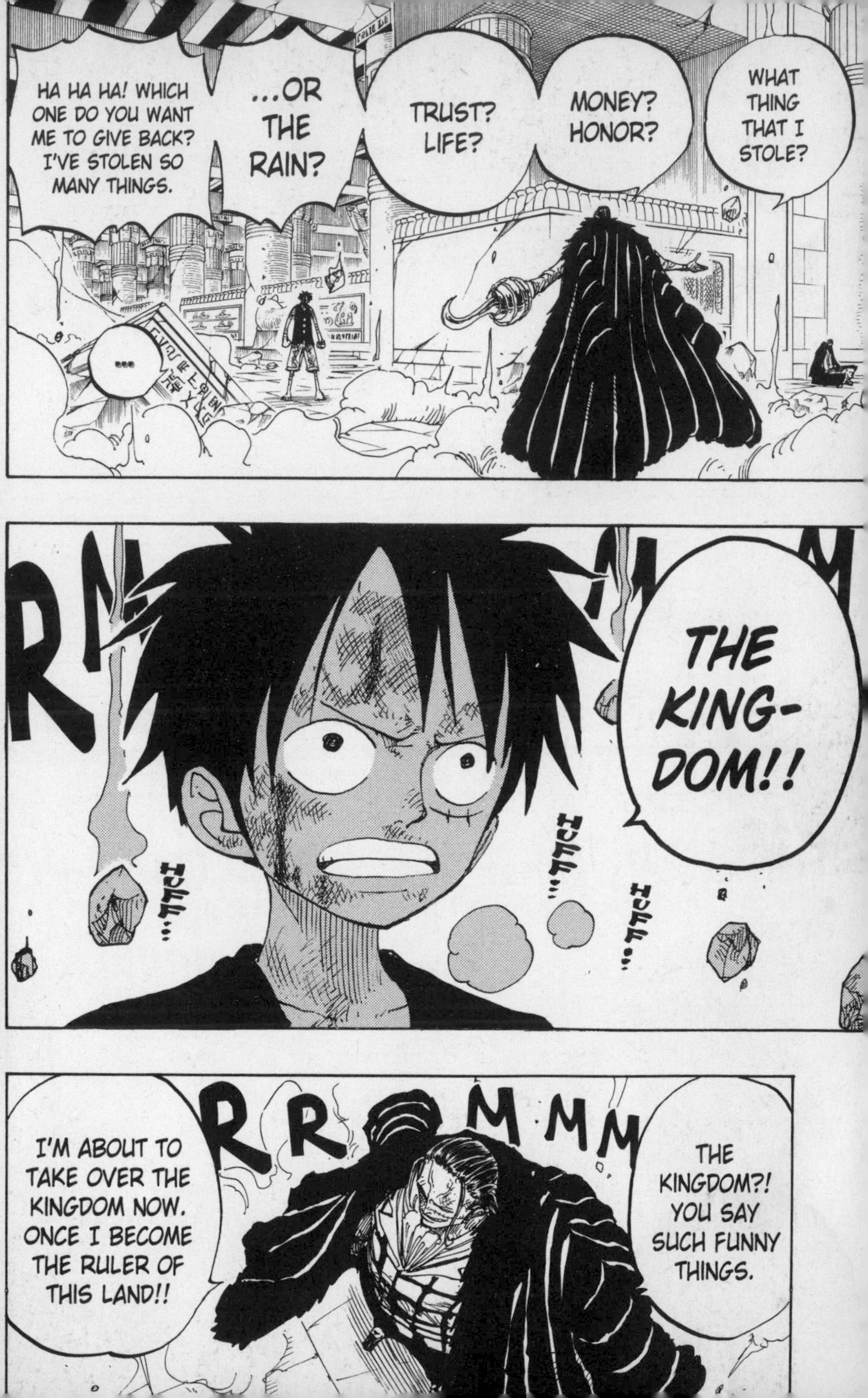
WHAT THING THAT I STOLE?
MONEY? HONOR?
TRUST? LIFE?
...OR THE RAIN?
HA HA HA! WHICH ONE DO YOU WANT ME TO GIVE BACK? I'VE STOLEN SO MANY THINGS.
...
THE KING-DOM!!
HUFF...
HUFF...
HUFF...
THE KINGDOM?! YOU SAY SUCH FUNNY THINGS.
RRRMMM
I'M ABOUT TO TAKE OVER THE KINGDOM NOW. ONCE I BECOME THE RULER OF THIS LAND!!

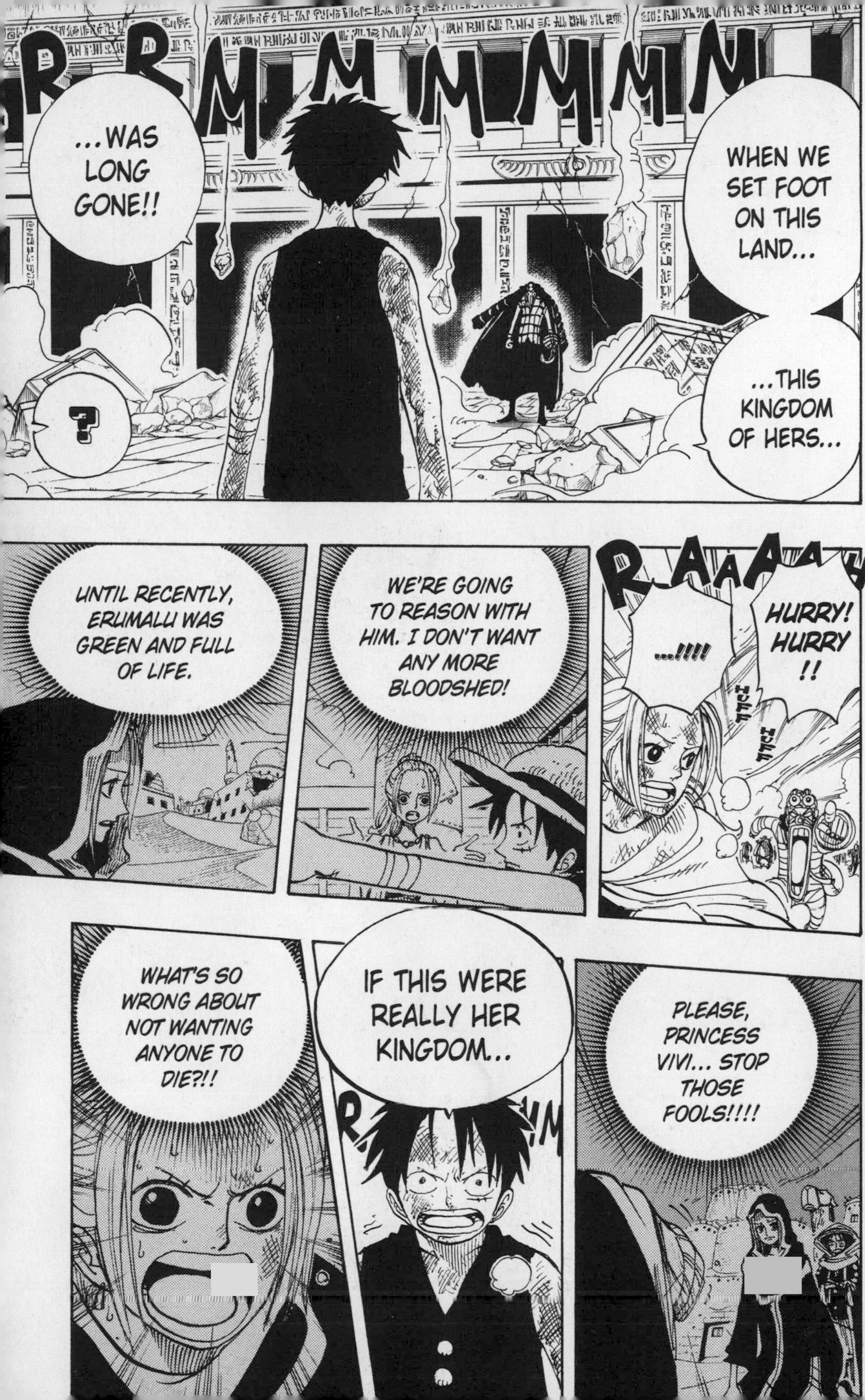
RRMMMMMMM
WHEN WE SET FOOT ON THIS LAND...
...THIS KINGDOM OF HERS...
...WAS LONG GONE!!
?
RAAAAH
HURRY! HURRY!!
...!!!!
HUFF
HUFF
WE'RE GOING TO REASON WITH HIM. I DON'T WANT ANY MORE BLOODSHED!
UNTIL RECENTLY, ERUMALU WAS GREEN AND FULL OF LIFE.
PLEASE, PRINCESS VIVI... STOP THOSE FOOLS!!!!
IF THIS WERE REALLY HER KINGDOM...
WHAT'S SO WRONG ABOUT NOT WANTING ANYONE TO DIE?!!

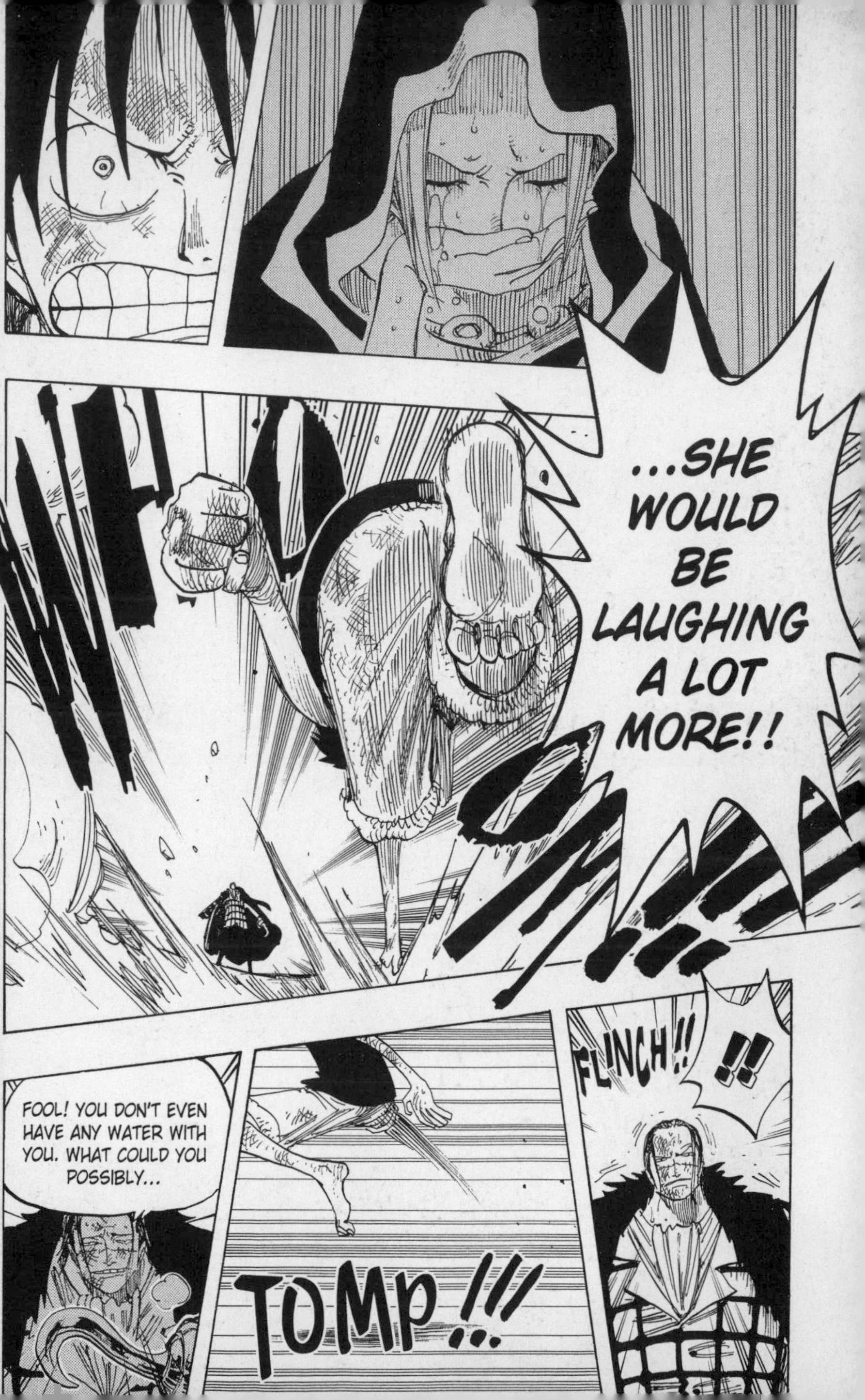
...SHE WOULD BE LAUGHING A LOT MORE!!
FLINCH!!
!!
TOMP!!!
FOOL! YOU DON'T EVEN HAVE ANY WATER WITH YOU. WHAT COULD YOU POSSIBLY...

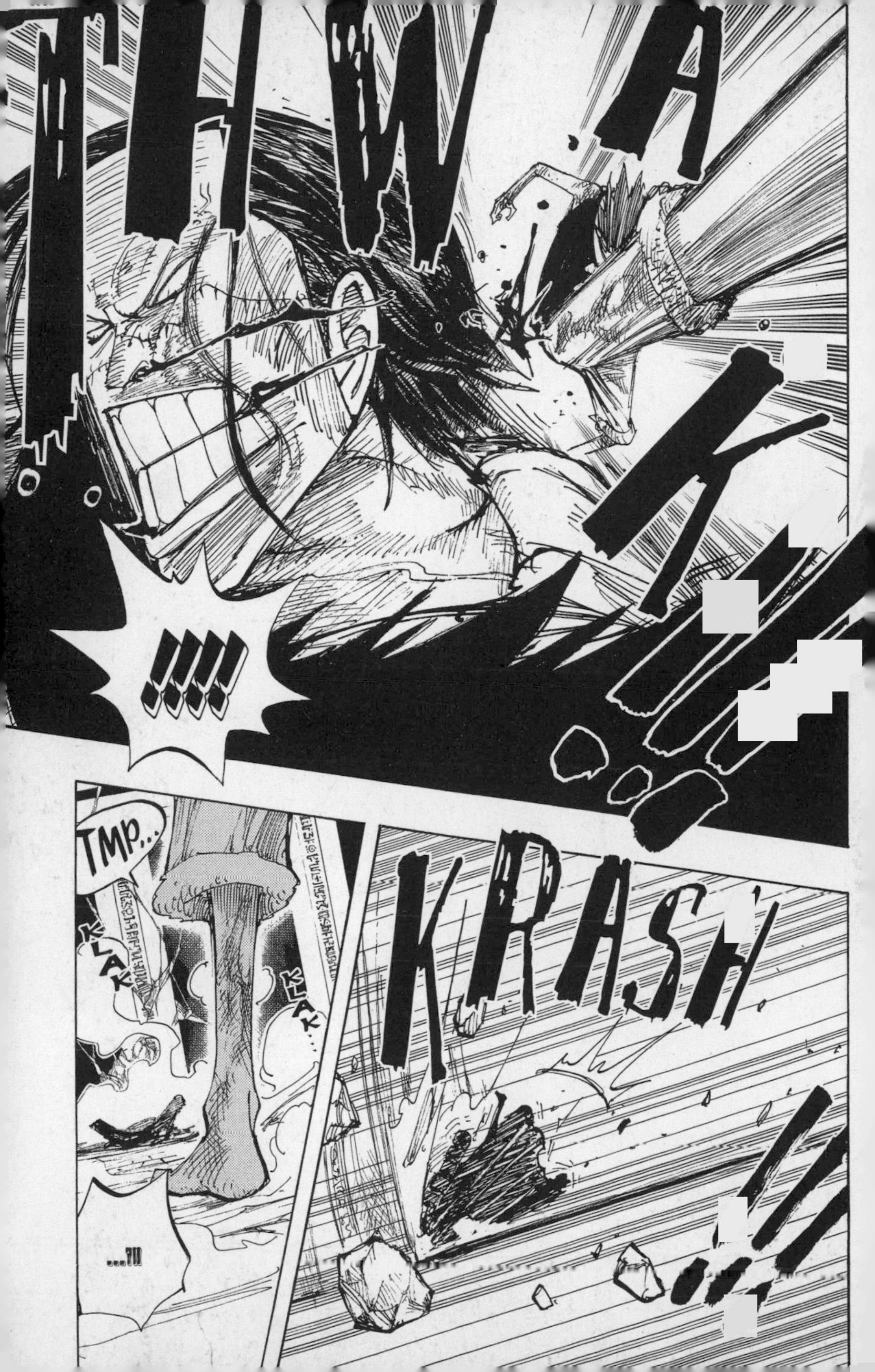
THWAKK
!!!!
KRASH
!!
TMP...
KLAK
KLAK...
...?!!

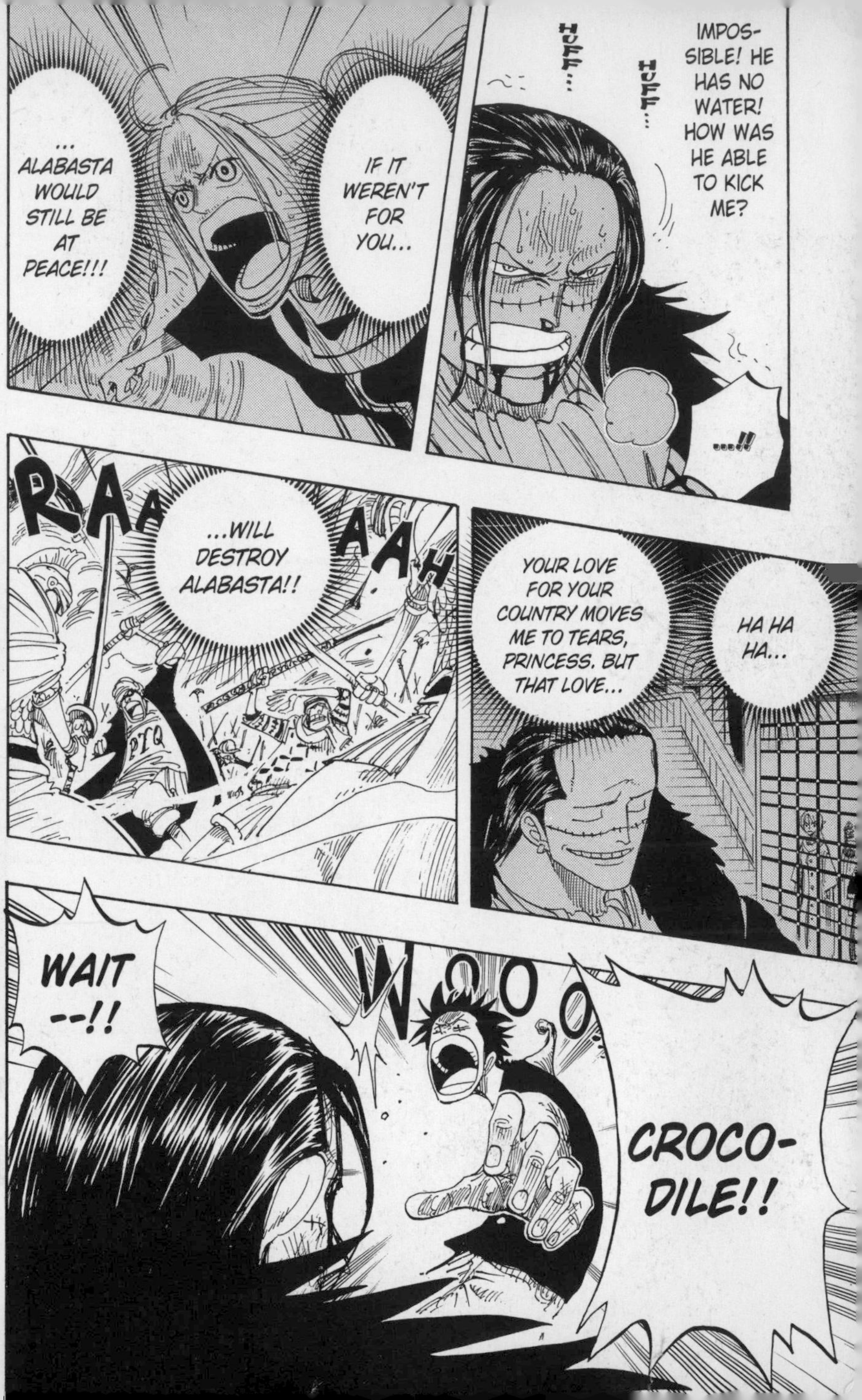
HUFF...
HUFF...
IMPOSSIBLE! HE HAS NO WATER! HOW WAS HE ABLE TO KICK ME?
...!!
IF IT WEREN'T FOR YOU...
...ALABASTA WOULD STILL BE AT PEACE!!!
HA HA HA...
YOUR LOVE FOR YOUR COUNTRY MOVES ME TO TEARS, PRINCESS. BUT THAT LOVE...
AAH
...WILL DESTROY ALABASTA!!
RAA
PTQ
WOOO
WAIT --!!
CROCO-DILE!!

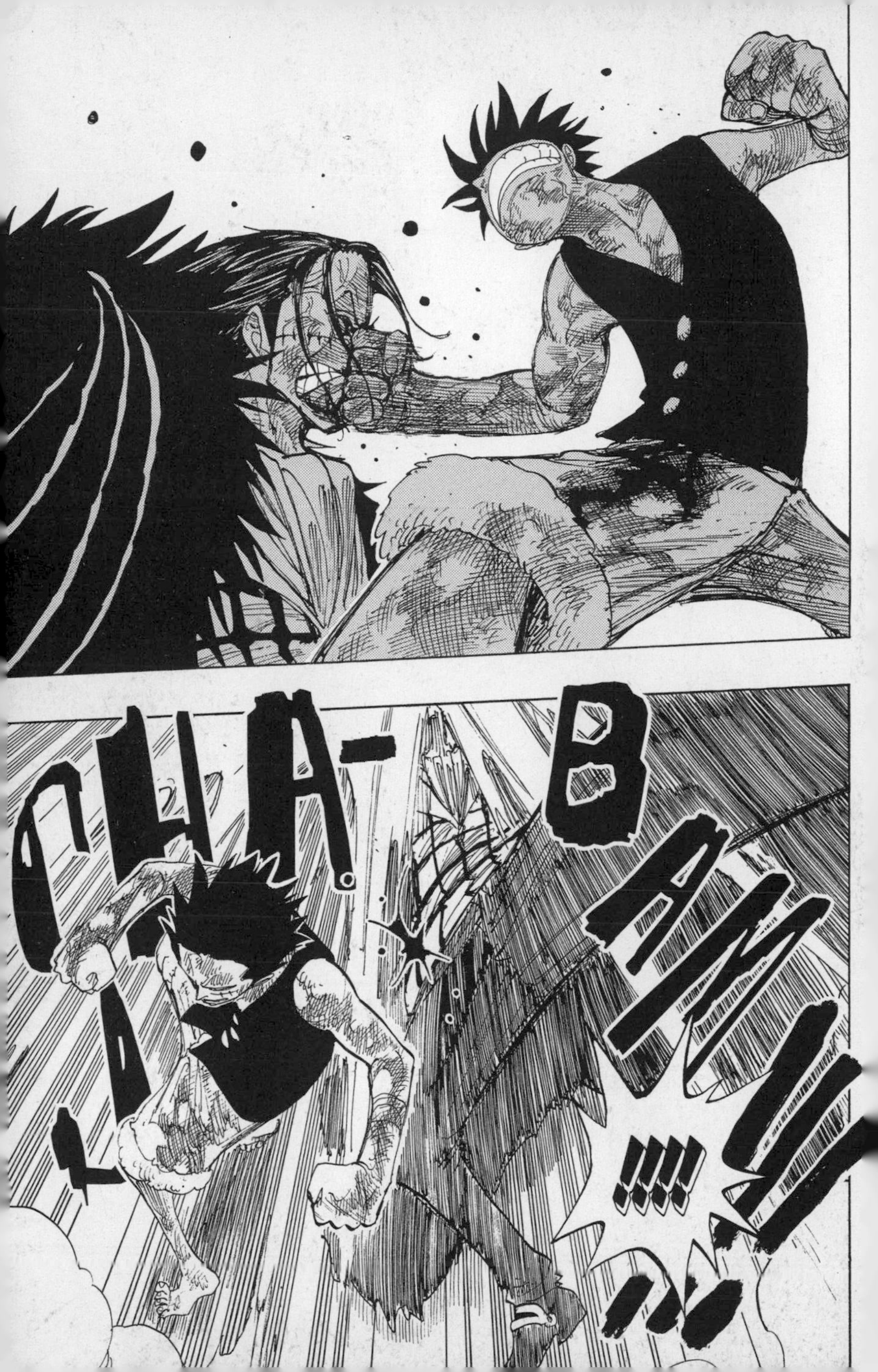
CHA-BAMM!!!!

BA-BOOM!!!

SHAKE

WOBBLE...

UGH... KOFF!!

SHAKE

...USE BLOOD?!!

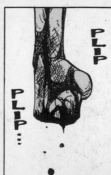

PLIP

PLIP...

DID YOU... YOU...!

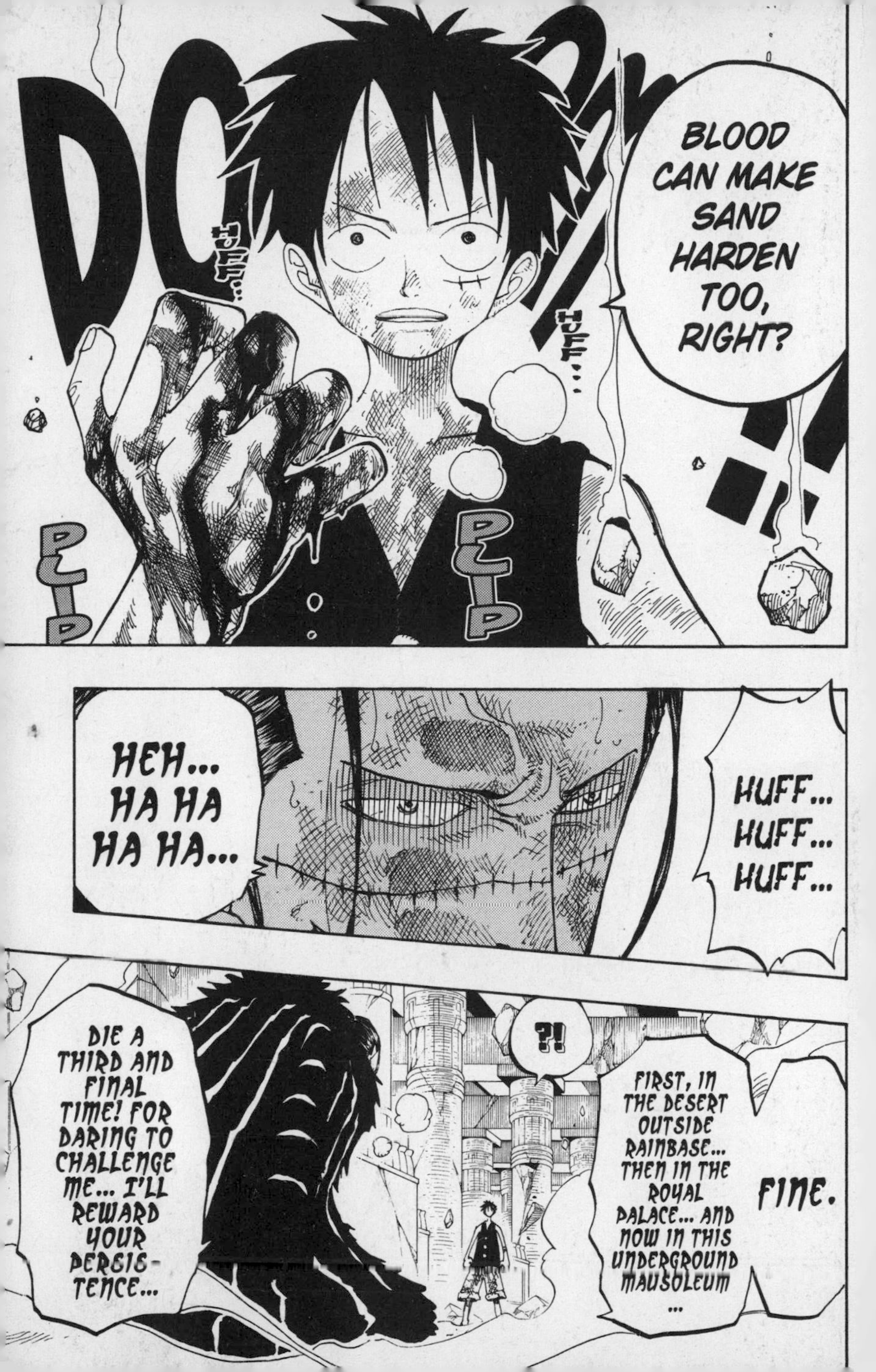
BLOOD CAN MAKE SAND HARDEN TOO, RIGHT?
HUFF...
HUFF...
DO
PLIP
PLIP
HUFF... HUFF... HUFF...
HEH... HA HA HA HA...
FINE.
FIRST, IN THE DESERT OUTSIDE RAINBASE... THEN IN THE ROYAL PALACE... AND NOW IN THIS UNDERGROUND MAUSOLEUM ...
?!
DIE A THIRD AND FINAL TIME! FOR DARING TO CHALLENGE ME... I'LL REWARD YOUR PERSIS-TENCE...

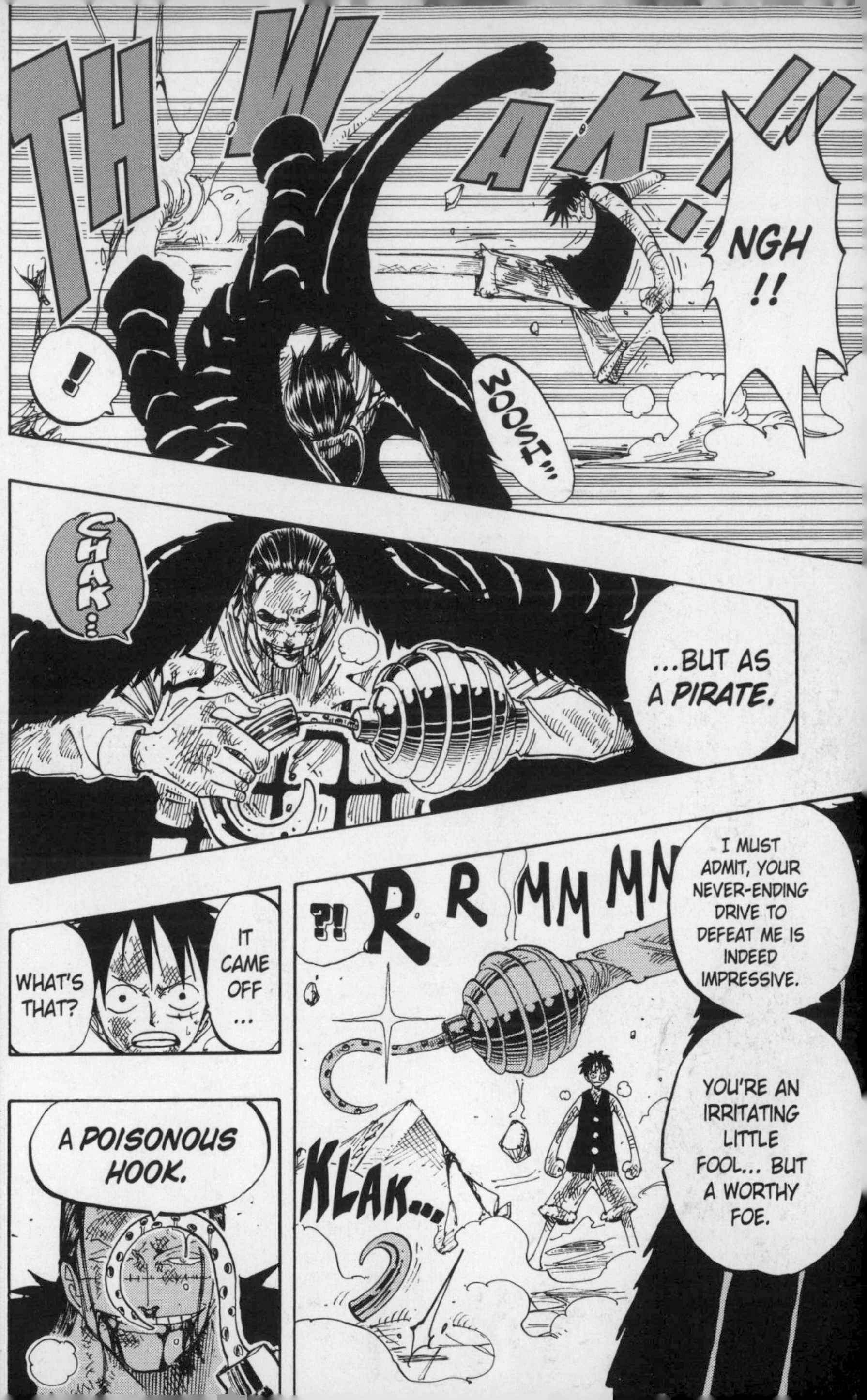
THWAK!!
NGH !!
WOOSH!!
!
...BUT AS A PIRATE.
CHAK...
I MUST ADMIT, YOUR NEVER-ENDING DRIVE TO DEFEAT ME IS INDEED IMPRESSIVE.
RRMMMMN
?!
YOU'RE AN IRRITATING LITTLE FOOL... BUT A WORTHY FOE.
KLAK...
IT CAME OFF ...
WHAT'S THAT?
A POISONOUS HOOK.

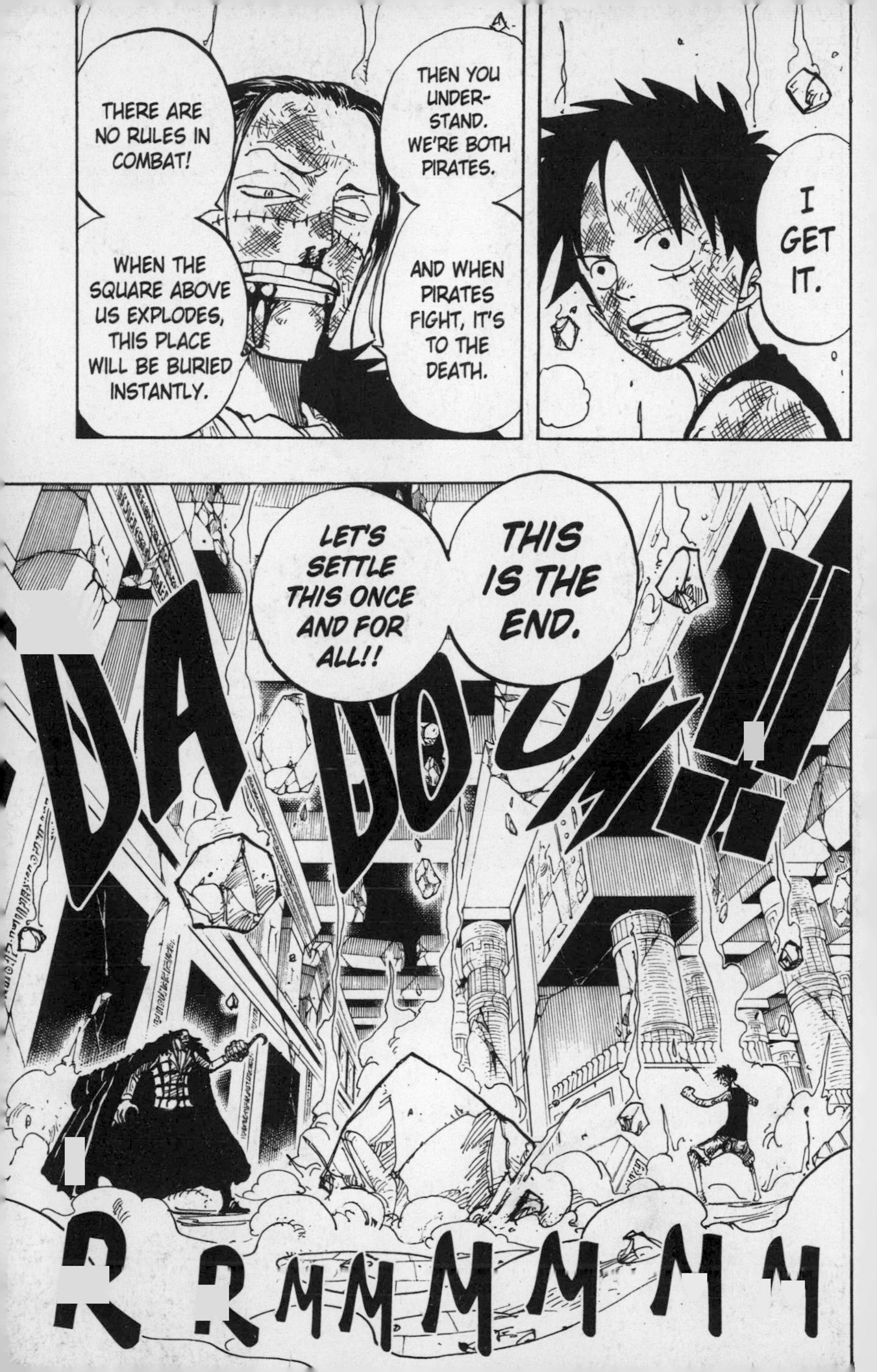
I GET IT.
THEN YOU UNDERSTAND. WE'RE BOTH PIRATES.
THERE ARE NO RULES IN COMBAT!
AND WHEN PIRATES FIGHT, IT'S TO THE DEATH.
WHEN THE SQUARE ABOVE US EXPLODES, THIS PLACE WILL BE BURIED INSTANTLY.
THIS IS THE END.
LET'S SETTLE THIS ONCE AND FOR ALL!!
DA DOOM!!
RRMMMMMMM

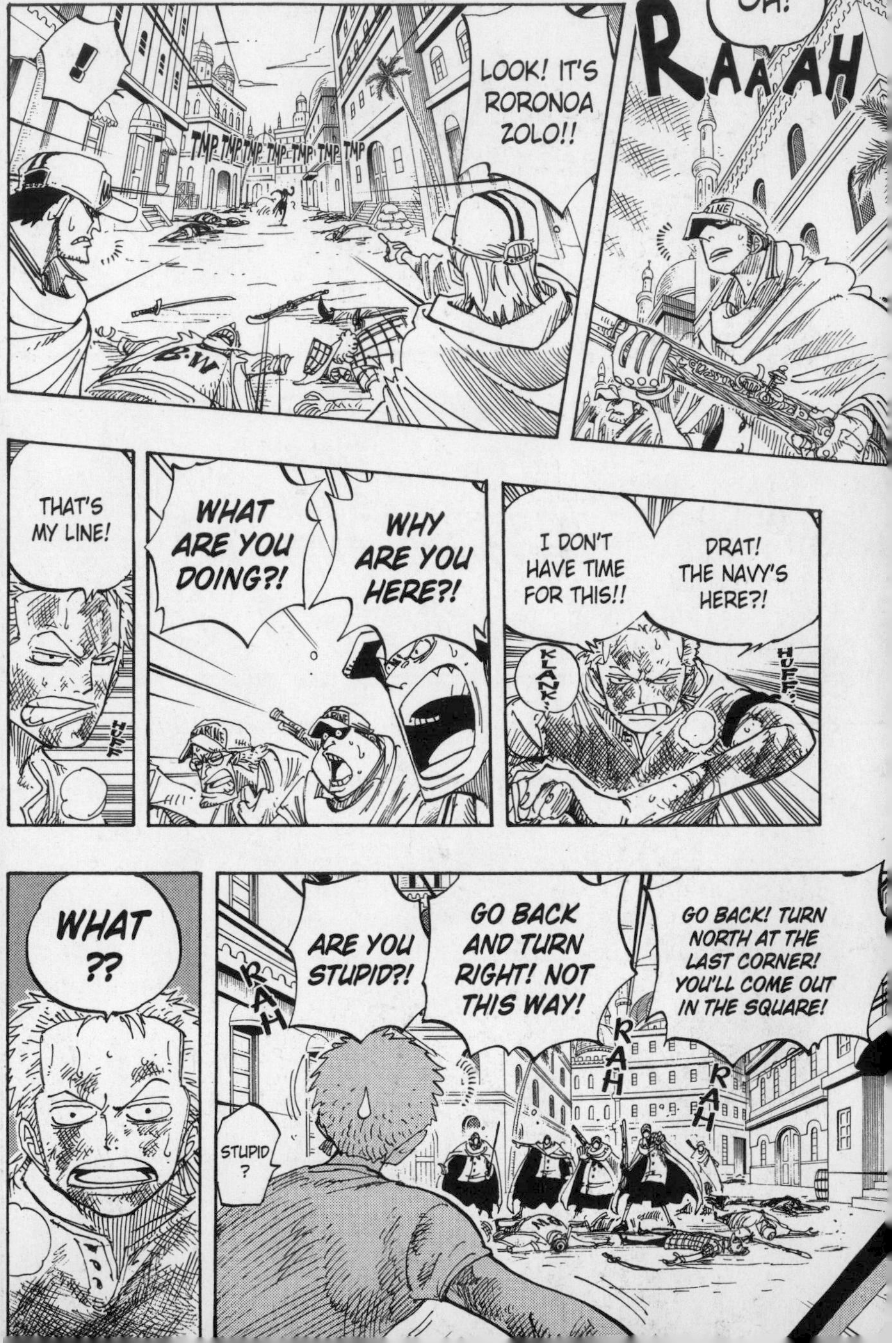
OH!
RAAAH
LOOK! IT'S RORONOA ZOLO!!
!
TMP TMP TMP TMP TMP TMP TMP
DRAT! THE NAVY'S HERE?!
I DON'T HAVE TIME FOR THIS!!
KLANK
HUFF
WHY ARE YOU HERE?!
WHAT ARE YOU DOING?!
THAT'S MY LINE!
HUFF
GO BACK! TURN NORTH AT THE LAST CORNER! YOU'LL COME OUT IN THE SQUARE!
GO BACK AND TURN RIGHT! NOT THIS WAY!
ARE YOU STUPID?!
RAH
RAH
RAH
STUPID ?
WHAT ??

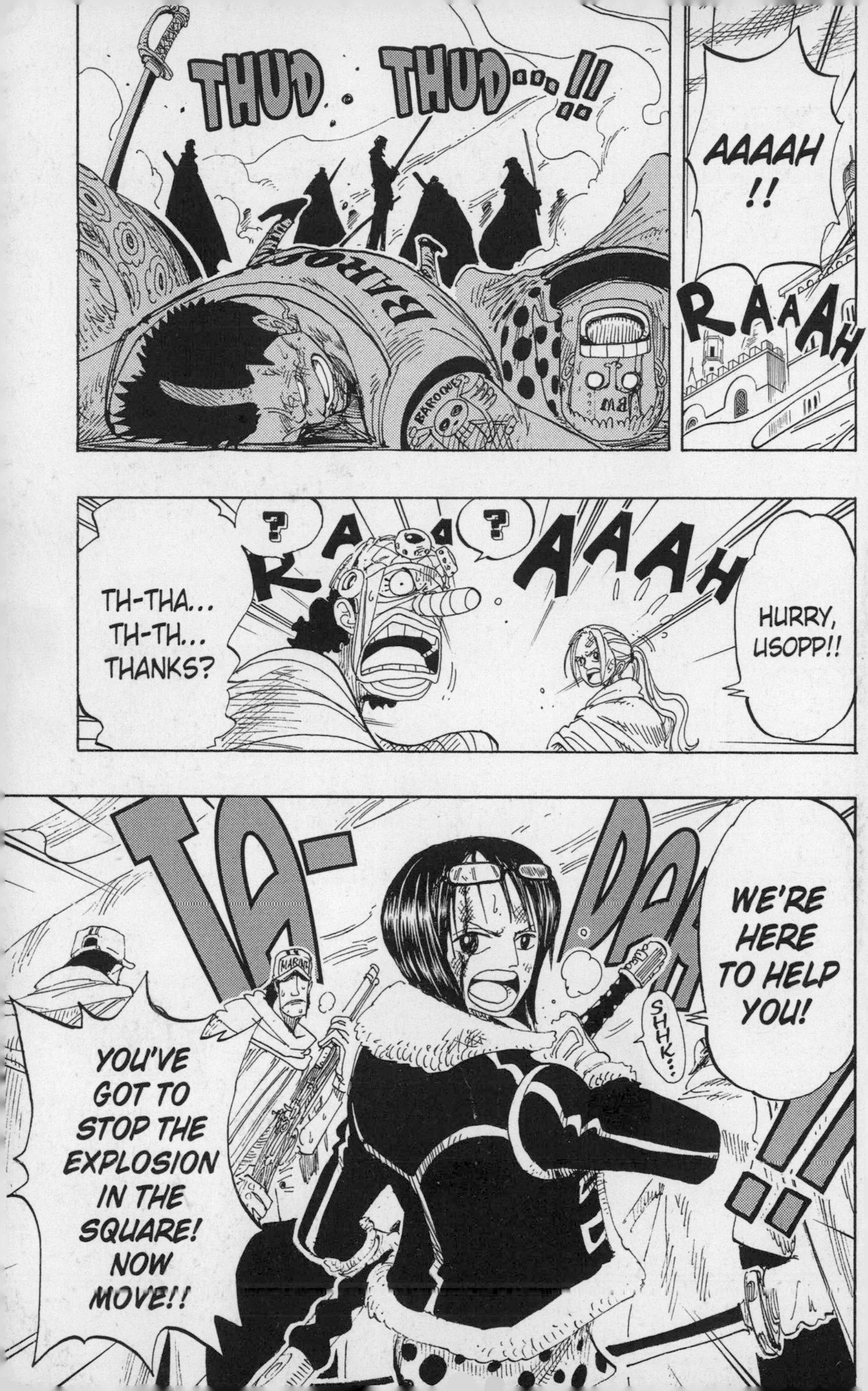
AAAAH!!
RAAAAH
THUD THUD...!!
? ?
RAAAAH
HURRY, USOPP!!
TH-THA... TH-TH... THANKS?
WE'RE HERE TO HELP YOU!
TA-DA
SHHK...
!!
YOU'VE GOT TO STOP THE EXPLOSION IN THE SQUARE! NOW MOVE!!

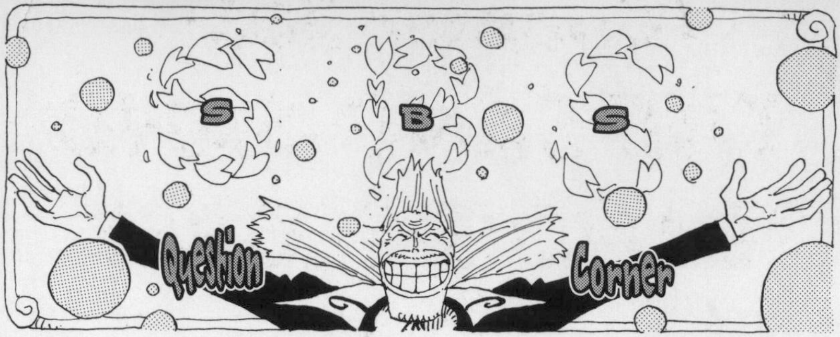
SBS
Question Corner

Reader: Umm, I have a question for Mr. Oda. In Volume 20, page 174, panel one, where Ms. Merry Christmas dives in a hole, the sound effect "woosh" (→) has a fish in it. Why did you do that? I have to know!

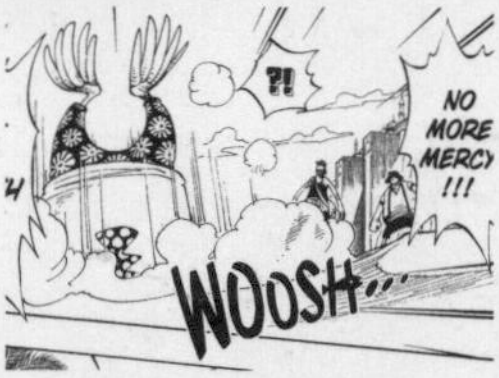
?!
NO MORE MERCY !!!
WOOSH...

Oda: Oh, it was just because she was doing her Mole Swimming Stealth Style. Why don't we try it? How to say "woosh." 1) Arch your eyebrows as high as you can. 2) Without moving your face, look up as high as you can. 3) Push out your lower teeth. Ready? **WOOSH...**

Were you able to do it? Go ahead and show your parents and friends. (But they're going to think you're a goofball!)

Reader: Even though Nami and Ms. All Sunday were wearing short skirts when they're fighting, we never see their undies. What color are they? Please tell me.

Oda: That's rather personal. What a question... And yet you seem so casual about it, as though you'd be surprised if anyone thought that was weird. You shouldn't be asking these things. But if I were to take a guess... Back in volume 14, Nami was wearing a black bra, so... Uh, we'd better end it right there. I value my life, you know.

Reader: Hello, Mr. Oda. What's next week's Question Corner gonna be about? How about "Usopp Lies," "Luffy Finds a Treasure Chest," and "Chopper's Nose Turns Red"? Okay? ♪ I'll be looking forward to it!

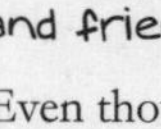
(PAPER)

Rock-paper-scissors!
Hee hee hee... ☆
Well, that's it for the Question Corner!

--President All-Brand Kiri, The Question Corner Conclusion Club

Oda: Darn it!! I was going to do scissors!! I overthought it too much!! Darn it!! I knew I should've gone with scissors!! Oh well, see you in the next volume. Darn it...

*Sazae-san,* a popular and long-running anime, always ends each episode with a game of rock-paper-scissors. --Editor

# Chapter 205:
# THE SAND-SAND BAND'S SECRET FORT

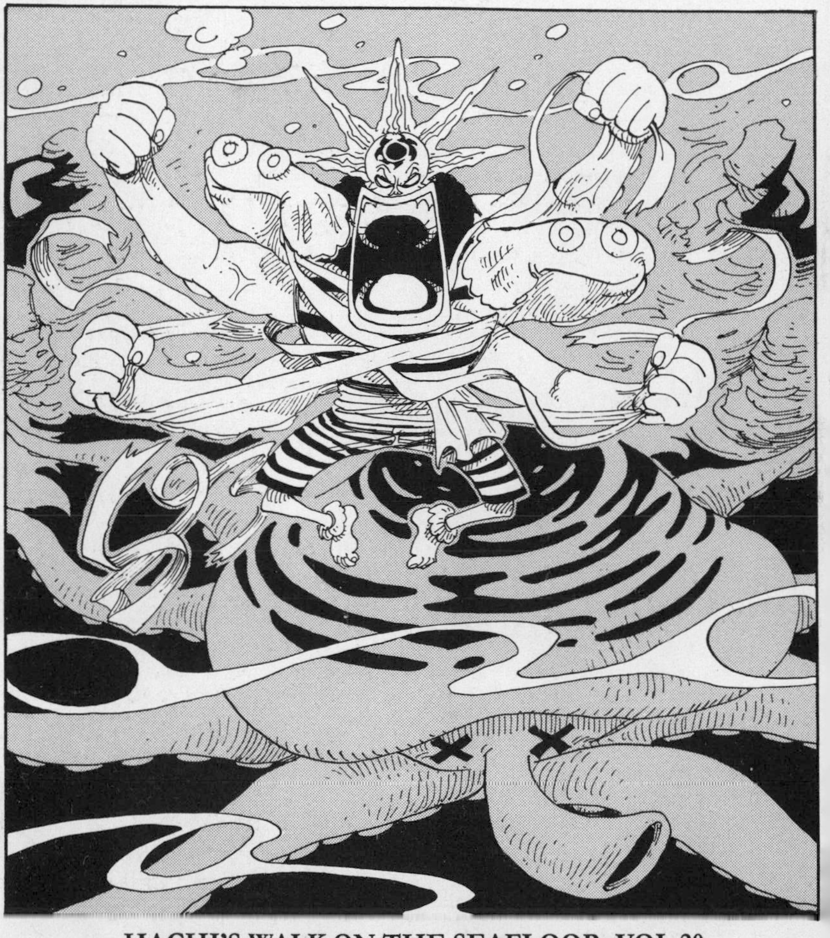

HACHI'S WALK ON THE SEAFLOOR, VOL.20:
"HACHI'S RAGE AT BEING FOOLED"

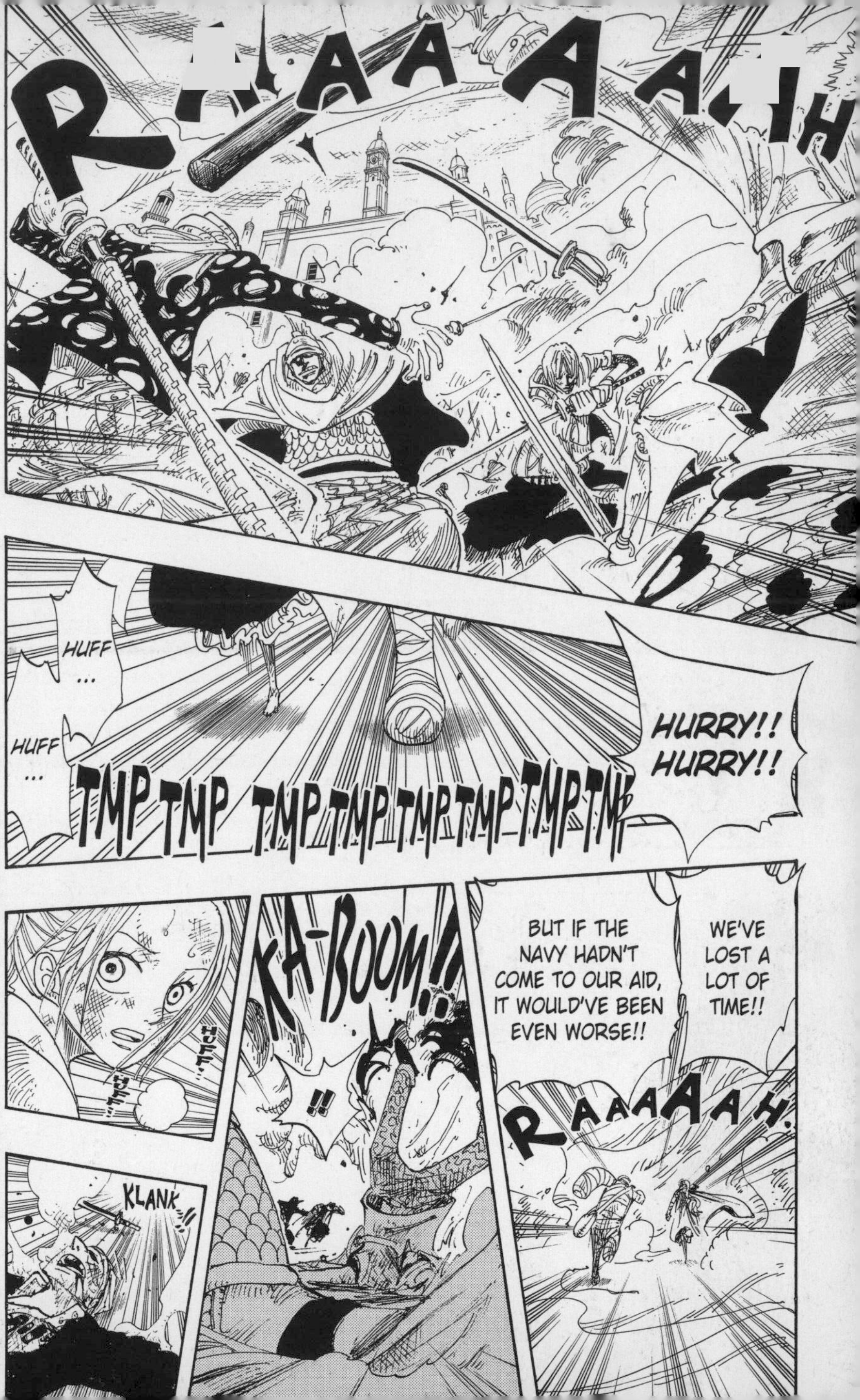
RAAAAAH
HURRY!! HURRY!!
TMP TMP TMP TMP TMP TMP TMP TMP
HUFF ...
HUFF ...
WE'VE LOST A LOT OF TIME!!
BUT IF THE NAVY HADN'T COME TO OUR AID, IT WOULD'VE BEEN EVEN WORSE!!
RAAAAAH
KA-BOOM!!
!!
HUFF
HUFF
KLANK!!

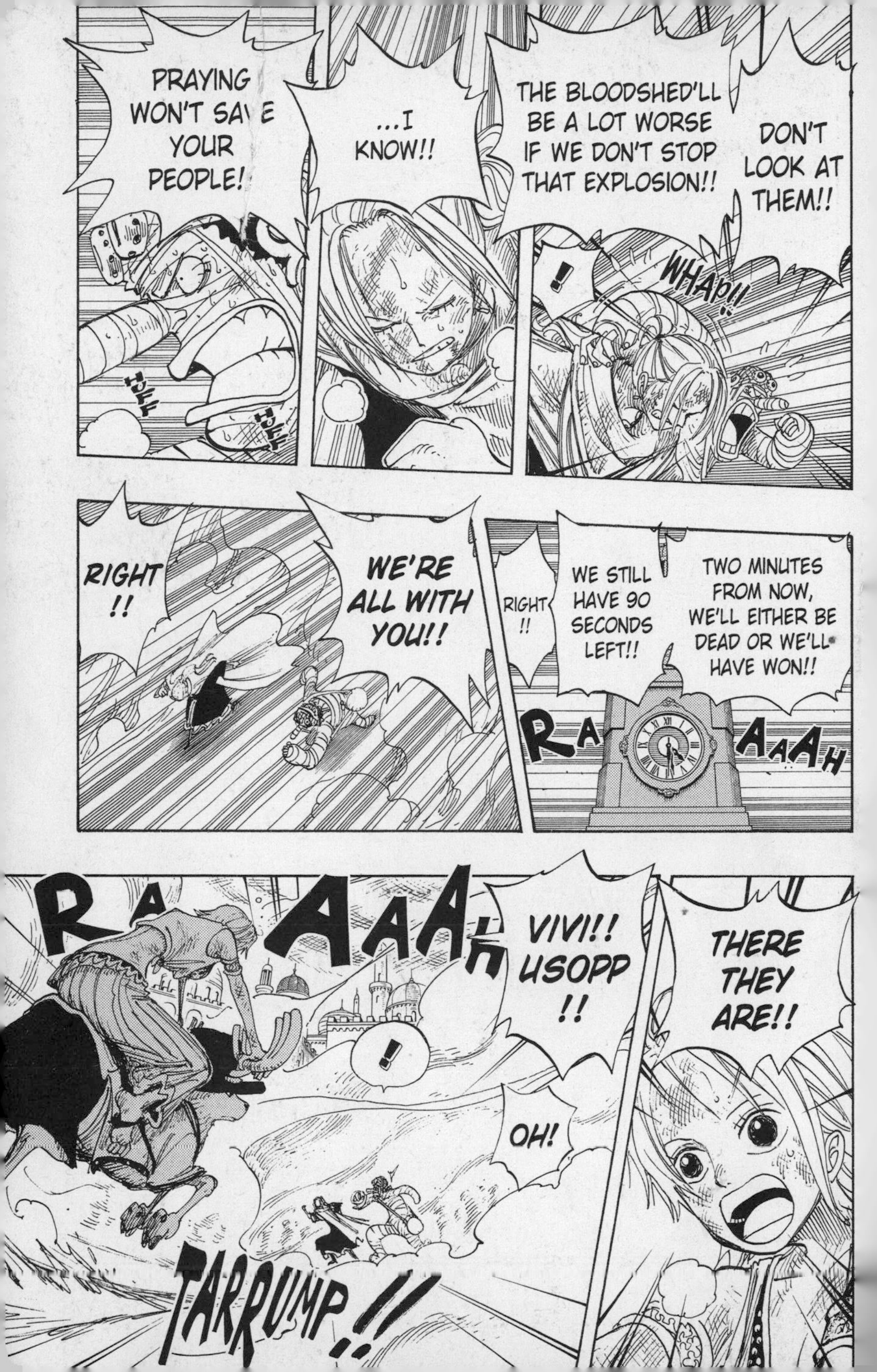
DON'T LOOK AT THEM!!
THE BLOODSHED'LL BE A LOT WORSE IF WE DON'T STOP THAT EXPLOSION!!
!
WHAP!!
...I KNOW!!
PRAYING WON'T SAVE YOUR PEOPLE!
HUFF
HUFF
TWO MINUTES FROM NOW, WE'LL EITHER BE DEAD OR WE'LL HAVE WON!!
WE STILL HAVE 90 SECONDS LEFT!!
RIGHT!!
RAAAAH
WE'RE ALL WITH YOU!!
RIGHT!!
THERE THEY ARE!!
VIVI!! USOPP!!
OH!
!
RAAAAH
TARRUMP!!

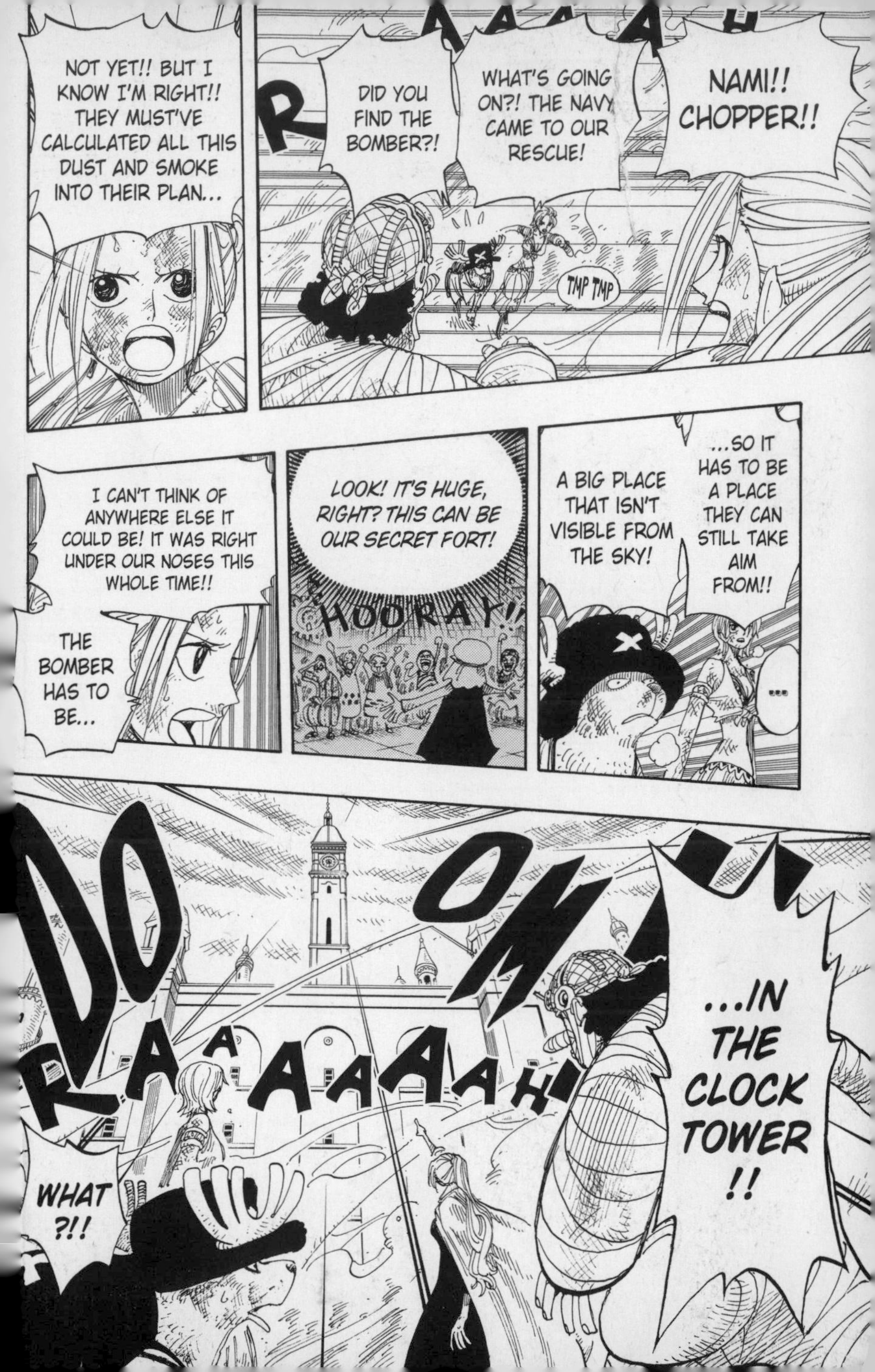
RAAAAH
NAMI!! CHOPPER!!
WHAT'S GOING ON?! THE NAVY CAME TO OUR RESCUE!
DID YOU FIND THE BOMBER?!
TMP TMP
NOT YET!! BUT I KNOW I'M RIGHT!! THEY MUST'VE CALCULATED ALL THIS DUST AND SMOKE INTO THEIR PLAN...
...SO IT HAS TO BE A PLACE THEY CAN STILL TAKE AIM FROM!!
A BIG PLACE THAT ISN'T VISIBLE FROM THE SKY!
...
LOOK! IT'S HUGE, RIGHT? THIS CAN BE OUR SECRET FORT!
HOORAY!!
I CAN'T THINK OF ANYWHERE ELSE IT COULD BE! IT WAS RIGHT UNDER OUR NOSES THIS WHOLE TIME!!
THE BOMBER HAS TO BE...
DOOM
...IN THE CLOCK TOWER!!
RAAAAAAAH
WHAT?!!

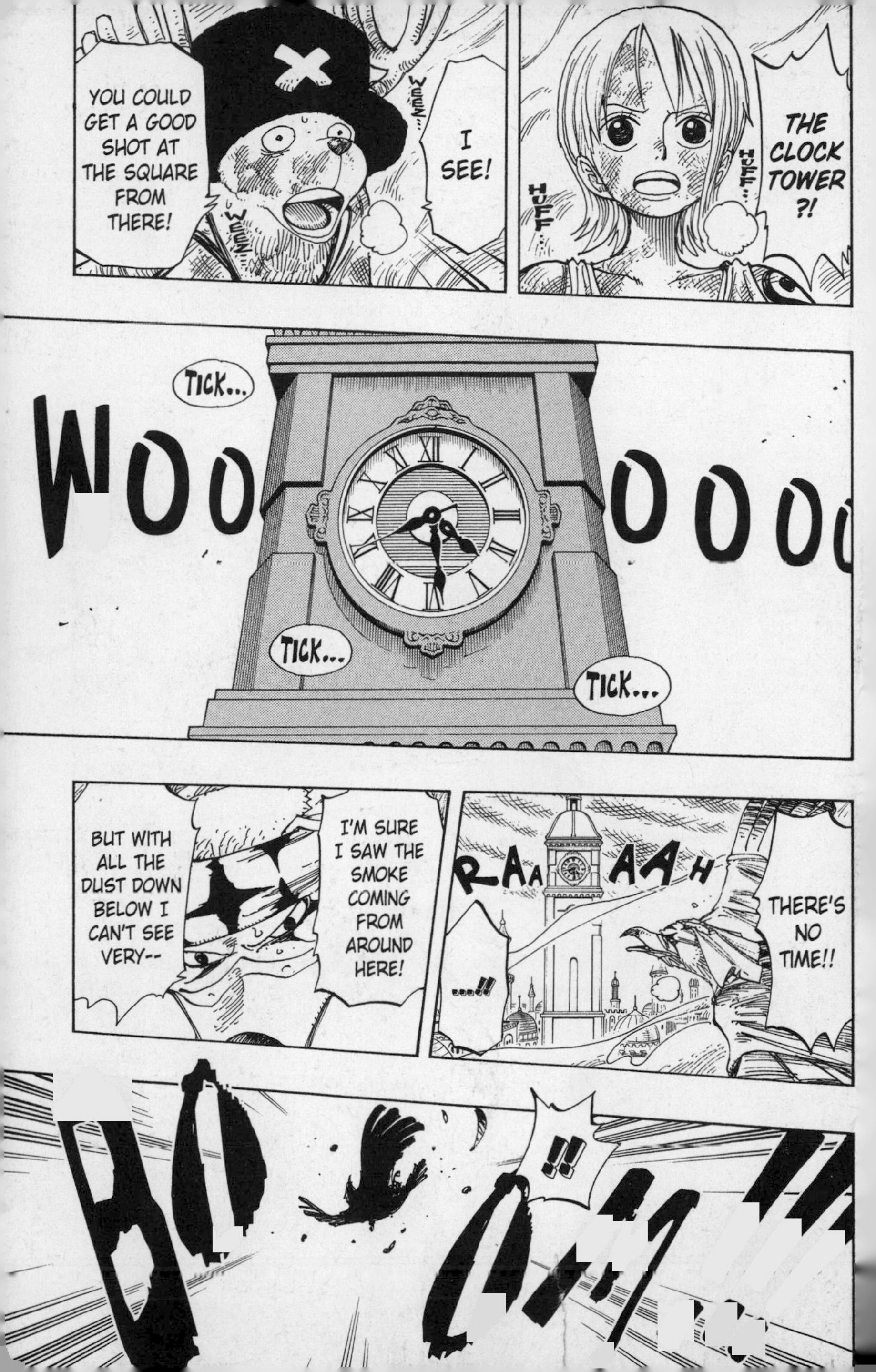
HUFF...
HUFF...
THE CLOCK TOWER?!
WEEN...
I SEE!
YOU COULD GET A GOOD SHOT AT THE SQUARE FROM THERE!
WEEN...
WOOOOOOO
TICK...
TICK...
TICK...
THERE'S NO TIME!!
RAAAAH
...!!
I'M SURE I SAW THE SMOKE COMING FROM AROUND HERE!
BUT WITH ALL THE DUST DOWN BELOW I CAN'T SEE VERY--
!!

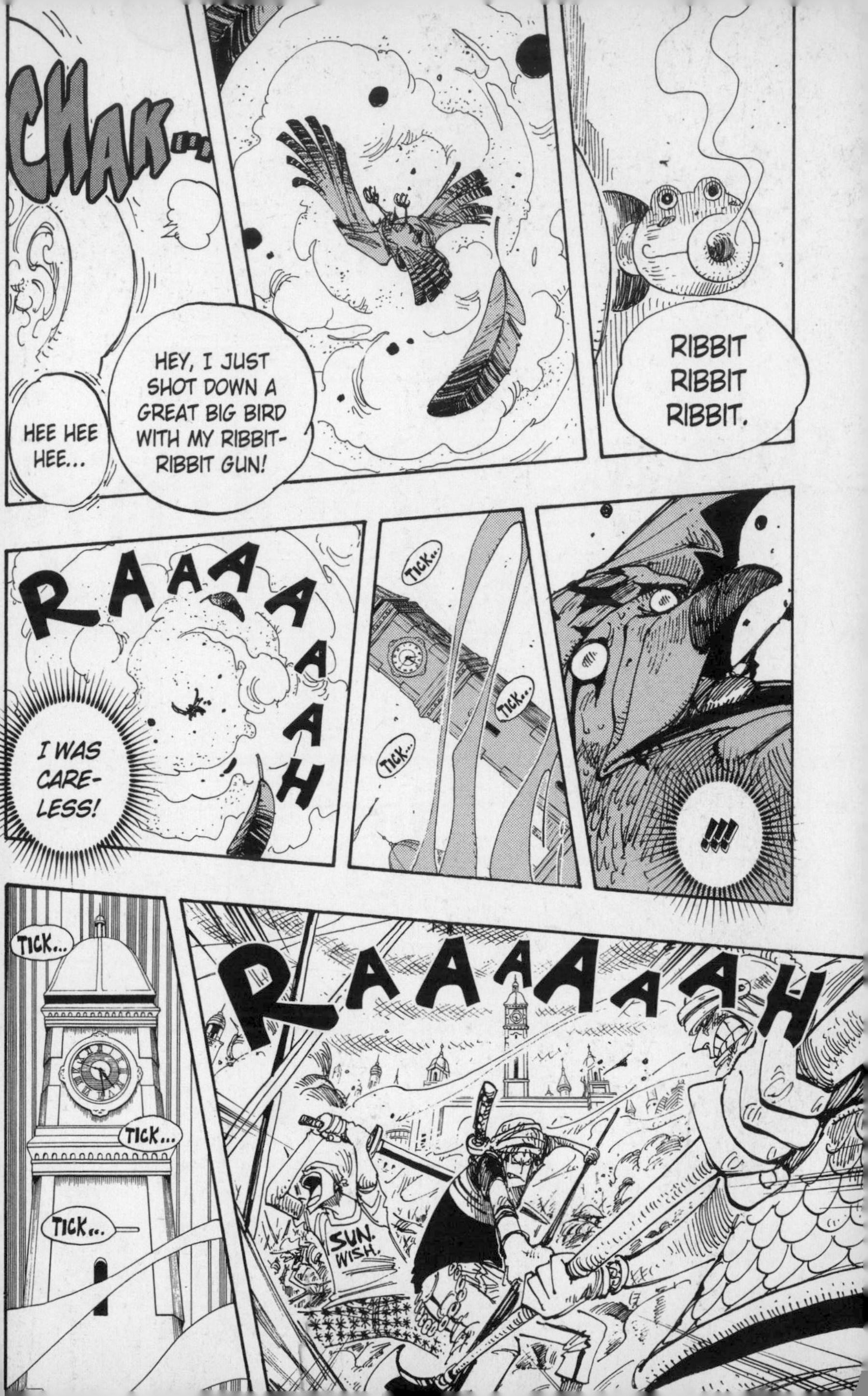
RIBBIT RIBBIT RIBBIT.
CHAK...
HEY, I JUST SHOT DOWN A GREAT BIG BIRD WITH MY RIBBIT-RIBBIT GUN!
HEE HEE HEE...
!!!
TICK...
TICK...
TICK...
RAAAAAAH
I WAS CARE-LESS!
RAAAAAAAH
SUN. WISH.
TICK...
TICK...
TICK...

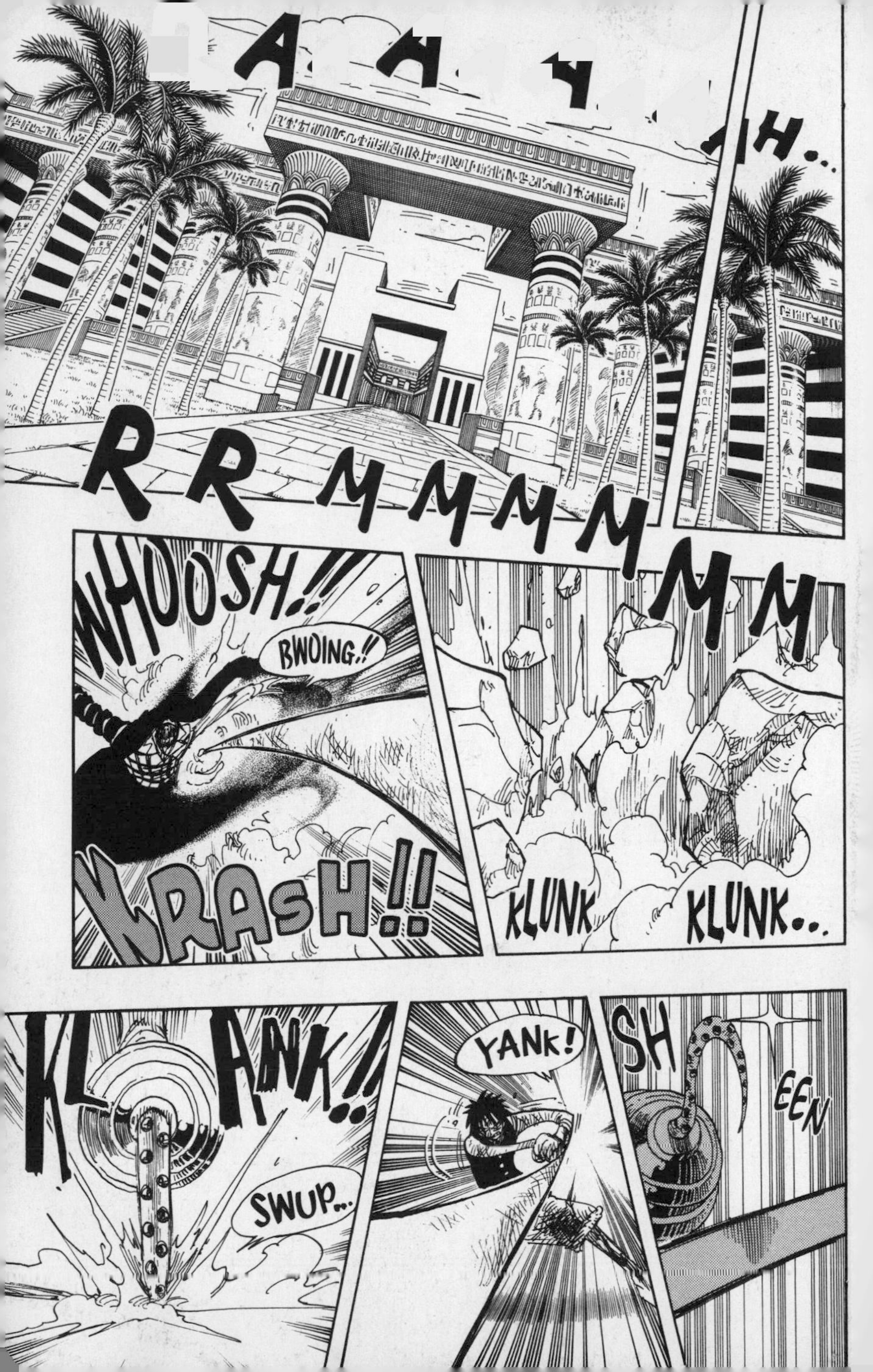

A A A AH...
RRMMMMMMMM
KLUNK KLUNK...
WHOOSH!!
BWOING!!
KRASH!!
SHEEN
YANK!
KLANK!!
SWUP...

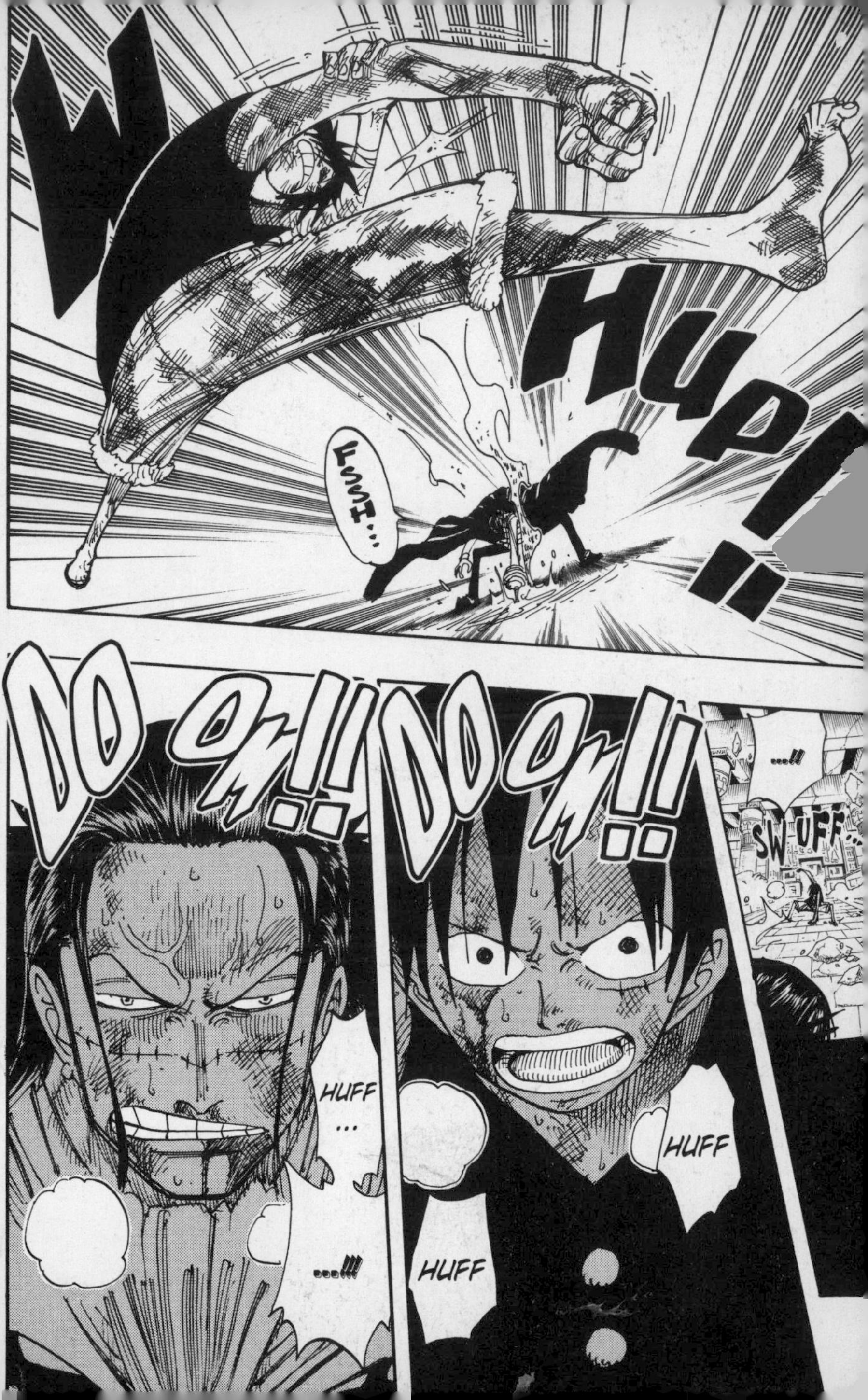
HUP!!
FSSH...
W
...!!
SWUFF...
DOOM!!
HUFF
HUFF
DOOM!!
HUFF
...
...!!!

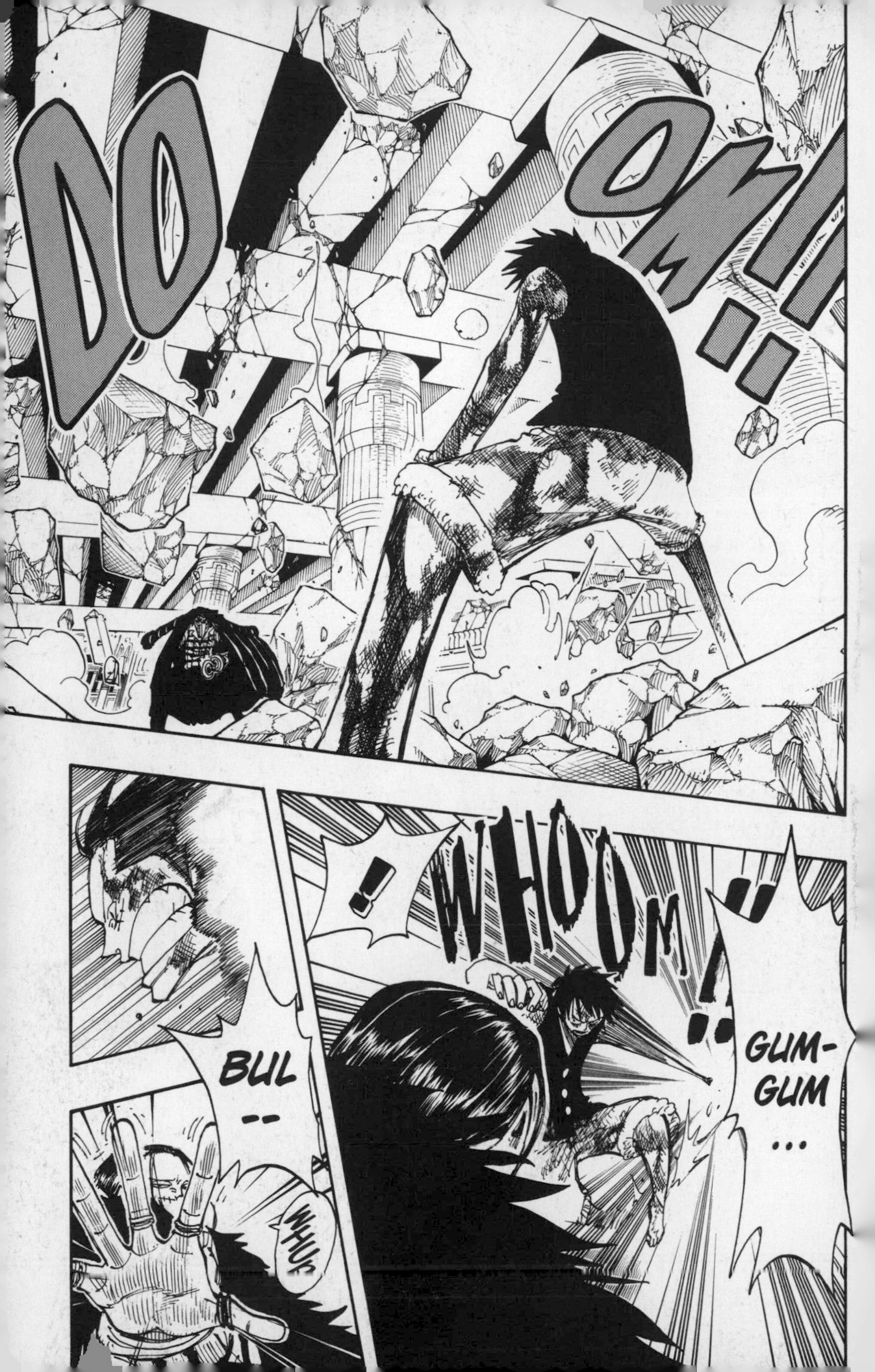
DOOM!!
!
WHOOM!!
GUM-GUM
...
BUL
--
WHUS

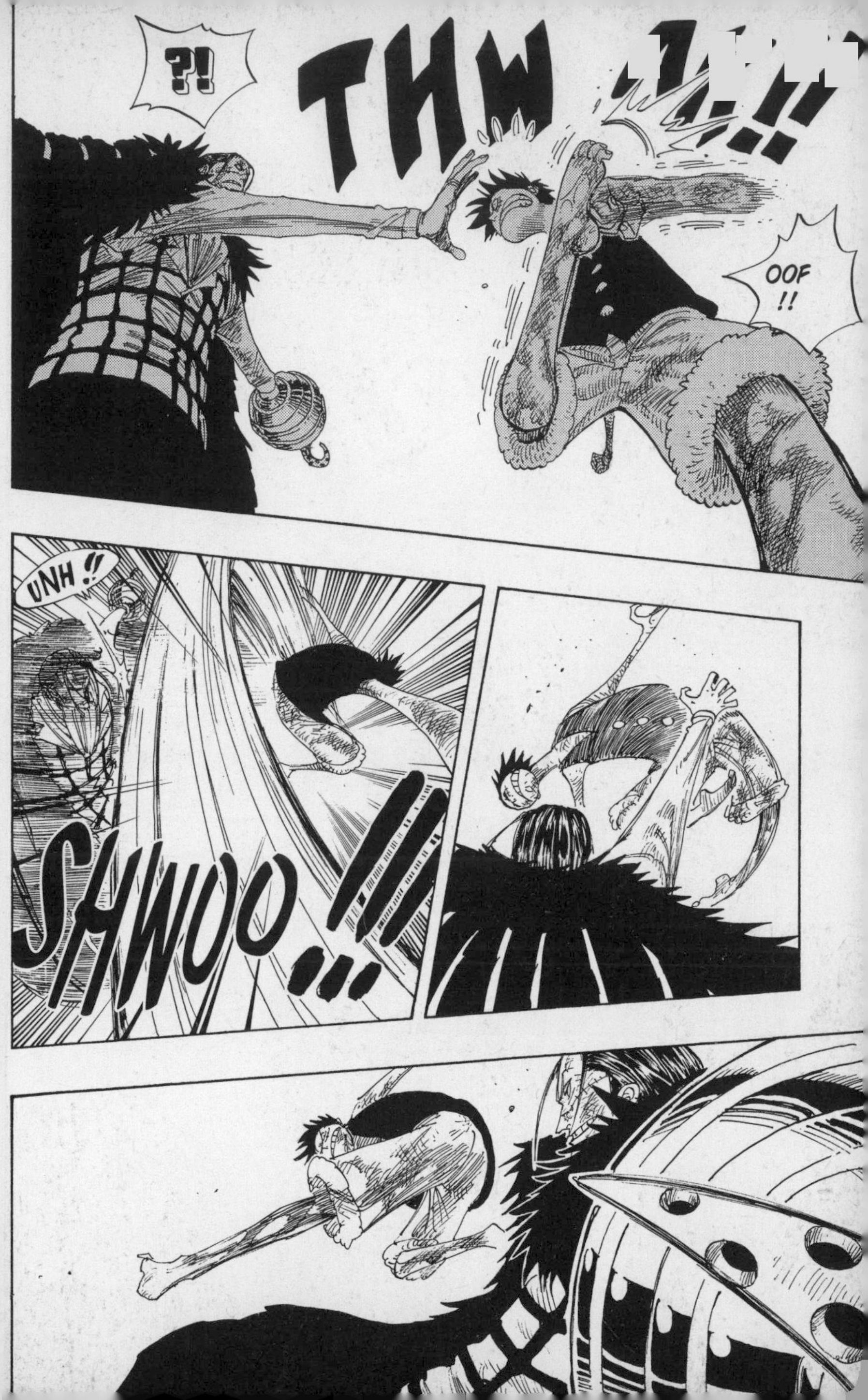
THW
?!
OOF !!
UNH !!
SHWOO...!!!

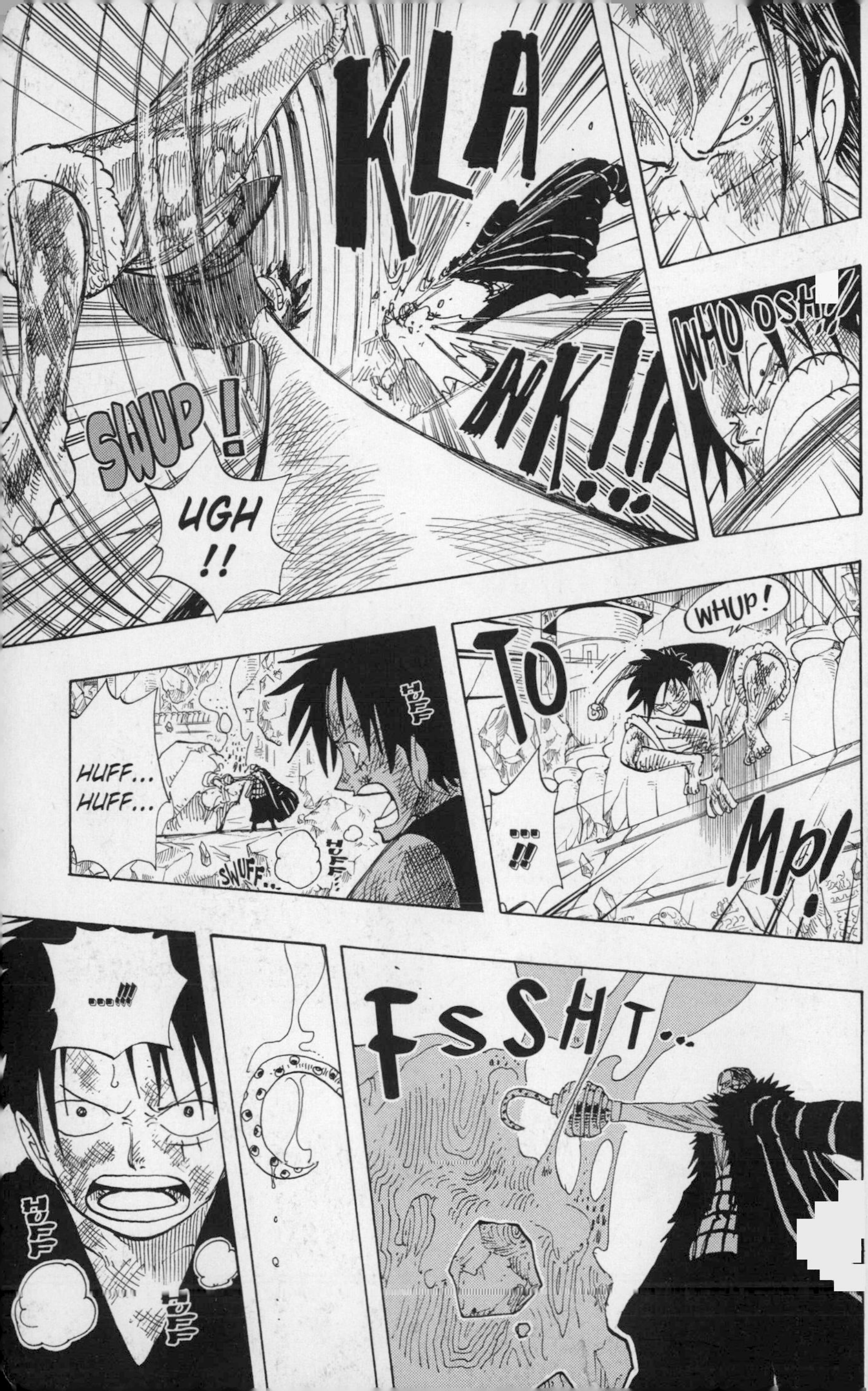
WHOOSH!!
KLANK!!!...
SWUP!
UGH!!
WHUP!
TOMP!
...!!
HUFF
HUFF...
SNUFF...
HUFF... HUFF...
FSSHT...
...!!!
HUFF
HUFF

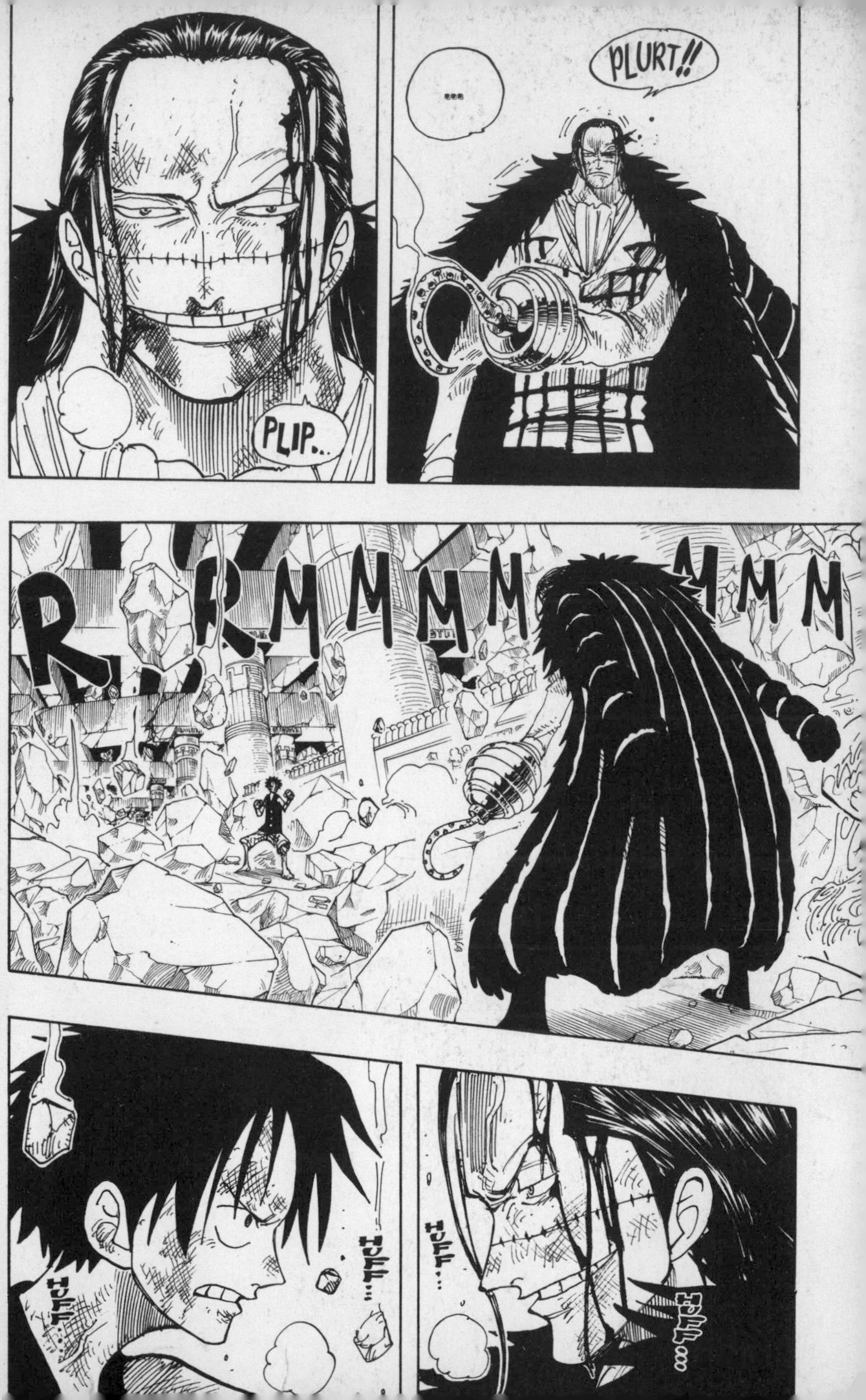
PLURT!!
...
PLIP...
RRMMMMMMM
HUFF...
HUFF...
HUFF...
HUFF...

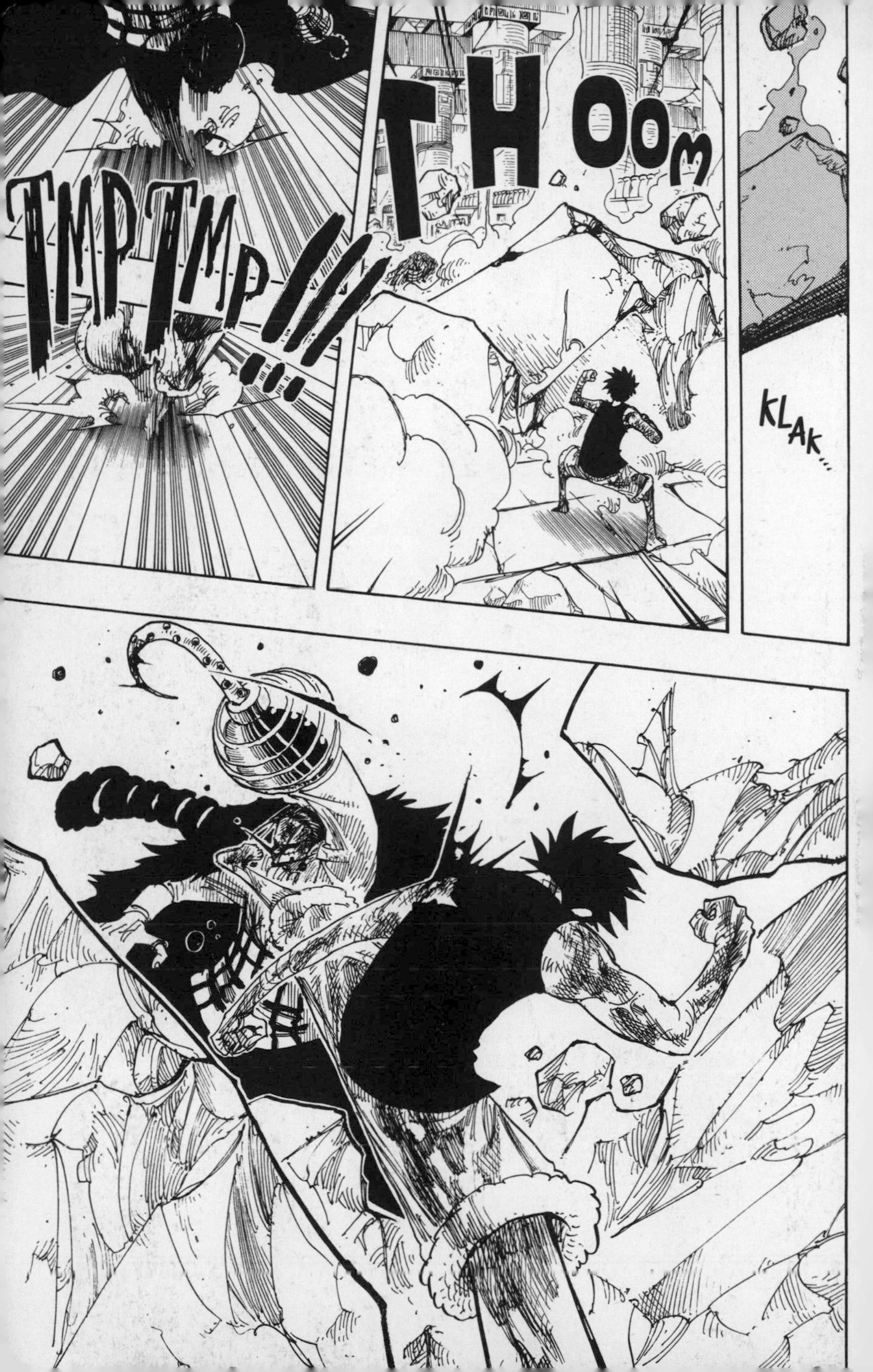
KLAK...
THOOM
TMP TMP!!!

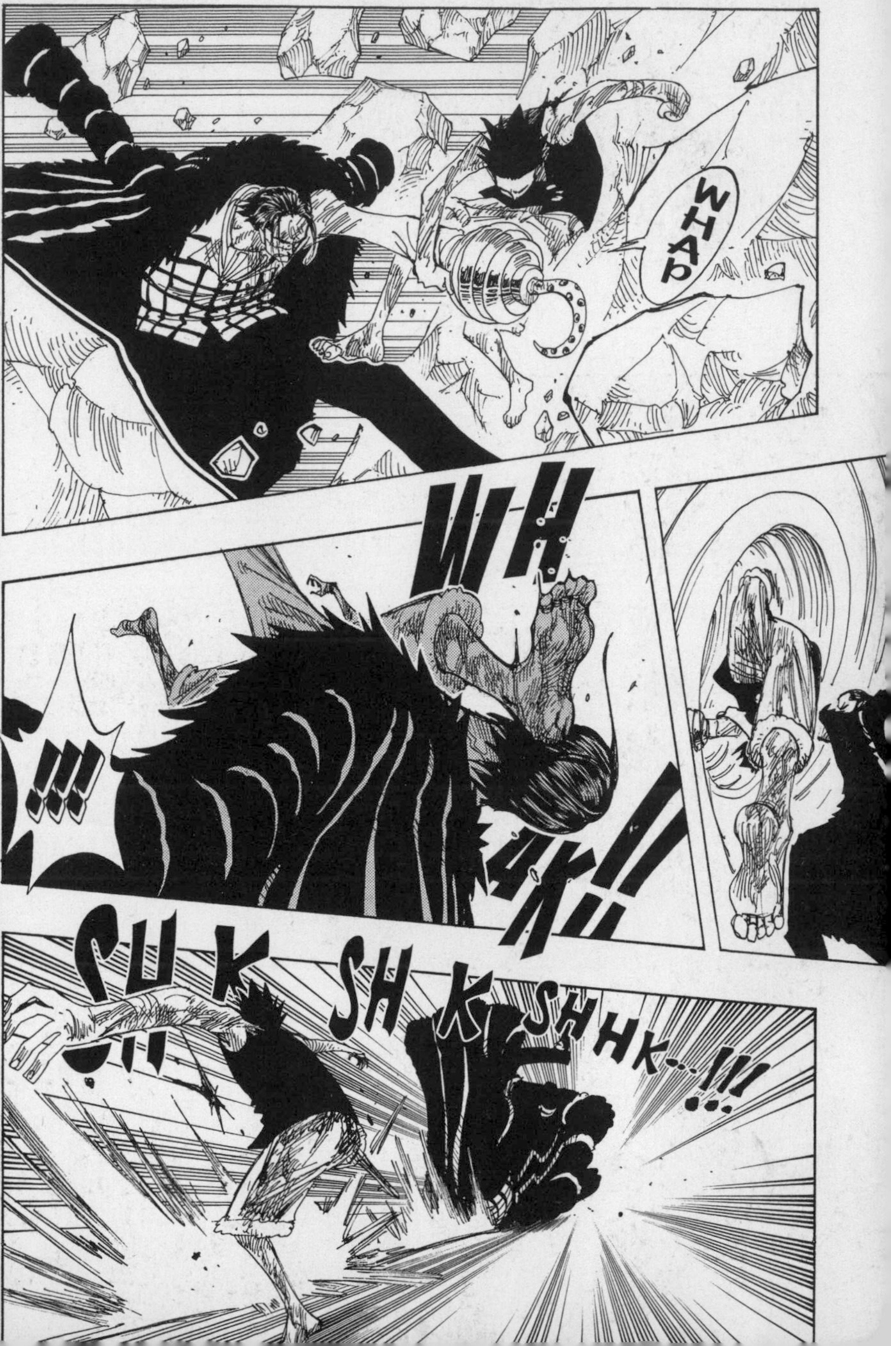
WHAP
WHUK!!
!!!
CUK!!
SH K
SHHK...!!!

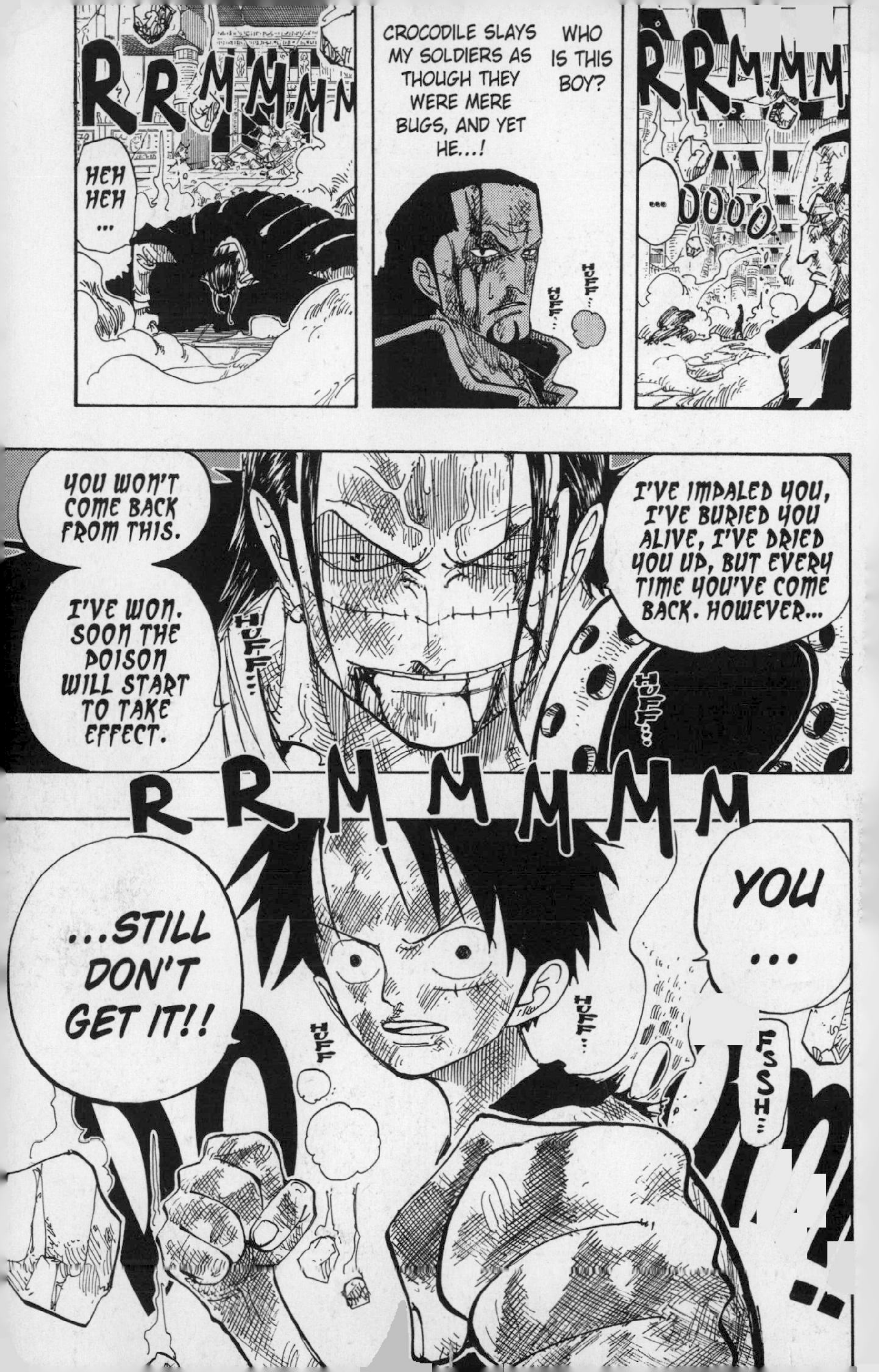
RRMMM
...
OOOO
WHO IS THIS BOY?
CROCODILE SLAYS MY SOLDIERS AS THOUGH THEY WERE MERE BUGS, AND YET HE...!
HUFF HUFF...
RRMMMMM
HEH HEH ...
I'VE IMPALED YOU, I'VE BURIED YOU ALIVE, I'VE DRIED YOU UP, BUT EVERY TIME YOU'VE COME BACK. HOWEVER...
HUFF...
YOU WON'T COME BACK FROM THIS.
I'VE WON. SOON THE POISON WILL START TO TAKE EFFECT.
HUFF...
RRMMMMMM
YOU ...
FSSH!!
HUFF...
HUFF
...STILL DON'T GET IT!!

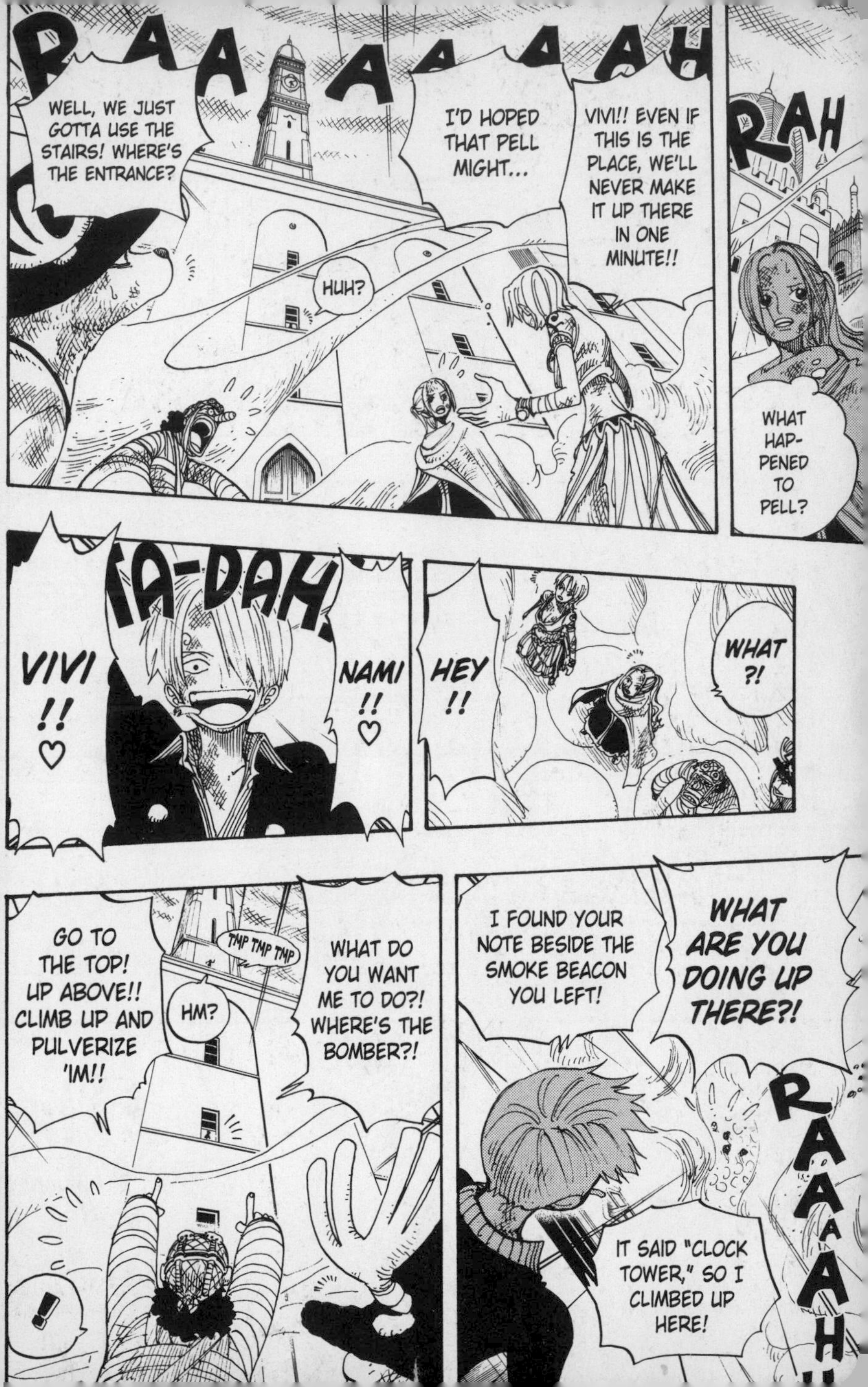
RAH
WHAT HAPPENED TO PELL?
RAAAAAAH
VIVI!! EVEN IF THIS IS THE PLACE, WE'LL NEVER MAKE IT UP THERE IN ONE MINUTE!!
I'D HOPED THAT PELL MIGHT...
WELL, WE JUST GOTTA USE THE STAIRS! WHERE'S THE ENTRANCE?
HUH?
WHAT ?!
HEY !!
TA-DAH.
NAMI !! ♡
VIVI !! ♡
WHAT ARE YOU DOING UP THERE?!
I FOUND YOUR NOTE BESIDE THE SMOKE BEACON YOU LEFT!
RAAAAAH
IT SAID "CLOCK TOWER," SO I CLIMBED UP HERE!
WHAT DO YOU WANT ME TO DO?! WHERE'S THE BOMBER?!
TMP TMP TMP
HM?
GO TO THE TOP! UP ABOVE!! CLIMB UP AND PULVERIZE 'IM!!
!

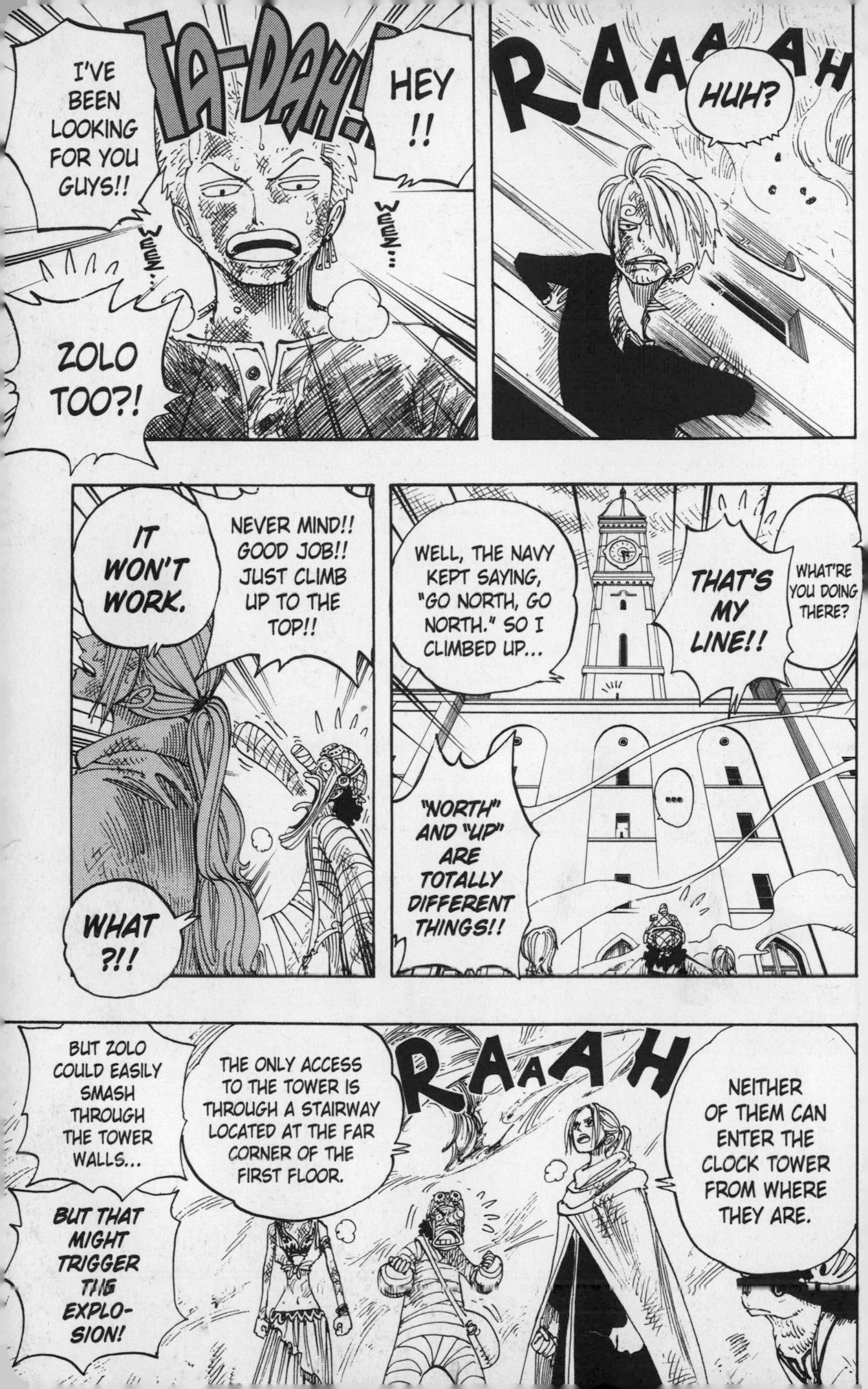
RAAAAAH
HUH?
HEY !!
TA-DAH!!
I'VE BEEN LOOKING FOR YOU GUYS!!
WEEN...
WEEN...
ZOLO TOO?!
WHAT'RE YOU DOING THERE?
THAT'S MY LINE!!
WELL, THE NAVY KEPT SAYING, "GO NORTH, GO NORTH." SO I CLIMBED UP...
...
"NORTH" AND "UP" ARE TOTALLY DIFFERENT THINGS!!
NEVER MIND!! GOOD JOB!! JUST CLIMB UP TO THE TOP!!
IT WON'T WORK.
WHAT ?!!
NEITHER OF THEM CAN ENTER THE CLOCK TOWER FROM WHERE THEY ARE.
RAAAH
THE ONLY ACCESS TO THE TOWER IS THROUGH A STAIRWAY LOCATED AT THE FAR CORNER OF THE FIRST FLOOR.
BUT ZOLO COULD EASILY SMASH THROUGH THE TOWER WALLS...
BUT THAT MIGHT TRIGGER THE EXPLOSION!

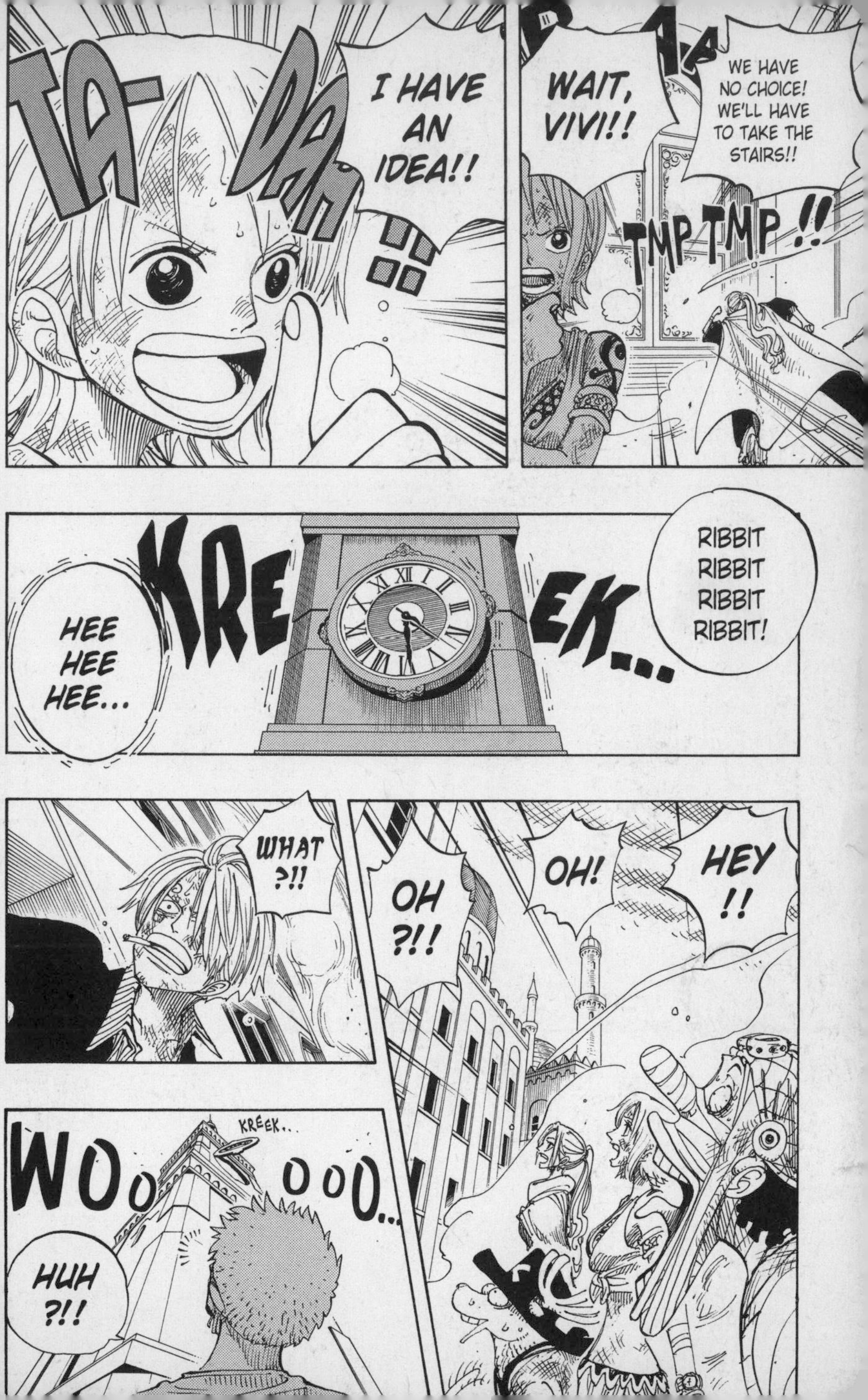
WAIT, VIVI!!
WE HAVE NO CHOICE! WE'LL HAVE TO TAKE THE STAIRS!!
TMP TMP !!
TA-DA
I HAVE AN IDEA!!
RIBBIT RIBBIT RIBBIT RIBBIT!
KRE EK...
HEE HEE HEE...
HEY !!
OH!
OH ?!!
WHAT ?!!
KREEK..
WOO OOO...
HUH ?!!

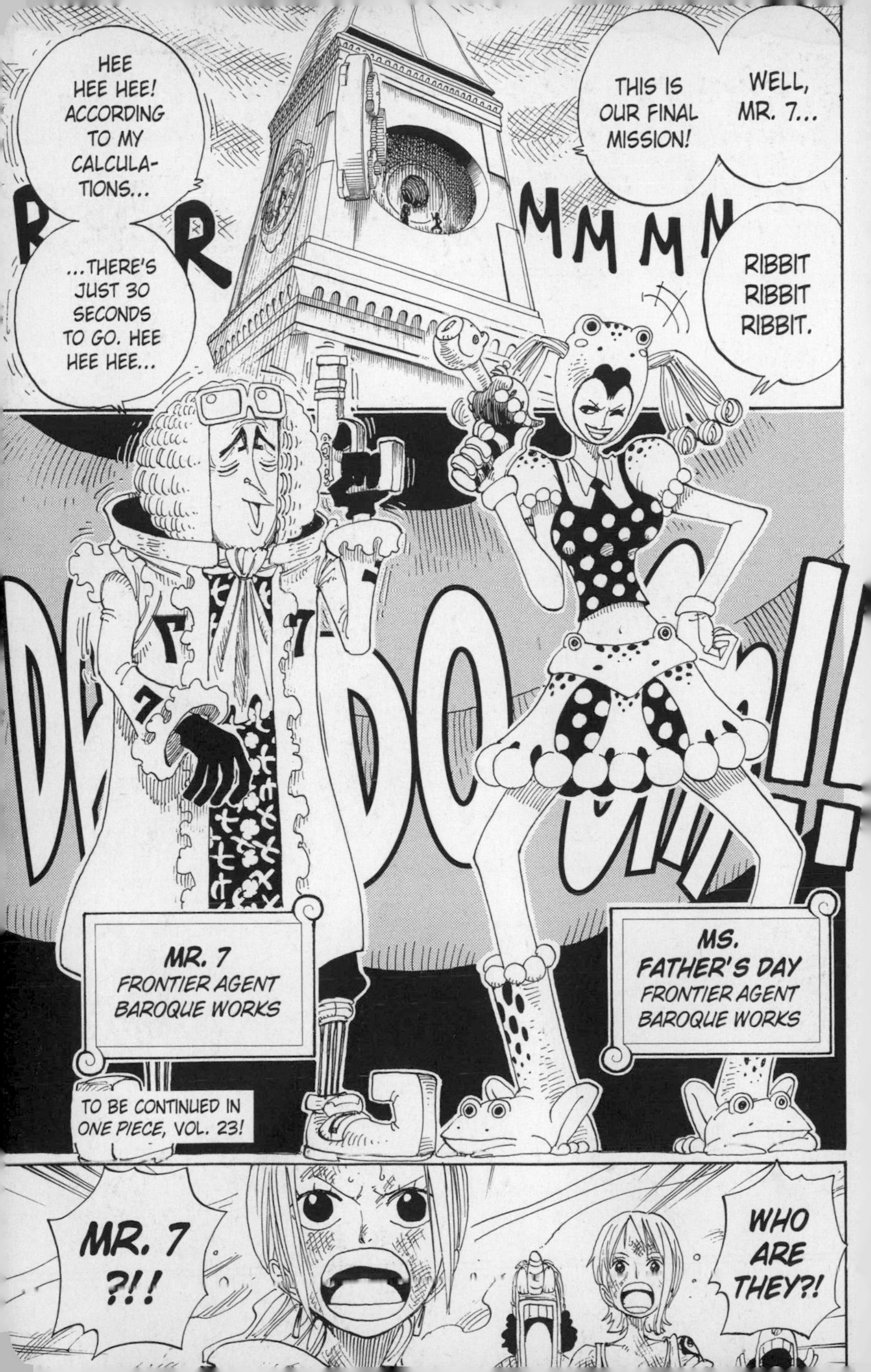
WELL, MR. 7...
THIS IS OUR FINAL MISSION!
HEE HEE HEE! ACCORDING TO MY CALCULATIONS...
RIBBIT RIBBIT RIBBIT.
...THERE'S JUST 30 SECONDS TO GO. HEE HEE HEE...
MS. FATHER'S DAY FRONTIER AGENT BAROQUE WORKS
MR. 7 FRONTIER AGENT BAROQUE WORKS
TO BE CONTINUED IN ONE PIECE, VOL. 23!
WHO ARE THEY?!
MR. 7 ?!!

# COMING NEXT VOLUME:

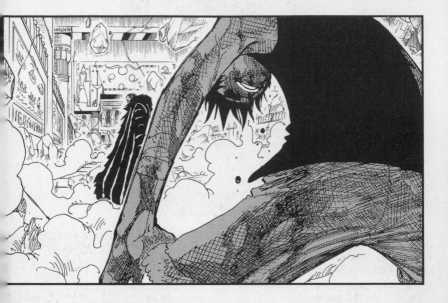

Vivi and the Straw Hats have located the bomb, but now they have to find a way to reach it in time to stop it. And with only seconds to go before it blows up, they'll have to get past the two Agents guarding it! Meanwhile, with the walls of the royal tomb caving in all around them, Luffy's trying to settle the score with Crocodile before they're buried alive!

## ON SALE NOW!

# You're Reading in the Wrong Direction!!

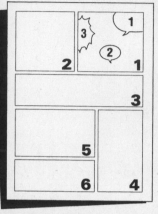

**W**hoops! Guess what? You're starting at the wrong end of the comic!

...It's true! In keeping with the original Japanese format, **One Piece** is meant to be read from right to left, starting in the upper-right corner.

Unlike English, which is read from left to right, Japanese is read from right to left, meaning that action, sound effects and word-balloon order are completely reversed...something which can make readers unfamiliar with Japanese feel pretty backwards themselves. For this reason, manga or Japanese comics published in the U.S. in English have sometimes been published "flopped"— that is, printed in exact reverse order, as though seen from the other side of a mirror.

By flopping pages, U.S. publishers can avoid confusing readers, but the compromise is not without its downside. For one thing, a character in a flopped manga series who once wore in the original Japanese version a T-shirt emblazoned with "M A Y" (as in "the merry month of") now wears one which reads "Y A M"! Additionally, many manga creators in Japan are themselves unhappy with the process, as some feel the mirror-imaging of their art skews their original intentions.

We are proud to bring you Eiichiro Oda's **One Piece** in the original unflopped format. For now, though, turn to the other side of the book and let the journey begin...!

—Editor